AUTHORITY AND FREEDOM
IN EDUCATION

Other Books by Paul Nash

The Educated Man: Studies in the History of Educational Thought,
New York: John Wiley & Sons, 1965 (with Kazamias and Perkinson).

Culture and the State: Matthew Arnold and Continental Education,
New York: Columbia University, T. C. Press, 1966.

AUTHORITY AND FREEDOM IN EDUCATION

An Introduction to the Philosophy of Education

PAUL NASH

Boston University

JOHN WILEY & SONS, INC.,
NEW YORK · LONDON · SYDNEY

Library of Congress Catalog Card Number: 66-17624
Printed in the United States of America

For Anne

with whom life has been an education in freedom

PREFACE

In the course of exploring the ideas treated in this book, I have been assisted by the suggestions, ideas, and criticisms of many people. Although they are not, of course, responsible for the ways in which I have used and interpreted their ideas, I should like to mention the following as among those whose thinking has been especially valuable to me: T. S. Ashton, H. L. Beales, the late Harold J. Laski, and the late R. H. Tawney of the London School of Economics; Charlotte Fleming, R. S. Peters, Louis Arnaud Reid, and Philip Vernon of the University of London Institute of Education; Raymond Klibansky, Gino Lorcini, and Alistair McKinnon of McGill University; Israel Scheffler and Robert Ulich of Harvard University; James McClellan of Temple University; Harold Loukes of Oxford University; John Strain of Tufts University; and Peter Bertocci, Theodore Brameld, Paul Deats, Gene Phillips, and Marx Wartofsky of Boston University. I am also grateful to my students at McGill, Harvard, and Boston Universities who have helped me to clarify my ideas through their criticisms. Above all, I am indebted to my wife, whose support has been cheerful, continuous, and indispensable.

Paul Nash

Boston, Massachusetts
March, 1966

CONTENTS

INTRODUCTION

As an introduction to the study of philosophy of education, this book was written with two purposes, which can be epitomized as *clarity* and *commitment*. It is appropriate here to say a word about each of these purposes.

It is well-known that much recent philosophy has been marked by a critical, analytical, and scientific spirit. In the last few years, some philosophers have begun to apply this method of linguistic analysis to the concepts of education.[1] This development has not been welcomed without reservations: indeed, some philosophers of education, especially those who see the very foundations of their traditional strongholds being undermined, have bitterly condemned this form of philosophizing as a timid, petty, hairsplitting, fruitless, intellectual game. I, however, welcome the advent of this analytical approach. It serves excellently my first purpose, which is to help students and others concerned with education to think as clearly, carefully, rigorously, and systematically as they can about the educational concept or problem that faces them.

Israel Scheffler has splendidly summed up the characteristic features of the analytical temper of linguistic philosophy—features, as he points out, that it shares with varieties of realism, pragmatism, and the philosophy of science. These approaches have

what might be described as an "inductive" way of going about things, a willingness to tackle single problems in piecemeal fashion, and a subjection of general assertions to the twin tests of fact and logical clarity. . . . There is a unanimous distrust of large generalizations about the universe, of attempts to interpret all of human life in terms of a single idea, of systems whose air of profundity and deductive strength is bought at the expense of a disparagement of common experience. In addition, there is hostility not alone to philosophizing that in practice reveals impatience with evidence

1

or that, in its haste to edify, substitutes rhetoric for reasons, but also, and above all, to philosophies that scorn reasoned discourse in principle, that glory in the vague and the subjective, and make a virtue of paradox.[2]

The analytical philosopher does more than analyze concepts: he is also concerned with arguments, with the substantiation of assertions, including occasionally assertions about morality and values. However, although he may analyze value-claims and logically evaluate moral arguments, he does not try, as a philosopher, to persuade others to adopt a particular moral position or commitment. He prefers to retain, at least explicitly, a morally neutral position in philosophy. This moral neutrality or detachment does not meet with universal approval. John Wild, for example, has severely criticized the "detachment from the actual concerns of everyday life in which many analysts seem to take great pride. Thus they are not so much concerned with ethics, the making of value judgments, as with meta-ethics, the objective analysis (in itself neutral) of the meaning of such judgments." [3]

I do not share the common condemnation of the analytical philosopher on the grounds of his moral neutrality, for I feel that such condemnation confuses his role as a philosopher with his role as a man. We might, indeed, be alarmed at the man who refused to commit himself to any moral position; but, in his professional task of philosophizing, a philosopher has the right to narrow or extend his range, within reason, in any way that seems to him fruitful. To confine oneself, as a philosopher, to the logical analysis of concepts and arguments, is a perfectly defensible procedure. What would be indefensible, of course, would be for the analytical philosopher to claim that *all* philosophers must adopt this same mode of restriction on their philosophical endeavors.

Personally, I find it most productive to adopt the analytical philosopher's goal of clarity, but to add to it the further goal of commitment. One might take as an example of the attitude I am advocating the work of a man like G.E. Moore, the Cambridge philosopher, who had a considerable influence on those analytical philosophers who came to believe that the sole task of philosophy is to analyze concepts and statements. In his major work, *Principia Ethica*, Moore did indeed lay the groundwork for a systematic clarification of ethical statements and questions. But in the final chapter, he went on to commit himself to a substantive ethical position, presenting his own conclusions with regard to the proper answer to the question "What is good in itself?" [4]

It is because I prefer an inclusive to an exclusive approach to the study of educational problems that I find the analytical method invaluable but inadequate. It is my purpose to urge students of education to commit themselves to a moral position. And since, if I do so, these students have a right to demand that I do the same, I shall not stay within the confines of analysis. I shall go on from there, where it seems appropriate, into diagnosis and prescription. In so doing, I have a frankly pedagogical purpose: my experience leads me to believe that students learn to think not so much by manipulating ideas held at a moral and emotional arm's length, but rather by taking a sincere stand on an important issue and learning its justifications and weaknesses in dialogue with teacher and fellow students. Involvement carries a learning power for which there is no substitute. The analytical philosopher is justified in his suspicion of teachers who try to persuade their students to adopt a *particular* moral position. But he perhaps underestimates the pedagogical value of helping students to come to *some* commitment, whatever it may be. I am declaring my personal commitments in these pages not to make converts, but to stimulate students to sharpen their own minds and justify their own commitments by criticizing and evaluating mine.

It is clear, then, that I am using the term "philosophy of education" in a wider sense than that employed to describe the activity of the philosopher acting in his capacity as a professional expert. It was this latter sense that Scheffler had in mind [5] when he wrote:

The assignment of value-determination to the philosopher on the one hand absurdly exaggerates his moral wisdom and good judgment, whereas on the other it underestimates the contribution he *can* make by his professional striving for generality and system, clarity and logical rigor.[6]

One can agree with Scheffler that the philosopher, as a philosopher, is not a moral or judgmental "expert" (although one would hope that the philosopher's concern with clear thinking would not be entirely without beneficial consequences in terms of his ability to make sound judgments), and yet still view the role of the philosopher of education, in the sense in which I am using the term, as including the making of recommendations, value judgments, and prescriptions for educational practice. The distinction I am making is similar to the one that Paul Hirst has made between philosophy and educational theory.[7] He suggested that philosophy should be considered as a specialist activity, concerned primarily with the clarification of terms and meanings and the substantiation of arguments, while educational theory should be thought of as philosophy (in the strict sense) plus the relevant findings of psychology, sociology, history, common sense, and so on, synthesized and applied to the practical problem of making educational recommendations and value judgments. I have no objection to this conception of "educational theory," and the present book could be considered an introduction to educational theory in Hirst's sense. However, because of the relative lack of currency of the term, I have chosen to use the more common, if somewhat more ambiguous term, philosophy of education. In this sense, it would no more exaggerate the moral wisdom and good judgment of the philosopher of education to ask him to make moral judgments than it would exaggerate the moral wisdom and good judgment of a school child to ask him what he thinks about cheating. We would not be asking for Absolute Truth, or immutable certainty, or even that the philosopher of education be right. We are merely saying that the enterprise of educational philosophizing is advanced more rapidly when we seek both clarity and commitment. In the first place, we harness more sustained effort when we discuss with people who involve themselves seriously and personally in educational and moral issues, rather than regarding them as intellectual exercises. Secondly, we might consider that the educational philosopher who refuses to take a value position provides a poor model for students in a profession like teaching, where moral choices and decisions are inescapable. And thirdly, there is less chance of introducing moral positions by way of implicit assumption when we must lay our moral cards on the table.

It will be noted that this is not an introduction to the philosophy of education in the sense of a purportedly comprehensive treatment of the whole field, through the study of various "schools of thought." Such a comprehensive approach has often been attempted in the past, has almost invariably been done badly, and is increasingly regarded as vestigial and anachronistic. The present study is an introduction in what it is hoped will be a more fruitful sense, that is, an examination of a single theme—one that I see both as the most important single theme in the philosophy of education and as a lens through which some of the major problems in the field can be studied. As an introduction for students who may have had no formal study in philosophy, it is designed to show how such a theme or problem can be approached. Many kinds of data have been introduced, and many methods, besides philosophical analysis, used. The approach may shock some purists by the breadth and eclecticism of its methodology; it may dismay some academic pedants by its use of many fields and disciplines. But the treatment is intended to have two consequences: it is intended not to satisfy the student but to stimulate him to react to the position here presented, to clarify his own thinking on the subject, and to formulate a justifiable position of personal commitment on it. It is also intended to provide a model that the student can use to go on to the study of other problems in education.

This is a study of authority and freedom in education for two reasons: it is suggested that the concepts of authority and freedom are the principal concepts, for the person concerned with education today, that need clarification and in terms of which personal commitment must be worked out; furthermore, this is a study of the *relationship* between authority and freedom because, it is suggested, there are some fruitful consequences of the *dialectical* approach to educational problems.

This use of the dialectic is influenced by Hegel, but it is not pursued in the rigid and absolute manner he used. Hegel suggested that a concept may contain its own opposite hidden away within itself and that this opposite can be extricated or deduced from it. This opposite can be "united in comprehension" with the concept to yield a higher level of insight. The three members of this triadic arrangement are sometimes called the thesis, antithesis, and synthesis, respectively.[8] However, no attempt will be made here to follow this triadic pattern rigidly; nor will it be suggested that there is anything of an inexorably logical nature about the dialectical approach. J.N. Findlay has pungently pointed out that, in the main, the dialectical triad stressed by Hegel is "merely an expository integument, and one that often positively masks, rather than reveals, the actual course of his thinking. . . . The attempted use of a rigorous triadic method is plainly the source of all that is unpersuasive in Hegel's conclusions, as it is the source of all that is obscure in his language."[9] The use of the dialectical approach here is merely a device that may serve to bring fresh insights to some familiar educational problems while at the same time keeping us open to aspects of the truth that will be hidden from those whose rigorously analytical methods compel them to reject paradox, the coexistence of contradictions, and the reconciliation of opposites.[10] We can agree wholeheartedly with Scheffler that one should not "make a virtue out of paradox." It is quite another thing, however, to be open to the possible truth in a paradox that experience forces on one's attention.

This dialectical approach can be seen as another example of the desire to be inclusive rather than exclusive—to choose, where possible, "both . . . and" in preference to "either . . . or." It represents an attempt to resist the strong contemporary tendency to be satisfied with simple and partial solutions. We are witnessing today the disturbing rise of extremist groups, which represent outlets for people who cannot face the complications of reality and who seek to withdraw into the dangerous ease of totalistic formulas. Not only must we resist such easy comforts, but we must also beware of the opposite temptation—that of letting the dangers of extremism frighten us into moral neutrality. The necessity for moral commitment does not permit us to add up the account hastily and draw a firm line under it. We must resist the temptation of premature closure; we must be aware that the finite can often be apparently self-contradictory, and that the truth is almost always complex and sometimes paradoxical; we must try always to rise to a higher level of understanding and inclusiveness rather than cut off investigation for the sake of a cheap certainty; we must resist the weariness that comes with a continued search and avoid the misleading embrace of peace of mind. The dialectical approach is suggested as one that enables us to work through to a position of commitment while avoiding these dangers.

The general approach to this investigation of the problem of authority and freedom in education can be gauged from the table of contents. The principal polarity of authority and freedom has been broken down into a number of subpolarities, each of which represents both an aspect of the main polarity and one of the main problems in the philosophy of education. The whole, then, constitutes both a treatment in breadth of some of the major issues in educational philosophy and a treatment in depth of the central and pervasive problem of authority and freedom. In each chapter the meaning of each part of the polarity is analyzed, the relationship between them is examined, and the implications of this relationship for education are explored. While it is possible to think of the "authority" polarity as the thesis, the "freedom" polarity as the antithesis, and the educational implications as the synthesis, this arrangement should be viewed as suggestive and convenient, rather than logical and necessary. This will quickly become clear in the first chapter, where it will be seen that a reversal of the polarities is quite possible. The titles of the chapters should be taken not as dogmatic summaries but as pedagogically useful starting points.

A word should be said at this point about definitions of the principal terms. For those who grow restless without early definition, we might define "authority" as that which exercises a force or influence over us, and "freedom" as the power to achieve, choose, or become. But such loose definitions are not intended to encapsulate these complex terms. No single definition of a widely used (and abused) term like "authority" or "freedom" would suffice. Furthermore, an attempt to encapsulate these terms now would be inappropriate, since the entire book is an extended attempt to explore their various contextual meanings, and an important intention is to stimulate the reader to carry out such explorations for himself.

With respect to the meaning of "education," it will be seen that this term is given a wide interpretation: the meaning is not confined to activities carried on in institutions of formal learning. This interpretation is affected by important contemporary developments, in which vital educational enterprises—such as preschool, adult literacy, job-training, and other programs—are being taken out of the hands of institutions of formal learning, partly because of the conservatism and resistance to change manifested by schools and colleges. The interpretation also reflects the steadily increasing willingness of scholars to give serious attention to the power of informal agencies to affect the educational development of the individual.

NOTES

1 Israel Scheffler, *Philosophy and Education* (Boston: Allyn & Bacon, 1958) and B. Othanel Smith and Robert H. Ennis, eds., *Language and Concepts in Education* (Chicago: Rand McNally, 1961) have gathered together some representative writings of this type.

2 Scheffler, *op. cit.*, 6–7.

3 John Wild, *Existence and the World of Freedom* (Englewood Cliffs, N.J.: Prentice-Hall, 1963), 104.

4 George E. Moore, *Principia Ethica* (Cambridge University Press, 1903), ch. 6.

5 He has assured me, in private conversation.

6 Scheffler, *op. cit.*, 4.

7 Paul H. Hirst, "Philosophy and Educational Theory," *British Journal of Educational Studies*, Vol. XII, No. 1 (November, 1963), 51–64. See also Louis Arnaud Reid, *Philosophy and Education* (London: Heinemann, 1962), ch. 6. I am grateful to Israel Scheffler for helping me to clarify this distinction, although he is not, of course, responsible for the way in which I have expressed it.

8 For Hegel's own definition of the dialectic, see Georg W.F. Hegel, *Encyclopedia of Philosophy*, Gustav E. Mueller, trans. (New York: Philosophical Library, 1959), 82; and *The Logic of Hegel*, William Wallace, trans. (Oxford: Clarendon Press, 1874), 125–29. For explication of this difficult concept, see W.T. Stace, *The Philosophy of Hegel: A Systematic Exposition* (London: Macmillan, 1924), 88–115; and John M.E. McTaggart, *Studies in the Hegelian Dialectic* (Cambridge University Press, 1896), ch. 4.

9 J.N. Findlay, *Hegel: A Re-examination* (London: Allen & Unwin, 1958), 353. See also ch. 3, "The Dialectical Method."

10 Norman Brown, in a provocative study of psychoanalysis and history, has suggested that there are times when it is appropriate to substitute for the law of contradiction the principle of the unity of opposites. He saw the dialectical process as the struggle of the mind to circumvent repression and to make the unconscious conscious. "As an attempt to unify and to cure, the 'dialectical' consciousness would be a manifestation of Eros. And, as consciousness trying to throw off the fetters of negation, the 'dialectical' consciousness would be a step toward that Dionysian ego which does not negate any more. What the great world needs, of course, is a little more Eros and less strife; but the intellectual world needs it just as much." Norman O. Brown, *Life Against Death: The Psychoanalytical Meaning of History* (Middletown, Connecticut: Wesleyan University Press, 1959), 320–22.

I

THE AUTHORITY OF WORK
The Freedom to Play

I HOMO FABER

Man Is Not Born Free

Man is nowhere born free and yet is nowhere completely enslaved. Rousseau, whose *Social Contract* was influential in setting the early pattern of American thinking on the subject of independence, said that all men are born free. Shaw called this claim "The most flagrant lie ever told by a sane man." [1] Man is born helplessly dependent, and without parental care he would die in a few days. Moreover, he needs more comprehensive and protracted care than any other animal. Even primitive man far exceeds the animals in the length of his dependence and the depth of his needs. With the development of civilization, these needs become vastly multiplied and sophisticated. A young person today who becomes a member of one of the liberal professions has usually been dependent on parents, the State, or some other body for a quarter of a century, or one-third of his lifetime.

Man Must Work

When this initial period of dependence has passed, moreover, man is still not completely free, for he is then dependent on his own labor. The only alternatives to work that present themselves to man are to depend on the work of his ancestors or his contemporaries, or to enslave his fellow man. These alternatives neither benefit the character nor provide a release from dependence. The slaveowner is no more free than the slave: his dependence on the slave's labor enslaves him. [2] The majority of mankind, we can assume, will continue to have to work.

Why must man work? If we look first at the economic reasons, we

8

find that they fall along a continuum of basic needs and preferences. At one end of the continuum are basic needs, which can be defined as the things we feel we cannot do without. For most people, these include adequate food and drink to maintain life and, if possible, provide health and energy; and shelter, clothing, and fuel to provide protection from rain and cold. Of course, these "basic" needs are susceptible to almost indefinite extension: we seem able to persuade ourselves that we cannot possibly do without the most refined developments of these fundamental requirements. All the needs that we consider basic serve to reduce our freedom, because we become bound by what we cannot do without. It is obvious that the alcoholic is not free, for he is bound by his need for alcohol. It is less obvious but no less true that those of us who consider ourselves free from such compulsive addictions are nevertheless dominated by the necessity of satisfying what we consider basic needs.

At the other end of the continuum lie man's preferences. These may range from a taste for cognac to a desire for family life, with its concomitant economic responsibilities. The existence of my family removes all sorts of freedoms that I enjoyed as a bachelor. But I do not *want* to be free from these family responsibilities, because in return for the loss of certain freedoms I obtain certain gains—in terms of emotional security, physical comfort, the giving and receiving of love and tenderness—that more than compensate. And for these compensations I am prepared to pay, and work. Even those of us who are fortunate enough to be doing work of our choice find within it many particular tasks that are distasteful (marking examinations and sitting on committees are frequent nominations for this category among members of the academic profession). Yet these, too, are entered into and executed with willingness and, often, a good spirit, because they are an integral part of the whole campaign of work by which we satisfy our needs and preferences.

Obligation of the Individual

Apart from these personal and rather egocentric considerations, however, man is also obliged to work because he is born not in isolation but into a society. This society has provided him from birth with protection, support, and security. Moreover, when he enters society he finds himself the heir of a vast legacy of culture: a great fund of knowledge and learning; the fruits of years of economic activity in the form of capital goods; long-nurtured skills and insights in the art of social intercourse; and generations of increasing refinement in the appreciation of beauty. All of this is the product of the efforts of his ancestors. And in the present, the individual rests on the continuing work of those who constitute his society. It is a responsibility of adults to make clear to the child his debt to society past and present; to show him that it is through work that this debt is paid—honest, productive, and useful work that will in its turn make a contribution to the health of society and so help to bring to fruition the potentialities of his unborn successors. An understanding of this reciprocal debt can do much to improve the individual's attitude toward his lifework by helping him to perceive its significance and dignity.

Obligation of Society

Since the debt between the individual and society is reciprocal, it follows that society must also continue to discharge its responsibility. In the early stages of the child's life, much of the burden is carried by the parents, but increasingly the State must take over where the resources of the parents prove inadequate. Where exactly this point comes is a matter of great controversy among politicians, economists, educators, religious leaders, and others. Even the most versatile of parents are today daunted by the protean challenges of a complex society. In such circumstances the State must assume a wide range of responsibilities. The welfare state is an inevitable corollary of technology, and nations that ignore this fact because of a primitive loyalty to the fetish of "free" enterprise merely make the passage of the inevitable more painful.

While man must be willing to perform useful work, the State has the duty to provide him with employment. Unemployment is one of the most destructive of diseases, and the nation that tolerates it deserves the consequent moral decline. The State must also provide social security in the form of safeguards against the hazards of sickness, accident, and old age. Only when man has achieved freedom *from* gross want, fear of economic disaster, and lack of opportunity to work, can he aspire toward freedom *to* live creatively and constructively. If the child's education in school prepares him for a freedom that he will later be unable to exercise in adult society because of economic, social, or political conditions over which the State can, if it wishes, exercise control, then that education is misleading and dishonest.

The danger of the welfare state, of course, is that if it is organized unwisely it can lower individual incentive and encourage indolence. The indolent man lacks inner freedom because he is dominated by his indolence. Hence, inner freedom may be harder to attain in an ill-organized welfare state. There is no intrinsic need, however, for the welfare state to be ill-organized, since it can draw on greater potential resources of skill and materials than private enterprise. It is the task of the State, therefore, to find that delicate balance where the citizen's outer freedom is enhanced through the removal of social and economic hindrances, and yet the incentive for him to achieve inner freedom is not reduced.

It must be recognized that this problem presents particular difficulties in contemporary America. To some extent this is because the country has never really worked out a satisfactory reconciliation of the Hamiltonian and Jeffersonian concepts of democracy, with their inconsistent views on the duty of the Federal Government to foster the welfare of the people through positive action. But in part, American politicians must bear responsibility for having failed to educate themselves and the people in the economics of federal intervention and budget-balancing. On this question, as Gunnar Myrdal has pointed out, "large sections of the public and Congress hold . . . an opinion that has no support in economic theory and is not commonly held in other advanced countries: that, in principle, expenditures of the federal budget should be balanced by taxation." [3] What is required is not a balanced *budget* but a balanced *economy*, and this may, at any one time, necessitate an unbalanced budget.

America has reached an unprecedented and critical economic condition: while there is an unsatisfied demand for highly skilled and professional manpower, there is at the same time a large, apparently irreducible, and socially dangerous body of unemployed and underemployed, notably among the unskilled, the young, and Negroes. At the same time, the country is blighted by unnecessary squalor in the form of urban and rural slums, dirty streets, and poor public transport. Massive efforts will be needed to train and retrain people who cannot at present find a productive place in the economic structure and to direct some of these unharnessed energies to the cure of our public ills. But this will require enormously increased federal intervention and expenditure. Myrdal has written,

> In the future society toward which we are moving, where our productive efforts will increasingly have to be devoted to the care of human beings, health, education, research and culture, and to making our local communities more effective instruments for living and working, public spending will be an ever larger part of total spending.[4]

Work, Guilt, and Anxiety

Although most men have been driven to work to satisfy their basic needs, there has arisen, especially in the Protestant world, another motive, less externally obvious but often even more rigorous in its effects. According to Max Weber, man drives himself to work in a self-denying, sacrificial way because of his need to find acceptance in the eyes of God.[5] The Calvinist Puritan developed this attitude even further along the road of compulsiveness by the assumption that man's worldly efforts were a manifestation of his predestined fate of salvation or damnation. The decline of religion was not accompanied by a corresponding decline in compulsive work, however, because with the loss of the traditional religious framework came an increased fear of death as complete oblivion. Work became used as a way of exorcising death from the consciousness and, hence, assuaging the fear.[6]

Under such circumstances, work became a compulsion divorced from any basic economic necessity. Thus we find men, in North America especially, already enjoying economic affluence and yet taking on second, third, and even fourth jobs. Dr. N.R. Martin, speaking at the World Federation for Mental Health at Edinburgh, in 1960, pointed out that many men today suffer from an inner compulsion to work and a feeling of guilt when they are not working. This is producing what he called "Sunday neuroses." He cited as illustration the fact that a greater number of depressions and suicides occur during vacations and weekends than on workdays.[7]

People who are beset by anxiety often try to assuage their inner turmoil by turning to work. There can, thus, develop a form of work addiction: [8] the tensions of work are used to suppress other, less tolerable, inner tensions. Many people in America, especially business executives and professional men, are work addicts who are not free to refrain from the compulsion of overwork.

Work and Health

Nevertheless, scientific, medical, and psychiatric evidence has accumulated during the past half-century to support the belief that, despite neurotic aberrations such as those mentioned above, there is a connection between work and physical and mental health. Physical muscles deteriorate when not used. Attempts to preserve the body through inaction result in destroying it. Similarly, most men seem to need work in order to retain mental equanimity and salubrity.

On the negative side, we have been made aware of the pernicious psychological and moral effects of unemployment. James Conant has suggested as a hypothesis "that the correlation between desirable social attitudes (including attitudes of youth) and job opportunities is far higher than between the former and housing conditions, as measured by plumbing and heating facilities and space per family." [9] On the positive side, we have seen the balancing or therapeutic effects of work on certain people suffering from mental illness. The playwright August Strindberg was an extreme introvert and almost certainly a schizophrenic.

Sylvia Sprigge has suggested that, "if he had not been able to write, surely he would have quite succumbed to his illness; his work was his outlet, his therapy." [10] The mentally sick person is isolated from his fellows, and his major task is to re-establish lines of communication. The unemployed worker suffers from a similar disability in being cut off from the working community. Mental health seems to require at a very deep level a conviction that one is a contributing and communicating member of the world of work.

II DEHUMANIZATION

Man Versus Machine

Modern science and technology have given man the possibility of greater freedom by increasing his mastery over and independence of nature. Medical science can help to free us from unnecessary pain and premature death; the automobile and the airplane can free us from the limits imposed by our own physical nature; household technology can free us from spending our energies in merely keeping warm, clean, and comfortable.

The wise *use* of the fruits of science and technology can enhance our freedom. But the *production* of these fruits raises special problems for the worker in an industrialized society. These can be summed up as what Berdyaev, Jaspers, Marcel, and others have called "dehumanization." The individual becomes divested of part of his humanity and freedom because of his subordination to the needs and nature of the mechanical equipment. Between the worker and his product there now intervenes the machine, whose size and complexity prevent the worker from seeing his completed product as a whole and useful contribution to the economic life of society and, hence, hinder him from finding sense and meaning in his work. "Inert matter," read a Papal Encyclical, "comes from the factory or work-shop with a nobility added to it, while men emerge from it in a state of degradation." [11]

To the employer, the significant aspect of the worker is not his personality but his output. Inherited from nineteenth-century capitalism is the view of the relationship between employer and worker as based on contract, with money the nexus. The employer who pays money for labor tends to regard it as a commodity like any other part of his costs. Efficiency becomes the watchword, but efficiency is seen entirely in terms of material production, with the intangibles of human happiness excluded from consideration as long as they do not impinge on that production. A good example of this is seen in the problem of the transportation of workers to and from the factory. The steady improvement in transportation facilities could have eased the tedium and strain of the journey to and from work. But, as Bertrand Russell has pointed out, there seems to be a law that improvements in transportation do not reduce traveling time but only increase the distance over which people have to travel. The reason is that better transportation has been used by industry to achieve centralization into larger units for greater technical efficiency. The worker's traveling time and conditions are ignored by industry because it does not have to pay him for the time spent in this way. But to the worker himself, of course, the problem of the journey to work has a crucial bearing on his happiness and welfare.

Another important pressure toward dehumanization lies in the fact that in the factory the tempo of work tends to be set by the machine and not the worker. Samuel Miller has said,

Here at the very apex of a highly developed individualism, sustained by centuries of freedom, education, and technological advance, man is caught in a situation where he counts for less and less. . . . Emotional rapport, intuitive insights, flexible variation, alert discrimination, original possibilities, fade before the huge juggernaut of mechanistic perfection and uniformity.[12]

The industrial worker clocks-in in the morning, and until he clocks-out again at night his life is dominated by a sense of order, time, and rhythm that derives from mechanical requirements. Factory life is scaled to the machine rather than to man, making his task of understanding and mastering the machine more difficult. Furthermore, the greater the gap between the power of the machine and man's understanding, the more man's freedom is reduced. "The peril of nuclear physics," wrote Charles Morgan, "consists in the disproportion of its power to the wisdom of mankind and . . . this disproportion remains whether the power is used to make a bomb or to drive a machine." [13] At the other end of the scale, anyone who has used a power lawn mower will be aware of the ease with which the machine can take over from man the task of setting the pace of work and of imposing on him the demands inherent in its own nature. Often the worker reacts against this domination by the tempo of the machine with behavior that is an understandable, if not always prudent, gesture of independence: constant evasion of thought about work, obsessive reveries while on the job, substitution of the glamour of leisure for the drudgery of work, crazy racing against the clock to vary the deadly monotony, slowdowns, wildcat strikes against "speedups." [14] Perhaps the most significant gesture toward a lost freedom is the usually unrealistic talk about "having my own little business" some day. Although the middle classes have largely abandoned this dream in favor of the security of the large corporation or the profession, the vision of independence through individual enterprise still acts for many members of the working class as a hypothetical escape from the tyranny of the machine.

Specialization

One of the greatest threats to industrial man's humanity comes from an essential feature of modern factory production—the division of labor. It has been regarded as essential since before Adam Smith's famous statement of its advantages in *The Wealth of Nations*.[15] Today, it is not too much to say, it is the "philosophers' stone" of industrial mass production, turning the lead of raw materials into the gold of our high material standard of living.

From the consumer's point of view, it makes possible a life of unprecedented comfort, ease, and material luxury. But from the worker's point of view it is accompanied by some less fortunate consequences: it becomes increasingly difficult for the worker to remain "whole" when, in his work, he is never related to any wholes. He is only a part of a vast process whose beginning, end, meaning, and purpose he cannot see. Work has always been man's chief medium for introducing meaning into his life: if his work loses meaning, where is he to find his life's significance? As the division of labor becomes ever more refined and minute, it seems likely that the individual's work will become more blind and compulsive.

Division of labor in the factory is matched by increasing specialization of function at the professional and managerial level. Again, this has borne considerable fruits in the greater depth of knowledge and power of concentration of the expert. But again it is accompanied by the dangers of fragmentation and imbalance, which extract a payment in terms of a loss of human freedom. In one form this is seen in the reduced freedom of communication between professional people in different disciplines. The physicist finds himself with less and less to say to the architect; the doctor scratches desperately for a topic of conversation that will engage the attention of the business man. "It's not that the educated person lacks curiosity nowadays;" said Richard Wilbur, "it's that he feels he must ruthlessly prune his curiosity in order to make it bear fruit. . . . One's sense of the magnitude of one's own field dissuades one from trespassing idly on any other." [16]

This development into increasing specialization represents another aspect of the dehumanizing of man, for man's uniqueness lies in his general nature. Unlike the animals, man has refused to be shut up in a narrow specialization that would forever limit the direction and scope of his development. The wings of the bird, the gills of the fish, and the immense size of the brontosaurus all took them into closed avenues of evolution; man, however, maintained the general intelligence and non-specialized form that enabled him to invent tools and technology and to develop psychologically. The chief danger in the increasing specialization of man's work is that it will make him into a mere technician— albeit an expert one—with an imagination that has dried up from lack of the nourishment that comes from the cross-fertilization, the unexpected analogies, and the fruitful comparisons that are the stimulus of the non-specialist. Peter Viereck has written,

Ultimately freedom's advantage over totalitarianism lies in the greater imaginative resourcefulness of the non-specializing free individual. His imagination overcomes the advantage in discipline that totalitarianism has over freedom, whether in war or peace.[17]

The Challenge to Capitalism

Nineteenth-century capitalism was bound to be challenged because it operated against man's constant striving for personal significance and full humanity. Based on the profit motive, it necessarily placed human considerations in a subordinate position—if anywhere. The most important challenge to this degradation and exploitation of the worker came from Karl Marx. He correctly diagnosed and condemned this system as an exploitation of the weak by the strong—as the dictatorship of the capitalist. But in his remedy he fell into an error remarkably similar to that of capitalism: he recommended simply another type of dictatorship—that of the workers. There is no ultimate hope for a system that rests on the dictatorship of the many, the few, or the single one. We have seen in the recent history of American trade unionism that workers are blessed with no special built-in mechanism to save them from exercising as ruthless a tyranny as any boss when they are in a position to do so. Moreover, communism shares with capitalism the view of society as made up of conflicting interests: a view that again reduces man's humanity and freedom by demanding that he be true to his class or group rather than to himself and to mankind. In the last analysis, it is the mechanical and static nature of the communist-capitalist interpretation of society and its relationships that renders it anachronistic: relationships between people can be harmonized only by taking a dynamic view and by regarding people (workers and employers) as persons rather than as members of groups.

While Continental socialism owes much to Marx, other socialist groups have attempted to formulate a more humane and flexible brand of social democracy. This is true of the Labour Party in Britain, the C.C.F. party (and now the New Democratic Party) in Canada, and the

Scandinavian socialist parties. The emphasis here has been on eliminating the grosser forms of inequality and exploitation through a varied and pragmatic program of social ownership. Much of this process is healthy, since social ownership in one form or another seems inevitable everywhere as the scale of technology increases. Thus, the nation that adopts a carefully thought-out policy of industrial modification will be better prepared for the future than one that passively accepts or struggles against the tide of economic evolution. However, there have been disappointments accompanying this process, and it is clear now that nationalization is no panacea for the problem of work in modern society. Despite the high hopes with which the British workers took over "their own" railways, coal, and other industries under the Attlee government, the old problems of production, incentive, and management-worker relations today remain obstinately extant. It is perhaps not surprising that the coal miner should fail to regard and treat the mine in which he works as his own. After all, we do not expect the soldier to regard himself as the owner of the army, although it is no less than a nationalized industry under the ultimate control of the government and the people. We are here up against a problem that faces and threatens to defeat all economic systems—capitalist, communist, or socialist—the problem of the vast size of modern industry and its consequently impersonal nature.

Decentralization

William Morris, Eric Gill, and others have proposed as a solution to this problem of the impersonal atmosphere of large-scale industry the method of decentralization. Collect men together in small, local units, where the manager can know all the workers personally, where the journey to work will not be a hell of tedium or tension, and where the life of the community can be to a degree reflected in the life of the factory. Under these conditions, it is argued, man will be able to comprehend the scale of his workplace and will begin to realize his personal responsibility and recover his identity. The principal flaw in this argument until now has been that it ignores a basic economic fact: modern industry largely depends, for the maintenance and enlargement of its profit margin, on the economies of scale that follow heavily concentrated production. No industry considers that it can afford to neglect the competitive pressures driving it always in pursuit of an efficiency measured in terms of material production. Samuel Courtauld has courageously stated, "The quality of the workers who leave the factory doors every evening is an even more important thing than the quality of the products which it delivers to the customers," [18] But private industry still remains unconvinced of this order of responsibilities, and if it is to be persuaded of the importance of its human task it must be convinced in terms of economic efficiency.

In recent years, however, a new element in the economic situation brings renewed hope to the apostles of decentralization. Automation represents in some ways a threat to the worker; its advent often means a painful period of transition during which many may lose their jobs because their old tasks are rendered redundant and new work cannot be found for them under the changed conditions. But in other ways automation holds promise of a better life, because ultimately the factory that introduces automation will find itself less dependent on the large reservoirs of labor concentrated in the great conurbations. Consequently, factories can be located according to other criteria, such as the aesthetic or hygienic, away from the deadening atmosphere of large cities. The easier transportation of modern fuels, such as electricity and nuclear power, as opposed to that of the older fuels, such as coal and oil, is another factor of encouragement in this direction.

Industrialism and Manual Labor

Although the satisfactions of the life of the preindustrial artisan have often been exaggerated, he did possess one advantage, the lack of which impoverishes modern man. There was an integrity about his work because he was involved in the whole process of production from beginning to end, and because his whole being—hand, heart, and head—was employed in the work. When we are wholly involved in an undertaking there seems to flow from the work to us a sort of healing power. Etymologically, "whole," "heal," and "health" all derive from the same Anglo-Saxon root. It is this activation of the whole person that is so frequently denied to the modern industrial worker. Indeed, modern man in general seems condemned to be a worker with *either* hand or brain, but not both.

In this we are in a position analogous to that of the citizens of the Greek city-states and later of Rome. Plato and Aristotle agreed that manual labor was degrading and favored the use of slaves to discharge such tasks. In Rome, similarly, the value and meaning of manual labor were lost through reliance on the institution of slavery. It was primarily through monasticism that the significance and dignity of labor were restored to Europe. Today we have instead of the slave the industrial machine—although there is more doubt now which is master and which is slave. There are some today who would attempt a solution by repudiating industrialism as we repudiated slavery. Particularly in the case of so-called underdeveloped countries, some observers feel that the industrialization these countries so eagerly seek should be discouraged because it will inevitably bring with it the loss of those qualities of integrity, spontaneity, and mental health at present enjoyed by people who work in preindustrial economies.

Quite apart from the validity of such an analysis of the people of the underdeveloped countries, it is futile to attempt to repudiate industrialism. The industrialized nations cannot go back on it, for their way of life is too deeply committed to it. And we cannot take the decision for anyone else. Although we may find that parts of our apple are rotten, we cannot forbid others who are tempted by the rosy skin to take one and try it for themselves. C.P. Snow has expressed bitingly the choice we face:

It is all very well for us, sitting pretty, to think that material standards of living don't matter all that much. It is all very well for one, as a personal choice, to reject industrialisation—do a modern Walden, if you like, and if you do without much food, see most of your children die in infancy, despise the comforts of literacy, accept twenty years off your own life, then I respect you for the strength of your aesthetic revulsion. But I don't respect you in the slightest if, even passively, you try to impose the same choice on others who are not free to choose.[19]

We must, then, accept the pattern of industrialism but at the same time try to fight its dehumanizing effects. One approach is through the reintroduction of the idea and practice of meaningful manual work. Although this task is formidable, its importance renders the effort worthwhile, and we can take heart from some attempts that are already showing fruitful results. The work-camp movement, the "do-it-yourself" trend, the Peace Corps, the VISTA program, and the work programs in colleges like Antioch and Wilmington in Ohio and Berea in Kentucky all are examples of man coming to grips with a real problem of understandable size and tackling it with his whole person. The food shortages that led to the widespread creation and cultivation of garden allotments in Britain and the United States during the Second World War brought unexpected dividends to thousands of people in the form of a new-found delight in the interaction of a person with the earth. There is no knowing how many neuroses have been avoided in industrial societies through the therapy of gardening. An old Negro in Ohio, who had been brought up on a farm but had spent most of his adult life in industrial work, in later years found himself a plot of land to cultivate. He told me, speaking of the long, barren years of industrial work: "Oh, how I missed that scratchin' in the ground." It may well be that through the medium of working together on a task where mind and body are fully employed men can find some of the communication and reconciliation that are necessary to withstand the psychological and spiritual impoverishment of industrialism.

It must be acknowledged, however, that manual work can be at best only a palliative to the human problems of industrialism. It works only on the fringes of the situation in the senses that it can usually be reintroduced only into the leisure sector of life rather than into the work sector; it accepts the economic *status quo* with the profit motive in the center of the picture, and it attempts to patch up when a radical reformation of the industrial system may be necessary.

Human Relations

A number of far-sighted men have observed the developing dilemma of man in industrialized societies and have tried to work out a cure in terms of an emphasis on the human relationships operating in the factory. This approach grew partly out of the work of Elton Mayo, of the Harvard School of Business Administration, and his disciples. They stressed the need for management to be aware that the worker is a person and that the factory is a miniature society. The relationships within that society are a crucial factor in determining the development of the worker's personality and, hence, play a vital role in controlling morale and efficiency.

As a consequence, industries persuaded by this "human-relations" assumption place great store by such factors as two-way communication between management and workers, substantial worker participation in details and principles of production, concern for the health of the social atmosphere of the factory, and the selection of foremen with the ability to lead through gentle persuasion rather than loud authoritarianism. There can be no doubt that the advent of "human relations" into the factory has done much to make it a pleasanter place to work in and has brought benefits to both workers and management.

The Polaroid Corporation is an outstanding example of a company that has successfully concerned itself with human relations without losing its concern for product-efficiency. Workers are treated as creative persons who would rather do a good day's work than not. It is made clear to them that they are regarded as people who are capable of preparing themselves through further training and education to take on more interesting, responsible, and creative work. Polaroid has found that productivity has gone up, morale is high, workers are loyal. It is even claimed that the relationships of workers with their families have improved: better human relations in the factory lead to better human relations in other areas of life.

Another approach that utilizes insights gained in the study of human relations is the production team. Kimball and McClellan, who are optimistic about the direction of technology in America, have suggested the well-designed production team as the ideal of the kind of human relationship they would like to foster: first, each person has a determinate role in the team, a role he can perceive as an indispensable element in his own self-concept; second, this role, which is more than technical skill, is recognized in the group as performing a function; and third, the work of the team as a whole is disciplined and supported by objectively defined purposes.[20]

However, before we accept it as the millennium, we should be aware of at least three implications of the "human-relations" approach. In the first place, we must realize that although the worker is thus treated more humanely, he is treated this way for exactly the reason the nineteenth-century worker was often treated brutally—because it is believed that this is the way to induce him to produce most efficiently. In other words, the factory remains firmly product-centered and not man-centered. It is also significant that the change in factory relations closely parallels other changes in society—reflections of a move away from physical coercion and toward psychological manipulation as a favored method of control. The worker today no doubt feels fewer constraints than did his nineteenth-century predecessor. But is he, therefore, objectively freer if he is equally controlled by other means? In fact, might not his position be more dangerously submissive in that he is less aware of the forces that reduce his freedom? If one were pessimistic, one might liken the difference to that between the overtly coercive atmosphere of George Orwell's *1984* and the more gentle but more terrifying atmosphere of Aldous Huxley's *Brave New World*. Moreover, while this "human-relations" approach may help the worker's morale by concentrating his attention on social factors and group relationships, it may in the process direct his attention away from the work itself. If it does so, it would seem to have a limited prospect as a solution to the central problem of the worker's relation to his work.

All of these attempts to deal with the problem of dehumanization are vitiated in part because they fail to hold man firmly in the center of the industrial picture. They are ultimately product-centered or profit-centered or efficiency-centered. The situation will remain discouraging as long as the principal capitalist country, the United States, and the principal communist country, the Soviet Union, are engaged in a race to see whose economic system is more "productive"—that is, productive of material goods irrespective of human cost. Our real task is to raise our sights above this miserable goal. However, the affluent society that is coming into existence through these efforts may present new opportunities as well as new dangers.

III THE AFFLUENT SOCIETY

Work and Affluence

In the underdeveloped countries of the world, man is in bondage because he is not yet free from material want and disease. The principal motivation to work is hunger or the threat of hunger. In industrial countries, material prosperity has lifted man above the level of starvation and physical debility but has introduced new hungers, with their attendant problems. Education in materially backward countries must be primarily enlisted in the campaign against basic physical handicaps —inefficient methods of agriculture, medical and sanitary ignorance, and illiteracy. Moreover, as has been pointed out, we cannot advocate that such countries avoid industrialization on the grounds that we ourselves see in it certain dangers and disenchantments. But this does not mean that industrialized nations should follow a formula that is appropriate for underdeveloped countries by concentrating on material production and consumption oblivious of other considerations, educating young people to be able to produce always more, and developing their taste for affluence.

For we have seen in the affluent societies of Europe and North America that the progressive acquisition of material goods guarantees neither happiness nor satiety. Hunger and Puritanism have increasingly given way as motivating forces to the desire for more and more of the world's goods and services. Those people in poorer countries who look forward to a Utopia of contentment when every family will own an automobile and a television set should observe more carefully the level of material contentment in North America, which has approached this standard of consumption only to find that second automobiles and second television sets are increasingly regarded as necessities. The important aspect of this development is not the fact that man has material demands—this is universal—but that the satisfaction of these demands leads in modern societies to their replacement by even more urgent demands, which in turn have to be paid for by extra work. The proverbial Chinese coolie today compares unfavorably as a worker with the New York business executive.

Affluence and Social Control

There can be no radical solution to the problems of work in an affluent society that does not come to grips with the structure of the external environment, rather than just tinker with the internal arrangements of factory life. Eli Ginzberg has endorsed Karl Marx's contention that "a meaningful consideration of work and freedom must be set within the broad framework of the total pattern of life rather than limited to the factory and its hours and conditions of employment." [21] A major feature of this external environment that must be examined is the power of business and industry to direct and control the individual's work-pattern by their manipulation of his material desires.

In this area of consumption, an enormous investment has been made in techniques that are designed to increase man's desire for material goods and to steer those desires in profitable directions. As Erich Fromm has pointed out, the very size of the capital investment in consumer-goods industries and the competition among a few giant firms make it necessary not to allow the consumer a free choice of whether and what he wants to buy. "His appetites have to be constantly whetted; his tastes have to be manipulated, managed, and made predictable. Man is transformed into the 'consumer,' the eternal suckling, whose one wish is to consume more and 'better' things." [22] The twin tempters of advertising and installment-buying create in the individual demands that do not arise spontaneously and then persuade him to satisfy these demands in the present by working harder in the future. Work becomes primarily not a way of making the individual's life more creative, enjoyable, and interesting, but a way of supporting the automobile or cosmetic or liquor industry.

The only ways to protect the individual from this external control of his life are social control and planning, and education. The greatest enemy of social control and planning is the doctrine—or its modern interpretations—of *laissez-faire* individualism. One of the most significant features of this doctrine is the fact that it was originally conceived to treat circumstances radically different from those of twentieth-century industrialism. It originated with the physiocrats of eighteenth-century France and was taken up and reinterpreted in late eighteenth- and early nineteenth-century England by Adam Smith, Thomas Malthus, and David Ricardo. These men believed that there are natural laws governing economic, social, and political life that, if left to themselves without harmful governmental interference, will result in a natural and beneficial harmony. Subsequently, individualism received support from the English utilitarians, like Bentham and Mill, and from the theory of evolution, which maintained that a process of natural, unimpeded evolution would result in the survival of the fittest. Writers like Herbert Spencer and John Stuart Mill advocated that education, for example, should remain outside the province of government. The doctrine has survived in the twentieth century through such writers as Friedrich Hayek [23] and Ludwig von Mises. [24]

Unfortunately, the issue is often misrepresented by the advocates of *laissez-faire* as one of freedom *versus* control. One should rather ask what *kind* and *extent* of control over *whom* will enhance the freedom of most people? This will entail a careful study of prevailing conditions, for the kinds of control necessary will alter as conditions change. When, as in the eighteenth century, road traffic was horse-drawn and relatively sparse, a minimum of traffic control would maximize the individual's freedom of movement. In the twentieth century, the speed and quantity of motor traffic ensure that a *laissez-faire* traffic policy reduces rather than increases the road users' freedom. Moreover, a *laissez-faire* policy for the business community results in a loss of freedom for the wider community. This has become increasingly clear with the exploitation by the advertising industry of the mass media of communication. Advertisers who are allowed complete freedom from government interference in their use of the channels of mass communication to disseminate propaganda on behalf of their products infringe the liberty of choice of the consumer. It might be asked how much freedom of choice the buyer is exercising when he reaches automatically for a packet on the eye-level shelf at the supermarket, after having had the name of the product hammered into him visually and aurally (and perhaps subliminally) every day for years? [25] Even more seriously, we must ask what power a young person has today to make a "free" decision whether or not to smoke cigarettes? The six largest tobacco manufacturers in America spend more than $200,000,000 annually to promote their products. Much of this advertising is directed at young people. The uninformed teenager, who is concerned to be one of the gang, sophisticated, grown-up, has a difficult task in combating the influence of this enormous campaign of persuasion. Although many countries in Europe have controlled tobacco advertising, the Federal Trade Commission in America has displayed a fundamental incapacity to regulate the tobacco industry in order to protect the consumer.[26]

If the individual in the affluent society is to be given a fair chance of freeing himself from the mud of materialism and rising to a level of higher aspiration, he must—because of the power of the mass media— be provided with assistance from the government in the form of control over advertising and business. There is no good reason why the family who drive out to the countryside to refresh themselves with natural beauty should be prevented from seeing the beauty by billboards exhorting them to buy products for which they have no genuine need. Nor is there a good reason why they should not be able to listen to a radio concert or watch a television play without having their mood interrupted and their aesthetic sense jarred by similar advertisements. If the government will play its part in the protection of the individual—

through laws, regulations, and restraints on the business community, through strengthening such agencies as the Federal Trade Commission and the Federal Communications Commission, and through direct intervention in mass media along the lines of the British Broadcasting Corporation or the Canadian Broadcasting Corporation—then education can play its part in attempting to make him more autonomous, self-reliant, and free, with reasonable hope of success.

The productive power of the affluent society brings with it, for the first time in the history of industrialism, the real opportunity to put man in the center of the picture and move the machine to one side, where it will still be able to produce the goods needed for a life of material affluence. But this will require federal intervention, planning, and control on a scale that America up till now has not been prepared to envision. W.H. Ferry, Vice-President of the Fund for the Republic, has suggested that "In an abundant society the problem is not an economic one of keeping the machine running regardless of what it puts out, but a political one of achieving the common good. And planning is one of its major means." [27] He envisages the affluent society as one where there is a six-month work year and retirement at fifty at full pay, accompanied by the continuation of education well into adult years, at public expense. There should also be payment from the public treasury for "non-productive" effort, such as writing novels, painting pictures, composing music, doing graduate work, and taking part in the expanding functions of government.[28]

We have the productive power now to base the pattern of work on man the creator instead of on man the consumer. Whether we shall choose to do so will depend largely on whether we can rid ourselves in time of anachronistic political and economic notions of *laissez-faire* individualism that may have had some relevance to eighteenth-century conditions but are a fatally expensive indulgence in the second half of the twentieth century.

Cybernation and Poverty

An unprecedented challenge and an unprecedented opportunity are being presented to the industrialized nations of the world by the introduction of cybernation—that is, the use of computers and automated devices. Although cybernation is still young and its use has been limited, we are already beginning to realize that its large-scale employment will both make possible an era of unparalleled affluence and raise social and educational problems of formidable magnitude. It will be possible to continue to raise the average material standard of living and at the same time to reduce drastically the working-day, working-week, working-year, and working-life of most people.

One of the problems that will be exacerbated by cybernation, however, is that there will be increased tendencies in industrialized countries toward the development of a growing gap between the rich and the poor. We are already seeing in America the danger of "two nations" growing up side by side, with little knowledge of or contact with each other. There is J.K. Galbraith's "affluent society"—those with the education, skills, knowledge, and ability to participate in the increasingly difficult and complex but rewarding activities of a highly technological society. And there is Michael Harrington's "other America"—those who, for reasons of age, race, sex, social class, background, or education, have missed the benefits of the affluent society and lack the skills that would enable them to contribute to its progress. It has been estimated that about one-fifth of the American people live in poverty amidst surrounding affluence. Moreover, because the level of education required for participation in a technological economy is constantly rising, the distance between the haves and the have-nots is increasing. The proportion of total income received by the poorest 20 percent of the American population fell from 4.9 percent in 1944 to 4.7 percent in 1963.[29] This process bears a significant similarity to the growing difference between the developed countries and the undeveloped countries of the world.

This trend carries with it a host of important implications, most of which cannot be fully explored here. One or two of the educationally significant might, however, be mentioned. In the first place, it seems certain that the traditional connection between work and income will be seriously weakened and, in many cases, broken. The apparently irremovable pool of unemployment that we have at present may be the harbinger of a growing body of people—especially Negroes, teenagers, old people, geographically immobile people—for whom no income-earning work can be found in the economic system. If the economy is not to break down because of lack of effective demand from large numbers of the population, there will have to be an important change in American attitudes, so that we can pay people from public funds even though they do not work in traditional ways.

The economy of abundance can sustain all citizens in comfort and economic security whether or not they engage in what is commonly reckoned as work. . . . Society, through its appropriate legal and governmental institutions [should] undertake an unqualified commitment to provide every individual and every family with an adequate income as a matter of right.[30]

Secondly, the traditional distinction between work and play is likely to become less clear, and there will be new opportunities for interpreting "work" in ways that have previously been associated with leisure or education.

The present system encourages activities which can lead to private profit and neglects those activities which can enhance the wealth and the quality of life of our society. . . . The era of cybernation can reverse this emphasis. . . . Society as a whole must encourage new modes of constructive, rewarding and ennobling activity. Principal among these are activities, such as teaching and learning, that relate people to people rather than people to things.[31]

Education for the Affluent Society

The educational implications of this technological revolution and economic affluence are vast. Some of them, as they relate to work and leisure, will be explored later. For the present, we shall look at one of the less obvious but still crucial implications.

One of the first educational needs of the student in the affluent society is for an introduction to the economics of affluence. This does not mean a course in orthodox economic theory; it means bringing the student to an awareness of the pressures that bear on him, their varying validities, and the defenses he possesses to resist them. Thoreau's complaint about nineteenth-century college economics can still be read with amusement and profit: "Even the *poor* student studies and is taught only *political* economy, while that economy of living which is synonymous with philosophy is not even sincerely professed in our college. The consequence is, that while he is reading Adam Smith, Ricardo, and Say, he runs his father in debt irretrievably." [32] For the wise, mature person, material comfort can be a boon that releases in him forces of productivity and creativity. But for the immature, it can be a grave moral danger. We can see in some of the less pleasant aspects of teenage life in modern industrial societies that the combination of material opulence with immaturity brings not contentment or creativity but dissatisfaction and moral degeneration. Schools and colleges can help their students to avoid this fate. The first step in doing so is to help them to become economically realistic and restrained.

Part of this education consists of showing the student that he has the freedom not only to read or listen or watch but also to refrain from reading, listening, or watching. George Bernard Shaw once named as the most valuable invention of the twentieth century the switch that turns off the radio. Schools can show students that not all reading is good or beneficial, that it is as important to know *what* to read as *how* to read, and that this implies knowing what *not* to read. The teaching of skills is insufficient: it must be supplemented by training in discrimination or it stands the risk of being a destructive force.

A more vital part of this educational process, however—because it is a more positive part—consists of helping young people to envision and aspire toward a kind of life that is richer and more satisfying than the materially affluent and the frenetically acquisitive.[33] But this is a tall order, for it means that the school must operate in opposition to the prevailing values of society. Nevertheless, the attempt must be made, for if man in modern society ultimately loses his freedom, it is less likely to occur as a result of an Orwellian dictatorship crushing him by physical force than by a Huxleyan seduction of his moral fibre by the temptations of material well-being. In the latter case, life would externally be little changed, but man would essentially be a slave by virtue of having given up the striving for a higher and freer way of life and having settled for the lowest level of aspiration available to him.

The chief danger in affluence is that when we surround ourselves by material abundance we tend to expect joy and life from these external things rather than from some center within ourselves. This causes the power for life and joy within us to atrophy while we look for these benefits to material things that are incapable of providing them. But most people in the West seem unwilling to acknowledge themselves to be unmitigated materialists. We aspire to something else for ourselves and our children: we claim that we do not hold material values as primary. However, if we observe current practice in the countries of Western Europe and North America, it appears that we pay lip service to this position in our teachings but ignore it in our behavior. In this it seems that a country like the Soviet Union has a great advantage, in that its official doctrine of materialism and its practice are entirely consistent. Many writers in the West criticize the Soviet Union on the grounds of its materialism. Surely we ought either to desist from such criticism and agree with the Soviet Union that we share their materialistic values, or, alternatively, if we claim to espouse other, superior values, we should begin to organize our society and our educational system along lines that will make those superior values operative in the realm of behavior. If we choose this second course, however, it will involve encouraging our children to question the whole basis of our present way of life and to attempt to formulate a better substitute. Central to this endeavor will be a consideration of the concept of simplicity.

IV SIMPLICITY

Freedom and Desire

Subjective freedom can be defined as the ratio between the individual's desires and his capacity to satisfy them; between what he intends and what he can achieve; between "wanting" and "power." [34] For this reason, a society in which great differences of wealth and power prevail will be marked by a relative lack of subjective freedom: the poor and unprivileged will see all around them evidence of the greater command of resources enjoyed by their neighbors and, hence, will be more liable to suffer increases in their own desires without a corresponding increase in their ability to satisfy them. If my neighbor, Mr. Jones, a successful business executive, enjoys an income twice as great as mine, and if I am possessed by an ambition to "keep up" with him, then my subjective freedom is diminished by the enlarged gap between my material wishes and my means.

It is clear, then, that my subjective freedom may be increased by an increase in my means. What is not so frequently recognized is that it may equally be increased by a decrease in my desires. The man who succeeds in making his demands simple enhances his freedom accordingly: the greater our wants the greater our dependence. He who masters the art of the simple life gives himself greater command over those aspects of life that are truly enriching and cuts out of his life much that is dispersing and impoverishing. If we are enriched by our means we are also impoverished by our wants.

This truth has been rediscovered and transmitted by generation after generation of sages and thinkers, but apparently we still fail to heed it. Twenty-five centuries ago Lao Tze said in the *Tao-Te King*,

> Appear in plainness and hold to simplicity:
> Restrain selfishness and curtail desires.[35]

Of princes and kings, he said,

> I would restrain them by the nameless Simplicity,
> In order to make them free from desire.
> Free from desire, they would be at rest;
> And the world would of itself become rectified.[36]

More than a century ago, Thoreau made his famous attempt to attain freedom through simplicity. By curtailing his material desires he found that he could meet all the expenses of living by working with his hands for about six weeks in a year. The rest of the time he then had free for study, contemplation, and the cultivation of the art of living. "My greatest skill," he wrote, "has been to want but little. . . . A man is rich in proportion to the number of things which he can afford to let alone." [37] He talked pityingly of "that seemingly wealthy, but most terribly impoverished class of all, who have accumulated dross, but know not how to use it, or get rid of it, and thus have forged their own golden or silver fetters." [38] In this century, Bede Griffiths has told in his autobiography how he and two companions, disillusioned by the futile complexity and materialistic pettiness of modern civilization, tried to recapture the life and spirit of the simple culture of the Cotswolds in England. By living simply and concentrating on essentials, they found that the annual cost of living for three of them was £100 for everything (including books!). Griffiths distinguished between a complex civilization and a simple culture as follows: "While a civilization is concerned with the continual extension of material luxury, often at the cost of the health and happiness of those who work for it, a culture like that of the Cotswolds, in which we were living, is based first of all on the necessities of human life, on the need for food and clothing and shelter." [39] The simplicity that Griffiths achieved released him for the activities that he considered central to his life—prayer, reading, and contemplation.

Simplicity and Responsibility

Just as in the society marked by gross disparities of wealth, so in a world characterized by both luxurious affluence and grinding poverty, the subjective freedom of the poor—individuals or nations—is diminished. This awareness of lack of means is a factor of instability in the world. The African bushman, living near or below the starvation level, isolated from white men, may be relatively content and uninterested in change. But the well-fed, well-clothed, educated African of Rhodesia is made restless and discontented by the sight of his fellow workers with white skins enjoying an income several times as large as his own. It is useless for the overfed white minority of the world's population to claim that they have a right to their material superiority over the underfed colored majority by virtue of their superior productivity. The colored man now knows as well as the white man that this higher productivity has been made possible in part by the white man's good fortune in living in areas of the world with a plenitude of natural resources and an invigorating climate, to say nothing of his willingness to exploit for his own advantage the natural and human resources of the underdeveloped areas of the world through political or economic colonialism.

The history and extent of the division of the world into rich and poor imposes on the affluent an economic responsibility toward the needy. This responsibility coincides with economic and political self-interest, for there are already signs that the industrialized nations cannot keep their economies going without the markets represented by the peoples of the underdeveloped nations who, however, cannot afford to pay for the goods they need. There is a need for a drastic reorganization of the economies of the wealthy countries in order to support the hungry ones. Arnold Toynbee has said,

The marginal production of the minority's technology will have to be redirected, away from its present prostitution to the frivolous purpose of supplying a satiated minority with superfluities, and towards supplying the majority's elementary needs. And the productive minority will have to become convinced that paying to meet other people's basic needs is a more satisfactory way of disposing of the product of one's economic labors than spending the same amount of purchasing power on superfluities for themselves.[40]

In other words, the discharge of our responsibility to the less fortunate among our fellow men means that we of the more prosperous countries must rise to a greater simplicity in our lives. In order to be fit enough to carry our brothers along with us, we must strip away many hampering and debilitating luxuries and complexities. The Taizé Community, in France, a Christian community devoted to the loving service of mankind, says in its *Rule:* "Your disposability implies a simplification of your existence, not by fear but by faith. . . . Reject useless burdens so that you may better carry to Christ your Lord those of other men, your brothers." [41]

Education for Simplicity

In an affluent society there is a sense in which an education for simplicity must be antecedent to an education for work. It has been pointed out that there are multiple pressures operating on the individual in such a society influencing him to work for spurious goals. If we are going to submit to the authority of work, it is good to know why. This is how an education for simplicity can help—by clarifying our values, putting things into perspective, and helping to ensure that we are working for goals that we genuinely hold as primary.

We do not serve children by training them to increase their ability to earn unless we also show them that to become bogged down in ever-increasing material demands constitutes a loss, not an increment, of freedom. Charles Wagner wrote,

The man who gives himself up entirely to the service of his appetites makes them grow and multiply so well that they become stronger than he; and once their slave, he loses his moral sense, loses his energy, and becomes incapable of discerning and practicing the good. He has surrendered himself to the inner anarchy of desire, which in the end gives birth to outer anarchy. In the moral life we govern ourselves. In the immoral life we are governed by our needs and passions; thus, little by little, the bases of the moral life shift, and the law of judgment deviates.[42]

To educate young people for simplicity means to bring them to an understanding of the importance of distinguishing the essential from the secondary. Essential simplicity involves more than ridding ourselves of superfluous material possessions, important as this might be in clearing the ground. It involves reaching a clear view of what is centrally important in our lives, and then cutting away all the peripheral encumbrances that hinder us from achieving this central purpose. Consequently, a vital part of the program will consist of teaching children discrimination and appreciation. Hence, they must not be indulged; for the child who is provided with all luxuries is thereby prevented from learning to appreciate the true value of things.

The educated man is he whose life is not dissipated by the tyranny of a thousand details, who can keep his eye on the main endeavor despite the multifarious press of the mundane. He must have developed the power of intellect and will ruthlessly to cut out of his life all those things that are dispersing and that prevent his concentration on the highest aspiration that his talents make possible. Simplicity releases him for nobler work than a further round in the amassing of yet another load of acquisitions. When man

has obtained those things which are necessary to life, there is another alternative than to obtain the superfluities; and that is, to adventure on life now, his vacation from humbler toil having commenced. The soil, it appears, is suited to the seed, for it has sent its radical downward, and it may now send its shoot upward also with confidence. Why has man rooted himself thus firmly in the earth, but that he may rise in the same proportion into the heavens above?—for the nobler plants are valued for the fruit they bear at last in the air and light, far from the ground.[43]

V   EDUCATION FOR WORK

Man and Worker

Education must produce in the same person both man and worker. Moreover, the two goals must be achieved in the same process. The relationship between man and worker is structural rather than additive: the worker is part of the man and not stuck onto him. Hence, we must question whether the popular distinction between liberal and vocational education is a fruitful one. Men like Robert Hutchins have not made their most helpful contribution in trying to maintain the classical superiority of a "pure" liberal education. Where the liberal and the vocational are clearly divorced, both suffer. Vocational and practical education carried on in separate trade schools too often becomes an introduction to the tricks of the trade and to a knowledge of particular examples without an analysis of the underlying theoretical principles. Such isolated vocational education has usually operated as a conservative force in society, keeping children from the lower strata of society in their places. This is because much of it has constituted a training in skills that were already outmoded, or would be by the time the young person was ready for work. This tendency toward rapid skill-obsolescence is certain to increase with the introduction of cybernation. Even some of those who support vocational education recognize that it must be transformed in the affluent society. "What Negro youth in the cotton districts need," Myrdal has written, "is not perfection in growing cotton . . . but a training that will help them to get out of the cotton districts and to compete for jobs in the expanding sectors of the American economy." [44]

On the other hand, a "liberal" or "gentlemanly" education that rigorously keeps itself untainted by manual or practical work often produces pupils who fail to relate the concepts dealt with to any percepts and, hence, fail to make the knowledge really their own—which means that they do not become educated. We are seeing the fruits of this snobbish "liberal" education today in various nations of Asia and Africa, where university graduates with no hope of employment in white-collar jobs (because the economy cannot yet carry so many bureaucrats or professional people) hang around the capitals and other big cities, enduring a debilitating unemployment, rather than soil their hands with a manual job that will serve their struggling country. [45]

The Soviet Union, too, is finding its university graduates disinclined to work with their hands. As a result, recent reforms in education place great emphasis on manual work at all levels. In kindergartens, all children are taught to share in the manual and menial work connected with their communal lives. Even children of three take their turn in such activities as cleaning tables. When the reforms are complete, it is planned that there will be a program of useful manual labor or work experience in all grades, with one-third of the six-day school week devoted to it in the ninth, tenth, and eleventh grades.

A liberal education is an education that liberates. But what liberates man must be rediscovered in each age. No easy resting on the solutions of past ages will suffice. In a technological society man can be liberated from the dominance of the machine only by an education that helps him to regain the integrity of hand and brain that technology removes or threatens. No education in an industrial society can be considered liberal, therefore, that does not include a carefully conceived program of manual work. Schools that carry on an extensive program of expensive sports to engage the physical energies of the students while at the same time hiring gardeners and workmen to keep the buildings and grounds in repair are misconceiving their educational task and losing their practical opportunities.

And schools that appeal to the purity of the Middle Ages as authority for their lack of concern with the practical application of their studies are misinformed about that period of history. Medieval students studied with a definite vocational end in view. Medieval universities were predominantly utilitarian and realistic in their approach. Masters who made their livelihood from students' fees were well-aware of the wisdom of appealing to the realistic demands of their pupils. One twelfth-century Italian master advertised his course as "short and practical, with no time wasted on out-grown classical authors, but everything fresh . . . and up-to-date, ready to be applied the same day if need be." [46]

Transition Periods

The problems of freedom and security are particularly difficult between the ages of fifteen and eighteen. In many countries these are the first years of freedom from formal education. From being a leading member of his relatively secure school community, the youth is moved rapidly into a working world characterized by impersonal relationships, where he is an insignificant part of a vast machine. At the same time, he is liable to be undergoing a period of increased psychological detachment from home and family and often finds it necessary to challenge parental authority or repudiate family help.

At this crucial time, it is important for young men and women to receive guidance and assistance to enable them to meet the problems associated with greater freedom. The fortunate youth finds a mature, understanding adult to whom he can look up and on whom he can model himself to some extent. Sometimes this can be achieved vicariously through studying the life and ideas of an admired figure. Much more investigation is needed concerning ways to bring desirable models to the notice and emulation of young people. At present, military leaders and ruthlessly successful politicians are often the models in totalitarian countries, while in freer countries sports heroes and film stars prevail. Since none of these models is able to draw out the best qualities in young people, and since the chances of finding a mature adult to take an interest in a young person's development are most uncertain, this form of guidance needs to be institutionalized.

It is to be hoped that when County Colleges become widely attended in England they will play an important role in this work and will be emulated elsewhere. Many successful attempts have been made in England to ease this transition from school to work through the use of

Continuation Classes and Day Release Schools in which young workers are given an opportunity to continue their schooling for one or two days out of the working week. Where they have been tried, these experiments have nearly always been accompanied by considerable gains in the morale and maturity of the young men and women involved. Unfortunately, due to lack of government support, these efforts have been confined to a few enlightened firms, since the firm itself has to provide the facilities and teachers and pay the workers' wages while they are at school. It seems futile to expect that such schemes will become widespread without official and generous government support.

Similarly, at the other end of the working life, there is need for educational assistance in overcoming the adjustments of retirement. When a man who has worked hard and usefully all his life is overnight released from all further vocational responsibilities, it is not surprising that he often feels his life is ended and, accordingly, dies. Retirement is a killer, but it need not be. There is no unanswerable reason why retirement should not be spread over five or ten years, during which time the worker could be spending at first one day, and later most of the week, "at school." The limitations to be placed on the forms that this education for retirement would take need be imposed only by the bounds of man's ingenuity. But, in particular, for the worker who has a degree of financial security, perhaps his retirement education could show him ways in which he could begin a second career of *service*—not only to his family as hitherto, but also, or alternatively, to the community, to an underprivileged group or individual, to a foreign country, to a cause that stirs him, to a religious or political organization, to an art or craft.

Such an education is to be firmly distinguished from a training in some type of hobby or "tinkering" or self-amusement, which is often advocated as a solution to the problems of retirement. These activities are purely egocentric and cannot solve the central problem of the retiring worker. It might be argued that he has given a lifetime of work and service and now deserves a rest and some self-indulgence. This is the formula that kills. The egocentric solution drives the individual further in on himself and increases his feeling of futility and pointlessness. Obviously, the type of service chosen will be dependent on the worker's physical health and strength; but infinite gradations of physical demand can be made, for the kind of help one's neighbor needs does not always require muscles. Besides, we need to consider the possibility that it is the futility of the retired person's life that makes him feel tired and infirm—not *vice versa*. Judging from the lives of those who have worked at a precious cause until late in life, we should have more faith in the

power of purpose and commitment to elicit unsuspected reserves of
vigor and well-being, even in the very old.

Education of the Adult Worker

In addition to all of these peripheral campaigns, however, it is
essential that the workplace itself should become an educational agency
in a more self-conscious way than it is at present. The adult worker is
representative of the great body of the population, and his degree of
success or failure in coping with the problems of living greatly affects
the tone of society. It has already been pointed out that one of the
factors militating against his success is the social divisiveness engendered
by specialization of vocation. In such circumstances it is more than ever
necessary that programs of adult education be made available to the
worker to reinforce and emphasize the common cultural factors and
traditions that make communication easier and more significant. It is, of
course, the task of elementary and early secondary education to introduce children to a common body of knowledge, beliefs, and values.
Freedom cannot exist in a society without a basic unity—at least enough
to ensure stable and effective government. But it is not enough for adult
education merely to repeat these early programs of common education.
On the contrary, a good program of adult education will re-evoke the
unity created by early educational experiences only to use it as a stable
basis for the development of critical analyses and judgments of society's
practices and beliefs. This is why education must be a process continuing throughout life: because the education obtained during the years of
compulsory schooling will not bear fruit unless it is re-examined and
pruned in the light of experience and maturity; and because long practice of a particular vocation or profession leads to a rigidity of mental
outlook that adult education should break open.

Quantitatively, adult education is booming, a fact that offers specious grounds for self-congratulation. On the basis of studies made for
the United States Office of Education, for instance, it is estimated that,
in this country, the almost incredible total of more than 35 million
adults are enrolled in various types of organized educational activities.
Such activities include those sponsored by health and welfare agencies,
labor unions, local and national church organizations, business and industry, and various government agencies. But it might be doubted
whether much of this laudable activity is of the quality necessary to
bring about a transformation of society. The vast majority of these
efforts, while commendable as manifestations of energy and ambition,
are purely ego-serving, with no relation to the wider problems of society.
The sort of program that *would* have the power to transform both

society and the individuals involved would be one similar to those followed in some of the better Scandinavian Folk High Schools where,
especially in Denmark, the reforming and redeeming effects on the
whole society are both magnificent and well-known; or to some of the
more ambitious Workers' Educational Association programs in England, where miners and factory workers follow the most rigorous and
demanding courses in economics, politics, and sociology, sometimes over
several years.

Rehumanization of Work

While these attempts to re-establish bonds of commonality, and to
move out from this common level into the regions of social criticism and
concern, are important, they can hardly stand by themselves and seem
doomed to fail, unless they are implemented by men of full human
stature. Therefore, the crucial aspect of this endeavor lies in the attempted rehumanization of work. "It should not be necessary," said Sir
Fred Clarke, "and even economically it may well be disastrous, that a
man should have to divest himself of a large part of his full humanity
and his social nature when he goes to his daily task." [47] In order to
achieve economic prosperity with freedom we need an education in
humane work. Such an education must be approached from two sides:
the institutional and the personal. There is first of all a need for a
revolution in factory management that will enable workers to be recognized, and to recognize each other, as persons rather than interests. A
man cannot be free as long as he is regarded as a piece of machinery or
raw material. The factory that does most to raise man's stature will be
the one whose atmosphere approaches that of a family, where the members may all be different (and, hence, receive different rewards) but are
nevertheless interconnected and valued primarily as human beings. To
balance and support this revolution in factory management, there is a
need for a revolution in trade-union practices in a complementary direction. Too often the creativity and humanity of the worker are stifled by
restrictive and inhumane trade-union regulations.

Then on the personal level, the individual worker must be helped
to recapture a sense of wholeness and purpose in his work. Education,
both in school and in factory, can contribute here by consciously striving
to show *connections* between the individual's work, the total product
and industrial endeavor, and the whole life of society. The differences in
moral and creative energy between purposeful and purposeless activity
are immense. Sir Richard Livingstone wrote to Alfred North Whitehead that to him the most significant sentence in Whitehead's *Aims of
Education* was the one that said the common man needs to be convinced of the importance of the work he is doing.[48] There is a vital

educational task waiting to be done in helping the worker to become aware of what Douglas Steere has called the "frame of meaning" [49] of his work. Seen in this framework, a man's work can act creatively on him: without it, his work can be a destructive force. When man is working as a human being, and not as an automaton, he feels the need to become the best of which he is capable. To reach this level of seeking for full humanity and personal excellence, he must, in Gerald Heard's words, "grasp the reasons why he is thus called upon to strive, how his conditions have aligned him for this destiny, what forces have energized him for this effort, what goal his trained powers could attain." [50]

Educators are under a special responsibility to abandon those time-worn school practices, well-loved by tidy-minded administrators, that prepare young people to take their places uncomplainingly as dehumanized cogs in a mechanically efficient industrial machine. Education should help to free man from "those pressures which mechanize the mind, which make for routine thinking, which divorce thinking from feeling, which permit custom to dominate intelligence, which freeze awareness of the human spirit and its potentialities." [51]

We need, for example, to make room in school for the operation of subjective time—Bergson's *durée*—as well as clock time. One of our main problems, as Lewis Mumford has pointed out, is to "reconcile the external, mechanical, public time-schedule that now governs so much of our activities with organic, personal, self-controlled time, associated with metabolism, memory, the cumulative human experience, dependent upon the rate of growth, the intensity and extent of activity, the capacity for assimilation." [52] Do we not prepare children in school too effectively for a mechanical future by the inexorable tyranny of the bell? Does the development of deep concentration not need some open-ended class periods where the student can immerse himself in a problem without fear of being jerked out of it by a jangling summons? Are we not making young people too accepting of the often meaningless, petty tasks of industrial life by "keeping them busy" in school, even when the busyness prevents the undertaking of more serious, longer-lasting, more creative, but less predictable and controllable tasks?

Above all, the rehumanization of work requires that work be again made a *reflective activity*. This is the secret of finding freedom through the authority of work. When work is carried on mechanically, automatically, unthinkingly, it is slavery. Freedom is gained only by infusing work with meaning and purpose through reflection. This means becoming conscious of *relationships*: between worker and worker; between worker and management; between the individual contribution and the whole; between a man's work and society's need; between the intention and the execution; between the present activity, past benefits, and future promise.

This radical change in the conditions and nature of work cannot occur without a revision of the current concept of efficiency. Industry must learn to view efficiency as a problem of the worker's spirit as well as of his physical output. No industrial organization should be viewed as efficient that does not enlist the free co-operation of all workers in the clear definition of the ends to be pursued and the methods of attaining them. This means overturning many traditional notions of industrial control and measurement. Roger Wilson, who has had much experience in organizing nonauthoritarian working groups in connection with Quaker relief work, summarized his experience as follows:

> Efficiency . . . is a by-product of intelligent co-operation; where this exists, so will efficiency. . . . When a general atmosphere of intelligent co-operation is low, authoritarian sanctions are prominent, and the infliction of them tends to a still further degradation of voluntary responsibility. In healthy societies large and small, authoritarian sanctions are hardly noticeable.[53]

It may be objected that the problems of Quaker relief work are not those of modern industry, and that industry will never agree to an abandonment of the profit measure of efficiency. This may be true, and yet two reservations seem appropriate. First, we may well find in such ventures of free co-operation valuable clues for building a model of healthy human relations in the factory or workplace. And secondly, examples from France, Italy, and elsewhere give reason to suppose that co-operative methods of manufacturing can combine efficiency in the traditional sense with a man-centered regime.[54]

Vocation

Perhaps the greatest contribution that education can make to the contemporary problem of work is a revival of the idea of *vocation*. There is a great deal of industriousness today in educational institutions, in factories, and among professional people, but comparatively little of this activity is carried out with a deep sense of commitment. It is too often done in a passionless way, efficiently perhaps, but with an efficiency that is merely striving to complete the present task as quickly and painlessly as possible so that one can begin the next one—which will, in turn, be done in the same, passionless, future-concentrated spirit. Speaking of the intellectual worker, Jacques Barzun has condemned activity that lacks passion, which he considers the essential element of work.

It is passion in work and for work that gives it its dramatic quality, that makes the outcome a possession of the worker. . . . Of all the deprivations that modern life imposes on intellectual man, the abandonment of work is the cruelest, for all other occupations kill time and drain the spirit, whereas work fills both, and in the doing satisfies at once love and aggression. . . . No man who works in the sense I mean can despise himself, even if the work is below his deserts, or its perfection short of his ideal.[55]

In recent years some observers claim to have noticed an abandonment of, or a deterioration in, the commitment that the intellectual worker brings to his work. This has been especially noted among young people. A sociologist who has had unusual opportunities for studying American college students is David Riesman. One of the marked traits he has noticed in college students today is "a certain withdrawal of emotional adherence to work." [56] They come to believe that work cannot be worth doing for its own sake and fear overcommitment, even while they are at the workplace. Often they find their work lacking in meaning, but they tend too readily to accept it as it comes, without trying to make it more meaningful. This is one of the reasons why young people withdraw emotional allegiance from their work: they feel they have no control over it anyway, that it is all in the mysterious hands of the men upstairs who run the show. Does education bear any responsibility for the development of this attitude? Riesman thinks it does, for he suggests that the attitude is learned in part at college because students feel they have no control over their own education. This feeling, Riesman agrees, is partly of the students' own making. They could do something to change the curriculum, to improve their own education, if they took the initiative. And when, on rare occasion, they do, they often find that the administration is not invulnerable to change. But usually they do not want to be too involved in and committed to their own education, because if one becomes too interested in something he is tempted to spend too much time on it, "at the expense of that optimal distribution of effort which will produce the best grades." [57]

The educational implications of this analysis are obvious. In the first place, we must find ways, both in school and college, of allowing students to develop a sense of the significance of their personal efforts. Because of the scale of power available to governments today, it is fatally dangerous to acquiesce in the current feeling of individual helplessness. The best way to overcome this on the national level is to give students an experience of accomplishing minor change at the institutional level. And secondly, if we find that the use of grades is hindering the students' attempts to gain an education, then the education should be safeguarded rather than the grades. No matter how much grades may appeal to the administrator's desire for consistent order and safe predictability, they should be swept away and replaced by substitutes of less educational virulence.

One reason why it is vitally important for young people who are preparing for a professional career to find some fulfilling sense of vocation in their work is the fact, underlined by recent sociological research, that professional workers, in contrast to factory workers, tend to find their central life interests in their work. Louis Orzack, in a study of nurses, found that for four-fifths of them, work and the workplace, rather than leisure activities, provided their central life interests. They preferred to derive their deepest personal satisfactions from work. Orzack speculated that this tendency may be even stronger in more male-dominated professions.[58]

These vocationally committed people tend to hold what Robert Havighurst calls "ego-involving" jobs rather than "society-maintaining" jobs. For the person with an ego-involving job, his work tends to be the organizing force of his life. He lives for his work and life would be empty without it. He does not count his working hours. He takes his job home with him at night. His vacations tend to be related to his work. Havighurst estimated that about 35 percent of young people will eventually take up such work. One of the principal tasks of the educational system, in Havighurst's view, is to help boys and girls of appropriate ability to get into occupations that they are likely to find ego-involving.[59]

We need also to re-examine the concept of "liberal" education for future professional workers. If they are going to focus on work as their central life interest, perhaps we should concentrate on their professional or vocational education and recast it so that it can be a liberalizing experience. Rather than follow the traditional pattern, which often consists of tacking "liberal arts" courses onto professional courses in the hope that some alchemy within the individual will transform the ingredients into a liberating education, we should experiment with the use of the individual's professional interest as a *focus* from which he can move out in a liberating exploration of its wider and wider human implications. In this way we can use the authority of work as a route to freedom.

Part of the campaign to achieve this must involve an examination of the place of the liberal arts college in American education. The narrow utilitarianism and materialism that prevail among many students in liberal arts colleges are partly due to this institution having become a catch-all into which it is assumed that virtually all intelligent—or even all middle-class—children should be thrown. A sense of vocation, or what Havighurst calls ego-involvement, will not come from such automatic procedures. Young people need the opportunity to see whether they can be creative and effective in a field that they can wholeheartedly commit themselves to, whether or not it fits into the prevailing pattern of American middle-class assumptions and prejudices. This means that strong efforts should be made to raise the prestige and increase the availability of art, music, dance, and craft schools and institutes of technology, as well as to create new types of institutions in which an education for vocation can be encouraged.

These institutional reforms and professional opportunities, however, are only permissive measures. Of much more importance in making the authority of work a freeing force in the life of the individual is the positive development of a personal spirit of vocation from the earliest days of school. "Work is love made visible," wrote Gibran.[60] Something of this idea can be caught by children if they are shown what deep satisfaction can be gained from effectively applying acquired skill and knowledge to the solution of a problem about which they care seriously. This satisfaction through effectiveness in work can be far more profound and lasting than that obtained through grades, monetary reward, or other external inducements. While working only for external reward results ultimately in boredom or resentment, a spirit of vocation can infuse *all* aspects of a person's life, rekindling it with vitality, purpose, and meaning.

VI WORK AND PLAY

Leisure and Industrialism

In the Western cultural tradition leisure, rather than work, has usually been regarded as the area of life in which the highest measure of freedom can be attained. The slave-supported societies of Greece and Rome deprecated the vulgarizing effects of work—especially manual work—and saw in man's leisure the best opportunities for the development of the specifically human attribute of reason, in which lay the only possibilities of freedom. Aristotle insisted in the *Politics* that children should be taught "only such kinds of knowledge as will be useful to them without vulgarizing them. . . . We call those arts vulgar which tend to deform the body, and likewise all paid employments; they absorb and degrade the mind." [61] Work may be necessary but it is inferior in value to leisure and gains its value only through making leisure possible. "We occupy ourselves in order that we may have leisure, just as we make war for the sake of peace," Aristotle stated in the *Ethics;* [62] and elsewhere he said, "The prime end of all action is leisure." [63]

This emphasis has had a profound effect on Western culture and education. It is an emphasis that receives reiteration today in many quarters. Josef Pieper has made an eloquent defense of leisure as the preserve of "freedom, of education and culture, and of that undiminished humanity which views the world as a whole." [64] He strongly opposes the view that holds work as central and leisure as serving it. A pause in work for the sake of refreshing man for more work is still part of the world of work, he has argued. Genuine leisure is altogether different: it cuts at right angles to work.

> The point and the justification of leisure are not that the functionary should function faultlessly and without a breakdown, but that the functionary should continue to be a man—and that means that he should not be wholly absorbed in the clear-cut milieu of his strictly limited function.[65]

It is in this spirit that Pieper contemned the proletarian as "the man who is fettered to the process of work." [66]

This attitude is at the basis of the sharp distinction between the *artes liberales* and the *artes serviles*. It is partly responsible for the low valuation of manual work that was mentioned earlier. And it bears some of the blame for much of the irrelevant trivia that are perpetuated under the protective custody of "liberal arts." It is an attitude that must be questioned and examined in the light of the drastic changes that have occurred and are occurring in the conditions of work in industrialized societies.

One of the most challenging of the factors to be considered is the remarkably rapid increase in the amount of leisure time available for industrial workers. In the century from 1850 to 1950 the average work week in America was reduced from 70.6 hours to 40.8 hours. This tendency, it has already been suggested, is likely to continue under the impact of cybernation. Donald Michael has asked what people will *do* with all their leisure, "day after day, four-day week-end after week-end, vacation after vacation, in a more and more crowded world. . . . What will they believe in and aspire to?" [67] He has warned that, if we fail to solve the problems of cybernation, the frustration and pointlessness produced may evoke, in turn, a war of desperation—ostensibly a war "against some external enemy but, in fact, a war to make the world safe for human beings by destroying most of society's sophisticated technological base." [68]

These developments and portents have prompted many writers to suggest that schools should direct their attention increasingly toward preparing young people to use wisely the ever-widening leisure sector of their lives. Such educational directions have been reinforced by a resignation in the face of the steadily advancing impersonal and mechanical nature of industrial work. If it is hopeless to find meaning and satisfaction in work, it is felt, then let us accept work as something to be endured as stoically as possible, continue to cut down working hours, and concentrate on the educational and cultural possibilities of leisure.

One of the most persuasive of these writers is David Riesman. In his influential book, *The Lonely Crowd*,[69] Riesman suggested that one of the chief obstacles to the achievement of autonomy—or freedom—is what he called the "false personalization" of work. In Riesman's opinion, we should try to reduce the emotional demands of work through automation and through making productive processes more impersonal. He condemned those who would try to bring joy and meaning into industrialism, who would like, in a "fallacy of misplaced participation," to personalize, emotionalize, and moralize the factory and the white-collar world. On the contrary, he thought we should work *with* the grain of impersonality in modern industry. This should be done for the sake of the important sector of life—that of leisure, pleasure, and consumption. Leisure should no longer be the residue sphere left over from worktime and work-feeling; it should become the sphere for the development of skill and competence in the art of living. Riesman looked on leisure as the sphere in which man can "reclaim his individual character from the pervasive demands of his social character" [70] and aspire to autonomy. In other words, he was saying, let us withdraw as much as possible from the authority of work, physically and emotionally, and save ourselves for the leisure sector where, as the Greeks would agree, freedom can be attained.

There can be no doubt that the majority of industrial workers share some of this attitude. It is well-known that in hard or unpleasant occupations like mining an increase in the hourly wage-rate is often followed by a drop in production. The men can now make money faster: usually they will choose to earn the same money as before and increase their leisure time rather than raise their income. No one can blame the worker in a mechanical, repetitive job if he looks on his leisure time as the part of the day when he begins to live. Robert Dubin found in his investigation of industrial workers that for about three-quarters of them work and the workplace were *not* central life interests. "Industrial man," said Dubin, "seems to perceive his life history as having its center outside of work for his intimate human relationships and for his feelings of enjoyment, happiness, and worth." [71] These are the people Havighurst called the maintainers of society, who make up about 50 percent of the population, and who find their main self-fulfillment from leisure activities.[72]

Nevertheless, while these attitudes can be viewed with sympathy, they cannot be looked on with enthusiasm. Nor can we condone or support views like those of Aristotle, Pieper, or Riesman, for the desertion of the attempt to make work more meaningful can hold nothing but disaster for the future. Certainly the task of helping men spend their leisure wisely is laudable, but it is doomed if that leisure is only a waiting interval before the start of another round of futile activity. "The mass of men lead lives of quiet desperation," said Thoreau a century ago. "A stereotyped but unconscious despair is concealed even under what are called the games and amusements of mankind. There is no play in them, for this comes after work." [73] The relationship between work and play is mutually dependent: true work and true play serve each other in an essential way.[74] But the stored-up tensions of dull, grinding, unrelated work result only in a leisure spent in the semistupor of television-viewing or in the directly or vicariously experienced violence of contemporary "sports."

A friend of mine who is an artist has in his studio a "worktable" and a "playtable." When he finds himself at his worktable seizing up or running dry or becoming too serious about the project he is working on, he turns to the playtable and plays there for a while. Usually he finds that he returns to his worktable refreshed, often with new ideas. Many of his most creative ideas have come from the playtable. Work and play are essentially interconnected: real play constitutes a creative feeding of genuine work, and *vice versa*. This is one reason why early specialization is achieved only at a cost—it tends to harden the borderline between work and play and, consequently, kills some of the creative zest that produces original work. Richard Wilbur has suggested that "when the various human creature is docked of his divergent impulses, and forced wholly into the mould of the specialist, . . . it is done at a sacrifice in spontaneity; and . . . his work ceases in great measure to be play. When work ceases to be play, it ceases to be vital and inventive." [75]

Leavis and Thompson have pointed out that "Men are now incapacitated by their work . . . from using their leisure for *humane* recreation, that is, in pursuits that make them feel self-fulfilled and make life significant, dignified and satisfying." [76] When the preindustrial craftsman found a self-fulfilling satisfaction in work, he did not need leisure to redeem him. His work was interesting, varied, demanding, and purposeful. He worked long hours but was not as exhausted as a modern factory worker is after a shorter working day, because there was less tension involved: his day was not spent battling a machine for supremacy. What he mainly needed from leisure was rest so that he could the next day be refreshed for his work-activity. It was primarily in the work sector of his life that he made (or failed to make) a success of

living. The modern industrial worker works primarily for money and
waits for release from monotonous work so that he can begin in leisure
time to cultivate the art of living, with the aid of the money earned.
And, of course, commercial interests have not been slow to exploit this
development, for they have seen in it the possibilities of profit on a vast
scale. But, since work is meaningless, this attempt to infuse leisure with
meaning usually fails. Man's attempts to find in leisure the freedom for
genuine play are constantly being undermined, unless he has experienced the authority of meaningful work.

Leisure, Rest, and Play

Hard work over a long period of time brings genuine tiredness, to
which body and mind eventually make the natural response of sleep.
But long before this point is reached we are often afflicted with lassi-
tude. After a day's work, for instance, we settle down in an easy chair to
watch television. Before long we feel drowsy and nod off to sleep; perhaps we stay in front of the screen all evening, intermittently dozing,
until finally we decide that our day's work was exhausting and we retire
to bed early. On another occasion, after a similar day's work, we may
spend the evening playing tennis, or building a needed bookcase, or
mapping out a planned addition to the house, or in delightful conversation with charming friends, without any feeling of exhaustion or weariness. Now, on the television evening, were we genuinely tired or not?
And is such an evening refreshing or debilitating?

There is a need for much more careful study of the nature of play,
rest, and fatigue, and the relationship between them. Cyril Burt carried
out an experiment with two matched groups of children who were very
backward in arithmetic. One group was given an extra arithmetic lesson
every afternoon while the other group slept. At the end of the term the
"sleepers" had improved in arithmetic more than those specially
coached.[77] Of course, there are many variables that might be causally
involved here, but the results should make us question the assumption
that "work" is the productive sphere and "play" the unproductive
sphere.

We all need to rest. But in order to understand the *kind* of rest an
organism needs, we must study the nature of the organism. After running to catch a train, our lungs are overworked and need to rest. The
way in which they rest, however, is by gradually reverting to the normal
rhythm of breathing, not by stopping. This is because they are built for
action. Similarly, everything intended to act, from muscles to minds, can
find rest in natural action as well as in inertia. "To act in obedience to
the hidden precepts of nature—that is rest," said Maria Montessori;

"and in this special case, since man is meant to be an intelligent creature, the more intelligent his acts are the more he finds repose in them." [78] Leisure should be regarded not as an opportunity to collapse, but as an opportunity to seek out ways of acting that are suitable to our nature but are not encouraged or permitted by our working conditions.

This action that Montessori called rest is identical with play. It is play that is needed to bring balance to the personality of the worker. At its best, play has a resuscitating and liberating effect on man's mind and body. It releases creativity, provides an emotional safety-valve, and nourishes the spirit. "Play is the purest, most spiritual activity of man," said Froebel. "It gives . . . joy, freedom, contentment, inner and outer rest, peace with the world. It holds the sources of all that is good." [79] Schiller, with his concern for the aesthetic education of man, has suggested that "Man only plays, when, in the full signification of the word, he is a man, and *he is only entirely a man when he plays.*" [80] Jean-Paul Sartre, with his concern for existential freedom has written, "As soon as a man apprehends himself as free and wishes to use his freedom . . . then his activity is play." [81]

Norman Brown, in a penetrating and provocative study of the psychoanalytical aspects of work and play, has contrasted the view of Marx, who defined the essence of man as labor, with that of Freud, for whom work and economic necessity were the essence of the "reality-principle," but for whom the essence of man lay not in the reality-principle but in repressed unconscious desires. "What is the pattern of activity, free from work, the serious business of life, and the reality-principle, which is adumbrated in the life of children?" Brown has asked. "The answer is that children play. . . . Play is the essential character of activity governed by the pleasure-principle rather than the reality-principle." [82] The life instinct or sexual instinct demands a kind of activity, in Brown's view, quite different from most people's work. It needs activity that can best be called play. The leisure problem of the affluent, cybernated society may appear less insoluble in this light. From the Freudian point of view, "every ordinary man has tasted the paradise of play in his own childhood. Underneath the habits of work in every man lies the immortal instinct for play. The foundation on which the man of the future will be built is already there, in the repressed unconscious." [83]

A.S. Neill has claimed that "the evils of civilization are due to the fact that no child has had enough play. . . . every child has been hot-housed into an adult long before he has reached adulthood." [84] Certainly, when one considers the phenomenon of the millions of adults in America who spend time watching children or young men playing games one is tempted to link it with the pressure put on American children to grow up quickly and to be "adult" and sophisticated in certain superficial ways. Neill's view is that, if children are allowed fully to live through their self-centered fantasy stage through play, they will be able as adults to face the demands of work without unconscious longing for the play of childhood.[85]

Adults need to play, too, but theirs may be different from childish play. One form of adult play that will have to be increasingly explored in the affluent society is the regular paid sabbatical—not just for university professors but for factory workers, office workers, and others—to engage in the development of mind, body, and spirit. In the face of chronic underemployment, such measures can be a substitute for—or an addition to—shorter working hours, earlier retirement, or shorter work weeks. Moreover, since the workers can be expected to return to work after their sabbatical years, summers, or months at a higher level of productiveness, the nation should be prepared to support such programs. It is preferable to establish such a balance between work and play throughout life rather than to work excessively hard all one's life until one is discarded onto the retirement pile at sixty-five, too worn-out to be able to enjoy the now embarrassing opportunities for play.

Education for Leisure

It has been pointed out that writers like Josef Pieper view leisure as the area of life in which culture and freedom can flourish, in which the liberal arts, as opposed to servile work, can be followed. Such a concept leads naturally to a type of education that prepares men to follow gentlemanly pursuits as fully, intelligently, and gracefully as possible. This is the educational motive that has prevailed, for example, in the English Public Schools at least since the time of Thomas Arnold's reforms in the second quarter of the nineteenth century. But this approach to education presupposes a particular class structure—with a small, privileged, leisured class in command, served by a large, docile, working class—that is not typical of North America and is disappearing in Europe. The developing pattern is one where leisure is a reality—if a problem—for the working man, and where the gentleman—if he continues to exist—must work.

What sort of education for leisure is appropriate for such a society? In what ways can we prepare children to understand and benefit from leisure? One of the first and most essential tasks of the school in this regard should be to bring young people to a realization that, in a working world, leisure is *negotiable*. We can trade part of our leisure for more goods and services, or *vice versa*. This choice needs to be made much more conscious and rational than it is at present. Children should be shown the essential economic relationship between work, material consumption, and leisure so that as adults they can understand as clearly as possible what they are doing when they work 18 hours per day, or insist on buying a second automobile, or demand to loaf all summer. All of these may be choices the individual *wishes* to make: but more often they are courses taken for the wrong reason, or for no reason, or through lack of awareness of consequences and alternatives.

Young people will benefit from learning the distinctions between work and play and between genuine, renewing play and enervating, destructive play. They can be shown that an emphasis on action in man's play should not be confused with a frenetic drive for overt activity. In pedagogy, we are more aware now of the pitfalls of "activity methods." We know that in a classroom full of bustle and movement there may be virtually no purposeful and constructive activity: and in a classroom that is outwardly still and quiet the students may be most intensely active. Similarly, in play, the still person may be following what is the most appropriate action for him at that moment. We need to devote part of our leisure to the enjoyment of reflective idleness, a state that is to be strictly distinguished from apathy or inertia. In reflective idleness we find time for what can well be the most vital action of our lives. It is necessary to withdraw regularly from the level of overt activity to deepen ourselves at the level of reflection. We grow through *being* as well as through *doing*, and there is an eternal rhythm between the two dimensions that steady growth demands. To maintain a pace of ceaseless activity is the surest way to deny ourselves the opportunity to develop the depth and wholeness of which we are potentially capable. "The laboring man has not leisure for a true integrity day by day," wrote Thoreau. "He has no time to be anything but a machine. How can he remember well his ignorance—which his growth requires—who has so often to use his knowledge?" [86] We can prepare for this reflective use of leisure by deliberately making opportunities in school for such periods of reflective idleness.

Above all we need a new concept of liberal education to help the majority of young people to enhance their freedom through leisure. Havighurst has suggested that for most people, who are in society-maintaining rather than ego-involving jobs, and who find their main self-fulfillment through leisure, the educational system should attempt to find some sort of ego-involving socially constructive activity apart from work.[87] The research of Dubin and Orzack, showing that professionals tend to be work-oriented and factory workers to be leisure-oriented, might lead one to speculate that perhaps we should reverse the customary emphasis in which future professionals receive more "liberal" education and future factory workers more "vocational" education. For the future leisure-oriented society-maintainers, there is a need not so much for *more* liberal education as a *different* kind of liberal education. It will be an education that is liberating because it helps these young people to explore areas of leisure activities that are the potential source of serious commitments, deliberate decision-making, and reflective behavior. In a word, it will help them to bring a spirit of *vocation* to some aspect or aspects of the leisure sector of life.

One of the great challenges that increasing leisure presents to education is that people with time to spare will be able—perhaps for the first time—to look inward and reflect on ultimate concerns. "In a workless or semi-workless society," W.H. Ferry has said, "men will have to confront themselves in a new way, and ask the old questions about where they came from and whither they are bound. This, I am sure, will be an agonizing experience." [88] But he is optimistic about the long-term prospects: "One might hope for a spiritual rejuvenation when there are no alibis for failure to meditate and take counsel of one's self." [89] This kind of optimism seems justified, however, only if young people are encouraged to drop the evasion of self-confrontation that our educational system engenders.

Work, Play, and Education

It is unlikely that, in the near future, work for the average man can be made so pleasant that, leaving aside economic considerations, he will prefer it to leisure. Teachers and parents, therefore, can help most children by clarifying for them the distinction between work and play, by showing them how to make leisure constructive and creative, and by encouraging them to submit to the authority of work in a positive and disciplined spirit.

But there are already many men and women who are fortunate enough to have found work that is so congenial that, even without additional material reward, they are happy to continue performing it long after they could be enjoying leisure. They prefer this work to play and often seem to be able to dispense with play altogether without harmful effects. Among this group would be some scientists, research workers, scholars, writers, religious leaders, artists, musicians, and others. If we analyze the nature of their attitude to work we realize that the distinction between work and play is for them very shadowy, and neat, clear generalizations become impossible. Moreover, their education raises special problems. It is by no means obvious that for them we *should* try to make clear the difference between work and play. These are the students who we hope will find genuine joy in study, who will catch fire with the excitement of intellectual ideas, who will be the creative workers and innovators of the future. For them, the usual play activities of the school may be superfluous or irrelevant; they are able to surmount the dull, tedious aspects of sustained intellectual work through the passion that drives them. It is of such people that Jacques Barzun has written:

That is the sense in which work is "fun", with an irresistible appeal to man's love of difficulty conquered—a pleasure altogether different from that for which educators have turned school subjects into activities and play. Under the habit of play, drudgery, when it comes, remains drudgery, instead of an accepted purgatory close to the heaven of work.[90]

It is necessary for teachers to remain flexible in their approach to such students, for to make uniform demands of all students with regard, for example, to sports and athletics is to ignore the fact that some students have comparatively little *psychological* need for this contrasting type of activity, as long as adequate physical exercise is taken. They can wring from their commitment to work much that we expect from play for the average student. The "first ecstatic increment of voluntarily chosen work," said Douglas Steere, "is hardly to be distinguished from play. It is, in fact, more full of self-losing and of excitement than most artificial forms of play." [91]

One might add that it is also potentially the source of freedom. And this is a realization that can transform the life of a young person. There is great danger in thinking of work as the area of authority, compulsion, seriousness, purpose, and discipline; and of play as the area of freedom, ease, pleasure, process, and interest. It is true that these elements are often present, but it matters greatly whether they are mutually exclusive or merely emphases. John Dewey, who admitted that in play interest centers in activity without much reference to its outcome, while in work the emphasis is on the product or result in which the activity terminates, nevertheless claimed that "when comparative prominence in consciousness of activity or outcome is transformed into isolation of one from the other, play degenerates into fooling, and work into drudgery." [92] In other words, fooling occurs when all reference to outcome is eliminated from play: drudgery occurs when the worker cares only for what is to be gained at the end of his work and has no interest in the activity itself. Play is a source of freedom when it is enriched by the authority of outcome or purpose. Work is a source of freedom when it is enriched by a reflective interest in the activity itself.

There is a need for deeper and more sustained exploration of the possibilities in school and in adult life for various ways to synthesize the elements of work and play. "To be playful and serious at the same time is possible," Dewey has written, "and it defines the ideal mental condition." [93] And elsewhere he has said, "Work which remains permeated with the play attitude is art." [94] Each of the fine arts as we know them is continuous with some form—often a humble form—of work: sculpture with masonry and welding; music with manual labor (through rhythm and worksongs); painting with decorating and house-repair. This connection gives the arts a social basis and provides a link between the artist and his audience. With the growth of industrialization and the division of labor, however, an increasing number of people are losing their experience of the simple techniques on which artistic activities are based.[95] As a result, art is coming to appear more and more unnatural and arbitrary. The artist is often looked on as a queer, playful fellow who does not work, and he evokes little sympathy in society as a whole. This is a source of alienation for the artist and of impoverishment for society. The school has a great opportunity to reverse this tendency by introducing students to the experience of a work-play synthesis of fine arts and practical arts and by explicating the links between them.

Whether an activity should be considered work or play is to be determined not only by the external description of the activity, but also by the internal spirit in which it is carried on. This is clearly seen in the way young children will often carry out in a spirit of joyous play tasks that would be regarded as work by an adult. The mental attitude determines whether the task is done because of the compulsion of the outcome or because of a free enjoyment of the activity. There is danger in many contemporary pedagogical practices because they concentrate so fully on the *results* of the work. This may induce the student to produce more in the short run, but it often leads eventually to a loss of zest, to dullness, and to boredom. This can be seen in characteristically future-oriented academic activities such as thinking of the next assignment while working on the present one, turning to the end of the chapter to see how far there is to go before release, calculating the payoff on all scholastic efforts, and so on. An education for freedom through work must be marked by activities in which the interest in completing the work is fused with an enjoyment of the task in the present.

Work is not achieved only under the compulsion of external pressure or threat. It can be done freely and joyously if we are wholly attracted by it and committed to it. Most of the finest creative work is done in this work-play spirit. Children should be introduced to this experience in school if we expect them to demand it later in life. Too many people acquiesce in a lifetime of drudgery because their sights have never been raised above this level of expectation. We should examine the whole structure of external pressures and rewards in pedagogy to see whether they do not hinder the development of an experience of work that is truly liberating. A school that envisages both work and play as vehicles of freedom will give attention to both ends and means in the pedagogical process. It will try to make work a reflective activity through the development of purpose and commitment in the student and, at the same time, help him to lose himself playfully in the work-task of the moment.

NOTES

1 George Bernard Shaw, "Coercions and Sanctions," *Everybody's Political What's What?* (London: His Majesty's Stationery Office, 1945), 284.

2 Suggestive evidence to support this assertion can be found in the adjustment difficulties of colonial servant-holders who, because of changed circumstances or the end of colonial rule, have been compelled to give up their servants.

3 Gunnar Myrdal, "The War on Poverty," *New Republic* (February 8, 1964), 16. See, also, Gunnar Myrdal, *Challenge to Affluence* (New York: Random House, 1962), 69.

4 Myrdal, "The War on Poverty," *loc. cit.*

5 Max Weber, *The Protestant Ethic and the Spirit of Capitalism*, Talcott Parsons, trans. (New York: Scribner's, 1930), ch. 5.

6 See Daniel Bell, *Work and Its Discontents* (Boston: Beacon Press, 1956), 54–56. Bell is one of the most stimulating of contemporary writers on the subject of work: parts of this chapter owe much to his thinking.

7 *The Guardian* (Manchester), August 12, 1960, 2. Gilbert Wrenn has suggested that America has a heritage of work as a moral value but not of leisure. In such a society freedom from work may merely induce anxiety. C. Gilbert Wrenn, "Human Values and Work in American Life," in *Man in a World at Work*, Henry Borow, ed. (Boston: Houghton Mifflin, 1964), 24–44.

8 See Alan Phillips, "Work Addiction," *Maclean's* (November 4, 1961), 13, 64–68.

9 James B. Conant, *Slums and Suburbs: A Commentary on Schools in Metropolitan Areas* (New York: McGraw-Hill, 1961), 33.

10 Sylvia Sprigge, "Mordant Alchemy," *Manchester Guardian Weekly*, September 13, 1962, 14.

11 Quoted by Douglas V. Steere, *Work and Contemplation* (New York: Harper, 1957), 88.

12 Samuel H. Miller, "Worship and Work in the Industrial Age," *Pastoral Psychology* (March, 1960), 25.

13 Charles Morgan, *Liberties of the Mind* (London: Macmillan, 1951), 40.

14 See Bell, *op. cit.*, 15–16.

15 Adam Smith, *An Inquiry into the Nature and Causes of the Wealth of Nations*, 2 vols. (London: Strahan & Cadell, 1778), I, 5–7.

16 Richard Wilbur, *Commencement Address*, Lawrence College, June 12, 1960.

17 Peter Viereck, *Inner Liberty: The Stubborn Grit in the Machine* (Wallingford, Pa.: Pendle Hill, 1957), 11–12.

18 Samuel Courtauld, *Ideals and Industry: War-Time Papers* (Cambridge: The University Press, 1949), 26.

19 C.P. Snow, *The Two Cultures and the Scientific Revolution* (New York: Cambridge University Press, 1959), 27.

20 Solon T. Kimball and James E. McClellan, *Education and the New America* (New York: Random House, 1962), 265–68.

21 Eli Ginzberg, "Work and Freedom," in *Freedom and Authority in Our Time*, Lyman Bryson, *et al.*, eds. (New York: Harper, 1953), 355.

22 Erich Fromm, *May Man Prevail? An Inquiry Into the Facts and Fictions of Foreign Policy* (Garden City, N.Y.: Doubleday, 1961), 80.

23 Friedrich A. Hayek, *The Road to Serfdom* (Chicago: University of Chicago Press, 1944).

24 "What is called a planned economy is no economy at all. It is just a system of groping about in the dark. There is no question of a rational choice of means for the best possible attainment of the ultimate ends sought. What is called conscious planning is precisely the elimination of conscious purposive action." Ludwig von Mises, *Human Action: A Treatise on Economics* (New Haven: Yale University Press, 1949), 696–97. See also his *Bureaucracy* (New Haven: Yale University Press, 1944).

25 For a popular treatment of this problem, see Vance Packard, *The Hidden Persuaders* (New York: McKay, 1957).

26 See Ruth and Edward Brecher, *et al.*, *The Consumers Union Report on Smoking and the Public Interest* (Mount Vernon, N.Y.: Consumers Union, 1963), for a thoughtful treatment of this problem.

27 W.H. Ferry, *Caught on the Horn of Plenty* (Santa Barbara, Calif.: Center for the Study of Democratic Institutions, 1962), 7.

28 *Ibid.*

29 Donald G. Agger, *et al.*, "Triple Revolution," *Liberation* (April, 1964), 4. See also W.H. Ferry, "Further Reflections on the Triple Revolution," *Fellowship*, vol. 31, no. 1 (January, 1965), 13–17; Donald N. Michael, *Cybernation and Social Change* (Washington, D.C.: U.S. Department of Labor: Manpower Administration: Office of Manpower, Automation and Training, 1964), 19–20; Donald N. Michael, *Cybernation: The Silent Conquest* (Santa Barbara, Calif.: Center for the Study of Democratic Institutions, 1962); Robert Hamill, *et al.*, "Moral and Technological Implications of Peace on Earth," *Fellowship*, vol. 31, no. 5, (May, 1965), 3–39.

30 Agger, *et al.*, *loc. cit.*, 5.

31 *Ibid.*

32 Henry David Thoreau, *Walden: or, Life in the Woods* (New York: Mentor, 1942), 40.

33 "The industrial problem arises from the base forcing of all human energy into a competition of mere acquisition." D.H. Lawrence, *Architectural Review* (August, 1930), quoted by F.R. Leavis and Denys Thompson, *Culture and Environment: The Training of Critical Awareness* (London: Chatto and Windus, 1933), 96.

34 John Macmurray, "Freedom in the Personal Nexus," in *Freedom: Its Meaning*, Ruth N. Anshen, ed. (New York: Harcourt, Brace, 1940), 5–9; Bertrand de Jouvenel, "A Discussion of Freedom," *The Cambridge Journal*, vol. VI, no. 12 (September, 1953), 710.

35 From the *Tao-Te King*, in *World Bible*, Robert O. Ballou, ed. (New York: Viking, 1950), 545.
36 *Ibid.*, 548.
37 Thoreau, *op. cit.*, 52, 60.
38 *Ibid.*, 16.
39 Bede Griffiths, *The Golden String* (London: Harville, 1954), 66.
40 Arnold Toynbee, *Globe and Mail* (Toronto), July 4, 1961, 7. It should be added that this support for the principle of foreign aid in no way endorses all the specific ways in which American foreign aid has been given in the past. It is not military aid that is being supported here; nor is it aid to bolster corrupt minority regimes. The *way* in which aid is given is vital: it should be given only in return for demonstrated social reform in the receiving country; it should reach the people who need it; it should encourage self-help; it should make the donor progressively more dispensable. See Sidney Lens, *Revolution and Cold War* (Philadelphia: American Friends Service Committee, 1962); William J. Lederer and Eugene Burdick, *The Ugly American* (Greenwich, Conn.: Fawcett, 1960), 240.
41 *Rule of Taizé*, 41. Quoted by Malcolm Boyd, "The Taizé Community," *Theology Today*, vol. XV, no. 4 (January, 1959), 505.
42 Charles Wagner, *The Simple Life* (New York: McClure, Phillips, 1904), 8.
43 Thoreau, *op. cit.*, 15.
44 Myrdal, *Challenge to Affluence*, 26.
45 For an analysis of the way this attitude operates in Southeast Asia, see Kenneth L. Neff, "Education and the Forces of Change," *International Development Review*, vol. IV, no. 1 (March, 1962).
46 Quoted by Murray G. Ross, "The University and Modern Man," *Education*, vol. 4, no. 9 (Toronto: Gage, 1961), 55.
47 Fred Clarke, *Freedom in the Educative Society* (London: University of London Press, 1948), 31.
48 Lucien Price, *Dialogues of Alfred North Whitehead* (New York: Mentor, 1956), 112.
19 Steere, *op. cit.*, 3.
50 Gerald Heard, *Training for a Life of Growth* (Santa Monica, Calif.: Wayfarer Press, 1959), 7.
51 Ross, *loc. cit.*, 57.
52 Lewis Mumford, *The Conduct of Life* (New York: Harcourt, Brace, 1951), 261.
53 Roger C. Wilson, *Authority, Leadership and Concern* (London: Allen & Unwin, 1949), 66.
54 See Steere, *op. cit.*, 71.
55 Jacques Barzun, *The House of Intellect* (New York: Harper, 1959), 125–26.
56 David Riesman, "Where is the Collége Generation Headed?" *Atlantic* (April, 1961), 40.
57 *Ibid.*, 42.
58 Louis H. Orzack, "Work as a 'Central Life Interest' of Professionals," *Work and Leisure: A Contemporary Social Problem*, Erwin O. Smigel, ed. (New Haven: College and University Press, 1963), 73–84. Subsequent unpublished research by Louis Orzack and Marie-Louise Frolen into the central life interests of accountants, insurance men, and graphic artists suggests that, for these professional people, work is about as important as it is for nurses.
59 Robert J. Havighurst, "Youth in Exploration and Man Emergent," *Man in a World at Work*, Henry Borow, ed. (Boston: Houghton Mifflin, 1964), 215–36.

60 Kahlil Gibran, *The Prophet* (New York: Knopf, 1956), 28.
61 Aristotle, *Politics* (New York: Black, 1943) Book VIII, ch. 2 (Jowett translation).
62 Aristotle, *Nicomachean Ethics* (Harmondsworth, Middlesex: Penguin, 1955) Book X, ch. 7 (Thomson translation).
63 Aristotle, *Politics* (New York: Black, 1943) Book VIII, ch. 3.
64 Josef Pieper, *Leisure the Basis of Culture*, Alexander Dru, trans. (New York: Pantheon, 1952), 59.
65 *Ibid.*, 56–57.
66 *Ibid.*, 64.
67 Michael, *Cybernation: The Silent Conquest*, 45–46.
68 *Ibid.*
69 David Riesman, *et al.*, *The Lonely Crowd: A Study of the Changing American Character* (New York: Doubleday, 1955), ch. 13, 14.
70 *Ibid.*, 315.
71 Robert Dubin, "Industrial Workers' Worlds: A Study of the 'Central Life Interests' of Industrial Workers," *Work and Leisure*, Smigel, ed., 53–72.
72 Havighurst, *loc. cit.*
73 Thoreau, *op. cit.*, 10.
74 In the preface to a later edition of *The Lonely Crowd*, Riesman admitted that he had failed earlier to recognize the full costs of the relocation of meaningfulness from work to leisure: "The burden put on leisure by the disintegration of work is too huge to be coped with; leisure itself cannot rescue work, but fails with it, and can only be meaningful for most men if work is meaningful." David Riesman, *The Lonely Crowd* (New Haven: Yale University, 1961), xliv–xlvi.
75 Wilbur, *loc. cit.*
76 Leavis and Thompson, *op. cit.*, 69.
77 Cited by A.G. Hughes and E.H. Hughes, *Learning and Teaching: An Introduction to Psychology and Education* (London: Longmans, Green, 1959), 450.
78 Maria Montessori, *The Montessori Method*, Anne E. George, trans. (London: Heinemann, 1912), 354.
79 Friedrich Froebel, *The Education of Man*, W.N. Hailmann, trans. (New York: Appleton, 1896), II, 55.
80 Johann von Schiller, "Upon the Aesthetic Culture of Man," *The Aesthetic Letters, Essays, and the Philosophical Letters*, J. Weiss, trans. (Boston: Little & Brown, 1845), 73 (italics in original).
81 Jean-Paul Sartre, *Being and Nothingness: An Essay on Phenomenological Ontology*, Hazel E. Barnes, trans. (New York: Philosophical Library, 1956), 580–81.
82 Norman O. Brown, *Life Against Death: The Psychoanalytical Meaning of History* (Middletown, Conn.: Wesleyan University Press, 1959), 32–33.
83 *Ibid.*, 36.
84 A.S. Neill, *Summerhill: A Radical Approach to Child Rearing* (New York: Hart, 1960), 64–65.
85 *Ibid.*, 60–61.
86 Thoreau, *op. cit.*, 9.
87 Havighurst, *loc. cit.*
88 W.H. Ferry, "Further Reflections on the Triple Revolution," *loc. cit.*, 15.
89 *Ibid.*
90 Barzun, *op. cit.*, 125–26.
91 Steere, *op. cit.*, 16.

92 John Dewey, *How We Think* (Boston: Heath, 1933), 284–85. See also pp. 209–15.

93 *Ibid.,* 286.

94 John Dewey, *Democracy and Education: An Introduction to the Philosophy of Education* (New York: Macmillan, 1916), 242.

95 It should be added, however, that in American society, surfeited with automatically produced articles, there are already developing signs of an increasing demand for the hand-made products of skilled craftsmen. Here lies an opportunity for education to nurture craftsmanship among those who will in the future have considerable leisure time to devote to such activities.

II

THE AUTHORITY OF INSTITUTIONS
The Freedom to Think, Teach, and Learn

I AUTHORITY OF THE CHURCH

Insufficiency of the Intellect

Much energy is wasted in discussing whether or not the aim of the school should be solely intellectual. This jejune debate is profitless because, whatever the *aim* of the school, the *practice* will not be bound by any such limitation. The human personality cannot be neatly dissevered in this way. If educators confine their attention to the intellectual development of their pupils they will find that their failure to regard the whole personality vitiates even their attempts at intellectual training. The mind, body, and emotions are so integrated that an underfed body or disturbed emotions will hinder or prevent the proper functioning of the mind. To ignore this essential interdependence is to render our intellectual task unnecessarily difficult. Mental training proceeds most efficiently when the body is properly warmed, clothed, fed, and exercised, and when the emotions are positively aroused in favor of the learning activity. Although these mundane details may be anathema to the "pure" intellectual teacher, he ignores them at his pedagogical peril.

There is an additional reason why intellectual training is inadequate as a sole educational aim. Intellectual power and skill can be used toward evil ends as well as good. Paul Goebbels was a man of considerable mental agility: it might have been well for mankind if he had been less so. The fact that immoral ends are more likely to be achieved when allied with trained and able intellects has caused many educators to refuse to hold mental training as their sole or even their primary goal. An allegiance to sound ethical principles is more neccessary for the

58

student than intellectual discipline, from the point of view of the healthy progress of society. It is, indeed, the disastrous example of some of the most highly educated, cultured, and intellectually disciplined nations in the world that has brought about a revival of the demand for an essential moral content to education.

A growing skepticism about the ability of science and empirical investigation to solve all of man's problems and to unravel all secrets has also led to a feeling of the insufficiency of the intellect. Especially in the West, where the scientific method has been used and refined for centuries, there is a seeking for adjuvant methods of inquiry to provide a multidimensioned picture of man and the universe. The methods of insight, mysticism, and revelation are being given fresh consideration, and there is a growing willingness to submit to various forms of religious authority. Some of this submission stems from a pusillanimous fear of communism and, hence, is worthless as an educating or maturing force. But some of it grows out of a genuine desire to seek the truth in the widest, most all-embracing and catholic way, without rejecting out of hand any method of inquiry, even if it is personal, nonliteral or symbolic, and not susceptible to scientific proof.

Finally, the times are such as to render security a highly prized value. We may offer young people an intellectual freedom for which they are psychologically and emotionally unready. Often they will reject the gift in a manner that shocks and disillusions us. Liberal parents and teachers who bring up their children in an "enlightened" way are sometimes disappointed and bewildered when the children turn to traditional, authoritarian dogmas. If the freedom offered lacks a solid content and a clear, transcending purpose the children may be unable to live with it. Instead, they turn to a dogma that gives them security and purpose, although it may also make it impossible to achieve freedom.

Religion and the Church

There are at least two possible motives for turning to the spiritual or religious dimension of life. It may be to seek a greater freedom of inquiry than is permitted when one is confined solely to the narrow limits of the intellectual or the scientific dimension. Or it may, on the other hand, be to escape from the burden of freedom into the womb of security and authority. When life is complicated and bewildering, and we are weary of the long and unsuccessful search for answers and solutions, it is tempting to avoid further seeking by accepting the authority of a strong, dogmatic religion. The initial weariness may be stronger than the initial conviction, but the conviction may come when we have become accustomed to accepting the truth from above.

An individual or a society that fails to grasp the significance and necessity of a spiritual dimension to life is destined to achieve at best only a thin and stunted measure of freedom. But the preservation and transmission of spiritual values is primarily the function of a fallible, human institution—the Church. Reverence for religious values is different from submission to the Church, even a church that purports to represent those values. Like all institutions, the Church is committed to the purpose of maintaining its own existence.[1] It must concern itself, therefore, with the drive for membership, the attainment of material prosperity, and—above all—the indoctrination of the young through education. When it concentrates on these organizational and institutional aims, it may—and often does—lose sight of its religious and ultimate purpose; but it sees the alternative as failure and disappearance as an institution.

Hence, religious education frequently becomes a means of inculcating the virtues of loyalty and fidelity, rather than a means of liberating the mind and spirit. The Christian Church, for instance, departs far from the example and methods of Jesus in its attitude toward the truth. Where the Church has controlled education, its power has been used predominantly to produce religious and intellectual conformity and to suppress rebels and heretics, of which Jesus was the prototype. The most brilliant portrayal of the distinction between religion and the Church is Ivan's story of "The Grand Inquisitor" in Dostoyevsky's *The Brothers Karamazov*.[2] Jesus returns to earth, to Seville in Spain, at the most terrible time of the Inquisition when heretics are burned daily for the glory of God. He is recognized by the people, who flock to him and follow him. But the Cardinal himself, the Grand Inquisitor, passes by, sees Jesus, and orders his guards to seize him and take him to the prison in the palace of the Holy Inquisition. Here the Cardinal comes to visit Jesus alone and tells him what the Church is trying to do. In the face of a completely silent Jesus, the Cardinal accuses him of having come back only to meddle in things that the Church can do better without his interference. The Inquisition must burn him, the Cardinal tells Jesus, for if they allow him to live he will destroy all the work they have accomplished in fifteen centuries. Jesus offered the people freedom, but the Church has in its wisdom vanquished that freedom to give the people happiness. "Nothing has ever been more insupportable for a man and a human society than freedom," says the Cardinal. But now the people "have brought their freedom to us and laid it humbly at our feet." Only the Church itself can endure freedom: it rules over the people, even deceives them, and, hence, suffers for their sakes. It has lifted from the people the burden of suffering and freedom that Jesus offered: "We have corrected Thy work and have founded it upon *mira-cle, mystery* and authority." Under the rule of the Church, there will be no more rebellion, no more struggling with conscience, no more restless seeking and inquiry. The people will have peace, bread, happiness, and security. And Jesus cannot be allowed to spoil this state of affairs with his dangerous offer of freedom. In reply to all this Jesus says nothing, but, at the end, approaches the old Cardinal in silence and "softly kissed him on his bloodless aged lips." The Cardinal shudders, opens the door and says to him, "Go, and come no more." Christ and Christianity are incompatible.

Authoritarian Religion and Intellectual Freedom

All religious faiths are susceptible to the temptation of authoritarianism. Not all are equal in this respect: some have built-in tendencies that make them more susceptible than others. There are several examples in the following discussion from the Roman Catholic Church. This is not because it lies at the extreme end of the spectrum of authoritarianism. Much more authoritarian are certain Protestant fundamentalist sects. But they are not particularly important in a world-wide context. The Catholic Church *is* important: it stands for something of universal significance; the direction in which it moves will affect us all; it cannot be ignored. That there are authoritarian tendencies and liberating tendencies in all faiths should be remembered in interpreting the terms "authoritarian religion" or "authoritarian faith." These terms should be taken to mean not a particular religion or type of religion but any religion inasmuch as it is emphasizing or submitting to the temptation of its authoritarian tendencies.

Authoritarian faiths tend to produce fanaticism rather than freedom. Almost inevitably they become linked with fanatical, authoritarian politics. It was a Christian minister, William J. Simmons, who revived the Ku Klux Klan in 1915 with the slogan of Protestant Christianity and White Supremacy.[3] In its most successful form, the religion achieves a theocracy, as in Calvin's Geneva or Czarist Russia. Theocracies tend to become much more strictly authoritarian and severely disciplinary than secular states because they are ruling and controlling the people not only for the good of society but for the glory of God. Minor points of order and behavior become measured according to the fearful standards of God's judgment and cosmic law.

The temptation for a religion to ally itself with government is always great, for history shows us many examples of admirable faiths that declined or disappeared because of lack of secular support; it shows us other faiths, apparently no more intrinsically worthy, that grew and prospered once they received state recognition and protection. Zarathustra, the founder of Zoroastrianism, for many years sought converts in vain in Persia. Then, after long pleading, he succeeded in converting the monarch Vishtaspa, and under royal patronage the success of the new religion became assured. According to Max Müller, had it not been for the Persian defeats at Marathon and Salamis, which halted the western march of the Persian Empire, Zoroastrianism, rather than Judeo-Christianity, would undoubtedly have been the prevailing religion of Europe and the Americas.[4] However, after the conquest of Persia by Alexander the Great, the decline of Zoroastrianism began; it continued under the Mohammedans, and today the followers of Zarathustra are a minor sect.

Christianity and Islam have been particularly prone to theocratic tendencies. Despite the fact that it was founded by a rebellious law-breaker who defied the power of the State, the Christian Church has, at least since the time of Constantine in the fourth century, tried to gain power and protection by associating itself with secular governments. The result has been that it has maintained its existence, but at a cost—the distortion of its essential message and a loss of certain freedoms for its people. Those countries—like Spain, Portugal, Ireland, Quebec, and parts of Latin America—where the Church has obtained power and influence through an alliance with government, are not distinguished by their inquiring spirit, religious vitality, or intellectual freedom.

Institutional prosperity and success are dangerous experiences for religious organizations. They make the institution and its leaders more vulnerable to moral temptation in times of crisis. Rolf Hochhuth's play, *Der Stellvertreter*, deals with such a moral crisis for the Catholic Church during the Second World War; it concerns the failure of Pope Pius XII to denounce Hitler for exterminating the Jews of Europe. In spite of the controversy and contradictions that have surrounded this play, some facts have been established beyond reasonable doubt. In the first place, Pius XII did *not* issue a public protest against the Nazi murders. Secondly, he *did* know of the existence of the murders, and that they were running into the millions. He did not hesitate to protest directly to Roosevelt against the bombs dropped on Rome. It is known that German officials lived in fear of the public effect of a papal interdict: there were 35 million Catholics in Germany alone. It has been suggested that protests to Hitler were nugatory. But in the same period the King of Denmark, a defenseless man, threatened Hitler that he and every member of his household would wear a Star of David if the Jews of Denmark were forced to do so. The protest was successful. Gordon Zahn has written that Hochhuth raises the question:

Is it not the duty of the Church and its responsible leaders at all times . . . to speak out against all major violations of its moral law, regardless of who the violators might be, regardless of what the penalties she and her members might have to suffer for giving expression to the conscience of humankind? Hochhuth—and this writer, too—would answer this in the affirmative; in this, we would be taking as our model of "the Church" the church of the prophets and the martyrs. Others will answer negatively; for them, the smoothly-operating, sacrament-dispensing, politically competent and influential institution is the preferred model. The first will stress the virtue of fortitude: the second, the virtue of prudence. And if the one risks erring in the direction of rashness, the other has proved all too often that it can lead the Church into a silent acquiescence to evil.[5]

When they have the power and the opportunity, authoritarian religions use their strength to enforce censorship and intellectual homogeneity. The Christian Church has practiced censorship since the Council of Nicaea in A.D. 325, which judged heretical and banned Arius' *Thalia*. A system of censorship continued throughout the medieval period. In 1467, soon after the invention of printing, Pope Innocent VIII ordered all books to be examined and approved by Church authorities before publication. In the sixteenth century, the Council of Trent listed a general catalogue of forbidden books. The present censorship policy of the Roman Catholic Church stems from the 1918 Code of Canon Law: all books defending atheism, materialism, divorce, dueling, suicide, abortion, and contraception are banned.[6] There is at present a fresh wind of ideas blowing in the Catholic Church, but when Hans Küng, the brilliant young German Catholic theologian and a harbinger of this fresh wind, came to speak in the United States, he was forbidden to speak in Los Angeles by Cardinal McIntyre, an ex-real estate man, whose principal preoccupation is reportedly the investments and real estate holdings of the Church. Protestant sects have acted similarly when they have had the opportunity. Luther, who demanded the right to preach unorthodox doctrines, found support among secular princes who used their power to make Luther's message a new orthodoxy. The American colonists, who left England in the name of religious freedom, wasted no time in their new home in setting up established churches, devising religious tests for teachers, introducing compulsory religious education in their schools, and viciously stamping out heretical thinking.

Authoritarian religions are antithetical to the development of intellectual freedom because they assume that they are the holders of absolute truth. This arrogant doctrine leads to fanaticism, under which intellectual inquiry wilts. There is usually a Leader, such as Frank Buchman for Moral Rearmament, Joseph Smith for the Mormons, or the Pope for Catholics, who has been blessed with special insight, revelation, or infallibility, thus making inquiry into ultimate questions unnecessary. Such fanaticism and leader-worship lead ultimately to intellectual stagnation, for many subjects of investigation are taboo. It becomes impossible to take a dispassionate view of opposing ideas or other faiths. The miserable history of fanatical religious hatred—Christianity *versus* Judaism, Protestantism *versus* Catholicism, M.R.A. *versus* communism—has been made possible only because fallible men are prepared to endow their own ideas with an infallibility and an absolutism that blinds them entirely to the possibility of truth in other ideas and of error in their own.

No religion is completely safe from these dangers. All religions face the difficulty of combining doctrinal aspiration—which often engenders feelings of brotherhood—with institutional reality—which often engenders bigotry. Milton Rokeach [7] has analyzed a considerable body of research gathered by himself and others, clearly showing that those who identify themselves with a religious organization express more intolerance toward racial and ethnic groups other than their own than do nonbelievers or Communists. Religious people express more antihumanitarian attitudes, bigotry, and anxiety than nonbelievers.

Individual Autonomy

The attempt by authoritarian religions to achieve—with the aid of secular power—a "closed-shop" situation works against the flexibility and communication that freedom requires. Fear of the fresh wind of contrasting ideas or of contamination by infidels brings the faithful to a crepuscular condition that is the harbinger of intellectual moribundity. The Archbishop of Dublin, in his 1961 Lenten pastoral, forbade Catholic youth "under pain of mortal sin" to attend Trinity College, Dublin, forbade parents and guardians to send their charges there, and forbade clergy to give help and counsel to those who wished to enter. The pastoral stated that a student of university age is not mature enough to be exposed without danger to the environment of a neutral or Protestant University.[8] This type of "ghetto" mentality seems suited only to faiths that are incapable of thriving in contact with the outside world, and brings to mind the fact that it is the invertebrates who need shells.[9] Authoritarian faiths represent closed frontiers. The elasticity goes out of old containers, and if we pour in new ideas the old skins burst. One can understand, therefore, the owners of the old skins protecting them from new wine, but this caution does nothing to assuage the thirst of the individual seeker after truth.

In order to be able to move toward the truth, the individual must be free to seek it in any direction. Diversity of faiths seems to be a prerequisite of religious freedom. In the seventeenth and eighteenth centuries, religious freedom and toleration were won not where religious uniformity prevailed but where a multiplicity of sects sprang up, each demanding the right to exist and none able to destroy its competitors. Even authoritarian faiths benefited from this situation, as we can see when we compare the spirit of the Catholic Church in countries where its version of truth remains unchallenged (such as Spain, Ireland, and Latin America) with that in countries such as France, and the German Rhineland, where the Church is not in a dominant position. Reinhold Niebuhr said,

> The truth of the church is purer in the nations where it is possible to challenge it as error. . . . The most effective way of freeing the mind of restraints placed upon it by corruptions in its religious commitments is to have enough political freedom to challenge those corruptions.[10]

The excessive paternalism and protectiveness of authoritarian religion is based on a particular view of the nature of man. The Christian authoritarian, for instance, claims that the Church and—in a theocracy —the State must have absolute authority over the individual because of man's original sin. Man is naturally sinful and depraved and, therefore, needs the firm guidance and close direction of the Church to protect him from his own evil tendencies. It is not necessary to dispute the doctrine of original sin to question this authoritarian thesis. The concept of original sin refers to man's fallen state in the eyes of *God*. We cannot translate this concept into a view of man by *man*. Earthly authorities and governments are themselves composed of men and are, therefore, also sinful. Sinful man has not the right to wield absolute authority over his fellow men on the grounds of a depravity that he shares. The Catholic Church, basing itself on the text of Matthew 16:18–19,[11] considers itself directly authorized and empowered by God. But this makes no essential difference. Taking isolated texts from the Bible for authority is notoriously dangerous. Moreover, what should be included in or excluded from what we today call the Bible was decided by sinful men over a period lasting from the first to the fourth century. And sinful men are still needed to interpret this difficult and often contradictory book to find a basis for their authority.

Authoritarian rule inevitably leads to the development of an *élite* and of dual standards of morality, with a resulting intellectual decline for the masses and grave moral dangers for the *élite*. Plato's *Republic* envisaged an *élite* of Guardians who were permitted to lie and deceive, although the people were not allowed this freedom. The *élite* of the Catholic Church—the clergy—are permitted to study certain heretical writings to become acquainted with their opponents' arguments and be able to refute them for the benefit of the laity, for whom such knowledge is considered too dangerous. Thus, the masses become intellectually dependent and slothful, while the hieratic *élite* are faced with a moral temptation to which many succumb.

Ultimately, authoritarian faiths destroy themselves; they can survive only as long as they provide security and certainty for the people, and they can do this only as long as the people are not exposed to conflicting ideas. This is why the Church confined itself in the Middle Ages largely to the fixed forms of deductive reasoning, and why it has subsequently been often inhospitable to the inductive method of science. Once people become infected by the restless inquiring spirit, the habit of free investigation, and the capacity for doubt that characterize the scientific method, they are liable to carry their attitude of doubt over into the religious domain. When that process begins, religious authority is imperiled. In this age, when science has gained prestige by demonstrating its power in a limited field, and when developments in transportation and communication make it increasingly difficult to protect any group of people from exposure to unfamiliar ideas, the only faiths that can survive are those that openly welcome the application of the scientific spirit of inquiry to their growth and refinement. Man's nature demands in the long run the freedom to explore for himself the spiritual world in the same way that science explores the physical world. As man emerges from the depths of ignorance, he invariably demands the freedom to become an autonomous creature, deriving his ethical principles and his intellectual ideas not from some external authority but from insights into his own experience.

The development of moral autonomy requires the individual to determine for himself criteria by which legal and social rules can be judged. Religion can foster this process by helping the individual to realize that as both citizen and man he bears a double responsibility to both the State and God; and that where these loyalties contradict each other he must make a personal choice between them. When a religion demands unquestioning obedience to ecclesiastical authority it hinders the development of moral autonomy by discouraging the search for individual criteria of judgment. A religion strengthens the development of moral autonomy when it encourages individual inquiry, private seeking after truth, and the examining of one's own conscience.

II AUTHORITY OF THE STATE

The State as a Protector of Freedom

F.R. Scott has suggested a useful tripartite division of the subject of human rights and liberties.[12] First there is liberty *through* government: rights and freedoms that can be realized only through governmental action, laws to free men from the forces in society that can destroy liberty. Second, there is liberty *against* the government: through efforts to curb governmental power, by Bills of Rights, concepts of natural law, doctrines of the separation of powers, and theories of checks and balances. And third, there is the liberalization of attitudes and practices: recognizing that the greatest restrictions on human rights come not from governmental action, or governmental inaction in the face of social needs, but from our own behavior toward one another.

With reference to the first concept—liberty *through* government —we must acknowledge that freedom for the individual is increasingly dependent in complex societies on the willingness of the State to intervene in the nation's life to establish the social, economic, educational, and cultural conditions essential to the full development of the individual citizens. What this degree of intervention comprises, of course, still remains to be judged. Those who fear any extension of State activity on the grounds that it presages totalitarianism surely misread the lessons of history. Dictatorships have usually followed weak governments rather than strong ones. Totalitarianism does not typically arise as a result of the slow, steady acquisition of power by a central government. On the contrary, it flows rapidly into the political vacuum left when the government fails to exercise proper authority and responsibility. The unwillingness of good men to take responsibility when in positions of political leadership results in the sort of weakness that invites the worst of men to attempt to exploit the situation for personal gain or power. A strong government can use its authority to intervene in the life of the nation to encourage variety and freedom as well as, or rather than, constraint and uniformity.

The State does not ensure freedom for the individual by leaving him alone. John Stuart Mill argued in his essay, *On Liberty*, that the State can justifiably interfere with the freedom of the individual only for the protection of others, not for the individual's own good. Where one's actions affect others, interference is legitimate; where they are purely self-regarding, no interference is warranted.[13] But this doctrine can be —and was in the nineteenth century—distorted to justify the worst excesses of industrial capitalism. It can be used (and was so used by

Mill)[14] as an argument against the State's providing universal education. It can be used by extension to prevent the school from interfering if it knows that a student is a secret drug taker. James Fitzjames Stephen, in his criticism of Mill's views, described his experiences in India, from 1869 to 1872, where he observed that freedom was enhanced not by diminishing governmental interference but by increasing it.[15] To ensure the welfare of the many it may be necessary not only to check the liberty of the few to exploit the many, but also to control the freedom of the many to destroy themselves through their own ignorance or weakness.[16]

"Free" is a word with strongly favorable connotations: hence it is often difficult to defend the need for restraint by government. The onus of justification is on the defender of governmental interference. One way to justify it is to demonstrate that the same freedom can operate differentially for different sorts of people. For example, freedom from restraint for advertisers can mean loss of freedom for consumers; freedom from restraint for employers can mean loss of freedom for employees, especially in dangerous occupations; freedom from restraint for racial bigots and Ku Klux Klansmen can mean loss of freedom for Negroes and civil rights workers; freedom from restraint for slumlords can mean loss of freedom for slum tenants. It is hypocrisy to say that people in slums are "free" to send their sons to Harvard, unless the government is prepared to intervene through such means as compulsory education (a loss of freedom of choice), provision of first-class schools in slums (a loss of freedom for taxpayers), and scholarship aid (a restraint on the rich).

A democratic government can justify itself only by interfering sufficiently to safeguard certain freedoms of minority groups, where these are threatened by a policy of *laissez-faire*. This responsibility is particularly heavy in a capitalist society where the mass media of communication are used by business to advertise its products. Especially in a medium like television, where costs are so grossly exorbitant, advertisers literally cannot afford (it is a matter of economic necessity, not evil intention) to let any other consideration supersede the paramount one of mass appeal. If the viewer happens to belong to a minority group that wants to see unpopular or controversial or culturally esoteric subjects on television, he is in this situation liable to be disappointed. Hence, we arrive at the position that the greatest freedom (in the sense of freedom from control for advertising and business) leads to the least freedom (in the sense of freedom of choice for the minority-group viewer). In this case, intervention by the government, in the form of State-sponsored stations and programs (like the British Broadcasting Corporation's

Third Programme) that provide entertainment and education for many diverse groups in the population, is fully warranted. A promising approach to this provision for minorities in the United States is the Pacifica Foundation, a group of three radio stations in New York, Los Angeles, and Berkeley. But, despite great listener support and the use of large numbers of unpaid volunteer workers, the Pacifica stations are always in financial crisis. About half of their staff have to be utilized in fund-raising activities. [17]

State Absolutism

State intervention is a prime safeguard against State absolutism. Unless the State actively intervenes to create an educated, cultured, responsible people who are aware of the value and delicacy of freedom, a social situation is liable to ensue that will encourage dogmatists to declare that the people are hopeless, irresponsible, ignorant, and not ready for freedom, and that the State must lead them like little children, taking all responsibility out of their hands. An identification is made of the State and the nation. The former claims to represent and speak for the latter in all matters and with absolute certainty. The people are encouraged to look up to their rulers as an infallible *élite* who do not merely hold opinions or theories but who know the truth. This conviction of holding absolute truth has been shared, in varying degrees, by Plato, the Calvinists of Geneva, Fascists, and Communists.

With the decline of religious belief, people become more anxious to seek security in the authority of the State and more willing to surrender decision and responsibility in return for that security. Absolutist governments have taken advantage of this anxiety by setting up the nation-state as an idol to be worshiped: no individual considerations or loyalties may prevail against loyalty and obedience to the State. The Fascist ruler does not hesitate to demand a service to the State that transcends all conflicting demands of morality and decency. The Communist believes that the revelations of Marx, Engels, and Lenin have given him a knowledge of the laws that govern history, thus empowering him with the exclusive rights to change society and control its direction. An absolutist government claims to know better than the individual citizen what is good for him, and it is going to give it to him even if it kills him.

The State as a Suppressor of Freedom

The authority of the State can be used as an active force for widening and deepening the freedom of all members of the nation. This means that the emphasis of governmental intervention must be on supporting the citizen from below rather than checking him from above. State support for freedom involves the removal of stultifying poverty, the diminution of unjustifiable inequalities of opportunity, the provision of free educational services at all levels, the subvention of cultural activities, the support of disinterested research. At the same time, it must resist the temptation to control the *outcomes* of all these activities. The people must be assisted from below, but the State must have sufficient faith in men to stand back and permit the opportunities it has given them to lead them in directions that are awkward or embarrassing for the government.

History is replete with examples of governments that have failed to resist this temptation, and whose contribution, therefore, has been deadening rather than creative. Education, research, and the pursuit of truth will always be dangerous, unpredictable enterprises. New insights, original ideas, heretical theories will always be offensive and unwelcome to those who are comfortable in the old ways, or who stand to lose wealth, power, or privilege by the adoption of new ways. Such reactionary forces use their power and influence with various degrees of subtlety to suppress intellectual freedom. More than 2000 years ago a Chinese emperor tried to destroy Confucianism by burning all books by and about Confucius. Biologists in nineteenth-century England were attacked for supporting views on evolution that are now accepted. In the Soviet Union under Stalin geneticists had to accept the officially supported Lysenko theories. The State legislature at Iowa a few years ago tried to suppress the findings of scientists in the state university showing that margarine had certain advantages over butter.

Nazi Germany between 1933 and 1945 represented a clear example of an unashamed attempt to achieve State control over the minds of the people. Hitler stated explicitly in *Mein Kampf*:

> Propaganda's task is . . . not to evaluate the various rights, but far more to stress exclusively the one that is to be represented by it. It has not to search into truth as far as this is favorable to others . . . but it has rather to serve its own truth uninterruptedly. . . . As soon as by one's own propaganda even a glimpse of right on the other side is admitted, the cause for doubting one's own right is laid.[18]

On May 13, 1933, 25,000 books were burned by the Nazis outside the University of Berlin before an audience of 40,000. All the books were "un-German." Some were by Jews, Communists, or liberals. Nine heralds came forward in turn and consigned an author to the flames. For example, the fourth herald declaimed:

Concerning the corrosion of the soul by the exaggeration of the dangers of war! Upholding the nobility of the human spirit, I consign to the flames the writings of Sigmund Freud!

The seventh herald announced:

Concerning the literary betrayal of the World War Soldier! Upholding the education of our people in the spirit of reality, I consign to the flames the writings of Eric Marie Remarque! [19]

The fruits of this attitude toward intellectual freedom can be seen in the contemptible achievements of Germany between 1933 and 1945 in the fields of art, literature, philosophy, and pure science.

No country is exempt from the need for vigilance in this matter: the temptation to control and suppress reaches right down to the petty levels of power. Sergeant Edward Kohout, of the Chicago Police Department Movie Censorship Board's office, was quoted as saying that "Anything that would be derogatory to the [United States] government" is ruled out of foreign films, and that "nothing red or pink is allowed." [20] Moreover, the pressures of the State can be exercised in devious and indirect ways. In 1960, State teacher magazines in Virginia refused to accept advertisements for H.H. Giles' *The Integrated Classroom* on the grounds that subject was "too touchy." [21] In August, 1961, the Louisiana State Attorney General ordered all Louisiana teachers to resign from the National Education Association because it supported school integration.[22] Nathan Pusey has summarized some of the manifestations of the repressive spirit of the age at work in education: "in renewed efforts to require special oaths of teachers; in attempts on the part of persons other than those professionally concerned to legislate or to dictate what may or may not be taught; in efforts, in community after community, to curb and restrain, and to make teaching 'safe.' " [23]

Intellectual Freedom and Individual Responsibility

The full flowering of the human mind requires intellectual freedom in the most comprehensive sense. This includes the second part of Scott's three-fold division of human liberties—liberty *against* the government. It is necessary to distinguish between restraints on *actions* (such as the exploitation of our fellow men), which may require government intervention to maximize freedom, and restraints on expression of *opinion* (such as speech or writing that advocates unpopular views), which in the free society should be at an absolute minimum. Man needs to be able to enjoy complete freedom of thought on all subjects, no matter how heretical, embarrassing, unfashionable, or dangerous; he needs to be able to read, discuss, and write about whatever impresses him as worthy of his serious concern; he needs to be free to publish his ideas without fear of persecution from government or vested interests. The State must work both to protect him from such threats to his freedom and to create an atmosphere in which his intellect will thrive.

Teachers, writers, artists, and scholars need an atmosphere of freedom before they can produce their best work. If they are afraid that their honest efforts will bring recriminations, their creative zest is killed and they themselves are changed. They develop the habit of reining in their intellectual adventurousness, of curbing their feelings, of restraining their expressions of enthusiasm and revulsion, until they become incapable of thinking daringly, of feeling sensitively, or of expressing acutely. Censorship affects not only the particular piece of work censored but also every other piece of work the writer or artist might produce in the future, as well as the work of all those who are aware of the act of censorship. Moreover, the public must have the freedom to enjoy the fruits of these labors to grow into intellectual maturity. "Only people who have been allowed to practise freedom," said E.M. Forster, "can have a grown-up look in their eyes." [24]

Admittedly, government control is needed to discourage the production of libelous and obscene works. But this should be effected by courts of law applying clearly stated legislation *after* the event, not by previous suppression carried out by petty officials, police departments, or self-appointed vigilantes. Furthermore, the legislation enacted should be a bare minimum, and it should be interpreted leniently. There are always forces trying to include within the concept of "obscenity" everything they oppose and would like to see suppressed. Since we cannot be infallible in judging what is obscene, let us err on the side of freedom and of confidence in man's resilience to rise above the dirt, rather than on the side of suppression, fear, and timidity. And let us keep in mind the possibility that even work that seems scandalous or obscene to us today may in fact contain the germs of future growth and beauty. "Nature from manure brings forth flowers and fruit," wrote Charles Erskine Scott Wood. "It might be by the same wonderful alchemy she would make from obscenity something vital and fine." [25]

This concept of freedom means that philosophies and theories that threaten the way of life of the nation must also be tolerated and permitted expression. Although fascism and communism are anathema to most people in Western countries, unless we allow men to advocate these doctrines we fall guilty of the very defects we see in them. The outlawing of Communist and Fascist parties, and the denial of the rights of free speech, assembly, and publication to such groups is to be heartily condemned. Even when men put forward hateful doctrines like anti-Semitism, they must be protected by the State while they are doing so. Unless freedom of expression is granted to the worst of men, we have no guarantee that it will be afforded to any. As Justice Hugo Black of the United States Supreme Court put it, "The freedoms of speech, press, petition and assembly . . . must be accorded to the ideas we hate or sooner or later they will be denied to the ideas we cherish." [26] The model of ideal behavior in this regard is represented by the English policeman standing at Hyde Park Corner, listening to a speaker exhorting his audience to join him in marching on Buckingham Palace to burn it down and murder the Royal Family. The policeman's duty is to protect, not the Royal Family, but the speaker, in case his safety is threatened by the crowd.

It is not an individual luxury but a collective necessity that we protect the right to express unpopular views and criticize the accepted ways. The health and growth of society depend on it. Criticism provides the goad to improvement that no society can afford to spurn. In an open society the government will be more criticized than in a closed society because critics in the former see that their criticism may have some effect in improving conditions. This valuable spur to progress is lost in a closed society. John K. Galbraith has described the task he had after the Second World War to unravel the way the Germans had used their totalitarian power to wage the war. In many respects they were more dilatory than the much-criticized Allies. Most German factories remained on a single shift throughout the war; women were never mobilized; luxury consumption was preserved until late in the war; the leaders were very cautious about imposing sacrifices on a people they did not trust. The German authorities did not suffer the critical onslaught of the public and press, as the Allies did. They presented an imposing façade to the world and to some extent to the German leaders themselves. In fooling the world they also fooled each other. "We may lay it down as a law that, without public criticism, all governments look much better and are much worse." [27]

John Stuart Mill argued that "all restraint, *qua* restraint, is an evil. . . . leaving people to themselves is always better, *caeteris paribus*, than controlling them." [28] He did not mean that all unrestrained actions are good but rather that the onus of moral justification should be on the restrainer rather than on the person who would be free. S.I. Benn and R.S. Peters, in a most helpful discussion,[29] have criticized Mill's view of restraint on the grounds that, when it came to freedom of discussion, Mill did not distinguish between descriptive (that is, factual, scientific) statements and prescriptive (that is, normative, hortatory) statements. Benn and Peters agreed with Mill with regard to descriptive statements: this is the basis of the scientific method; we can be sure of a truth only after watching opponents try, and fail, to refute it. But they differed with regard to prescriptive statements. A government, they argued, may be right in suppressing a book that would have a morally pernicious influence. "If we have a duty to combat an evil when it is within our power to do so, it is a pusillanimous morality that shrinks from acting upon conviction, on the principle: 'who knows? the other fellow may be right after all.' " [30] This view is persuasive but it ignores the evidence of history. They admitted that "Though some men have certainly been persecuted for false beliefs, many more have suffered for dangerous ones. And the dangerous ones are those that prescribe conduct, not those that simply describe facts." [31] Now we have two dangers to consider: the persecution of holders of beliefs that the government or majority consider dangerous (but that may be right); and the moral evil that may ensue from allowing such ideas to be discussed. We have much historical evidence of the loss to mankind from the suppression of so called "dangerous" ideas. But I am not aware of any evidence of the evil that ensues *in the long run* from the free discussion of ideas, however unpopular. Benn and Peters are right to suggest that freedom of discussion cannot be absolute: we must except, for example, defamation and military secrets. But to include in this category ideas that the government may consider morally pernicious is to open the door to complete governmental control. Does not in fact every totalitarian government suppress free discussion on precisely these grounds of the moral welfare (as it interprets it) of the people?

The government's right to suppress freedom of assembly was also defended by Benn and Peters on the grounds that "public meetings may degenerate into riots. . . . The most elementary duty of a government . . . is to preserve the public peace; when a public meeting *threatens* to turn from airing grievances to smashing windows, the time has come to disperse it." [32] This argument, also, must be firmly combated. The time to disperse the meeting comes when it *turns* to smashing windows. And the penalties must be strictly in accordance with previous laws. To allow suppression when violence *threatens* is to open the door to interpretation, by police and others, of the climate of opinion—a situation that can lead to unlimited abuse. Violence is without doubt a danger to be avoided if possible, but the risk of violence is much less grave than the risk of placing the responsibility for making interpretations and predictions onto fallible, emotional, interested groups like the police.

It is claimed that the State cannot afford to permit the freedom to advocate its own overthrow, especially by violence. But it is exactly the need to avoid violence that necessitates complete freedom of speech and writing. Without this freedom, discussion goes underground and the government becomes ignorant of and unresponsive to common attitudes and moods. It is when the government, through repressive measures, has grown out of touch with popular thinking and has failed to institute desirable changes peacefully that violent change comes about. He who tries to prevent the escape of steam by screwing down the safety valve inherits an explosion.

In the last analysis, however, the State cannot *guarantee* intellectual freedom. Its efforts are confined to providing the best soil in which freedom can grow. The protection and nurture of the plant must be carried out by individual citizens. This involves the third element of Scott's tripartite division—our attitudes and conduct toward one another and the degree of personal responsibility we are prepared to assume in the guardianship of freedom. "Liberty," said Learned Hand, "lies in the hearts of men and women; when it dies there, no constitution, no law, no court can save it." [33] Only that country can count itself blessed in this respect whose citizens are vigilant to detect signs of the erosion of freedom and have the courage to sacrifice themselves in freedom's defense. A writer in the *Times* (London) wrote in 1846:

> The greatest tyranny has the smallest beginning. From precedents overlooked, from remonstrances despised, from grievances treated with ridicule, from powerless men oppressed with impunity, and overbearing men tolerated with complacence, springs the tyrannical usage which generations of wise and good men may hereafter perceive and lament and resist in vain. At present, common minds no more see a crushing tyranny in a trivial unfairness or a ludicrous indignity, than the eye uninformed by reason can discern the oak in the acorn, or the utter desolation of winter in the first autumnal fall. Hence the necessity of denouncing with unwearied and even troublesome perseverance a single act of oppression.[34]

III   THE DIALOGUE

The Dialogue and Intellectual Freedom

Intellectual freedom requires that men be permitted to exchange ideas and to contradict each other without being subjected to direct or indirect persecution. To suppress opinion is to impoverish ourselves by hindering our attempts to approximate to the truth. And men as different as Buddha, Socrates, Jesus, and Freud have agreed that truth is the power that can make man free. Unless we assume our own infallibility, we cannot justifiably silence those who disagree with us; they *may* be right, in which case we shall have left ourselves in error by suppressing them. Moreover, it is unusual that one opinion is wholly true and another wholly false. More often both contain an element of truth. By suppressing one, we sentence ourselves to seeing by a partial light, which could have been enhanced by the clash of opposed ideas. The classic defense of this point of view was that made by John Stuart Mill:

> If all mankind minus one were of one opinion, and only one person were of a contrary opinion, mankind would be no more justified in silencing that one person, than he, if he had the power, would be justified in silencing mankind. . . . We can never be sure that the opinion we are endeavoring to stifle is a false opinion; and if we were sure, stifling it would be an evil still.[35]

And a century later, the same view was expressed thus by Raymond Williams:

> The practical liberty of thought and expression is less a natural right than a common necessity. The growth of understanding is so difficult that none of us can arrogate to himself, or to an institution or a class, the right to determine its channels of advance. . . . To tolerate only this or only that, according to some given formula, is to submit to the phantasy of having occupied the future and fenced it into fruitful or unfruitful ground.[36]

Intellectual freedom cannot be won until man is willing to submit his ideas to the scrutiny of others—in other words, to enter into the dialogue. If a man respects his fellows he must respect their freedom to criticize his ideas and beliefs, for to do otherwise is to assume the contemptuous attitude that nothing they can do or say can alter his opinions. The freer a man is, the wider will be the range of subjects on which he permits discussion and criticism. By this criterion, the Protestant is freer than the Catholic because, although both believe the truth to be contained in the Holy Bible, the Catholic believes the truth is in accordance with the interpretation of the Bible by the Church, while the Protestant allows its interpretation by the individual and his conscience, to a degree. That is, there is room for discussion of its meaning. This involves a great danger: the interpretation of the scriptures by any one individual may be in error. For the Protestant this is a risk worth taking, since the alternative of denying the right of his fellow men to freedom of conscience and discussion is an even greater danger.

What does the dialogue imply for our relationship with those who differ from us? What should be the attitude, for example, of the Christian missionary toward the heathen, or of the Western diplomat toward the Communist? He (the missionary or diplomat) may try to persuade the others of the superiority of his own beliefs, but he must do so believing in the right of the heathen or the Communist to attempt to do the same to him. Moreover, he must retain at the back of his mind the reservations that he *may* be wrong, that the heathen or the Communist may be right, and that, if the others persuade him of the superiority of their set of beliefs, he will embrace them, giving up his belief in Christianity or capitalism or whatever. If we do not enter the dialogue in this spirit, it is not a true dialogue, for we do not treat others as equally worthy of respect as human beings and equally worthy of the freedom to argue, discuss, bring evidence, and persuade. To enter the dialogue believing that our own opinions contain final truth, which no evidence or argument could possibly refute, is to act hypocritically. We demand for ourselves rights and privileges that we are unwilling to grant to others and, thus, hold our fellows in contempt as our inferiors.

The Dialogue and Education

To the extent that external pressures and controls hinder the individual from thinking, speaking, reading, and writing freely, they threaten his healthy growth as a human being. Moreover, the need for such freedom, as Robert Calhoun has pointed out, "is greater, not less, as persons become masters of more extensive and complex ranges of experience." [37] This is why intellectual freedom is always threatened by the ignorant and uneducated, who do not see clearly the precious nature of such freedom and the necessity of the dialogue. They prize more highly other values, such as material comfort, national pride, conformity, and "security," with the result that, in a case of conflict, they are apt to retain these values and let the freedom go. And they not only fail to see the importance of free discussion for themselves, but become impatient with the demands of others for the preservation of the dialogue.

With more education, man becomes more aware of the value of freedom of discussion and, hence, comes to prize it more. Free discussion is necessary, initially, to *gain* education. "Where there is much desire to learn," said Milton, "there of necessity will be much arguing, much writing, and many opinions; for opinion in good men is but knowledge in the making." [38] And once man has tasted the *fruits* of education he realizes that the retention of this freedom is worth the sacrifice of many lesser values. This is clearly shown in the way that concern with civil liberties grows with education. The American Civil Liberties Union, the chief guardian of civil liberties in the United States, demonstrates this in the composition of its membership. An investigation in 1959 showed that 18 percent of its members were university or college teachers, and another 7 percent were schoolteachers. Sixty-six percent said their last level of schooling was postgraduate university work, 24 percent said college, 7 percent said high school, and 2 percent said grade school. [39]

It is unnecessary to document the dramatic extent to which these figures diverge from a cross section of the population.

Conviction and Conduct

A society that aspires to foster intellectual freedom must encourage the dialogue, for otherwise it will find itself with a people who, although they may pay lip service to certain noble ideals and ethical maxims, fail to develop the kind of deep convictions that manifest themselves in conduct. The wise teacher knows that telling his students to be good, and having them memorize and repeat his precepts, hold no guarantees with respect to their subsequent behavior. We must genuinely and deeply understand the bases of and reasons for our beliefs if we hope to maintain those beliefs in the face of critical challenge and to translate them into action. This understanding can come only as a result of submitting our beliefs to the test of full and open discussion. Victor Gollancz, the publisher, who worked with tremendous energy and dedication to change the climate of British opinion through his Left Book Club, has subsequently criticized his own efforts in this field.

Passionately believing in certain ideas, I have allowed myself, I think, to become too much of a propagandist and too little of an educator. . . . my eagerness to express certain ideas has . . . tended to overlay what I hope I have never forgotten: namely, that only by the *clash* of ideas does a mind become truly free, and that no mind not free can have that utter conviction which will render it immune to any assault of passing circumstance.[40]

Those who hope for a Utopia in which man will have achieved perfect freedom and truth and will be able to pass them on to his children in a painless capsulated form are misled. Man can never reach such a state. By its nature, intellectual freedom demands that each person win it for himself by his own efforts. Beliefs, doctrines, and opinions that are inherited passively receive only formal, verbal, ritualistic loyalty. The behavior they exhort is followed only as long as no conflicting opinions are permitted to disturb their monopolistic but tenuous hold. They lack the fire of conviction, the power of growth, and the vitality of genuine knowledge that are essential if belief is to coincide with behavior. If we hesitate to enter the dialogue, placing our faith alongside others' for comparison, criticism, and correction, we shall never succeed in making that faith truly our own to the extent of being able to use it as a secure basis for rational action.

It is for this reason a double tragedy that the capitalist and communist blocs avoid studying each other's beliefs and practices. A genuine dialogue between the two would give each a clearer vision of its own weaknesses. We in the West, for example, are in the habit of comparing communist practices with our principles and claiming (with justification) the former to be inferior. In a genuine dialogue we would compare communist principles with our principles, or their practices with our practices. If we did so, we might discover with surprise that much was praiseworthy in communist principles, and that our own practices differ from our principles alarmingly. For example, we often attack communism for its atheism. But do our Christian principles in fact govern our practice of the division of goods and the holding of property? Or does communist practice in this matter more closely approximate to Christian principle? The purpose of such a dialogue is not to make all capitalists into Communists, or *vice versa*, but to help each to understand his own beliefs, to reject that which is merely an anachronistic residuum, and to reduce as far as possible the constant gap between profession and performance.

The contemporary attempts to teach about communism in American schools fall far short of constituting a genuine dialogue—even when they are not examples of pernicious chauvinism, as they often are. What is needed is an exchange of university professors and high school teachers on a huge scale between East and West. If American schools and colleges were flooded with Communist teachers, and Russian and Chinese schools and colleges flooded with Western teachers, each trying to clarify for the students the justification for his own views, we might have the beginnings of a true accommodation between the present power blocs. There is some indication that the Communists might be more open to this than the West. An English professor of political science was recently invited to lecture at the University of Warsaw. He chose to lecture on "Democratic Government." With official sanction he conducted a well-attended course.[41] It is doubtful if any Communist lecturer has had the chance to give an extended course to American university students on the advantages of communism.

Truth in the Dialogue

"The best test of truth," said Justice Holmes, "is the power of thought to get itself accepted in the competition of the market." [42] This is the *raison d'être* of the continuing dialogue, which Sir Fred Clarke calls the "Community of Persuasion." But faith in free discussion and in the toleration of differences carries an assumption that it is possible in the long run to reach a measure of agreement. This will be so only if all parties will ultimately accept certain common criteria of judgment. Unless they do so, their supposed "dialogue" becomes the sort of profitless wrangling engaged in by capitalist and Communist diplomats—each group uses the same words in different senses, so that even if a nominal agreement is reached it is unlikely to constitute an agreement in practice because each side's interpretation of the words is different. Hence, the mutual accusations of bad faith, hypocrisy, dishonesty, and so on.

Is the situation hopeless, then? Not at all, but there is no easy solution. For the solution demands the utmost of us as human beings. It demands that, in entering the dialogue, we maintain respect for our opponents on the deepest level, and a constant loyalty to truth no matter what penalties we may suffer for it. Margarethe Lachmund, a German Quaker who has lived in East Germany and in Berlin and has done much to encourage a genuine dialogue between East and West, has described her attempts to approach the Russian and East German Communists profitably.[43] She found that one *can* talk meaningfully with the Communists, but one must speak truthfully to them and in a spirit of love. Opposing views must not be abolished, or even veiled.

The courage for clarity and the strength to stand up for truth are repeatedly demanded of us. However, the secret lies in the way in which truth is spoken. If it is spoken with contempt, bitterness or hatred, it results in bitterness; if, however, truth is spoken in love the door to the other's heart can slowly open so that the truth can perhaps have some effect.[44]

She has told how she repeatedly experienced the subtle sensitivity of the Russians with regard to whether they were being lied to or told the truth. Often they reacted in a surprisingly positive way when she had to say what was for them an unpleasant truth and did so in a quiet manner. She asked,

Isn't there a natural feeling alive in every person against being lied to which should be respected? If we are unable to tell the truth there is something wrong with us, too; our relation to another lacks inner freedom because we simply do not meet him as another human being, but with bitterness, hate or contempt in our hearts.[45]

If we are to respect truth in the dialogue we must abandon the practice of using the arguments that we think will persuade our opponents, rather than the arguments that really convince us. The use of such hortatory arguments is less than truthful to ourselves and patronizes our opponents. Moreover, it perpetuates what David Riesman has called "pluralistic ignorance." That is, we hesitate to express the deep feelings that are the true well-springs of our opinions, and hence we fail to discover others who might share our feelings but who are similarly reluctant to express them. Of course, we cannot speak to our opponents as we might wish them to be; we must speak to them as they really are.

But if this "realism" induces us to sacrifice the honesty of our viewpoint to the needs of polemical argument, then we not only fail to achieve a true dialogue but also run the risk of missing the chance of a genuine, as opposed to a superficial, agreement with our opponent.

At its best, the dialogue digs down below the cultural relativism of different societies and reaches a type of communication that operates at the universally human level. Languages, cultural mores, and local conventions constitute barriers to communication, but they do not alter the nature of the basic truth to be communicated. The true dialogue strips away regional variations and reveals this common truth. In doing so, it puts local forms in their properly subordinate place and emphasizes the deeper level of common aspiration. For example, in the West, guests commonly decide when to take leave of their host. In India the host dismisses them. But in both cases the criterion of conduct is courtesy, and the responsibility of the individual is to act in the way that will manifest courtesy in this situation. There is a truth to be found in every situation, and respect and consideration for the other members of the dialogue can help us find it.

Responsibility in the Dialogue

It might be objected that, in fact, the free discussion of ideas has not justified the hopes placed in it. The faith of men like Condorcet and John Stuart Mill that the dialogue would lead inevitably to the substitution of truth for error has, undeniably, often been disappointed. Why is this so? One important reason is what Richard Wollheim calls "the systematic confusion of the seductive and enlightening aspects of communication." [46] Condorcet and Mill were aware of the potential influence of the writer on his audience but failed to see the potential influence of the audience on the writer—failed to foresee that in a commercialized society the rewards of popularity would tempt even writers and artists. This is not only a matter of "giving the public what it wants" but also of falling into the "other-directed" image of a writer, rather than maintaining an ultimate responsibility to the truth.

A warning example of this danger can be found in the treatment of Castro and Cuba by the American press, radio, and television before the infamous Bay of Pigs invasion. A huge mass of communication and discussion was devoted to the subject, and yet the total effect was to produce a disastrously misinformed public. Truth was an elusive commodity. Why? Principally because the writers, journalists, broadcasters, and other opinion leaders failed (with one or two honorable exceptions) to accept their responsibility to the dialogue. Instead, they bowed to current prejudice and preferred to seduce the American people with cath-phrases, simplifications, and headline scares rather than enlighten them with painful truth. Mere quantity of communication does not suffice for the dialogue. All those involved must see themselves as personally responsible for its integrity.

IV EDUCATION FOR INTELLECTUAL FREEDOM

Education in a Free Society

All societies require effective, dedicated leadership if they are to prosper. But for the free society this is not sufficient. A society that aspires toward intellectual freedom needs a large body of ordinary citizens who are prepared to give time and energy to the nurture and preservation of that freedom, if necessary at the cost of personal comfort and welfare. "Unlike the great pyramids," said John W. Gardner, "the monuments of the spirit will not stand unattended. They must be nourished in each generation by the allegiance of believing men and women." [47] No generation of men, however hard they work and however much they sacrifice, can ever guarantee freedom for their children. They may help to build up conditions that enhance their children's possibilities of achieving freedom; but the basic task remains to be done again by every generation.

This perennial task of winning freedom requires a people trained for the effort. Just as a generation cannot in this respect rest on the achievements of its predecessors, so a people cannot rest on the efforts of its leaders. The highest freedoms cannot be given: they must be won. The American people of the early national period were well-aware of this demanding law. That is why declamation found a place in the curriculum of the common school: it was realized that in a democracy all must be trained to safeguard liberty of opinion and conscience.

Indoctrination

It follows from the necessity of personal responsibility for winning intellectual freedom that deliberate indoctrination can have no place in the educational practices of a free society. This is not to deny that a certain degree of contingent indoctrination, occurring daily from birth onward, is both inevitable and—from the point of view of cultural unity and continuity—desirable. What is to be condemned is the forcible inculcation of ideas among young people whose rational powers would permit them to criticize and evaluate such ideas, given the opportunity of free discussion.[48]

Deliberate indoctrination, even in "desirable" values, is incompatible with a growth toward freedom, for it conditions rather than educates. Conditioning proceeds by keeping the individual away from competing influences and subjecting him totally to the influence that it is believed will bring about the desired behavior. Conditioning is successful when a given stimulus will evoke in the individual a fixed reaction without the intervention of rational processes. It appeals to what is most automatic and visceral in man and attempts to build up a stable connection between stimulus and response by bypassing the higher faculties, which are particularly concerned with man's possibilities of freedom.[49]

It is not enough to produce people whos evalues have been internalized. A totalitarian government or an authoritarian church can indoctrinate so that the individual will conform to its doctrines even when all external sanctions are removed. Voltaire estimated contemptuously that one priest was worth ten policemen. Education can be distinguished from indoctrination in that the former fosters intellectual freedom, while the latter reduces it. Nels Ferré said,

> Freedom is authentic not when people do what they want after they have once become indoctrinated by authoritarian standards, but rather when they do from personal insight and by personal choice the very things which accord with their fullest nature. *Authority can be judged as legitimate only by the genuineness with which it abrogates itself.*[50]

There is much criticism in the West of the indoctrination of youth in totalitarian countries. But many of these critics are apparently willing to accept the idea of indoctrination in the values of democracy, free enterprise, or capitalism, to say nothing of chauvinistic nationalism. Even some thoughtful writers argue that democratic indoctrination is quite different from totalitarian indoctrination, and that the former is permissible because of its built-in safeguards. Victor Gollancz, for instance, has suggested that democratic liberals can afford to be less scruplously fair than others in presenting their case for, he great liberal democratic principles—freedom of thought and discussion, the sanctity of the individual conscience, the paramount importance of moral and intellectual independence.

> For not only will they be creating a habit of mind that will *naturally* criticize, and so be annihilating the advantage that propaganda for particular principles and policies might otherwise give them, but, over and above that, propaganda for liberalism carries with it . . . the instrument for its own overthrow. . . . If the liberalism survives, it will survive on its own merits.[51]

This persuasive argument needs to be strenuously combated, on grounds both of principle and of tactics. Gollancz's viewpoint may be valid with respect to the three specific principles he enumerates, but it does not hold true for "liberalism," because "liberalism," like "democracy" or "socialism" or "free enterprise" or "communism," can be interpreted in a variety of ways, and once it is agreed that indoctrination in one of these ambiguous creeds is permissible, then the process of indoctrination is harmless only until it comes into the hands of unscrupulous leaders who are prepared to interpret the creed to suit their own purposes. Besides, it is tactically and psychologically unwise to claim for ourselves a right that we are not ready to grant to our opponents.

The school can justifiably act as an instrument of intentional indoctrination only in a totalitarian society. In a free society such a task is beyond its rightful jurisdiction. To insist that the school should take on this role, as Hullfish and Smith have pointed out, is to "remove from the culture the one agency it has created which is not committed in advance, as issues arise within society, to the support of special interests. Schools represent only the social interest in the large—an admittedly difficult task. Their responsibility is to contribute to society, through their graduates, an increasingly informed, sensitive, and critical intelligence." [52] In the classroom there can, therefore, be no "taboo" subjects. Everything must be liable to subjection to common scrutiny and rational analysis, subject always to the teacher's right to refuse to follow red herrings and to decide what is the appropriate allocation of time among various topics. The teacher, moreover, must admit the student to a level of equality in the dialogue. Although the teacher is in a position of superiority with regard to the organization of the learning situation, once the discussion has begun both teacher and pupil are equals in the quest for truth. Usually the teacher will exercise leadership by virtue of superior maturity, knowledge, or skill, but he must never use superiority of rank to alter the logical or evidential superiority of the student's argument. And, finally, the teacher must not use his position of authority to force even verbal acceptance of doctrines that the students have no opportunity to study or criticize, even if the teacher is himself convinced of the truth of the doctrines.

Rather than keeping the student shut up in the house of secure doctrine—however comfortable, safe, and "true" the house may be—the teacher should see his responsibility as that of opening the door so the student can explore the outdoors. The passive absorption by indoctrination of even the most desirable beliefs will not produce free men. Only when the student passes through the door in active search of new routes, personal experience, and extended horizons does he gain the possibility of freedom. And this opening of doors can be done at any level, if the maturity of the student is taken into consideration. How many doors, for example, are opened through learning to read.

Minority Viewpoints

The school, even in a democracy, operates within a society where many forces are acting on the child to render him intolerant and bigoted. It is not enough to remain neutral in the face of these forces: they must be actively opposed in the school. The teacher needs, said Howard K. Beale, "to habituate the child to the finding and facing of facts and to create in him a keen desire for intellectual integrity and fair-mindedness." [53] We are apt to teach children the meaning of democracy by holding elections for class secretary and by emphasizing the importance of majority rule. It would be well for democracy if we concentrated less on the rule of the majority and emphasized rather respect for minorities. After all, majority rule may be only another name for tyranny: the dictatorship of the proletariat is no better than the dictatorship of one man if you are not a member of the proletariat.

Respect for minorities means that their viewpoints must be fairly and sympathetically examined in the school. This will take the secondary school into the area of controversial and unpopular subjects. In this matter the school and society have reciprocal responsibilities. Society must permit the teacher to discuss with his class the crucial issues of the day, even when this involves the examination of doctrines that the community hates or fears. The teacher, for his part, must attempt to deal with these topics without prejudice and without forcing acceptance of his own views. The alternative to this degree of freedom is a generation of ignorant and prejudiced students. After the United States entered the First World War nearly half of the states passed legislation prohibiting the teaching of the German language. The fruits of this can be seen now in the pitiful condition of German-language teaching in American schools. It is still often considered unpatriotic to know what one's enemies are doing or thinking. There can be no doubt that young people *will* form views on communism, racial integration, unemployment, pacifism, atheism and so on. The alternatives are for them to pick up uninformed, biased, emotionally colored opinions through exposure to the mass media, or to have these views partly balanced by careful study and calm, rational discussion in school. The quality of the discussion will be partly determined by the extent to which there are members of minority groups in the school to take part in the interchange of fact and opinion. Segregation according to race, sex, class, or religion is harmful to the extent that it narrows the student's spectrum of experience and makes it subsequently more difficult for him to understand and communicate with members of those groups with which his education has denied him any contact.

Students must be encouraged to learn to judge people and ideas not by their labels but by their fruits. This is difficult and often painful, of course, because it means studying and thinking instead of merely reacting. They must also learn that a democratic attitude toward minority groups will often involve unpopular decisions, such as granting Communists in the West the same freedom of speech and association that we would like all people to enjoy in the Soviet Union, or granting Hutterite farmers in South Dakota the same right to buy land that is enjoyed by everyone else.[54] A free society can be built only on a foundation of toleration for different points of view, to the extent of granting others the right to work out their problems by means that we ourselves would not use.

Language Education

An educational program that fosters intellectual freedom will include as a cardinal feature a training in literacy and articulateness in the languages of human intercourse, both verbal and symbolic. In particular, students must be helped to read, listen to, and use their own language with understanding. They must be taught to distinguish between truth and propaganda, to judge the value of what they read and hear, to express themselves in speech and writing in such a way that their true intention emerges. They must be helped to avoid the unnecessary misunderstandings and conflicts that arise when their lack of articulateness prevents them from making their meaning clear. Just as the members of a free society must be trained in language to enable them to enter and continue the dialogue, so the building of a world community of free men and women demands the steady removal of illiteracy.

George Orwell has pointed out the close connection between freedom and language.[55] Politicians and bureaucrats, he argued, who want to destroy liberty tend to write and speak badly, and to use pompous or woolly or portmanteau phrases in which their true meaning or any meaning disappears. "Political language," he said, "is designed to make lies sound truthful and murder respectable, and to give an appearance of solidity to pure wind." [56] It is the duty of the citizen to be on the lookout for such language and to rend it to pieces. If we write and speak clearly we are more likely to think clearly, "and to think clearly is a necessary first step towards political regeneration: so that the fight against bad English is not frivolous and is not the exclusive concern of political writers." [57]

One of the most effective ways to help children to free themselves from the strangling coils of propaganda and half-truths is to encourage in them an urgent demand for accurate expression, both in themselves and in others. They should be shown the importance of not taking words at their face value but of approaching them with skepticism and with high demands for clarity. Hitler could not have come to power if he had had to define all his terms. "If names be not correct," said Confucius, "language is not in accordance with the truth of things. If language be not in accordance with the truth of things, affairs cannot be carried on to success. . . . Therefore a superior man considers it necessary that the names he uses may be spoken appropriately." [58] We now know enough about the structure and meaning of language to achieve through its analysis a form of education for intellectual freedom. But there are still powerful forces in all countries that oppose such a liberating process. If this claim is doubted by anyone, he should read Aldous Huxley's account of the history of the Institute for Propaganda Analysis.[59] Founded in 1937 by Mr. Filene, a New England philanthropist, the Institute was closed in 1941, with the Allied governments engaged in "psychological warfare." The analysis of propaganda carried on by the Institute during its short life was opposed by many groups: by educators, because it would make adolescents unduly cynical; by the military, because recruits might start analyzing the utterances of superiors; by the clergy, because it would undermine belief and diminish churchgoing; and by advertisers, because it would undermine brand loyalties and reduce sales.

Lastly, it must be pointed out that we enhance our freedom from unintelligent and distorted thinking through linguistic proficiency. This has been shown by several studies, one of the most interesting being W.H.O. Schmidt's report of the comparison of the intelligence and schooling of European, Indian, and Bantu children in Natal, South Africa.[60] It suggested that the school, through its teaching, creates language proficiency and that this, in its turn, raises the effectiveness of the pupil's thinking, as reflected in raised scores on both verbal and *nonverbal* intelligence tests. In all groups, Schmidt found positive correlations between years of schooling and scores on both verbal and nonverbal tests, age and socio-economic status being held constant. He concluded that the decisive factor in performance on intelligence tests, both verbal and nonverbal, is not maturation and biological growth but the influence of formal schooling on linguistic ability.[61] Since we think so predominantly through language, effective language training is essential for clear and intelligent thought.

Freedom and Behavior

"We profess to seek truth," said George Buttrick, "but would we try to do it if we knew it? If not, what right have we to ask to know?" [62]

Although mastery of language is a necessary condition of intellectual freedom, it is not a sufficient condition. The dangerous notion that it is sufficient is one that pedagogues and intellectuals are particularly liable to adopt. This is why educational schemes that promised much in the way of liberation have so often been disappointing in their fruits. Unless verbal commitments are translated into changed behavior, facility in language can serve as a smoke screen of complacency behind which the deep-lying beliefs that govern conduct can remain securely unaltered. If these conduct-governing beliefs are to be touched and penetrated, the student must be involved emotionally and morally, as well as intellectually, in the subject matter that he is examining. The division of the human being into the intellectual, emotional, and physical can be made only for purposes of convenience, and it corresponds to no clear-cut categorization of reality. The school that ignores this fact, tries rigidly to compartmentalize man, and places all its hopes in the power of one compartment to liberalize him, is destined to share the miserable fate of all such purely intellectual ventures in the history of education.

It is sad but instructive that some of the greatest failures in the campaign to achieve intellectual freedom have been suffered by nations that have achieved excellence in the domain of formal intellectual education. Two obvious examples are the Nazism that grew up in a Germany that had been looked up to by the world for its models of secondary and higher education; and the fascism, never far below the surface of French life, that appeared in all its ugliness under the Vichy government and in the Algerian War, springing from the nation that boasts a literary and linguistic education of unparalleled quality. The history of Germany since 1945 suggests that the defeat of Hitler was not the magic formula that brings a metamorphosis, but that the causes of the rise of authoritarianism and submissiveness still lie deep within the German character and educational system. George C. Allen has criticized contemporary German schools on the grounds that they are still producing students who are verbally and intellectually trained but who lack initiative, hesitate to make judgments, and are excessively submissive and respectful of experts. [63] Kurt P. Tauber has commented on the political apathy of German university students.[64] Interest and activity in politics means sacrifice of time and effort in the cause of something greater than oneself, and Tauber claimed that the German students' verbal allegiance to the processes of democracy is not enough to overcome their basic material selfishness. The postwar enthusiasm among young Germans for the rebirth of freedom that the fall of Hitler made possible has been "smothered under an avalanche of Volkswagens, television sets and other glitter." [65] Before the authoritarian tendencies in modern

Germany can be discouraged it will be necessary for more young people to be willing to translate their verbal statements about freedom into the material sacrifices necessary for the practical preservation and nurture of those liberties that die inevitably if neglected.

It is centrally important that teachers should themselves have made this transition from the verbal to the behavioral level if they are to help their students do the same. That we still have a long way to go in this direction has been shown by a study of the values of students at nine teachers' colleges in New England, New York, New Jersey, and Pennsylvania.[66] The study showed these future teachers to be very confused about freedom. They pay lip service to the liberties that they have been taught verbally from elementary school through college, but when faced with specific issues they often take a stand that is more authoritarian than libertarian. The majority of these students claim to believe in freedom of speech and inquiry and yet

> they would allow the censorship of speakers in schools, and the banning of textbooks which contain criticism of religious organizations. A large minority would deport or silence those who do not believe in our form of government. . . . These important young people . . . are already modifying their behavior to conform to the growing insistence that teachers do not join questionable groups, speak on controversial issues, or associate with individuals who believe in socialism or Communism.[67]

In a similar inquiry I made into the attitudes of future teachers toward the Bill of Rights, I found that not one of its provisions commanded unanimous approval among the students. Two provisions—the reserved rights of the people and the right to confront one's accuser—were rejected by a majority. Only one student in five thought that an accused person should always have the right to know who has given evidence against him.[68] Freedom cannot be safeguarded by people who mouth platitudes in its praise but who will not actively commit themselves to the painful, sacrificial behavior that its concrete defense involves.

V ACADEMIC FREEDOM

Education and Society

It is clear from the foregoing remarks that a key figure in the achievement of intellectual freedom is the teacher. His chances of success in guiding his students toward such freedom will depend in part on his own freedom to teach. It is for this reason that academic freedom has been a perennial subject of concern and discussion since the time of Socrates. The degree of freedom granted to the teacher in school and university will be determined by the community's prevailing concept of the true function of the teacher, the school, and the university. Clearly, a community that views the function of educational institutions as that of handing on a cultural and social order will not be as ready to permit freedom to the teacher as one that expects the school to select, criticize, evaluate, and innovate.

One of the central aspects of the problem of academic freedom lies in the element of financial support. In all countries, private schools and universities must obtain at least part of their support from nongovernmental sources. Thus, we find in the private sector of education both exciting, experimental innovations and desperately ill-paid and ill-qualified teachers. Public schools and state-supported universities are generally both more financially secure and more conservative in atmosphere. With rising costs it seems inevitable that the State will increasingly intervene even in private education with financial support. The question that arises in all cases, then, is: does he who pays the piper necessarily call the tune? Does control surely follow support? There are some discouraging examples from various parts of the world. Totalitarian nations unapologetically use the teacher, the school, and the university as instruments of indoctrination. But so-called free countries often fail to resist the temptations of financial patronage. The *Rhodesia Herald* of June 9, 1961, for example, reported that at a meeting in Salisbury, Southern Rhodesia, on June 8, Dr. T. Ranger, a lecturer in history at the University College of Rhodesia and Nyasaland, was elected chairman of the newly founded Citizens Against the Colour Bar Association. Members of the association were to "sit-in" in Salisbury's shops and hotels reserved for Europeans.[69] Only two days before, the same newspaper had reported that, on June 6, members of the Twentieth Annual Conference of the Southern Rhodesia Municipal Association at Victoria Falls condemned the staff of the University College of Rhodesia and Nyasaland for political activities. The total proposed grant in aid to the College from the thirty-one local authorities of Southern Rhodesia for the current year (£8200) was refused. Councillor H.D. Tanner, of Salisbury, said, "I hold that the University College should be a seat of Learning, and not in any way connected with political activities. I believe the University College has at least one cell which is a hot bed of political intrigue." The acting mayor of Que Que said his people were opposed to giving any future grants to the University College.[70] Courage and determination are needed by a university president if he is to stand up for a principle that turns away financial support.

In America, serious potential threats to academic freedom have developed since the Second World War because of the enormous amount of university research that is supported by the Federal Government, especially the Defense Department. Such massive financial support needs equally massive restraint and self-discipline on the part of those who dispense it. Perhaps this is too much to expect over a long period. But it is not impossible to set up intervening bodies whose composition will go far to ensure that research will not be distorted, dominated or corrupted by those who pay for it. The outstanding success of the University Grants Committee in Britain, which for many years has allocated government funds to universities without ever showing the least sign of wanting to determine how the money shall be used, is an encouraging example of what is possible with men of integrity and restraint.

In Europe and North America the principle of academic freedom has enjoyed the healthiest, although by no means an unimpeded, growth. The obstacles to it have been to a degree complementary in the two continents. In Europe there has developed a strong tradition of academic freedom, especially in the universities. The University of Berlin, and other nineteenth-century German universities, became exemplars of the freedom to teach, learn, and pursue research. But these same institutions were plunged into the depths of servitude in the Nazi period, partly through their own failure to exercise a wider leadership. Whatever may be said about the caricature of the "ivory tower," it remains true that if educational institutions segregate themselves from the vulgar details of the everyday world, they cannot justifiably complain when the leadership role they abdicate is taken over by other less disinterested agencies in society.

In North America the danger has been rather that of regarding the school and university as "service" institutions, and the teacher as a hired help of the community, employed by it to teach its children and young people as it thinks fit. While the North American University has largely escaped the irresponsibility of ivory-tower isolation, its freedom has been reduced by attempts to make it a reflector rather than a critic of society's values. The McCarthy period was not a unique, unrepeatable aberration. It was a manifestation of a tendency lying just below the surface of all societies, brought to ghastly focus in this case by the skill of an unscrupulous demagogue playing on the universal weaknesses of fear and cowardice. There are always forces in society trying to keep the teacher in line, trying to prevent him from advocating—or even examining—views that differ from those of the majority. And calm courage will always be required by those who try to combat these forces.

Controversial Issues

The issues on which the teacher is most liable to be silenced are those that touch man in his most sensitive spots or that involve his deep-lying—often unexamined—assumptions and beliefs. We are all irritated by having our sensitivities rasped and are made restless when our life-axioms are forced into the daylight. And if we are in a position of power or influence there is the temptation to use our strength to avoid such irritations and disquietude by preventing the raising of the painful issues. Hence, the question of academic freedom is often associated with topics like the relationships between the sexes or between people of different races, man's religious beliefs, and challenges from radical political ideologies.

The belief that disturbing topics, such as sex, slavery, segregation, atheism, and communism should be discussed in classrooms is relatively recent. In America, until the separation of church and state in the late eighteenth and early nineteenth centuries, most colleges were under church control and did not permit the free discussion of religious issues. Even in the nineteenth century, progress in this regard was extremely slow. Nor were controversial social and economic problems examined. It has been said that the Civil War might have been prevented if teachers had enjoyed the academic freedom to discuss the issue of slavery.[71] In the twentieth century, a greater professional consciousness among teachers brought demands by them for freedom to deal with topics that aroused controversy. Schoolteachers followed behind university teachers, who were led in this matter by the American Association of University Professors. Opposition to the granting of such freedom came from many groups, outstanding among whom were the American Legion, the Daughters of the American Revolution, and Chambers of Commerce, as well as various vigilante groups. State legislatures often acted as forces of reaction and constraint. In 1920, the Lusk Committee, appointed by New York State to investigate seditious activities, concluded that teachers should actively range themselves on the side of the *status quo* and against the forces of change. In Tennessee, it is still illegal to teach the facts of evolution, because they are considered contrary to the truths of revealed religion.

When a topic of controversy arouses fierce emotions and threatens vested interests, it is extremely likely that the tender plant of academic freedom will wither in the inhospitable climate. Such is the situation in the Southern states of the United States, with respect to the discussion of segregation. Surely here is a time and place where the problems of race relations should be objectively and rationally examined in the classroom, bringing to bear all the facts available in an effort to raise the matter above the level of primitive reaction. Instead, the subject is largely taboo in schools and colleges, and state legislatures use their power to impose a rigid uniformity of opinion. In 1961, Waldo F.

McNeir, who had been a professor of English at Louisiana State University, in Baton Rouge, for 11 years, was forced to resign because of his opposition to the efforts of the legislature to block desegregation. He resigned after General Troy H. Middleton, President of the university, told him that he was preparing to charge him with "showing disrespect for the Legislature." Middleton told McNeir that he regarded his outspoken expression of antisegregation views as "detrimental to the best interests of the University," which "as a tax-supported state agency can best perform its functions by avoiding participation in controversial matters." [72]

The subject that most beclouds the vision (with a red mist) in the United States is that of communism. Should communism be examined in the classroom? Clearly, if its study is educationally relevant, it should be undertaken, since no subject should be *a priori* taboo. Should Communist teachers be permitted in school and university? If an educational institution respects the principle of academic freedom, it cannot exclude a teacher because of his political views. This is not to oppose the dismissal of a teacher found guilty of professional misconduct. But the crucial aspect of the matter is that this should be a *professional* judgment. "A professor should be dismissed," said Carl Wittke, "for failing to get his students to think, not for getting them to think in a way that the board of trustees or some special group disapproves." [73] If a teacher performs his professional duties satisfactorily, his outside activities and private beliefs should not be considered in matters of appointment, promotion, and dismissal. It is essential to keep in mind the need for *relevance* between the teacher's professional activities and the heresy of which he is accused. Otherwise we find ourselves in the ludicrous situation of the Maryland Chess Federation, which in 1958 disqualified the State chess champion on the grounds that he had been described before a congressional sub-committee as a Communist organizer.[74] A Communist teacher accused of unprofessional conduct should—like any other teacher—be judged according to the substantiated facts of his individual case and not according to the unjust and undemocratic method of "guilt by association."

Contracts and Oaths

Because teachers hold a special position of influence in the community, employers and governments have frequently tried to limit and control their actions, thoughts, and associations by demanding that they swear adherence to the beliefs and customs of the majority. These demands have reached their most grotesque form in the case of young, unmarried women teachers who have neither the temerity nor the power to oppose a tyrannous community. For example, in 1923, a North Carolina teacher bound herself, in return for an annual salary of $637.50, as follows:

I promise to take a vital interest in all phases of Sunday-school work, donating of my time, service, and money without stint for the uplift and benefit of the community. I promise to abstain from all dancing, immodest dressing, and other conduct unbecoming a teacher and a lady. I promise not to go out with any young man except in so far as it may be necessary to stimulate Sunday-school work. I promise not to fall in love, to become engaged, or secretly married. I promise to remain in the dormitory or on the school grounds when not actively in school or church work elsewhere. I promise not to encourage or tolerate the least familiarity on the part of any of my boy pupils. I promise to sleep at least eight hours a night, to eat carefully, and to take every precaution to keep in the best of health and spirits in order that I may be better able to render efficient service to my pupils.[75]

More recently, in 1959, a school board in Montgomery County, Maryland, required a teacher to swear she believed "in God and in Rewards and Punishments." [76]

The social criticism that accompanied the depression of the 1930's in the United States brought a nervousness that resulted in demands upon teachers for oaths of loyalty to the government. True to its traditions from the colonial era, Massachusetts began this restrictive trend, which spread to other states. By 1960 about thirty states required loyalty oaths from public-school teachers. University teachers and scholars have also been diverted from their true work by such oaths and affidavits.

Loyalty oaths have no place in schools and universities, especially in America, where they contradict the spirit of freedom contained in the Bill of Rights. As Justice Douglas of the U.S. Supreme Court said in 1958, in his concurring opinion declaring unconstitutional California's law requiring a loyalty oath to obtain certain tax exemptions: "I know of no power that enables any government under our Constitution to become a monitor of thought, as this statute would have it become." Furthermore, loyalty oaths are completely ineffective in achieving their purpose, and are ultimately self-defeating. John Stuart Mill made this clear a century ago when he opposed the contemporary English practice of refusing to permit anyone to give evidence in a court of law who did not profess belief in God and in a future state. "The rule," said Mill, "is suicidal, and cuts away its own foundation. Under pretence that atheists must be liars, it admits the testimony of all atheists who are willing to lie, and rejects only those who brave the obloquy of publicly confessing a detested creed rather than affirm a falsehood." [77] The same is true of loyalty oaths for school and university teachers. No person seriously bent on sedition would hesitate to swear falsely his loyalty to the institution he wishes to overthrow. On the other hand, the integrity and loyalty of the honorable and responsible teacher will not be augmented in any way by swearing an oath. Justice Black, in the 1958 judgment cited above, said,

I am convinced that loyalty to the United States can never be secured by the endless proliferation of "loyalty" oaths; loyalty must arise spontaneously from the hearts of the people who love their country and respect their government.

The people principally eliminated from the teaching profession through loyalty oaths are those men of principle and courage who refuse on conscientious grounds to swear oaths of any kind.

It is claimed that loyalty oaths can in some cases be effective because of the hidden threat of trial for perjury that they contain. But such attempted intimidation is basically unjust, for it singles out one group of the population and demands that they swear to an allegiance that is taken for granted and left unexpressed in the case of the majority. It was largely for this reason that Harvard, Yale, Princeton, and other leading American universities refused to accept federal loan money under the student loan program of the National Defense Education Act, as long as the Act demanded that before receiving a loan the student had to take an affidavit that he did not support any organization that believes in or teaches the overthrow of the United States Government by force. In this case, a student's financial need singled him out for unusual and unnecessary demands with respect to his loyalty.

Most important of all, oaths are intellectually and educationally harmful, for they discourage teachers from being politically active and concerned, in case the cause or organization with which they associate themselves today may become the forbidden area of tomorrow. Particularly pernicious are those oaths that require statements about a man's past beliefs and activities. Abraham Lincoln, commenting on proposed post-Civil War loyalty oaths, said, "On principle I dislike an oath which requires a man to swear he has not done wrong. It rejects the Christian principle of forgiveness on terms of repentance. I think it is enough if a man does no wrong hereafter." [78] But all oaths serve as instruments of intellectual repression, for they create an atmosphere inhospitable to the germination and communication of ideas and innovations. Scholars and teachers working on the boundaries of knowledge will frequently find themselves in minority positions and will appear to be different, eccentric, or even disloyal. Such men must be protected from totalitarian mechanisms like loyalty oaths if they are to be free to concentrate on their intellectual task.

Academic Freedom and Professionalism

The basic components of academic freedom in the schools and universities of a free society include the freedom of teachers and students to conduct research and inquire into any subject that evokes their intellectual concern; the freedom of teachers to teach in the manner they feel is professionally appropriate; and the freedom of teachers and students to act in their private lives with all the rights and liberties enjoyed by other citizens. This degree of freedom, it will be noted from history, has more often been approached in countries with a high general level of education than in relatively backward countries and more often in universities than in public schools. This is because the issue of academic freedom is integrally bound up with the development of professionalism. Academic freedom must be *earned*—by the quality and professional discipline of the teachers who claim it. In nineteenth-century America, when some university professors were demanding the right to discuss controversial issues in the classroom, such a privilege was not even considered for public schoolteachers, because only a negligible number of the latter were qualified to take advantage of such freedom.

If the community is to be persuaded to take a tolerant, far-sighted, and enlightened attitude toward academic freedom, the teachers must prove themselves worthy of such freedom by demonstrated competence in their professional field. Academic freedom, then, must await the advent of well-trained, professionally minded teachers. We have already reached a level in Europe and North America where teachers in the better universities are permitted complete freedom to teach *within the field of their specialization*. It would not, for instance, be considered professional for a teacher of mathematics to use his class periods to attempt to indoctrinate his captive audience with Marxism or Roman Catholicism. But it would be appropriate for, say, a philosophy professor to "advocate" dialectical materialism as an exercise in philosophical criticism. No topic of inquiry that the competent teacher finds appropriate to his professional purpose should be forbidden.

Moreover, the canon of academic freedom demands that if a teacher is accused of abusing the privileges of his academic position his case should be examined not by a government committee or citizens' vigilante group but by the teaching profession, in the form of his own educational institution and his professional organization. It should be the responsibility of the school or university to make decisions arising out of such an investigation. This means that schools, especially, will have to be granted much more autonomy in matters of appointment, promotion, and dismissal of teachers. School boards and governments will have to learn that teachers will act maturely only when they are treated as mature people, and that schools will take responsible leadership in the community only when they are regarded as autonomous, responsible units. Eventually, it is to be hoped, all matters of professional discipline will be in the hands of the teaching profession itself. Only through this self-discipline can academic freedom be firmly established.

It must be made clear that academic freedom is necessary not for the comfort and pleasure of the teacher but for the sake of the community and the cause of truth. If teachers, scholars, and students are afforded intellectual freedom, their work will be discussed, criticized, refuted when in error, confirmed when correct. It is by this steady process of free inquiry, open criticism, and continuous correction that our knowledge of man and the universe is enhanced. It is an extremely risky process, of course, but then so is education and so is life. There is the risk that students will be exposed to teachers of undesirable or harmful views, that some students will be unable to carry the burden of freedom offered to them. But the alternative to academic freedom is indoctrination in current majority viewpoints, which may be false now and will almost certainly be false under the changed circumstances of the future. The risky, uncertain way of academic freedom is still the most effective way for the individual to develop independence and maturity and for mankind to discover truth.

Freedom to Learn

The principles of academic freedom that gave distinction to the nineteenth-century German universities can be epitomized as *Lehrfreiheit und Lernfreiheit*—the freedom to teach and the freedom to learn. The concept of *Lehrfreiheit* was brought back to America by the thousands of American scholars who studied at German universities. Unfortunately, they were not so effective in making an emigrant out of the complementary principle of *Lernfreiheit*. While professors in American universities have, during the past century, steadily strengthened their position with regard to their freedom to teach without outside interference, American university students have not made similar progress in their freedom to learn. Even at the better universities, administrations frequently treat students like schoolchildren, drawing up lists of regulations without consulting them and keeping them in a condition of intellectual subservience. Indeed, some observers consider that, with the pressure of numbers in universities, the situation is worsening and cite as evidence the prevalence of students "learning" by sitting passively in lecture halls with hundreds of others while a distant professor talks to them through a microphone.

In a sense, the offense is greater now because we know more about the process of learning. We know that an important aspect of the learning process is the student's active participation in and responsibility for his own education. How do students learn? One effective way is for them to take responsibility for arranging the conditions of their own learning. From the point of view of long-term learning, it is better for the student to take issue with his teacher and clarify his own views in the tempering experience of the dialogue than to copy faithfully the teacher's deathless (or more often deadly) prose into his notebook for subsequent obedient memorization.

Hence, it is important to get university students to take a stand on important (and, therefore, probably controversial) issues. The dialogue requires that the professor also take a stand. This procedure, of course, demands a pattern different from the prevailing one in which the student is rarely in a group small enough to permit it and, at that, is often with an inexperienced and insecure graduate student as teacher. Even when the conditions are right, it is often difficult to persuade American students to argue with the professor in this way. Why should this be? It is partly because of the narrow range of intellectual and ideological diversity in America. Partly it is because the students are *afraid*.

This fear is one of the greatest enemies of the freedom to learn. It stems from the students' distrust of their professors and administrations, even when these latter assure the student that they welcome controversy, originality, and disagreement. In looking around, students perceive that such statements are not translated into supporting behavior. They observe that the rewards for conformity, obedience, and docility are great and reliable, while the absence of these qualities is often punished in blatant or subtle ways. Education becomes a ritual: students quickly realize that by "playing the academic game"—keeping out of trouble, not annoying the professor or administration, not rocking the boat—they can get their degrees and go on with their professional careers.

In other words, academic life is beset by a great deal of hypocrisy and phoniness. Administration, faculty, and students connive tacitly in playing a game that all believe to be personally beneficial but which, in fact, is seriously destructive of genuine learning. The student protests, which began at the University of California at Berkeley and spread rapidly to other universities, were, at least in part, a gesture of opposition to this hypocrisy. Such protests are an extremely hopeful sign. If administrations and faculties cannot save the university, it may yet be saved by the students. These student rebels are demanding that verbal allegiance to freedom to learn be translated into behavioral terms. They want freedom to learn in the sense of participation in determining the conditions under which they will learn and be taught. Their professors have for years been teaching them about great liberal principles like intellectual freedom, and now the students are beginning to take these teachings seriously.

Needless to say, we do not always welcome being taken seriously, and the reaction from faculty and administration to these student protests has not always been admirable. University administrations, in particular, have lived too long with a paternalistic, authoritarian system of student government to change painlessly. There is, of course, a need for authority in the administration of a university and the teaching of students. There is a need for rules and regulations by which students' lives shall be organized. But these needs do not constitute a justification for authoritarianism, for the application of rules for their own sake or for the convenience of those in authority, or for the unreasonable, arbitrary, or irrelevant application of rules.

Rules governing student life and learning should be examined to see whether they are *relevant* to the accomplishment of the goals of the institution. Many rules are merely accretions that remain solely because of academic inertia. Since one of the principal goals of the university is the fostering of learning, it would seem imperative that students should be consulted as often as possible in the formation of rules that will affect their learning. It is necessary to look at authority in the university from the students' point of view. Rules that are consistent with the goal of *Lernfreiheit* will both be reasonable and *appear* to the student to be reasonable; they will be clearly understandable and relevant to the student's ability to comply; they will be compatible with his view of the purpose of the institution and, as far as possible, with his own interests and purposes.

NOTES

1 "All religious organizations, when their spiritual vitality burns low, become extremely proficient in the art of institutional self-defence." Daniel Jenkins, *Equality and Excellence: A Christian Comment on Britain's Life* (London: S.C.M. Press, 1961), 166.

2 Fyodor Dostoyevsky, *The Brothers Karamazov*, Constance Garnett, trans. (New York: Random House, 1950), Book 5, ch. V, 292–314.

3 See "Ku Klux Klan," in *Encyclopedia Britannica* (Chicago: Benton, 1964), vol. XIII, 512; Robert A. Wilson, "The Rebirth of the Ku Klux Klan," *Fact*, vol. I, no. 3 (May–June 1964), 10–17.

[4] See Robert O. Ballou, ed., *World Bible* (New York: Viking, 1950), 163–64.

[5] Gordon Zahn, " 'The Vicar': A Controversy and a Lesson," *The Critic*, vol. XXII, no. 2 (October–November 1963), 42–46.

[6] See Radhakrishnan, *Recovery of Faith* (London: Allen & Unwin, 1956), 13.

[7] Milton Rokeach, "Paradoxes of Religious Belief," *Trans-action*, vol. 2, no. 2 (January–February 1965), 9–12.

[8] *Observer* (London), February 26, 1961, 12.

[9] For a critical analysis of the way ghetto Catholicism operates in the Province of Quebec, see Gérard Dion and Louis O'Neill, "A Dispute on Religious Labels and Moral Principles," translation of an article published in *Ad Usum Sacerdotum* (Faculté des sciences sociales, Université Laval, Quebec), vol. 14, no. 9 (November, 1959).

[10] Reinhold Niebuhr, "The Commitment of the Self and the Freedom of the Mind," *Religion and Freedom of Thought* (New York: Doubleday, 1954), 59–60.

[11] "And I also say unto thee, that thou art Peter, and upon this rock I will build my church; and the gates of Hades shall not prevail against it. I will give unto Thee the keys of the kingdom of heaven: and whatsover thou shalt bind on earth shall be bound in heaven: and whatsoever thou shalt loose on earth shall be loosed in heaven."

[12] F.R. Scott, "Expanding Concepts of Human Rights," *Canadian Bar Journal*, vol. 3, no. 3 (June, 1960), 199–208.

[13] John Stuart Mill, *On Liberty* (Chicago: Regnery, 1955), ch. IV.

[14] *Ibid.*, 156–57.

[15] James Fitzjames Stephen, *Liberty, Equality, Fraternity* (New York: Holt, n.d.), ch. I–IV. For an extended discussion, by various writers, of Mill's view of freedom, see *Nomos IV—Liberty*, Carl J. Friedrich, ed. (New York: Atherton Press, 1962; Yearbook of the American Society for Political and Legal Philosophy).

[16] "Those who proclaim liberty as the supreme social goal often fail to realize that they themselves do approve of certain restrictions of interpersonal freedom, not only in order to make other freedoms possible but also for the sake of goals other than freedom." Felix E. Oppenheim, "Freedom—An Empirical Interpretation," *Nomos IV—Liberty*, Friedrich, ed., 284.

[17] Peter Davis, "Thinking Man's Radio," *Fact*, vol. I, no. 2 (March–April 1964), 22–29.

[18] Adolf Hitler, *Mein Kampf* (New York: Reynal & Hitchcock, 1939), 236–37.

[19] Author of *All Quiet on the Western Front*. See E.M. Forster, "What has Germany done to the Germans?" *Two Cheers for Democracy* (London: Arnold, 1951), 49.

[20] *Civil Liberties*, no. 173 (October, 1959), 4.

[21] *Civil Liberties*, no. 177 (February, 1960), 4.

[22] *Civil Liberties*, no. 191 (September, 1961), 4.

[23] Nathan M. Pusey, "Religion's Role in Liberal Education," *Religion and Freedom of Thought* (New York: Doubleday, 1954), 48.

[24] E.M. Forster, "Culture and Freedom," *Two Cheers for Democracy*, 45.

[25] Charles E.S. Wood, *Heavenly Discourse* (New York: Penguin, 1946), 131.

[26] In his dissenting opinion to the 1961 Supreme Court decision to uphold the McCarran Act.

[27] John K. Galbraith, "Dissent in a Free Society," *Atlantic* (February, 1962), 44–48.

28 John Stuart Mill, *On Liberty* (Chicago: Regnery, 1955), 140–41.

29 S.I. Benn and R.S. Peters, *Social Principles and the Democratic State* (London: Allen & Unwin, 1959), ch. 10, "Freedom as a Political Ideal."

30 *Ibid.*, 226–29.

31 *Ibid.*, 227.

32 *Ibid.*, 229. My italics.

33 *Civil Liberties*, no. 191 (September, 1961), 1.

34 Quoted by Clarence L. Barber, *Canadian Association of University Teachers Bulletin* (October, 1959), 12–13.

35 Mill, *op. cit.*, 24.

36 Raymond Williams, *Culture and Society, 1780–1950* (London: Chatto & Windus, 1958), 335.

37 Robert L. Calhoun, "The Historical Relations between Religion and Intellectual Freedom," *Religion and Freedom of Thought* (New York: Doubleday, 1954), 27.

38 John Milton, *Areopagitica* (London: Dent, 1927), 32.

39 *Civil Liberties*, no. 175 (December, 1959), 2.

40 Victor Gollancz, *More for Timothy* (London: Gollancz, 1953), 367.

41 Norman Z. Alcock, *The Bridge of Reason* (Oakville, Ontario: John Wilkes Press, 1961), 15–16.

42 Quoted in Harold B. Alberty and Boyd H. Bode, eds., *Educational Freedom and Democracy* (New York: Appleton-Century, 1938), 147.

43 Margarethe Lachmund, "Christians in a Divided World," *Friends Quarterly*, October, 1958. (Reprinted by Friends Peace Service, American Friends Service Committee, Philadelphia.)

44 *Ibid.*, 8.

45 *Ibid.*, 11.

46 Richard Wollheim, "The Consequences of Communication," *Times Literary Supplement* (July 15, 1960), 450.

47 John W. Gardner, "National Purpose," *New York Times* (June 9, 1960), 34.

48 On this point, Maurice Cranston has made a valuable distinction between "rational freedom" and "compulsory rational freedom": *Freedom: A New Analysis* (London: Longmans, Green, 1954), 23–62.

49 For an interesting Jesuit criticism of conditioning in the Catholic Church, see Louis Beirnaert, "The Problem of Conditioning in the Church," *Cross Currents*, vol. XII, no. 4 (Fall, 1962), 433–41.

50 Nels F.S. Ferré, "Authority and Freedom," in *Authority and Freedom in Our Time*, Lyman Bryson, *et al.*, eds. (New York: Harper, 1953), 502–503. Italics in original.

51 Gollancz, *op. cit.*, 318.

52 H. Gordon Hullfish and Philip G. Smith, *Reflective Thinking: The Method of Education* (New York: Dodd, Mead, 1961), 264.

53 Howard K. Beale, "The Present Status of Freedom in the Schools," in Alberty and Bode, eds., *op. cit.*, 90.

54 The Hutterites are a 300-year-old Christian sect. They are pacifists, live communally, and own no private property. They are forbidden by law in South Dakota to buy any more land.

55 George Orwell, "Politics and the English Language," *A Collection of Essays* (New York: Doubleday, 1954), 162–77.

56 *Ibid.*, 177.

57 *Ibid.*, 163.

58 From the Analects of Confucius, *World Bible*, Robert O. Ballou, ed., 506.

59 Aldous Huxley, *Brave New World Revisited* (New York: Harper, 1958), 131–32.

60 W.H.O. Schmidt, "School and Intelligence," *International Review of Education*, vol. VI, no. 4 (1960), 416–32.

61 *Ibid.*, 429.

62 George A. Buttrick, *Sermons Preached in a University Church* (New York: Abingdon Press, 1959), 86.

63 George C. Allen, "Germans at School," *Listener* (August 15, 1957), 235–36.

64 Kurt P. Tauber, "Over Germany: Shadows From the Past," *New York Times Magazine* (December 27, 1959), 34.

65 *Ibid.*

66 Fay L. Corey, *Values of Future Teachers: A Study of Attitudes Towards Contemporary Issues* (New York: Teachers College, 1955).

67 *Ibid.*, 46.

68 Paul Nash, "Should We Abandon the Bill of Rights?" *Social Education*, vol. XXIII, no. 8 (December, 1959), 371–78.

69 *Rhodesia Herald*, June 9, 1961, quoted by *Federation of Rhodesia and Nyasaland Newsletter* (June 9, 1961), 16.

70 *Rhodesia Herald*, June 7, 1961, quoted by *Federation of Rhodesia and Nyasaland Newsletter* (June 9, 1961), 11.

71 John S. Brubacher, *A History of the Problems of Education* (New York: McGraw-Hill, 1947), 633–34.

72 Quoted in *Civil Liberties*, no. 189 (May, 1961), 3.

73 Carl Wittke, "Educational Freedom in Colleges and Universities," in Alberty and Bode, eds., *op. cit.*, 151.

74 *Christian Science Monitor*, May 12, 1958, 1.

75 Quoted in Alberty and Bode, eds., *op. cit.*, 68–69.

76 *Civil Liberties*, no. 172 (September, 1959), 4.

77 Mill, *op. cit.*, 43.

78 Quoted in *Civil Liberties*, no. 187 (March, 1961), 1.

III

THE AUTHORITY OF DISCIPLINE
The Freedom to Develop One's Interests

I AUTHORITY, AUTHORITARIANISM, AND THE TEACHER

Authority and Power

> Behold, I was shapen in iniquity;
> And in sin did my mother conceive me.

Thus, in the Psalms (51:5), is the doctrine of original sin described. The Christian doctrine of the Fall, that man is born in sin and can reach a state of beatitude only through serving God and with the aid of divine grace, has deeply influenced education throughout the West. The idea seems to be firmly embedded in Western consciousness; it might be related to the sense of the tragic in life and to the Greek concept of Destiny or Fate. Because of it, education has been regarded as a moral discipline: the child is naturally evil and can be saved only with the aid of strict control, denial, and authority. His natural propensities will lead him astray and should, therefore, not be indulged. The function of the Christian teacher, consequently, is to teach with authority. Even Jesus, who came to bring men freedom, is reported to have gone into the synagogue and to have "taught them as having authority." (Mark I:22.) This authoritative position of the teacher with regard to the pupil is clearly stated in the Encyclical Letter of Pius XI on *The Christian Education of Youth* (1929):

> . . . every form of pedagogic naturalism which in any way excludes or weakens supernatural Christian formation in the teaching of youth, is false. Every method of education founded, wholly or in part, on the denial or forgetfulness of original sin and of grace, and relying on the sole powers of human nature, is unsound. Such, generally speaking, are those modern systems bearing various names which appeal to a pretended self-government

and unrestrained freedom on the part of the child, and which diminish or even suppress the teacher's authority and action, attributing to the child an exclusive primacy of initiative, and an activity independent of any higher law, natural or divine, in the work of his education.[1]

The principal danger associated with this doctrine is that the right to exercise authority often becomes, in man, mingled with a lust for power. In the Middle Ages, the Church was acknowledged to be the holder of this sacred trust of authority over men. With the Renaissance man grew out of his childlike state of dependence and demanded freedom. The Church was reluctant to give it, believing she would be violating a historical trust. But man saw her reluctance as a wish to cling to Rome's ancient mastery and the profits that went with it. In the event, the Church lost both her unity and her absolute authority and won a reputation as an enemy of freedom that is still with her. The nation-state took over much of the Church's authority and in its turn drifted into the same vice that the Church had fallen into—the lust for power and dominion over others. We are still suffering from this evil, and it may ultimately destroy us.

In the teaching situation, as in any situation in which problems of leadership arise, authority is a necessity. But the clearcut authority of the traditional Christian concept, with the Church and its official ordering, and sinful children obeying unquestioningly, is based on a serious oversimplification. It ignores at least two complicating factors: the sinfulness and fallibility of those in authority, and the necessity for a mutual responsibility between teacher and pupil for the conduct of the educational process. These two factors are linked, for where the feeling of mutual responsibility is absent or weak the one in authority will flee from the difficulties of true responsibility and take refuge in power and force. Those with a lust for power—which may take the form of an ambition for status, privilege, prestige, or the successful manipulation of others—are blinded by their lust and, hence, are unable to perceive accurately the objective situation and its demands on them and their pupils. They are apt to fall into the temptation of viewing persons as means rather than ends and of using their authority to subordinate or destroy the wills of others.

Authority and Authoritarianism

It is essential to differentiate clearly between authority—which is often necessary—and authoritarianism—which is always pernicious. T.E. Hulme was a convinced authoritarian. He wrote: "Nothing is bad in itself except disorder; all that is put in order in a hierarchy is good." [2]

The belief in the value of order for its own sake is a basic feature of an authoritarian philosophy. At a lower level, this becomes the exercise of authority and the achievement of order for one's *own* sake, rather than for the sake of the other person or the group. There is a constant danger in schools that authority will degenerate into authoritarianism, because teaching unfortunately attracts those who consciously or (more commonly) unconsciously wish to exercise authority in order to satisfy some unfulfilled need within themselves.

The authoritarian demands unquestioning obedience and is prepared to implant fear and to punish severely in order to produce it. An archetypical example of the authoritarian view was given by Hubbard Winslow in a lecture delivered before the American Institute of Instruction in 1834, entitled, *On the Dangerous Tendency to Innovations and Extremes in Education.*

Children left to their chosen way are left to ruin. Hence the first step towards their salvation is, to control their choice; that is, to subdue their *wills* to rightful authority. . . . Now the fundamental motive to obedience is *fear*. Other powerful motives operate, but all are ultimately *sustained* by this. Take this away, and all other motives lose their efficacy. Hence the first practical lesson for children is, that transgression is followed by punishment. If they *sin*, they will *suffer*.[3]

Such attitudes would have been less persistent if they had not been matched by a desire on the other side to obey and follow unquestioningly. For every one with a need to command and wield authority there are many with a need to obey and to accept authority. We are all insecure and fearful to a degree, and there is a recurring temptation to seek security and to silence our fears by finding a firm, stern authority that will tell us what to do and control our more dangerous tendencies. A revealing statement comes from a young eleventh-grade student in Canada, who was asked to contribute to a symposium on discipline an article outlining his own beliefs on the subject. He wrote in part:

. . . we cannot have the "right attitude" towards learning, if we consider our tutors our "pals", and if we have too much opportunity for what the progressive educators call "self-expression". . . we all need greater severity and discipline in school. . . . We have too often participated in what is shrugged off as "mischief" or "playfulness." . . . Some of this unorthodox behavior may be natural for our age, but the greater part is attributable to the fact that our elders too often "spared the rod" in our younger days. . . . In secondary institutions of learning we cannot afford levities. Inhibitions are products of maturity and intelligence.[4]

Whence comes this aged, humorless priggishness? It stems in part from the student's fear of his own natural impulses. He senses the stirring within himself of embarrassing or even vicious tendencies and is afraid of them. He feels a need for control but doubts his own ability to exercise it. Hence, he seeks a strong external authority that will not permit him to indulge the more primitive side of his nature.

Authoritarianism and the Degeneration of Personality

According to the existentialists, man possesses a "dreadful freedom": he is able to choose and he must choose before he is ready. We never have all the facts we would like to help us make a decision, but we must nevertheless decide and act in the light of the incomplete data. Similarly, colonial territories must be given political freedom before they are ready for it. Even the most advanced nations cannot be considered fully ready to govern themselves, judging by the percentage of the electorate who vote in elections and the extent of the voters' accurate knowledge of economics, politics, sociology, and international affairs. We cannot wait until colonies are completely fit for self-government before we grant it, although, as the example of the Congo shows, this does not absolve us from the responsibility of *preparing* them for this freedom. Children must be given a measure of free choice and self-determination before they are fully ready for it. They are *never* fully ready, and we must be prepared to take chances with them, while at the same time preparing them as fully as possible for the responsibilities of such freedom.

The reason that such chances must be taken is that the alternatives of paternalism, colonialism, prolonged dependence, and authoritarian rule lead to degeneration of personality in both the rulers and the ruled. The degeneration is often more serious in the rulers. From my experience with men who have lived for many years as members of colonial ruling groups, I am forced to the conclusion that such a life engenders a personality marked by a boyishness and even a childishness. There seems to be something in paternalism that prevents the "paters" from growing up. Perhaps the scarcity of equals and the lack of variety among them fail to provide the necessary challenge for personality development. We cannot grow through the limited range of interaction we can have with people we consider our inferiors. In the traditional English Public School the masters, after a lifetime of living and ruling in their little kingdoms, have often been found disastrously ill-equipped to meet their contemporaries in the outside world. The Public Schoolmaster has been called "a man among boys and a boy among men." Authoritarianism in the classroom or the colony largely denies the ruler the maturing experience of meeting his fellow men on everyday terms of approximate equality, and is thereby constantly making him less and less fit to rule.

On the other side, the personality of the governed also fails to mature under authoritarian rule. Experience in colonial Africa shows clearly that Africans who have no share in formulating laws fail to develop a mature sense of social responsibility and have no feelings of regret, repentance, or wrongdoing when they contravene laws made by white men that apply only to black men.[5] People who are kept in a state of infantile dependence, in which all major decisions are taken for them, fail to develop the strength of personality that would enable them to exercise freedom if they were offered it. In the Soviet Union, prisoners released from prison settlements have often preferred to remain there after the expiration of their sentences, rather than face the unpredictabilities of freedom. In the armed services, many servicemen regard their lack of freedom and responsibility as such an ideal state that they willingly re-enlist after a tour of duty and are stricken at their misfortune when at last they must retire. The individual under authoritarian rule may be able to perform adequately within the matrix of his society, but he is lost when taken out of his normal environment or when faced with an unprecedented problem. Spartan children were brought up under a severe, authoritarian regime. They were treated with great physical harshness and were taught unquestioning obedience and strict subordination to the State. At home, the Spartan was apparently a model citizen: brave, loyal, self-controlled, respectful to his elders, devoted to the State. But away from Sparta he became lax and licentious, and a prey to the very vice of avarice against which so many precautions had been taken.[6] His training had not fitted him for the greater world: his values were parochial and did not apply outside the Polis.

Children brought up under authoritarian influences are liable to suffer from many of the defects of the authoritarian personality, to which can be attributed some of the world's most serious ills. The authoritarian personality is characterized by an ambivalence toward authority. Men like Martin Luther and Adolf Hitler shared this inner conflict. Hitler, for example, suffered from an authoritarian, domineering father who (himself a minor customs official) opposed and blocked his son's ambition to be an artist. There was constant strife between father and son. Adolf hated and rebelled against the authority of his father. But he was at the same time impressed by the Catholic Church. He sang in the choir at Lambach Convent and considered becoming a monk. He admired the Church not for its religious teachings but for its imperious authority.[7] Luther suffered from this same ambivalent attitude of rebellion against his father and submission to the Church, which he later transferred to the Pope and God, respectively. As a result of this inner conflict and chaos, the authoritarian personality is relatively less able to tolerate outer ambiguities and variations. He tends to favor homogeneity and conformity and to support dogmatic beliefs and absolute doctrines. He admires strength, power, and aggressiveness and is prepared to use cruelty and physical violence to impose the rigidities of his espoused orthodoxy on all. He tends to see things in clear blacks and whites, favors sharp dichotomies, and is impatient of subtle distinctions and multiple criteria. He distinguishes sharply between his own "in-group" and the "out-group:" the latter he fears and considers a threat. He is apt to think in terms of stereotypes and clichés. He is contemptuous of gentleness, considerateness, tenderness, sentiment, and affection. He shies away from doubt, uncertainty, ambiguity, and paradox, preferring to press such difficulties down below the conscious level, where they fester and increase his inner chaos and fear. Later this fear re-emerges as the basis of a search for scapegoats.[8]

The Authority of the Teacher

The necessity for avoiding the personality degeneration associated with authoritarianism does not absolve the teacher from the responsibilities of leadership. It only makes the task of leading more subtle and difficult. To abdicate leadership is no better—and may be worse—than to wield authoritarian control. W.R. Niblett wrote,

Anyone who has been concerned with children soon discovers two situations in which any of them may go to pieces. One is a feeble environment which provides no firm response to anything that he may do so that he finally becomes lost in his own waywardness with no signposts to guide him into profitable activity. The other is an environment which responds firmly but mechanically; there is no resilience, no recognition of the individual in his unique situation.[9]

If the teacher provides too much guidance and leadership, if he tells the pupil everything he needs to know, if he exercises an indisputable and weighty authority, the pupil is liable to find himself on a path with the sun in his eyes, blinding him and preventing him from picking out the route for himself. On the other hand, if the teacher gives no guidance or leadership, if he tells the child nothing, and makes him find his own way unaided, the child finds himself on the same path, this time in total darkness, without even the minimal light necessary to see his way.

How can the teacher decide what form and degree of authority he should exercise in the best interests of his pupils? There is no easy answer, and the force of particular circumstances can make any rule inadequate. However, some generalizations can be made if it is remembered that they must be translated into the terms of the specific conditions prevailing. In the first place, there is a continuing relationship between power and humility. Whenever we find ourselves possessed of power we need to be on our guard against the concomitant moral dangers. In order to avoid these, the spirit of humility should increase in us alongside our power. As we become more powerful we do not rise above the law but ought to be more scrupulous in obedience to it. If we have power over a child it is incumbent on us to understand and respect the laws of the child's nature and its growth. We must, in a word, have reverence for the child. Bertrand Russell has suggested that

> the man who has reverence will not think it his duty to "mould" the young. He feels in all that lives, but especially in human beings, and most of all in children, something sacred, indefinable, unlimited, something individual and strangely precious, the growing principle of life, an embodied fragment of the dumb striving of the world. In the presence of a child he feels an unaccountable humility.[10]

It is this type of humility on the part of the teacher that was manifested in the story of the old German schoolmaster who courteously doffed his hat to his class each morning. When asked why he did so he explained that, although he did not know which one, he was nevertheless certain that a greater one than himself was present in the class.

It must be recognized, of course, that the modern school has undergone a considerable transformation that corresponds to the transformation in political and industrial life that has occurred in the last century. This might be termed the substitution for coercive authority of manipulative authority. Coercive authority used physical force: manipulative authority uses psychological persuasion. The change has been a response to the changing organizational needs of industrial society. Manipulative authority is more gentle, more subtle, and usually more pleasant: but it is important to realize that it does not necessarily imply any greater respect for the person who is manipulated. And gentle manipulation may create greater problems for some children than physical coercion. A.S. Neill, who has maintained that "When there is a boss, there is no real freedom," has claimed that "This applies even more to the benevolent boss than to the disciplinarian. The child of spirit can rebel against the hard boss, but the soft boss merely makes the child impotently soft and unsure of his real feelings." [11]

Anyone who feels that students in American public schools are emancipated from the hold of manipulative authority should familiarize himself with Edgar Friedenberg's searing indictment of the American public high school.[12] Friedenberg has documented in horrifying detail the ways in which high school students are denied the opportunities for growing up into mature, decision-making people and are kept in a state of infantile irresponsibility for the sake of administrative smoothness. He concluded that

High-school administrators do not . . . think of themselves as practitioners of a specialized instructional craft, who derive their authority from its requirements. They are specialists in keeping an essentially political enterprise from being strangled by conflicting community attitudes and pressures. They are problem-oriented, and the feelings and needs for growth of their captive and unenfranchised clientele are the least of their problems; for the status of the "teen-ager" in the community is so low that even if he rebels, the school is not blamed for the conditions against which he is rebelling. He is simply a truant or a juvenile delinquent; at worst the school has "failed to reach him." . . . Many students like high school; others loathe and fear it. But even the latter do not object to it on principle; the school effectively obstructs their learning of the principles on which objection might be based; though these are among the principles that, we boast, distinguish us from totalitarian societies.[13]

The proper authority to which the pupil must submit is not the arbitrary authority of the teacher but the authority of a third factor, above both teacher and pupil. This is found in the necessities of the situation, and the teacher must himself submit to it. Only if the teacher shows that he is not seeking his own selfish ends, or the accretion of his own power, but is acting selflessly in the disinterested pursuit of common ends, will the pupil in his turn willingly submit himself to the discipline necessary for the attainment of those ends. Rather than demand obedience, the good teacher inspires co-operation: rather than exert his power over his pupils, he creates new power with their help. It is the teacher's task to bring his students to a recognition of the authority of the learning situation, and the exercise of authoritarian power hinders this process by reducing the sensitivity of the child to the necessities of voluntary submission. Until the pupil himself recognizes the necessity for authority the process of self-education cannot begin.

II   RESTRAINT AND PUNISHMENT

The Meanings of Discipline

There are at least two conflicting aims of education: one, that man should be educated to become what he is; the other, that he should be educated to become what he is not. The first emphasizes the valuable potentialities of each individual from birth and sees the function of

education as providing an environment that will draw out those potentialities and help the individual reach the greatest heights of which he is
capable. The second aim attempts to formulate an ideal character to
which education should attempt to mold each individual. The first aim
emphasizes freedom: the second emphasizes discipline. Unfortunately,
this distinction has often developed into an "either-or" dichotomy that
is unnecessary and unproductive. The matter is complicated by the fact
that freedom and discipline can each be both a means and an end, and
by the fact that the words "freedom" and "discipline" are liable to a
variety of connotations. Moreover, it is not always clear which meaning
is intended when one of the words is used.

It will be helpful, therefore, to attempt to explore some of the
possible meanings of the term "discipline." The word comes from the
same root as the word "disciple," meaning a follower, pupil, or learner,
derived from the Latin *discere* (to learn). This meaning has been
largely lost in the military sense of the word, but at least partly retained
in the pedagogical sense. Even in education, however, the word has
developed a variety of distinctions and nuances of meaning. These lead
us often to talk at cross-purposes by using the word in a different sense
from that intended by the other members of the discussion, without
being aware of our differences. At least four of these distinctive senses
can be epitomized here in the following sentences:

1. Mr. Birchenough maintains good discipline.
2. Children who disobey will be disciplined.
3. What discipline is used in this school?
4. The study of Latin constitutes the best discipline.

In the first sentence the sense usually implied is that of control; in the
second sentence the word is usually synonymous with punishment; in
the third it is associated with some form of regulation or organization;
and in the fourth some concept of mental training is indicated. It is well
to keep in mind which sense is intended in discussing discipline. Nevertheless, all of these four meanings share something in common: they all
imply a degree of restraint on the spontaneous or natural impulses and
actions of the child.

The Need for Restraint

A more profitable line of educational enquiry than continuing the
dispute between freedom and discipline is to ask what degree and form
of discipline will best prepare the child for specific kinds of freedom.
There are few, if any, parents and educators who would advocate complete absence of discipline, in the sense of restraint, in the upbringing of

the child. Even A.S. Neill, who has shocked conventional opinion by the degree of freedom allowed the pupils in his school, Summerhill, permits them freedom to do as they wish only as long as they do not trespass on the freedom of others. Where they begin to endanger or annoy or hurt anyone else, restraint is exercised.[14]

We have been introduced, perhaps *ad nauseam*, to examples of the dangers that follow when parents are unwilling or afraid to exercise restraint and authority on their children. North American parents are notoriously uneasy about authority. Perhaps it is because the United States came into existence by defying legal authority. Perhaps it is because the rapid assimilation of the children of immigrants often left the parents in a position of cultural inferiority, leading to their rejection by the children as figures of respect, emulation, and authority. It is remarkable that, although juvenile delinquency is often associated with poor living conditions, America, with a high material standard of living, has one of the highest rates of juvenile delinquency in the Western world, while Italy, with a comparatively low standard of living, has one of the lowest rates. It is also remarkable that Italian immigrants to the United States find themselves members of a national group with a notorious reputation (deserved or not) as the seedbed of criminal elements. Italy is characterized by a predominantly patriarchal social pattern, with the father typically ruling his family with a sometimes kindly, but usually firm, hand.

The parent or teacher owes to the child in his care a responsibility that can be discharged only by restraining him. This discipline must not be exercised for its own sake: this is the fault of the disciplinarian, who achieves control, as the authoritarian wields authority, for the sake of order itself, or to enjoy the feel of power. Discipline must be exercised in the first place for the physical safety and survival of the child. Freedom is not granted to the child by the teacher's abdication. The child is still restrained—and perhaps imperiled—by the environment, by his own ignorance, and by some of his natural impulses.

It is necessary, in judging what is appropriate restraint, to distinguish between wishes and needs in the child. For example, the young child *wishes* to eat. He is hungry and probably *needs* to eat. There is little to be lost by feeding him. In another example, the child *wishes* to stay up late. He probably *needs* to go to bed. If we judge that the need must take precedence over the wish in this case, then discipline is involved. A.S. Neill reports that bedtime is one of the principal problems at Summerhill. Adults should respect genuine needs and permit the child to satisfy them unless their satisfaction would be dangerous, in which case substitutions should be worked out and suggested to the child. Wishes may be gratified unless they lead to danger or to a state of serious subsequent remorse too strong for the child to bear. Adults must take responsibility for restraining children from committing acts that will bear consequences with which the children will be unable to cope. It is less harmful to restrict a child's act than permit that act if it would later bring intolerable guilt feelings. For example, a boy may feel an impulse to hurt his little sister. If allowed to do so, the consequent feelings of remorse might be seriously destructive of his relationship with her and his parents.

Children are not naturally evil, as the medieval church taught, but they possess spontaneous impulses that sometimes endanger themselves and others. Ethel M. Rogers, who was imprisoned by the Japanese with hundreds of other women and children in Changi Prison, Singapore, from 1942 to 1945, has told in her account of her experiences how the Japanese forbade the women to discipline or restrain the children in any way. As a result, the children developed into young savages. Their games were solely concerned with murder, hangings, shootings, and stacking bodies. The author wrote, "Once, I came across a child hanging by a rope around his neck. Fortunately, we were able to cut him down before he died. His playmates pummeled us with their fists. One eight-year-old shouted, 'You've spoiled it all. We were just waiting to see the death kick.' " [15] A similar tale of the barbarism of young children left to their own devices was horrifyingly told by William Golding in *Lord of the Flies*.[16]

Order, Direction, and Restraint

Restraint and limitation are further necessary for the achievement of order and direction in life. What is limited is not necessarily hampered by those limitations: its limits can be the means of its achieving a certain freedom. The river is limited and confined by its banks but these same banks permit it to move onward freely to the sea. Without its banks the river would collapse into a swamp: only through limitation can it reach its goal. Man, similarly, needs limitations and discipline before he can find direction. Fullest expression of his degree of freedom is dependent on an ordering and limiting discipline. Lack of such discipline results in a wandering aimlessness, associated with ignorance, sickness of mind or body, indolence, or self-indulgence. "Discipline," said Montessori, "is . . . a path." In following this path the child "savours the supreme delights of that spiritual *order* which is attained indirectly through conquests directed towards determinate ends." [17] Discipline, being a path, is not an end in itself: the end is the kind of productive self-fulfillment that is possible only through discipline. This self-fulfillment is achieved partly through an inner ordering of the personality, making it harmonious with the order of the universe.

Studies of the development of young children have shown us that firm limits and recognizable boundary marks are necessary for the child to give it the kind of emotional security it requires before setting out to explore the world. Man needs order to be able to operate in freedom, and if order is lacking he will reject that freedom. The danger of freedom without order is that it will develop into chaos and that man will then place himself under a tyrant in the hope that order will be restored. In Spain, for example, the chaos and horror of the Civil War led the majority of the population to acquiesce to the dictatorship of Franco, who took away much of their political freedom but offered them order. It was the great achievement of John Locke, in *Two Treatises of Civil Government,* to show men that the path to the greatest possible freedom lies through law, authority, and order.[18] The importance of the family lies precisely in this: that the warmth, security, and order of family life are the foundation of a free personality. Later it is the teacher who must assume the difficult task of determining exactly where the balance should lie between the need for security, with the danger of an inflexible overprotection, and the need for growth, with the danger of anxiety. No one can tell in advance what is the appropriate formula for any child: hence, the importance of finding mature teachers who can make wise decisions on the spot.

Ideal Norms of Discipline

The necessity for external discipline does not mean that all types of restraint are to be recommended. Especially in group situations, the teacher finds himself often tempted to impose arbitrary control on a child for reasons other than that of the child's welfare. To obtain peace and quiet, to give vent to one's own feelings of irritation, to further the welfare of the majority, may all be understandable and even defensible motives for forcibly restraining an individual. But it is important not to fall into the error of believing, under such circumstances, that one is exercising restraint *for the good of the child.* This will be effected, as will be suggested later, only when external discipline begets self-discipline.

Piaget has written:

Society is the sum of social relations, and among these relations we can distinguish two extreme types: relations of constraint, whose characteristic is to impose upon the individual from outside a system of rules with obligatory content, and relations of cooperation, whose characteristic is to create within people's minds the consciousness of ideal norms at the back of all rules.[19]

It is only through these "relations of cooperation" that productive external discipline can be developed. The child must be brought to a realization of the wisdom of the rules he obeys and have a part, appropriate to his maturity, in framing them. As the one who imposes the discipline, the adult should take care to avoid coercion through personal authority. He should instead represent the impersonal authority of one who has himself submitted to the discipline he wishes the child to acknowledge. This means the avoidance of all petty, meaningless, unrealistic rules and restraints. The educator should appear to the child not as an unpredictable master whose tyrannous whims constitute a fearful suffocation for the timid and an irresistible challenge to the spirited, but rather as an intermediary through whom can be gained a knowledge of the "ideal norms," the ineluctable realities, the inexorable truths and laws, respect for which is the beginning of freedom.

Punishment

What is the proper place of punishment in such a framework? Ideally, it should be wholly dispensed with; in almost all situations reliance on it could be reduced without difficulty; but it is realistic to expect it to be a major disciplinary tool for some time to come. As such, it should be carefully examined so that its true nature can be understood and it can be used with a minimum of harm.

Since adults who have responsibility for children often find themselves involved in punishing, it is well to have in mind some general principles about the use of punishment. In the first place, the adult owes it to the child to be genuine and honest with him. The suppression of one's natural feelings for the sake of avoiding punishment can do no good to the adult, or to the child, or the relationship between them. Hypocrisy is betrayal. The respect due to the child demands that the adult relate to him sincerely, even if this involves acting toward him with irritation or ill-temper. "The flashing interchange of anger between parent and child is part of the responsible relationship, necessary to growth," wrote D.H. Lawrence. "The only rule is, do what you really, impulsively, wish to do. But always act on your own responsibility sincerely. And have the courage of your own strong emotions. They enrichen the child's soul." [20]

Secondly, it would clearly be a wise principle to punish only when the infliction of punishment can be judged to carry good consequences on the whole—that is, to the whole community, including the wrongdoer. In order for this to occur, the good flowing from the punishment must be judged to be greater than the suffering experienced by the one punished. Usually we become involved in punishment when we set up a rule that someone then transgresses. We should be careful, therefore, about setting up rules, because once they are established we must try to keep them. If a punishment seems terribly costly in terms of the suffering to the one punished, we should examine the rules to see whether they are satisfactory, necessary, and well-conceived and consider whether their continuation is worth the cost. There is a danger of forgetting that rules are set up for the benefit of the individuals to whom they apply. Sometimes the rules, once established, take on an apparent value of their own and must be upheld at *any* cost. But there may well be a cost so great that it is no longer worth upholding the rules.

The good that may flow from punishment can be seen in terms of reforming the individual advantageously, deterring him from repeating the offense, or deterring others from commiting this or similar offenses. In fact, punishment rarely reforms a wrongdoer, that is, changes his character so that he recognizes what he did as wrong, feels remorse for having done it, and resolves not to do it again. More commonly, punishment leads to a loss of self-respect, feelings of resentment, and a resolve to be more careful about detection next time. It is unlikely that any beneficial results can follow punishment—especially corporal punishment [21]—unless there is a relationship of genuine warmth and affection between the adult and the child. While this may often exist in the family, it is doubtful whether the necessary loving concern often accompanies classroom punishment. A wise nursery school teacher said, speaking of a problem-child: "I do not love him enough to spank him." [22] It is a mistake to assume that impersonal punishment is fairest and best. Unless the student who is punished is known, studied, and cared for, he will reject the intent of the punishment and with it, in most cases, the teachings of the one who punishes.

Moreover, punishment is dangerous because it encourages the student to look outside himself for judgments and evaluations of his actions. Punishment helps the student to make the conflict an external one between himself and the teacher and, hence, to avoid the necessity of internalizing it. And only when the conflict is taken within can it be resolved in terms of genuine reform of personality. All else is merely an expedient lying-low for the time being, or a craven submission to superior force. This is why we must question the traditional pedagogical dogma that punishment should always be consistent. If punishment is always the same for the same offense the student comes to expect it and in a sense rely on it. He rests on this dependable external restraint and has no incentive to internalize the struggle for improved behavior. If we are less consistent in punishing, the student may feel more need to control himself internally. Punishment should be designed to impel the child to raise questions about his own conduct, to take the true measure of his act, and ultimately to stand in self-judgment.

Usually, then, the justification of punishment must rest on its deterrent effect—to the wrongdoer or others. Unfortunately, it is precisely the consistency questioned above that is essential to make deterrence credible. To be effective, the threat of punishment should be supported by being seen to apply under normal circumstances of rule breaking. If a rule can be broken without punishment following regularly, the threat of punishment loses its power to deter. We may decide not to apply the punishment under a particular, extenuating set of circumstances. But unless these circumstances are obviously exceptional we may destroy the general deterrent effect.

Moreover, there are many cases where deterrence will not work. The person who deliberately breaks a rule on grounds of conscience may not be deterred by even extremely severe punishment, and such punishment can rarely be defended on the grounds of the advantages of inducing uniformity. The failure of excessive punishment to deter conscientious objectors to military service in France and Switzerland is an example of the inefficacy of deterrence in the face of deep conviction. Similarly, with the civil-disobedience movements in India, Denmark, the United States, and elsewhere, it is clear that no punishment within the law really deters such people. Their pleas must be examined carefully and sympathetically, and punishment is almost impossible to justify.

When we punish an individual *pour décourager les autres*—as a deterrent to others—we must be careful that we treat the individual as an end in himself and not as a means to other people's welfare. His welfare should not be placed above that of the others, but he should still be valued as of ultimate worth. A special case of this arises when we are faced with the problem of whether it is justifiable to punish someone who has committed no offense. For example, suppose a member of a class has stolen, and this is a punishable offense. If the thief will not admit his guilt, is the teacher justified in punishing the whole class? It depends on whether he thinks the maintenance of the rule against stealing and of general discipline is more important than the principle that the innocent should not be punished. The practice of punishing the whole group cannot be morally defended under school conditions, for no rule can be so important as to justify such inhuman methods. It is equivalent to a totalitarian government using the relatives of a missing criminal and punishing them for his offense. We threaten others in an attempt to bring pressure to bear on the individual to surrender. But this is using them as means rather than as ends.

The greatest indictment of external punishment is that it has little if any carrying power. If we control behavior through punishing it may well be that the behavior will change to an undesirable previous level once the external restraints are removed. If learning is stimulated only by punishment or the threat of punishment, we should not be surprised if that learning ceases when the threat is removed—at graduation. The only educated man is he who conceives his own education as a lifetask, based on a rigorous process of self-discipline. But punishment encourages man to escape this self-discipline and hence makes his self-education more difficult to attain.

III   SELF-DISCIPLINE

Restraint and Self-discipline

As previously stated, external restraint has an educative effect on the child only when it begets self-discipline. This happens much more rarely than we are apt to believe. There is a very natural tendency to think that when we restrain a child we are doing so for the child's sake alone. We do not usually like to think that we are placing our own comfort before the child's well-being. But energetic, ebullient, obstreperous children are hard to tolerate, so we achieve a combination of a quiet life and an easy conscience by simultaneously restraining them and telling ourselves that the restraint is beneficial to them.

It is not difficult to train children, as we train dogs or soldiers, by a process of conditioning, so that they will adopt apparently disciplined habits. The danger is that we come to accept these habits as evidence of an inner discipline. We are usually disabused of this illusion when a crisis shows that the conditioning is effective only under ideal circumstances and cannot withstand the strain of the unusual. In 1924, Leningrad, where Pavlov's laboratories were situated, was seriously flooded. The water entered the dogs' feeding room. When assistants arrived to rescue the dogs the cells where the dogs were housed were already two-thirds full of water. As the doors of the cells extended only one-third of the way up the cell the assistants had to submerge each dog's head under water in order to extricate it. All the dogs were rescued but it was subsequently found that several of them had lost their conditioned reflexes as if they had never been formed. Restoration of the reflexes had to start again from the beginning.[23] The discipline of the dogs, established by rigorous conditioning, broke down completely in the face of crisis. The military discipline of the parade-ground is equally ineffective in helping the soldier meet the unpredictable. Many American soldiers in Korean prison camps disintegrated morally after capture because they had never achieved self-discipline.[24] They lacked understanding of their own country and its ideals, of the nature of democracy, and above all of themselves. Similarly, German soldiers who had experienced the strict military discipline of the *Wehrmacht* broke down spiritually in prison camps in Russia after the Second World War. Helmut Gollwitzer, who was one of them, has attested that they refused to share food with sick comrades, they denounced to the Russians weak members unwilling to work, they spied on each other, and so on.[25]

Pavlovian or military discipline is not an effective way of helping children to achieve self-discipline, for it will fail them when they need it most. The traditional view of pedagogy maintains that the child achieves self-discipline by adapting himself to the authority of the teacher. In fact, however, the child achieves self-discipline by overcoming himself. Maria Montessori wrote,

> We do not consider an individual disciplined, only when he has been rendered as artificially silent as a mute and as immovable as a paralytic. He is an individual *annihilated*, not *disciplined*. We call an individual disciplined when he is master of himself, and can, therefore, regulate his own conduct when it shall be necessary to follow some rule of life.[26]

The criterion for judging the efficacy of discipline should not be how the child behaves *now*, when the teacher is nearby to help and remind him, but what *future* behavior the discipline encourages, what happens when the teacher's restraining hand is removed, what permanent pattern of self-control the child is helped to develop.

If self-discipline is effectively inculcated, it should help the child toward a free recognition of genuine authority. "When external authority is rejected," wrote Dewey, "it does not follow that all authority should be rejected, but rather that there is need to search for a more effective source of authority." [27] The more often external restraint and punishment are used to control the individual the less likely he is to develop the necessary sensitivity to and recognition of genuine authority. The sort of authority recognized by the self-disciplined person includes the authority of one's own considered experiences, the authority imposed by the nature of the material in art, the authority necessary for the preservation of community life, and the authority of one's own nature.[28] Appropriate respect for such authority is the disciplined person's alternative to both enervated apathy and destructive rebellion.

Self-mastery for Excellence

The necessity for self-mastery is an ancient part of man's knowledge. The Buddhist *Dhammapada* puts it thus: "One's own self conquered is better than all other people." [29] And in the *Tao-Te King* of Loa Tze it says:

> He who knows others is wise;
> He who knows himself is enlightened.
> He who conquers others is strong;
> He who conquers himself is mighty.[30]

While mastery of oneself is difficult, it is a mistake to think that it goes against the grain of man's nature. John Macmurray has maintained that there is in all human nature a craving for discipline that "is simply the longing to fulfill one's own nature. . . . Give this instinctive craving a chance, and human nature, especially when it is fresh and unspoiled, will respond to the call of discipline with a rush of spontaneous happiness." [31] Educators miss their greatest opportunity when they fail to show children how their voluntary submission to appropriate discipline will lead them to self-mastery, self-fulfillment, and joy. This can be achieved at any level. Even the youngest child can soon be made aware of the necessity for self-control, for giving up some petty desires, for resisting the temptation to give way to easy whim, in order to establish satisfactory personal relations with others. This checking of impulse is a demonstration of the child's capacity for undertaking the responsibilities of self-discipline.

Self-discipline is sometimes criticized because it is "unnatural," and we must follow nature. But this criticism is seriously misleading. There is a sense in which we cannot avoid following nature: we cannot do what nature does not permit. There is no reason why we should identify "nature" with our physical or emotional urges rather than with our rational self-restraints. Our reason is also part of our nature. To discipline oneself according to rational considerations is no more unnatural than to indulge oneself according to animal impulses.

Self-mastery begins with aspiration: we wish to achieve something in the sphere of human relations, art, knowledge, skill, or conduct. We look around us and see standards superior to our own. Thus arise in us the feelings of modesty for our own achievements and respect for those of others. Helped by man's love of overcoming difficulties, of successfully meeting challenges, we become willing to submit ourselves to the discipline that we now see is essential for the satisfaction of our aspiration.

The aim of self-mastery, then, is personal excellence. There is in all of us a continuing tension, the product of the gap between our aspirations and our capacity to achieve them. If the tension becomes too low, we stagnate: many people prepare all too effectively for death (the end of all tension) by ceasing to strive and, hence, by "dying" before their time. If the tension becomes too great, mental breakdown results. The task of education is to encourage young people to keep their sights high and to show them the path to the self-mastery that will bring their performance nearer to their professions. Teachers must avoid the false charity that shields young people from the dazzling glare of the highest standards. This is especially true in the case of the talented young who, too often, wrote Jacques Barzun, "remain innocently conceited and hurtfully ignorant of both the range of common achievement and the quality of genius." Their aims have been "measured by sheltered ambitions," he maintained.[32] The hardship necessary to achieve competence should never be disguised, but its worthiness should be extolled. An admirer told a great pianist on hearing him play, "I'd give anything to be able to play like that." The pianist replied, "Would you give five hours a day, six days a week, every week of the year, every year of your life?" Ease is the result of forgotten toil.

This is why the Beatnik writers and artists, despite all their love of freedom, their adventurousness, their originality, their sincerity, remain a sociological rather than a literary or artistic phenomenon. Their self-indulgence has undone them and renders their protest lacking in any serious creative import. Therefore, society tolerates them amusedly: they are the "licensed jesters of the Admass society." [33] They have failed to adopt the self-discipline necessary to achieve the freedom they seek.

Self-discipline as a Release from the Self

There is an unfortunate likelihood that the quest for self-discipline will involve us in one of the most prevalent diseases of the age—that turning in on the self that separates us disastrously from our fellow men. The constant and meticulous concern with his own moral improvement that characterizes the Puritan is a manifestation of the most pernicious type of self-centeredness. Self-discipline can lead to a release from these egocentric bonds if—and only if—it is not sought as an end in itself.

Self-discipline can, for example, serve as a means for making us of more use and less harm to our fellows by reducing our enslavement to self-indulgences and our subordination to compulsions. William Golding has brilliantly analyzed, in *Free Fall*, the way in which the individual who lacks self-discipline and who has lost his freedom to a sexual compulsion is forced to use others cruelly and selfishly.

They said the damned in hell were forced to torture the innocent live people with disease. But I know now that life is perhaps more terrible than that innocent medieval conception. We are forced here and now to torture each other. We can watch ourselves becoming automata; feel only terror as our alienated arms lift the instruments of their passion towards those we love. Those who lose their freedom can watch themselves forced helplessly to do this in daylight until who is torturing who? The obsession drove me at her.[34]

Only by mastering ourselves so that we are emancipated from driving compulsions can we avoid the evil of using others to feed our obsessive needs.

Self-denial for its own sake is a perversion. Buddhism, Christianity, Zoroastrianism, and other major religions agree that self-denial as an end in itself is worthless. But it is wise to deny ourselves those things that constitute impediments to worthy ends. "If any man would come after me," said Jesus, "let him deny himself, and take up his cross daily, and follow me." (Luke IX:23). To take up one's cross means to achieve a level of self-discipline in life that will enable one to concentrate his main energies on the pursuit of the highest values. There is no merit whatsoever in practicing self-denial, in suppressing desire, in undertaking drudgery, if it is unrelated to the conquest of a worthy goal. Fortunately, children are usually too positive in their attitude toward life to be persuaded to deny any aspect of it without good cause. It is useless to preach the virtues of self-discipline *per se*. But children can be shown that self-discipline is worth cultivating because it makes us ready, stripped for action, prepared for opportunity and for service.

IV   INTELLECTUAL DISCIPLINE

Formal Discipline and Transfer

In the Middle Ages the study of Latin was a vocational pursuit, since Latin was the language of the Church (which controlled education), as well as the language of international scholarship. By the seventeenth and eighteenth centuries, when the Church had lost its dominance and nationalism had raised the prestige of vernacular languages, Latin still remained the basis of the curriculum because of scholastic inertia and the social *cachet* afforded by the recital of Latin phrases. To make it academically respectable, however, it was necessary to find a new educational *raison d'être*. This was found in the doctrine of formal discipline: the idea that certain subjects, by virtue of their intellectual rigor and difficulty, were ideal educational instruments for exercising the "faculties" of the mind. The best subjects for this purpose were supposed to be the classics and, later, mathematics. This "disciplining" of the mind by strenuous effort was considered more important than the actual content of study, an attitude caricatured by the phrase, "It doesn't matter what you teach a boy as long as he hates it."

A more serious paradigm of this point of view was represented by the educational philosophy of the French writer, Paul Valéry. He tried to kindle in the young, as Laszlo Borbas has recounted, a spark of that rigorous mental effort—"the adorable rigor"—that was at the heart of his pedagogy, his writing, his way of life. He became a peer among "the heroes and martyrs of the resistance to the facile." He adopted the habit of a rigorous examination of all his thoughts, fundamental or random. He said he could never attach any importance to what his mind produced easily, believing that only effort had the power to transform a man into a better edition of himself. This worship of strenuous discipline led Valéry to admire that form of "creative constraint" that French classicism had brought to its culmination, the literary achievement that produced "the astonishing fruits of an extraordinary constraint." [35]

An important assumption underlying this doctrine was that the mental discipline, habits, skills, and power gained in the study of one subject "transferred" automatically to other subjects or fields. The best possible training for a British colonial administrator was considered to be a course in "Greats" (that is, classics) at Oxford, because the unpredictable and varied problems of administration in remote colonial areas could best be tackled by a mind that had gained clarity and power through classical studies. In the twentieth century this doctrine received some serious blows at the hands of empirical investigators. E.L. Thorndike and a large number of others set up experiments to demonstrate the extent of transfer of knowledge or skill from one situation to another. [36] The results destroyed the idea of automatic and complete transfer, and some researchers denied that *any* transfer takes place. "We learn what we learn." The carefully conducted Classical Investigation, whose results appeared shortly after the First World War, compelled supporters of classical studies to abandon or at least seriously modify the disciplinary justification for their subject. [37] More recent investigations, however, have suggested that the rejection of the idea of transfer in many cases went too far; that transfer not only *can* take place under appropriate learning conditions but is even the basis of the way in which we learn how to learn. Bruner has said,

. . . earlier learning renders later performance more efficient . . . through . . . nonspecific transfer or, more accurately, the transfer of principles and attitudes. In essence, it consists of learning initially not a skill but a general idea, which can then be used as a basis for recognizing subsequent problems as special cases of the idea originally mastered. This type of transfer is at the heart of the educational process—the continual broadening and deepening of knowledge in terms of basic and general ideas. [38]

Discipline of the Traditional Subjects

In the secondary schools of Europe and North America, the assumption of the existence of transfer has never been abandoned, although it is rarely made explicit. Despite the twentieth-century inrush of vocational, practical, and aesthetic studies, the high school remains predominantly centered on the traditional academic "disciplines" (that is, history, geography, mother-tongue, foreign languages, mathematics, and science). This predominance is due partly to inertia and to the fact that the majority of high school students are considered expendable in the cause of preparing the minority to enter university; but it is also partly the result of the assumption that the study of these traditional subjects will result in a transfer of intellectual power to other situations that the young person will encounter after leaving school. This assumption has been made explicit and stoutly defended by the supporters of "Basic Education," whose whole argument rests on the idea that "The primary job of the school is the efficient transmission and continual reappraisal of what we call tradition. Tradition is the mechanism by which all past men teach all future men." [39] The traditional basic subjects, it is claimed, possess *generative* power—that is, they are not self-terminating but lead on to something else, and their mastery makes it easier to learn this something else. These master subjects have a basic disciplinary value in themselves because man is a rational animal, and it is through the discipline of reason that he attains freedom.[40]

A similar viewpoint has been expressed by G.H. Bantock, who has suggested that freedom can come only through a rightful submission to due authority. The alternative is an egocentric assertion of self that is ultimately defeating. The due authority that Bantock envisages is a "third ground" that transcends the "otherwise fortuitous relationship of master and pupil." [41] This third ground should be a common object, the discipline imposed by the subject of study. Bantock conceives traditional subjects as having an objective reality of their own, irrespective of subjective human feelings or social needs. Learning requires on the part of the learner a respect for the unknown, a reverence before the unattained, and inevitably therefore a transcendence of the self. Acceptance of the authority and discipline of the unknown is an essential prerequisite of learning.[42]

Discipline of a Common Cultural Tradition

Individual growth is dependent on a rootedness in a cultural tradition. To grow healthily we vitally need a connection with a group, a community, a history. Freedom from these connections is a destructive freedom, for it threatens our development. The tree that is cut free from its roots dies. Similarly, some types of human freedom are pernicious because they sever us from sources that feed our healthy growth. It is possible to pursue individual development as an aim of education only within the discipline of a common culture. For example, one of the directions in which the individual's education can help him develop is that of language. But in no country do we teach the child "language": in England he is taught English; in France, French; in Spain, Spanish. His culture, in other words, determines the *form* of his individual development. Moreover, the particular form adopted will permanently shape his thinking. Certain concepts cannot be expressed in certain languages: for instance, some North American languages have an entirely different time-concept from that inherent in Indo-European languages. Similarly, the child's initial explorations into the fields of history, religion, social conduct, and so on, will be made not in general terms but in terms of a particular cultural interpretation. There is probably no way in which this can be avoided. It may be necessary for the individual to submit to the discipline of one religion, such as Christianity or Islam, before he can understand the meaning of "religion" as a force and aspiration in man's life.

Relevance, Structure, and Interest

In the context of the present educational scene in North America, there is need for a revival and reinterpretation of some of these basic requirements of intellectual discipline. In the course of such reinterpretation, however, it will be wise to study past pitfalls, recent research on learning, and the exigencies of contemporary circumstances. Discipline, to be effective, must be relevant and realistic. Too often in the past, especially in Europe, elementary education has failed to capture the loyalty and kindle the creativity of the working classes because its discipline has been imposed from above and has been largely unrelated to the genuine needs and aspirations of these groups. In such cases, it has often, despite some good intentions, resulted in negative opposition or apathy.

Furthermore, the traditional view of intellectual discipline as submission to the memorization of a mountain of data must be abandoned and replaced by a view that includes consideration of our knowledge of the learning process. We know that memorized material that lacks relevance, significance, and structure for the learner is rapidly forgotten. The work of Bruner has been important in demonstrating that the structure of a field of learning is vitally important in grasping and retaining knowledge.[43] We must throw off the tyranny of the isolated fact that still dominates our education. The student can best approach intellectual freedom through the discipline of thinking in terms of general or fundamental principles, for this approach to learning makes easier the transfer from an earlier learning situation to a later one; it makes knowledge more usable in different situations—hence, creating interest in the subject—and it minimizes the rate of memory loss.

There is no doubt that the teacher must introduce the child, as Bantock and others maintain, to the indubitable discipline of the fact, of the unknown, of intractable material. Without this discipline the child will never attain the reverence for truth that is the necessary stimulus for further enquiry. But what many of these traditional thinkers ignore is the concomitant demand that in the process of education the child must be brought to, and kept at, the level of interest and concern necessary to impel him to undertake the acquisition of knowledge. Before he can reach this level he must be shown, in most cases, that the knowledge, the facts, the material, are relevant to his life and important in terms of his own purposes. Herein lies the significance of pedagogy.

Imagination and Intuition

There is no ineluctable reason why the development of intellectual discipline should result in a loss of imaginative freedom, but this is often in fact the consequence. Our schools and universities too often fail to nourish the imaginative and intuitive powers of their students through an unduly narrow and short-sighted view of intellectual discipline. The inculcation, memorization, and regurgitation of facts, no matter how efficiently conducted, can never kindle fires in students, and even as a form of discipline such techniques are ultimately self-defeating. Unless the students learn to use the facts, to play with them in their imaginations, to relate them to previous knowledge, to speculate on their untested possibilities, the facts will fail to have a truly educative influence; they will remain dead and without personal significance.

If we wish to help our students become disciplined thinkers we would do well to study more closely exactly how the disciplined thinker works. We would find that the fact is only one of his many tools. He also uses the speculative hypothesis, the imaginative guess, the intuitive hunch. We are used to the idea of acting on incomplete data in everyday life but we forget or are ignorant of the extent to which the scholar, the scientist, and the researcher must also guess in this way. Do we impede the development of intuitive thinking in school by an unnecessarily discouraging attitude toward guessing? Students should be encouraged to guess in the interest of learning eventually how to make intelligent conjectures. Our students should be encouraged to make use of the degree of intellectual freedom that they are capable of exercising. Emphasis solely on analysis and data can discourage the kind of freedom that the potentially creative mind can reach. If done early enough and often enough, discouragement of guessing can kill the imaginative and intuitive potentialities of the original mind.

There is danger, too, in certain educational techniques and types of teachers. Objective examinations and emphasis on grades can make students intellectually timid by throwing attention on correct answers and verifiable data and by making the use of intuition and imagination too risky in terms of academic success. The teacher who is insecure can hinder the imaginative development of his students by consistently refusing to leave anything to chance, by having everything cut and dried, by never leaving himself vulnerable in working through an unprepared problem before his students.

Discipline, the Student, and the "Ritual Fallacy"

When we use the word "discipline" in the sense of a field of learning we must remember that this is a derivative sense. The original sense was connected with the instruction of disciples or scholars. In the derivative sense, it is too often forgotten that the field of learning or body of knowledge is meaningless without a disciple or pupil. All the academic disciplines of the world would be useless if a nuclear war or some other cataclysm was to destroy mankind, leaving intact his libraries, theses, and works of scholarship. The activity of pursuing knowledge is pointless in itself and for its own sake: it is only man's profit from the activity that gives it meaning.

Man must always be the measure of the value of intellectual discipline. If we forget this, we are liable to fall into the error of gaining a smaller good at the expense of a greater good. The effort to gain mastery in one discipline may leave the individual without the resources to gain a wider freedom and, hence, in a pitiful condition of servitude and blindness. A man may succeed, for example, in becoming an excellent scientist but may lend his efforts to support a totalitarian regime or to plan the more efficient destruction of his fellow man. We have seen many examples of this recently in Germany, the Soviet Union and the United States, and we shall probably continue to see them as long as the cold war continues. The scholar who becomes disciplined in his own field by cutting himself off from the wider concerns of the world makes himself into a political, social, and cultural simpleton who finally enjoys less freedom in the larger sense despite his self-discipline in the narrower.

If we consistently hold the individual student at the center of our concern we shall be less liable to the fault, committed by many apostles of intellectual discipline, that John Macdonald has called the "ritual fallacy" in education.[44] It is commonly thought that if a student has performed an assignment something significant has somehow been gained. Ritual, which plays a great part in the life of primitive man, is based on the belief that, if certain prescribed acts are properly performed, something important will result, although no one asks or knows how. This ritualism can be exemplified by the businessman who spends the better part of his life making his fortune and then tours the galleries of Europe to get his culture; by the teacher who thinks he has done enough when he has put his student through a course in grammar or geometry; by the student who "reads" a book by passing his eyes over the lines of print, or "takes" a course by sitting in lectures for a year, or "studies" by copying notes from a book. None of these ritualistic gestures has any necessary educational significance. They *may* have: but their performance alone does not guarantee this.

V   DISCIPLINE AND FREEDOM

Freedom as a Product of Discipline

It is necessary in education to distinguish freedom as a means and freedom as an end. Freedom as a means is used in school to encourage effective learning and self-activity in children. Freedom as an end concerns the condition of the whole person as influenced by the educational process. One of the central problems of education is how much and what kind of discipline the educational process should include to achieve the end of freedom. Freedom is not a gift. A. Whitney Griswold, the late President of Yale University, declared his opposition to the concept of freedom that "puts stress on the first syllable of the word and identifies the whole word as a gratuity, as something available to anyone who desires it without payment or cost. . . . there could be no more illusory commodity than free freedom. To assume its existence, as many of us do, is to assume an attitude that invites true freedom's destruction and demise." [45]

The essential relationship between discipline and freedom can be exemplified by the difference between the man who has submitted to the discipline of learning to swim and the one who has not. The former enjoys a freedom in the water that the latter lacks. Similarly, the person who demands the initial freedom of the "hunt-and-peck" method in learning to type cuts himself off from the possibilities of facility and freedom that can be gained by the person who goes through the tedious and often frustrating discipline of learning a "touch" system. A form of discipline that leads to freedom is that gained by learning the means of effective investigation and inference. This is why an element of compulsion in education can be defended by apostles of freedom. There is a sense in which appreciation of education comes only after education. The child who is given the freedom to choose the courses he will take in school before he has been introduced to the experiences that will enable him to choose wisely is not in effect able to make a genuinely free choice. Moreover, granting unrestricted choice to the immature may simply be a way of cutting them off from the possibilities of future freedom. For instance, the student who has chosen driver-training instead of mathematics is not subsequently free to choose physics, for he lacks the necessary mathematical training. Hence, there is a need in high school for an integrated curriculum—one that represents for the individual student an ordered and purposeful progression throughout his school life, rather than the mere accumulation of a number of isolated courses with no particular relation to one another. Each stage in the curriculum should be designed to provide the experience that will make the student free to attempt the next stage with confidence and, ultimately, to choose freely and wisely among a number of specialties.

Discipline as a Product of Freedom

It is nevertheless, if paradoxically, true that a self-disciplined responsibility comes only as a result of the exercise of freedom. Children in school must be granted a steadily increasing area in which to make their own decisions. Progressively, their authority in the school should grow, and with it should grow their responsibility for the consequences of their decisions. This self-direction should be seen in the increasing freedom they exercise in the matter of choosing their own subjects of study, in arranging their own timetables, in organizing societies for serving the school and community, and in writing and publishing school newspapers and journals. Moreover, we cannot in this respect ignore the remarkable results achieved by such educators as Maria Montessori in her *Case dei Bambini,* and A.S. Neill at Summerhill. These innovators claim that self-discipline flows from an experience of freedom—and from no other source.

In the view of Montessori, the child develops self-discipline not by being silenced, punished, or inhibited, but by being permitted to express and act on those longings that represent his deepest nature. We must not, therefore, suffocate the spontaneous actions of the child: these are the manifestations of individuality and if we stifle them we do irreparable harm to the child's development. Educational acts should help the unfolding of the child's unique life. To help in this process it is necessary rigorously to avoid the arrest of spontaneous movements and the imposition of arbitrary tasks.[46] Montessori does, however, distinguish between spontaneous, creative acts, which contain the makings of self-discipline, and useless or destructive acts, which are dangerous to the child himself or to others. These latter acts are to be at first hindered, and little by little suppressed. The freedom of the child should have as its limit the collective interest.[47]

A.S. Neill shares this view that this is the appropriate limitation of freedom. At Summerhill each child is free to do as he wishes as long as he is not trespassing on the freedom of others. But Neill would go much further than Montessori in avoiding the suppression of acts that adults feel are inconvenient, ill-mannered, unpleasant, or even (to a degree) harmful. In Summerhill, Neill set out to make a school in which children would be free to be themselves. He accordingly renounced all external discipline, direction, suggestion, moral training, and religious instruction. Neill wrote,

I believe that to impose anything by authority is wrong. The child should not do anything until he comes to the opinion—his own opinion—that it should be done. The curse of humanity is the external compulsion, whether it comes from the Pope or the state or the teacher or the parent. . . . Freedom means doing what you like, so long as you don't interfere with the freedom of others. The result is self-discipline.[48]

The practical success of Montessori and Neill compels us to consider their views with respect, although of course it does not prove the validity of their theories. They may have succeeded for quite different reasons—as, for example, the outstanding nature of their own personalities, which may have ensured that schools led by them would have flourished under an entirely different philosophy. However, no attempt to formulate a theory of the relationship between discipline and freedom can now afford to ignore the theoretical and practical contributions made by these apostles of freedom.

Discipline and Interest

Education is a risky business. There are no guaranteed results. No program will infallibly produce a self-disciplined person. Moreover, the most promising programs contain a considerable element of danger. It has been said that you have to risk youth in order to raise a generation of men. A university president said,

The university must take the chance that some of its students will "go to the dogs," rather than restrict the freedom in which the other young men will learn to make their own decisions, develop self-discipline and the capacity to act as persons of independent spirit. We must take risks, but no more effective way of developing character or of discovering truth has yet been discovered.[49]

It is imperative under such a regime of freedom to prepare young people as well as we can by helping them to develop clear, strong lines of interest. Strong interests are equivalent to strong will: what is called weakness of will is usually deficiency of interest. A person who can be persuaded to do something that he has no real desire to do has no clear conception of his true interests. The danger of excessive external discipline is that it helps to produce people who have no strongly developed interests, are weak-willed, and hence easily led.

One reason why strong external control is necessary in schools is that the children have not been given the opportunity to develop their own strong interests. A clear sense of purpose, based on interests that have relevance to the child's own view of the world, itself constitutes a form of discipline. Dewey has suggested that a school firmly oriented in the world of its pupils could dispense with discipline in the sense of keeping order through external force. Children whose interests are actively engaged in their studies do not need policing. They can be permitted considerable freedom, not to avoid genuine discipline, but to enable them to assume larger and less artificial responsibilities, the performance of which will evoke order from within.[50]

Sylvia Ashton-Warner, in teaching her Maori children in New Zealand, found that by using what she calls "organic teaching," that is, helping the children learn the words they are spontaneously interested in, however "difficult," unusual, or "improper," rather than words conventionally approved of for beginning readers, and by having the children compose their own readers, rather than submit to mass-market books, she was able to lead the most unpromising students to a willing submission to the discipline of reading. Moreover, she claims that once the freedom of this organic base is experienced by the child, the discipline of ordinary readers, static vocabularies, and other conventional teaching, can be imposed without harm. But the unrestricted choice of following unique interests must come *first*.[51]

It is necessary in this connection to distinguish between interest as means and interest as end. As means, interest is of course the stock-in-trade of the teacher. But it is as an end—the development of continuing, life-long interests of a creative, constructive nature—that interest represents the greater freedom. One of the difficulties of pedagogy is that the two concepts may be mutually injurious. Especially in a society where passive spectators vastly outnumber active participants, teachers must be on their guard in using techniques—such as audio-visual aids—

that succeed in capturing a temporary interest but do so at the cost of producing a generation of young people who can be aroused from a pervading lethargy only by dramatic tricks or colorful gimmicks. The disciplined person is he who has achieved an autonomous power of attention and interest. Schools must avoid interest-arousing techniques that militate against the development of this autonomy.

Discipline, Freedom and the Nature of Man

The educational practices of men like A.S. Neill are based on the belief that the child's nature is intrinsically good. The child has an innate wisdom and realism. "If left to himself without adult suggestion of any kind, he will develop as far as he is capable of developing." [52] If we *must* adopt a one-sided view of the human being, it is better to err in this Rousseauesque direction of freedom than in the medieval direction of punitive discipline. But it is not necessary to accept either of these limited concepts: a more comprehensive view of man would acknowledge the existence of his profound potentialities for good—which need an atmosphere of freedom to flourish—and yet recognize that he has also a dark side, with immense possibilities of evil—which needs discipline to control it. The ancient sages of China conceived human nature as stemming from the *Yang*, from which came a host of good spirits called *shen*; and the *Yin*, from which came a host of evil spirits called *kwei*. Counterparts and conflicting opposites, the *Yang* and the *Yin* were nevertheless considered to complement each other in the formation of a creative force whose product was heaven and earth with its fruits. Their symbol was a circle divided into two embryonic shapes, one white and one black, whose significance was life, universal power, and the mysterious polarities that inhere in the nature of man.

Psychology and psychiatry have more recently lent support to this ancient wisdom. Evil is in reality the equal and opposite partner of good. But we fail to recognize this complexity in ourselves. Rather we isolate evil in others. We cannot accept responsibility for the guilt that is ours by virtue of our humanity. We, therefore, localize evil onto delinquents, criminals, or other nations and assuage our conscience by punishing them or making war on them. At the same time we claim ourselves innocent. The Christian view exonerates man of a great burden of evil by placing it on the Devil.[53] By ignoring the dark side of the child we encourage or permit a license that can result in permanent damage to himself and others. By ignoring or undervaluing the good side, we discourage or prevent the development of the freedom that is essential for creative self-discipline.

It is infinitely easier to emphasize the dark side in education, for its implications are the strict control and authoritarian pedagogy that produce peaceful classrooms, polite, docile children, quick obedience, and unstrained teachers. But it is important to strive constantly to measure up to the more difficult implications of freeing the good side. The difference can be likened to that between the Confucian and the Taoist approaches. Confucius thought that human conduct must first be made correct, and then man's relation to God and the universe would take care of itself. Lao Tze thought that man must first establish himself in harmony with the universal principle (Tao) and righteous conduct would follow through its own intrinsic nature. While both of these emphases are needed at some stages, it is the Taoist approach that holds out the possibilities of a higher level of ultimate freedom. The relationship between good and evil within the individual is not fixed but is constantly fluctuating. The strengthening of the good in man is equivalent to a weakening of the evil and is an alternative to the external control or attempted suppression of that evil. Sir Herbert Read has likened freedom in education to a state of being with positive characteristics, and, he has suggested,

the development of these positive characteristics inevitably eliminates their opposites. We avoid hate by loving: we avoid sadism and masochism by community of feeling and action. We shall not need to repress because we shall have made education a process which . . . *prevents* us in the ways of evil.[54]

It is not necessary to accept Read's view on the inevitability of the process to recognize that the development of strong, creative, productive qualities in the child makes it less necessary to stamp out evil qualities; the positive qualities will work to shape his life in such a way that the evil propensities are largely preceded and precluded.[55] The great challenge of freedom and discipline is to frame educational theories, institutions, and practices that will express and support the *best* aspirations within man.

NOTES

1 "Encyclical Letter on Education," *Catholic Educational Review*, vol. XXVIII, no. 3 (March, 1930), 149.
2 *Times Literary Supplement* (June 24, 1960), 400: review of Alun Jones, *The Life and Opinions of T. E. Hulme*. See also T. E. Hulme, *Speculations*, Herbert Read, ed. (New York: Harcourt, Brace, 1924).
3 Hubbard Winslow, *On the Dangerous Tendency to Innovations and Extremes in Education* (Boston: Tuttle & Weeks, 1835), 17–18.
4 Andrew Roman, "Discipline: A Grade XI Boy's Point of View," *The Educational Record of the Province of Quebec*, vol. LXXV, no. 4 (October–December 1959), 232–33.
5 See paper by H.W. Chitepo (an African lawyer), "The Impact of Legislation on

the Community," presented at the Indaba in Salisbury, Southern Rhodesia, November 1, 1960. *Federation of Rhodesia and Nyasaland Newsletter*, November 4, 1960, 9–10.

[6] S.S. Laurie, *Historical Survey of Pre-Christian Education* (London: Longmans, Green, 1900), 247.

[7] See C.S. Bluemel, *War, Politics, and Insanity* (Denver, Colo.: World Press, 1950), 82–83.

[8] See T.W. Adorno, et al., *The Authoritarian Personality* (New York: Harper & Row, 1950), *passim*.

[9] W.R. Niblett, *Christian Education in a Secular Society* (London: Oxford University Press, 1960), 29.

[10] Bertrand Russell, *Principles of Social Reconstruction* (London: Allen & Unwin, 1916), 147. Ch. 5 contains an interesting discussion of the significance of reverence in education.

[11] A.S. Neill, *Summerhill: A Radical Approach to Child Rearing* (New York: Hart, 1960), 52.

[12] Edgar Z. Friedenberg, "The Modern High School: A Profile," *Commentary*, vol. 36, no. 5 (November, 1963), 373–80.

[13] *Ibid.*, 379.

[14] Neill, *op. cit.*, 155–61.

[15] Ethel M. Rogers, "Miracle at Changi Prison," *Maclean's* (August 12, 1961), 42.

[16] William Golding, *Lord of the Flies* (London: Faber & Faber, 1958). It is important, however, to recognize that the children in Golding's novel (as the children in Changi Prison) brought with them to the island a great deal of experience gained in English society. The evil that appeared in some of the more vicious of Golding's characters, such as Jack, Roger, and Maurice, may have been due not to tendencies inherent in their natures but to frustrations set up by their experiences in "civilization."

[17] Maria Montessori, *The Montessori Method*, Anne E. George, trans. (London: Heinemann, 1912), 353.

[18] See Maurice Cranston, "Two Treatises of Civil Government," *Listener* (November 19, 1959), 866–67.

[19] Jean Piaget, *The Moral Judgment of the Child*, Marjorie Gabain, trans. (Glencoe, Ill.: The Free Press, 1948), 402.

[20] D.H. Lawrence, *Fantasia of the Unconscious* (London: Secker, 1923), 44.

[21] For a more extended discussion of the assumptions and consequences of this form of punishment, see Paul Nash, "Corporal Punishment in an Age of Violence," *Educational Theory*, vol. XIII, no. 4 (October, 1963) 295–308.

[22] Josephine Moffett Benton, *The Pace of a Hen* (Philadelphia: Christian Education Press, 1961), 30.

[23] Y.P. Frolov, *Pavlov and His School: The Theory of Conditioned Reflexes* (London: Kegan Paul, Trench, Trubner, 1937), 214–15.

[24] See Eugene Kinkead, *In Every War But One* (New York: Norton, 1959).

[25] Helmut Gollwitzer, *Unwilling Journey: A Diary from Russia* (London: S.C.M. Press, 1953), 95–96.

[26] Montessori, *op. cit.*, 86.

[27] John Dewey, *Experience and Education* (New York: Collier, 1963), 21.

[28] See A.G. Hughes and E.H. Hughes, *Education: Some Fundamental Problems* (London: Longmans, Green, 1960), 209.

[29] From the *Dhammapada*, quoted in the *World Bible*, Robert O. Ballou, ed. (New York: Viking Press, 1950), 139.

30 From the *Tao-Te King*, quoted in the *World Bible*, 548.

31 John Macmurray, *Reason and Emotion* (New York: Barnes & Noble, 1962), 85.

32 Jacques Barzun, *The House of Intellect* (New York: Harper, 1959), 126.

33 Bernard Bergonzi, "Strictly for the Beat," *Manchester Guardian Weekly*, September 22, 1960, 11.

34 William Golding, *Free Fall* (London: Faber & Faber, 1959), 115.

35 See Laszlo Borbas, "Valéry and the Education of Youth," *French Review*, vol. XXXIV, no. 4 (February, 1961), 368.

36 E.L. Thorndike and R.S. Woodworth, "The Influence of Improvement in One Mental Function upon the Efficiency of Other Functions," *Psychological Review*, vol. VIII, no. 3 (May, 1901), 247–61; no. 4 (July, 1901), 384–95; no. 6 (November, 1901), 553–64.

37 See John S. Brubacher, A *History of the Problems of Education* (New York: McGraw-Hill, 1947), 262.

38 Jerome S. Bruner, *The Process of Education* (Cambridge, Mass.: Harvard University Press, 1960), 6, 17.

39 Clifton Fadiman, Introduction to *The Case for Basic Education: A Program of Aims for Public Schools*, James D. Koerner, ed. (Boston: Little, Brown, 1959), 5.

40 See also Jacques Maritain, *Education at the Crossroads* (New Haven: Yale University Press, 1943), 46; and Barzun, *op. cit.*, ch. 4.

41 G.H. Bantock, *Freedom and Authority in Education: A Criticism of Modern Cultural and Educational Assumptions* (London: Faber & Faber, 1953), 203.

42 *Ibid.*, 189.

43 Jerome S. Bruner, "Teaching Intuition," *Harvard Graduate School of Education Bulletin*, vol. V, no. 2 (Fall, 1960), 15–18; *Process of Education*, 8, 11–12, 24, 31–32.

44 John Macdonald, *Mind, School and Civilization* (Chicago: University of Chicago Press, 1952), 16–17.

45 Alfred Whitney Griswold, "The Cost of Freedom: An Academic View," *In the University Tradition* (New Haven: Yale University Press, 1957), 142.

46 Montessori, *op. cit.*, 86–88.

47 *Ibid.*, 87, 93.

48 Neill, *op. cit.*, 4–5, 114, 155.

49 Murray G. Ross, "The University and Modern Man," *Education*, vol. 4, no. 9 (Toronto: Gage, 1961), 56–57.

50 John Dewey, *The Child and the Curriculum* (Chicago: University of Chicago Press, 1902), 15; *Democracy and Education* (New York: Macmillan, 1916), ch. 10; *How We Think* (Boston: Heath, 1933), 284–88; see also Oscar Handlin, *John Dewey's Challenge to Education* (New York: Harper, 1959), 44–45.

51 Sylvia Ashton-Warner, *Teacher* (New York: Simon & Schuster, 1963), 95, 105.

52 Neill, *op. cit.*, 4.

53 See Carl G. Jung, "God, the Devil, and the Human Soul," *Atlantic* (November, 1957), 57–63.

54 Herbert Read, *Education Through Art* (London: Faber & Faber, 1943), 6.

55 "Through the vents of creativity forces can get out and away, leaving the lower levels relatively calm. . . . I get a precarious sense of some deep order." Ashton-Warner, *op. cit.*, 84–87.

IV

THE AUTHORITY OF THE GROUP
The Freedom to Become Oneself

I THE INDIVIDUAL IN THE GROUP

Self-interest, Protestantism, and Secularism

The drive to ensure the survival of the self seems to be innate in man. While this drive provides the energy for much of his endeavor, it is one that he shares with the animals and it does not reflect the most noble part of his nature. Nevertheless, it has been the frequent concern of theologians, who have spent much time speculating on the nature and possibilities of individual survival.

Protestantism has been especially concerned with the welfare and fate of the individual. The link between the individualism of Protestantism and the individualism of capitalism has been pointed out many times. In industrial economies where Protestantism is dominant, the individual worker is usually paid for the amount of work done. In countries where a Catholic social doctrine prevails, such as Italy, it is more common to find a "family-wage" system, under which a family man receives more than a bachelor who does the same work.[1]

The growth of secularism has not contributed to any decline in the emphasis on self-interest. As God has moved out of the center of men's lives, the commonest replacement has been the self. To be engrossed in self-preservation, self-indulgence, or self-improvement is a prominent pattern of the present day. It was characteristic of the Puritan to be constantly scrutinizing himself and his children for indications of individual salvation or damnation. With secularization, as Riesman has pointed out, such indications have been translated into signs predicting upward social mobility, that is, a future facility in passing not from hell to heaven but from a lower to a higher position in the status hierarchy.[2]

Education is customarily looked on not so much as a way of raising the overall quality of life of the group to which one belongs but as a means of raising oneself within the group or, preferably, into the next higher group.

Hedonism and Repression

The self-regarding tendencies of secular individualism received further support from the work of Freud. He showed that man's happiness is dependent on the gratification of certain instinctual drives, particularly the drives to obtain outlets for sexuality and aggressiveness. The survival of society depends on man's willingness to renounce immediate and constant gratification of these drives. But a thorough repression of them, Freud demonstrated, is harmful to the individual. Thus, from the beginning, there arises between man and society a conflict to which neither hedonism nor repression is a solution.

To a degree, this conflict is internalized within the infant by parental demands and assumptions. But a conflict internalized is not a conflict resolved: indeed, the internal struggle can be more painful for the individual. Modern society makes this problem more acute for the individual by encouraging and rewarding aggressiveness, but at the same time demanding an apparently complete repression of aggressive drives. Especially in a middle-class society, the child is urged to compete successfully against his fellows, but he is also urged to co-operate and get along with them. This ambivalent demand results in a sort of covert competition that is much more difficult to maintain than either open competition or the abandonment of competition altogether: the child must compete without appearing competitive.[3]

The Isolation of Modern Man

Many writers, including Erich Fromm, C.G. Jung, and Martin Buber, have described and analyzed a problem that compounds the difficulties of contemporary man—his isolation. With the vanishing of many traditional landmarks, man no longer finds the old certainties on which he used to depend. He finds himself free in a sense—free from the dominance of traditional authorities, such as church, state, family, culture—but it is a freedom that is largely unwelcome because it makes life a more frightening and lonely prospect. Man's isolation is increased by other developing forces in society, such as specialization, which engenders a fragmentation of society, and the increasing size of institutions, which encourages a feeling of individual impotence and social irresponsibility—that is, an isolation from human concerns in the wide sense.

Man often seems unable to overcome his isolation from his fellows even when it would seem simple and advantageous to do so. Anyone will appreciate this who has watched the evening traffic of people driving from work in a large city. Despite the problems of strangled congestion caused by the quantity of traffic, almost every car contains a single, isolated figure, sitting grim-faced in his little box of loneliness. At its worst, this isolation leads to mental illness, which might be called the exponential illness of today. The mental patient is in a condition of ultimate loneliness. He cannot combine or co-operate with his fellows for either good or evil purposes. In Karl Stern's novel, *Through Dooms of Love,* a sensitive study of the nature of contemporary loneliness, a doctor in a mental hospital says of his patients, "It's part and parcel of their very condition that there can never be any gang or leader, or any concerted action. And we cash in on that. Don't you fool yourself. Their sickness is *our* line of defense if you know what I mean. We're lucky they cannot get organized." [4] But worse than this, these mentally ill people are unable to sympathize, unable to cross the invisible barriers between men and feel sorrow for another's suffering. In a mental hospital all must suffer alone.

The Individual's Need for the Group

Such isolation is destructive because man has a fundamental need for society. There can be no such thing as bare and unrelated individuality. Some form of society is necessary for the development of self-consciousness and personality. This is clear from studying the development of the personality of the child in interaction with his mother, and as he learns to master language. To become a person one must be a conscious member of a group. Every healthy person is dependent on his fellow men in the sense that he wants to be like them (although he also wants to be different from them) and wants them to approve of him. Even the neurotic, who appears to *want* disapproval of the group, in reality *needs* their approval, which alone can help to cure him.

The work of men like Harry Stack Sullivan and George Herbert Mead has shown the essentially interactive nature of human development. "Many lines of inquiry have converged," Richard Niebuhr wrote, "on the recognition that the self is fundamentally social, in this sense that it is a being which not only knows itself in relation to other selves but exists as self only in that relation." [5]

The whole idea of education, indeed, is based on the assumption of the insufficiency of individual life and the necessity for incorporating external values into it. If we were satisfied with the isolated child as he is, we should not find it necessary to bring him together with other children in an institution to educate—that is to change—him. The dependence of the infant on his mother for his physical survival is only the initial stage of a continuing dependence of the individual on others for his economic welfare, his intellectual development, his emotional health, and his psychic maturity.

Law and Custom

The individual's relationship to the group becomes informally epitomized in custom and ultimately codified in law. In preliterate societies, customs and laws are not distinct. The rules by which men live are unquestioned and thought to be part of the nature of things. It is not necessary to explain or defend the rules. But when a society comes into contact with other societies questions arise when men see that life is not always lived according to the rules they follow. Then law arises: it is usually written, it is usually made by an authority or leader, and it is usually accompanied by certain penalties that follow nonobservance. Customs are wider than laws because not all customs are codified. Only social, not legal, sanctions support noncodified customs.

In preliterate societies, man lacks individual freedom but has greater security than man in modern society. The preliterate man is secure in the tight hold of the group: there is relatively little danger of social disintegration. The growth of individual freedom in literate societies raises new problems in terms of threats to group security. Accordingly, these societies usually seek alternative means of social control, such as stronger authority for the leader or government. Modern nations have typically sought this control through law. The codification of laws brings up the question of the appropriate relationship between the individual and the state. How can we best reconcile the claims of individual freedom and collective security? This, in a sense, is the basic question of social philosophy. The question becomes particularly acute in times of rapid social change or unrest, as in fifth-century Athens, seventeenth-century England, or, in the twentieth century, virtually the whole world.

In a modern society it is impossible to achieve individual freedom outside of a context of the authority of law. The problem of providing a large measure of freedom for each individual is not a matter of minimizing authority but of making authority serve the interests of freedom. "Those wise restraints which make men free," as Robert Carr has reminded us, are necessary in a civilized society. "We must never forget that civil liberty is *by definition* something more than natural freedom. It is civilized freedom, if you will; liberty enjoyed in a civil setting, that is, in the context of authority." [6]

II THE TYRANNY OF THE GROUP

Conformity

There are occasions when it is desirable or inevitable or appropriate for the individual to be subordinate to the group. But many observers feel that the greatest danger in modern society is that the individual is too often held in subordination to group interests, even when this is not desirable, inevitable, or appropriate. It is necessary, therefore, to examine some of the predominant manifestations of this danger to arrive at a judgment of the most productive relationship between the individual and his group.

An obvious manifestation is the conformity that has so often been condemned as a crippling and destructive feature of our lives. This is, of course, no new complaint. Men have for centuries been lamenting that their fellows are too prone to follow the crowd rather than think for themselves. "Every generation laughs at the old fashions," said Thoreau, "but follows religiously the new." [7] But there are forces operative in contemporary life that threaten to bring about a conformity more pervasive and comprehensive than at any time in the past. Such forces are the power of the mass media of communication, the general loss of religiously based inner certainties, the unprecedentedly rapid rate of change, which induces bewilderment and insecurity, and the greater plenitude and speed of transportation.

There is always a tendency for opinion to coagulate. Just as a bead of quicksilver is drawn into a pool of the same substance, so the opinion of the individual is constantly under pressure to merge itself with majority opinion. No one is completely immune to this pressure, but its effects are felt particularly acutely by young people. One recent study found that girls at tenth-grade level who were able to surpass boys did so, but that girls at twelfth-grade level who could make higher grades chose to make lower grades to avoid appearing unfeminine. Social approval was more important to them than academic success.[8]

Even apparently individualistic protests against an overuniform society may turn out, under closer examination, to be variations on a theme of conformity. Bohemianism, for instance, has its own rigid code of conformity. One of the first acts of the Beatnik is to seek to join a group of fellow Beatniks. Elias Wilentz, editor of *The Beat Scene*, who claims to speak with authority on the Beat phenomenon, has maintained that the only true Beats "are those who identify themselves with the ideas of Allan Ginsberg, Jack Kerouac, Gregory Corso, and Peter Orlovsky." [9] Identification with the ideas of a high priest can never result in individualism: a personality cult is incapable of producing free personalities among the followers. Similarly, the juvenile delinquent, whom many regard as a rebel against society, may in fact be the most slavish conformist to some of the basic values of American society, such as the "take now, pay later" principle and faith in the efficacy of the use or threat of violence.

A particularly pernicious feature of group conformity is the development of dual standards of morality. Man as a member of a group will commit or approve of acts that he would condemn as an individual. The individual may feel he has no right to force his private views on anyone else, but at the same time may be prepared to indoctrinate others through propaganda or force with the views of the political, religious, or national group to which he belongs. Double moral standards are also characteristic of the "organization man," who has permitted the organization's demands on his character and integrity to lead him into actions that he would never commit for his own sake. In the 1961 antitrust trials in the United States, twenty-nine firms, including virtually all the country's makers of electrical equipment, and forty-nine of their executives were fined nearly $2,000,000, and seven executives were jailed, for price-fixing and bid-rigging. In the judge's words, the culprits were "torn between conscience and an approved corporate policy." They were "organization or company men." [10]

It is true that we are not islands: we must be concerned with one another. When our fellows fall below the level of conventional morality we should not ignore them but should be concerned for their redemption. But how much pressure is it justifiable to exert on them to encourage them to conform to a moral code? Should we attempt to persuade them? Ostracize them? Actively persecute them? It would seem that our responsibility both permits and directs us to attempt to persuade them. But active intervention should end there. There are penalties enough for breaking social and moral rules without adding our personal penalty. For example, a person who goes to jail for an offense also suffers social obloquy when he comes out. Even an accused man found innocent suffers some loss of reputation because of his being accused. Moreover, we rarely have enough facts to make wise judgments of our neighbors. Even courts of law, which try to be impartial, to summon expert testimony, to inquire carefully and fully, are by no means infallible. Social opinion tends to be based on passion, prejudice, and bigotry, its penalties are liable to be severe, and its validity is suspect.

In-group Fanaticism

A more pressing danger than conformity—in that its consequences could be universally disastrous—is the development and strengthening of the amity-enmity complex. The loyalty to the in-group is accompanied

by hostility toward the out-group. The story of "love me, hate my enemies" is an old one. It has been perennially a feature of the relationships
between families, tribes, nations, and religious groups. In the Zoroastrian *Gathas*, it says:

> O Ahura Mazda, this I ask of thee: speak to me truly!
> How will love actually, in deeds, extend over those persons
> To whom thy spirit was announced as a doctrine?
> On account of whom I first was elected, and whom I love;
> All others I look upon with hostility of mentality! [11]

And in the *Koran*, it warns: "O believers! take not the Jews or Christians
as friends. They are but friends to one another[!]; and if any one of you
taketh them for his friends, then surely he is one of them!" [12] In our
day this is known as guilt by association.

Loyalty to our own group is necessary to a degree to maintain the
unity that survival demands. But when it excludes the possibility of
virtue in those outside the group such loyalty becomes a menacing force.
In-group feeling contains the danger of nourishing the stereotype of
"The Enemy." When we identify another group as The Enemy we are
more readily persuaded to attribute all right to our group and all fault to
them. We cannot trust them, for they are evil. We interpret all their
actions and statements to fit this stereotype. We suffer from what has
been called "hardening of the categories." [13] That is, we can no longer
attend to people and situations or see them as they really are. We relate
to a person as a member of a category, on which we have formed a pre-
judgment. If we meet individual members of the enemy group who we
find do not fit our stereotype, we do not change the stereotype: we assume either that they are deceiving us, or that they do not typify their
group, the majority and leaders of which remain evil in our opinion.

The consequences of The Enemy stereotype are pernicious. In the
first place, communication tends to break down. Individuals who want
to maintain contact with individuals in the other group (for instance,
Americans who visit Russia, have Russian friends, or read Russian literature) are regarded with suspicion at home. They are under pressure—
overt or subtle—to restrict or abandon their contacts. And the breakdown of communication is a prelude to disaster. Furthermore, the "self-
fulfilling prophecy" process tends to make the in-group's beliefs about
The Enemy come true. For example, if we distrust the Russians, and
act toward them as we act toward those who are untrustworthy, they are
liable, as a result, to act in a way that justifies our suspicion. And, finally,
the contemporary developments in belligerent nationalism and military

technology have combined to make in-group exclusiveness now more dangerous than it has ever been.

Totalitarianism

The subordination of individual interests to group interests reaches its ultimate stage of development under a totalitarian system. Under a fully realized totalitarianism the individual gains his significance *only* through the group. The liberalism and romanticism of the early nineteenth century in Europe encouraged the release of individual potentialities. But the failure of the liberal-democratic revolutions in mid-century led to a reaction that made possible the imperialistic, chauvinistic nationalism of the second half of the century. The earlier writings of Fichte and Hegel were used to propagate the view that man could become free and rational only through submitting himself to disciplined and dedicated service to the State. Education became looked on as the chief agency to develop this sense of national loyalty and service. Teacher-training institutions were the objects of particularly severe State pressure.

Totalitarianism advanced further in the twentieth century: between the two World Wars in the U.S.S.R, Italy, Germany, and Japan, and after the Second World War in China. As the State merged its identity with society in these countries, so education became virtually identical with citizenship training. The values of the dominant group in such societies prevail over all others and individuals who cannot or will not accept these values are considered expendable. André Schwarz-Bart's *The Last of the Just* gave a poignant and moving account of the difficulties of Jews who tried to obtain an education in Nazi Germany in the 1930's and of the fate of those non-Jews who tried to befriend and help them.[14] The preamble of the constitution of the All-China Federation of Trade Unions, as revised and adopted in 1957, states:

> Under the leadership of the working class, the interests of the state are identical with the common interests of the entire people and also with the fundamental interests of our working class. The trade unions should educate the workers and recognize the unity of interests between the state and the individual and, when these two conflict, realize that individual interests should be subordinated to state interests.[15]

The trial of Adolf Eichmann showed the consequences of totalitarian subordination of the individual to the group in an advanced form. Eichmann called himself an "idealist," that is, one who *lived* for his idea and who was prepared to sacrifice everything and everyone for it. He asserted that he would have sent his own father to his death if that had been required—to show the extent to which he was idealistically obedient to orders. For the "idealist," personal feelings must never be allowed to influence his actions. When asked if his conscience never disturbed him, Eichmann replied that he would have had a bad conscience only if he had not done what he had been ordered to do—to ship millions of men, women, and children to their death with great zeal and most meticulous care.[16] In other words, for the model totalitarian citizen, the conscience is not silent. It operates, but only to tell him whether he has fitted into the overall group design. It does not operate to permit him to evaluate the design itself.

Although totalitarian tendencies flourish best under fascist or communist regimes, they are by no means absent from the so-called democratic nations. The dangerous prevalence of what Aldous Huxley calls the "Social Ethic," [17] or what Charles Morgan calls "numerical thinking," [18] presents a constant threat that the individual will be sacrificed in the interests of the group. Democracy is based on the assumption that individuals *count*, but in practice it often becomes interpreted as a belief that individuals should *be counted*. We are in danger of raising the mechanical *means* of democracy to the status of an *end*. Head-counting is not democracy. There is no doubt that majority opinion should constitute the basis for policy and that minorities should conduct themselves in accordance with those policies. But this does not mean that the majority opinion is *right* or that the minority should give up their attempts to make their views prevail. Fifty-million Frenchmen can, indeed, be wrong. The fact that everyone at one time agreed that the earth was the motionless center of the universe in no way affected its regular orbit around the sun.

Mind Control

Developments in science and medicine have, in the last few years, presented new and dangerous possibilities in the realm of the control and subordination of the individual by the group in power. Until recently, it was difficult to deprive a man of freedom of thought: he could keep his thoughts to himself and so keep them inviolate. It was possible to attempt to control thought in a negative sense through censorship, that is, by denying men access to heretical ideas. But now we can operate more directly on men's minds through psychological persuasion, drugs, subliminal advertising, brain surgery, electric shock treatment, and other techniques. Some observers have pointed to communist trials, in which prisoners, apparently not subject to any physical torture, have made amazing confessions and self-accusations. Evidence is also beginning to gather of group persuasion techniques, used especially by the Chinese, that bear remarkably long-lasting results in terms of mental manipulation and conversion. Brain surgery and electric shock treatment can effect permanent changes in the patient's mind and personality. Aspects of these methods have been explored by a number of writers, including Charles Morgan, Aldous Huxley, Arthur Koestler, and George Orwell.[19]

There can be little doubt that in this field lies the possibility of a most serious threat to individual freedom from the tyranny of the group. Psychological control is potentially more dangerous and permanent than physical control, for the person under physical coercion is always aware of his lack of liberty and, hence, likely to strive to free himself, while the victim of mental manipulation is under the illusion that he acts of his own volition. Prison walls are a constant reminder to the prisoner of his servitude. The walls of the psychological slave are invisible and leave him with the dangerous impression that he is free.

It is, therefore, essential to restrict and guard carefully the practices of administering drugs and performing surgery that cause chemical or physical changes in the human brain. Mental freedom is basic to other freedoms. The loss of other freedoms is regrettable but not necessarily permanent. Given freedom of the mind, man may be able to regain other lost liberties through the exercise of his mental freedom. But, if man's mind comes under the control of another's, the loss of freedom is apt to be permanent, because the enslaved mind lacks knowledge of its own condition and will remain passively acquiescent in its slavery.

It is true that some of these mind-altering techniques can be used for laudable ends. But should they be? Mind control even for "good" ends must be opposed on the grounds that it does not basically respect the person controlled. If one attempts to influence a person's mind while still respecting him, one appeals to his reason. But these techniques attempt to control thought not by appealing to reason but by suspending its operations. If we decide what is good for someone and give it to him whether he likes it or not, we are ignoring a basic demand of morality— that we let other people tell us what they think they need and deserve and do not ignore these claims except for clearly defensible reasons. And these reasons must be brought into the open so that people can have a chance to oppose them.

III BECOMING ONESELF

Pluralism

The group pressures adumbrated here all serve to render more difficult the individual's major task of finding himself, of becoming a genuine person. A pluralistic society is more likely than a totalitarian society to contain a healthy number of genuine persons because, while the task for each man is ultimately a private, internal one, the chances of his success are greatly affected by the external climate of society. "So Two cheers for Democracy," said E.M. Forster: "one because it admits variety and two because it permits criticism." [20] The pluralistic society is based on the idea that all sorts of individuals are valuable in building a civilization. It does not sacrifice all variety to efficiency. People who want to create or discover or initiate something eccentric are given a chance to do so in a pluralistic society. Only people who perform orthodoxly succeed under an efficiency-regime.

One of the greatest virtues of a flourishing pluralistic society is tolerance. It is a basic value to be encouraged in the young, who should be shown the necessity for respecting the differences of others and for guarding their right to be different. "Mankind are greater gainers," wrote John Stuart Mill, "by suffering each other to live as seems good to themselves, than by compelling each to live as seems good to the rest." [21] Such tolerance should not be mistaken for weakness, for it necessitates not an abandonment of one's own beliefs but an acceptance of the views that there are many routes to truth and that life is enriched by diversity.

A pluralistic society, where many conflicting groups are permitted to coexist, is likely to enjoy more freedom than a monistic society—even if the single point of view is a most laudable and respected one. Perry Miller has analyzed the close connection between freedom and diversity in American life:

. . . both in education and in religion, we didn't aspire to freedom, we didn't march steadily toward it, we didn't unfold the inevitable propulsion of our hidden nature: we stumbled into it. We got a variety of sects as we got a college catalogue: the denominations and the sciences multiplied until there was nothing anybody could do about them. Wherefore we gave them permission to exist, and called the result freedom of the mind. Then we found, to our vast delight, that by thus negatively surrendering we could congratulate ourselves on a positive and heroic victory.[22]

This historical example prompts the speculation that perhaps an officially and uniformly held ideal of freedom is less efficacious in achieving individual liberty than is a tolerance of wide and fundamental diversity. Such a speculation should make us wary of arguments that we can best safeguard freedom by suppressing groups who do not support "democracy."

The Uniqueness of the Individual

Everyone is born unique—a uniquely combined bundle of hereditary potentialities. A good education will foster this uniqueness, for it is the source of variety, richness, innovation, creativity, and invention. The uniqueness of the individual gives him dignity and significance, for he appears on earth only once and his appearance makes a permanent difference to the stream of life. All the great religions share this view of the uniqueness of each man and of the importance of its nurture. In Buddhism everything is subordinate to the cultivation of the individual as suggested by the Eight-Fold Noble Path. In Confucianism, great stress is placed on the fullest possible realization of human nature at its best. In Hinduism, the individual self in its deepest experiences is the reflection of the absolute Self and is, therefore, to be cared for as a divine manifestation. In Christianity, everyone is looked on as a child of God and should be treated with respect for his intrinsic worth. Rabindranath Tagore has expressed it this way: "The universal is ever seeking its consummation in the unique, and the desire we have to keep our uniqueness intact is really the desire of the universe acting in us. It is our joy of the infinite in us that gives us our joy in ourselves." [23] And Martin Buber has written: ". . . the humanly right is ever the service of the single person who realizes the right uniqueness purposed for him in his creation." [24] "It is because things happen but once that the individual partakes in eternity. For the individual with his inextinguishable uniqueness is engraved in the heart of all and lies forever in the lap of the timeless as he who is constituted thus and not otherwise. Uniqueness is the essential good of man that is given to him to unfold." [25]

Autonomy

The genuine person is an autonomous person. It is today more than ever necessary to seek autonomy, for many of the traditional crutches that sustained our forefathers have been swept away. Young people need to be shown how to grow into a state of intellectual and emotional self-reliance that will enable them to face life without depending on old certainties that are no longer valid. The autonomous man is one who is able to understand his own thoughts and feelings, his own talents and limits, and who can act responsibly in the light of that understanding. The concept of autonomy is here used in a similar sense to that followed by David Riesman, who has contrasted the adjusted, the anomic, and the autonomous man. The adjusted man is one who reflects his society, his class or his group, with least distortion. He conforms because he must: he has no choice. The anomic man is one who is maladjusted, ruleless, ungoverned. He *fails* to conform with the same compulsiveness with which the adjusted man conforms: he *must* rebel. The autonomous man is capable of conforming to the norms of his group, and will usually do so, but he is equally capable of non-conformist action: he is free to choose.[26]

Autonomy is essential not only because of the withering away of alternative sources of support but also because of the danger that technological developments in transportation and communication will make us all more alike and, hence, less interesting to each other. The stimulating differences that have in the past been the result of our various national, regional, social, or racial origins will gradually melt into a homogeneity; they can best be replaced by an increasing emphasis on and development of those unique potentialities of intellect, emotion, and spirit lying within everyone but at present hardly tapped. In advocating the use of an individualized reading program in the primary grades, Sylvia Ashton-Warner has written: "I think we already have so much pressure towards sameness through radio, film and comic outside the school, that we can't afford to do a thing inside that is not toward individual development, and from this stance I can't see that we can indulge in the one imposed reading for all until the particular variety of a mind is set." [27]

To be autonomous is to be truly oneself. Many thinkers have held this up as the greatest goal.

> Be ye lamps unto yourselves.
> Be your own reliance.
> Hold to the truth within yourselves
>   as to the only lamp,

said the Buddha.[28] "Every individual," said D.H. Lawrence, in defining the goal of education, "is to be helped, wisely, reverently, towards his own natural fulfillment. . . . Every man shall be himself, shall have every opportunity to come to his own intrinsic fullness of being. . . . The final aim is not to *know* but *to be*." [29] In fiction, works like George Orwell's *Nineteen Eighty-Four* and J.D. Salinger's *The Catcher in the Rye* have variously described the problems of becoming and remaining an individual in totalitarian and conformist societies. The drive toward autonomy is complicated further by the fact that it is rarely a "pure" drive but is more usually part of an ambivalent mixture of feelings of dependence and independence. There is in us a desire to be like others, to be obedient to authority, to look up to a leader, to follow a clear doctrine. But there is also a desire to be different from others, to think for ourselves, to express our uniqueness, to be self-governing. It is important that the educator who wishes to help the child toward autonomy should recognize this ambivalence and create an atmosphere in which it can be brought to the surface and calmly examined.

Rebellion

Helping the individual to adjust to his environment is an inadequate aim of education, if for no other reason than that the environment is not healthy enough to make this wise. The juvenile delinquent is a model of adjustment to his delinquent group.[30] We must rather help the child to discriminate between the healthy and destructive elements of the culture and to resist those elements he considers pernicious. This means that we run the risk of involving young people in a conflict with society or the State. Nevertheless, if we abandon the task of living with a continuing tension between the individual and the State, we must settle for one of the less desirable alternatives of sacrificing the State to the individual, as the anarchists would, or sacrificing the individual to the State, as the totalitarians would.

The healthy person will want to conform to the prevailing mores and standards in most matters—especially inessentials. But he will also know that he *can* rebel against those standards on occasion, and that he *must* rebel if his conscience, after careful and repeated examination, tells him to. All great moral reformers were heretics: no moral progress comes from conformists. Socrates, Jesus, Thoreau, Gandhi, were all rebellious individualists. Jesus consistently put the individual before the institution—even if that institution was as sacred as the church or the sabbath. "The sabbath was made for man, and not man for the sabbath." (Mark II:27). "If a man does not keep pace with his companions," said Thoreau, "perhaps it is because he hears a different drummer. Let him step to the music which he hears, however measured or far away." [31] "The best way to judge a culture," said John Dewey, "is to see what kind of people are in the jails." [32]

It is never easy to decide, in any society, whether the people in the jails ought to be inside, and the people without the jails outside, or *vice versa*. The difficulty is compounded by the fact that the criminal and the saint are both nonconformists. One of the crucial tasks for the free society is to distinguish between the negative or destructive rebel and the positive or productive rebel and to treat them differently. The negative rebel is the criminal, the man who has sunk below the level of society's conformity. The positive rebel is the creative reformer, the man who has risen above the level of society, who sees further and more clearly than his contemporaries. In primitive and totalitarian societies, both types of rebel are treated alike: no deviation from the norm is permitted, and severe sanctions are used against those who persist in a pattern of nonconformity. In a mature society, the criminal is treated differently from the heretic, who is given the freedom to criticize, innovate, or create.

But how can we distinguish between these two types of nonconformity? One guide can be found in the degree of egotism in the individual's demands. If he is acting by himself, for himself, according to a principle that favors only him or his special group, then he is likely to belong to the inferior type of rebel. The white, American southerner who defies the law of the land because of his desire to maintain special privileges for members of his own race is an example of this type. The superior rebel rebels against a law only because he is obeying a higher law, and the principle to which he appeals has a universal applicability. Although his conscience will be the ultimate guide to conduct, it will be a conscience tested in the light of historical evidence and purified by sincere and repeated self-examination. The conscientious objector, who refuses to obey the law of conscription because of his obedience to what he considers the higher law of an ethical or religious code, is an example of this type.

Solitude

In order for the individual to grow to the degree of self-knowledge and firmness of conviction that will enable him, as an autonomous man, to rebel against the majority when it is right to do so, he must be prepared to withdraw from the group periodically. If we are always with others we can never know or become ourselves. Only through withdrawal into solitude can we renew and enrich ourselves so that we have something of significance to offer when we return to our fellows. "Society is commonly too cheap," said Thoreau. "We meet at very short intervals, not having had time to acquire any new value for each other. We meet at meals three times a day, and give each other a taste of that old musty cheese that we are." [33]

Many men have deepened their self-knowledge and developed great strength of conviction during periods of enforced separation from all society, as, for example, during solitary confinement in prison. One example of such was Christopher Burney, who, after being parachuted into France in 1942, was captured and kept in solitary confinement for 18 months. In his fascinating account of this period, he calls his 18 months of solitude "an exercise in liberty." [34] He was freed from the necessities of maintaining himself economically and of communicating with his fellow men. On the few occasions when intercourse was possible—shouting through windows, exercising, and so on—he found himself reluctant to break the precious solitude he had gained. In solitude he found his mental freedom enhanced and deepened because his thoughts were quite untrammeled and because he had no need to phrase them for transfer to another person. In the process of solitary contemplation he came to a remarkably deep level of self-knowledge.

Howard Thurman has told a story [35] that when he was a theology student in Rochester, New York, he was returning late one night to the seminary by way of Main Street. There was almost no traffic. Suddenly he became aware of the sound of rushing water, although no water was in sight. Next day he mentioned this to a professor who told him that for a distance under Main Street there ran a part of the old Erie Canal: this was the sound of water. The sound was continuous but the normal daytime traffic noises drowned it out. It was only when the surface noises had stopped that the sound of the water came through. This is analogous to the experience of a person who contemplates in quiet solitude and becomes aware of a dimension within him that is there all the time but cannot be experienced until the traffic of the surface life is stilled. At the end of Sartre's *Huis Clos*, Garcin says, "L'enfer, c'est les autres." Hell is being unable to get away from other people. Certainly, without regular periods of quiet solitariness, we cannot develop that private, personal life that is essential if we wish to bring, on our return, a contribution that can enrich society.

Self-examination and Freedom

The process of self-examination bears an essential relationship to the growth of personal freedom. Only as we begin to know ourselves dare we admit our own weakness—and this admission of weakness is, paradoxically, the beginning of emotional and spiritual strength. Philip Rieff has pointed out [36] that a weak person may consider himself strong, but others, near him, have to carry the burden of his weakness. Thus, a family may be dominated by its weakest member who, to the untrained eye, may appear strong only because he is aggressive, but who lacks powers of self-criticism. Eastern philosophy and religion have always been aware of the need for self-examination, but in the West it has been said that we are "shut up outside ourselves." [37] We need to enter again into ourselves, through meditation and self-analysis, to tap the rich sources of knowledge, strength, and energy that lie there.

Only through rigorous self-scrutiny can we come to see some of the amusing, pathetic, or dangerous subterfuges we perpetrate on ourselves by playing certain roles. It is fairly harmless to play the role of teacher or student or professor or parent as long as we maintain enough self-insight to regard our role-playing with a humorous detachment. But any role can be dangerous if we become uncritically absorbed by it. "The world tends to trap and immobilize you in the role you play," James Baldwin has warned; "and it is not always easy—in fact, it is always extremely hard—

to maintain a kind of watchful, mocking distance between oneself as one appears to be and oneself as one actually is." [38]

Above all, we need self-examination and self-knowledge to free ourselves from the fear of others that prevents us from entering into a deep and satisfying relationship with them. This fear arises because we project onto others the unrecognized malevolence that is in fact within ourselves. The fatal cost of this self-ignorance today makes it imperative that we withdraw these projections, which divide and alienate man from man. This can be done only through searching self-criticism. We must study ourselves so that we question our own assumptions, open ourselves to the possibility that some of our beliefs may be mistaken, and lay firmer hold on those values that are most deeply and genuinely ours.

IV THE PERSON IN THE COMMUNITY

The Return to the Group

Man begins as a member of a group—familial, tribal, cultural, political, religious. Before he can be a free person he must break away from this group: he must, as the prodigal son, take his inheritance and leave home. If he never throws off this early authority, he will never be able to rule himself. But if he remains there, he has not reached the fullness of freedom that comes only through the uncompelled reunion of autonomous persons. Only the prodigal son can know, on his return, the completeness of the father's love. Separation must precede the deepest and most mature level of relationship. But this relationship—in which lies the highest freedom—can be entered into only by a return to the group, this time a group of the person's own choosing.

As Plato showed in the Allegory of the Cave, the person who achieves a measure of insight, who approaches closer to the truth, must descend again into the cave to discharge his responsibility to his fellows. Men grow to their full stature only through a commitment to a purpose greater than their own little egocentric concerns. Full freedom is found not in isolation but in community. The group that constitutes a community, however, is to be distinguished from the group that forms a society.[39] Society is an organized form of political and economic relationships, springing from a functional co-operation in work, with the need for food, shelter, and safety as typical motivations. Community is a form of relationship arising from the impulse to share a common life: love, concern, and caring, are typical motivations. Society is a means to an end: community is an end in itself. Society can always be defined in terms of a common purpose that transcends the nexus of relationships that it establishes: community cannot. An illustrative example might be found in two business partners who are also friends. The society (the business partnership) has a purpose beyond itself. The community (the friendship) has no purpose beyond itself: its motive is found in the desire to share experience and live a common life of mutual relationship. With this distinction, it is easier to see that freedom necessitates treating people as ends rather than as means. We are free in our relationship only with people whom we treat as genuine friends—that is, we care for them as ends in themselves. There is constraint and lack of freedom to the degree that we depart from this type of relationship.

The concept of community rests on the beliefs that all men are connected and that freedom is indivisible. Abraham Lincoln, in his message to Congress in December, 1862, said, "In giving freedom to the slave we assure freedom to the free." Even more categorical was Eugene Debs' statement, "While any man is in prison, I am not free." Michael Bakunin, the nineteenth-century anarchist, put it thus, "I myself am a free man only so far as I recognize the humanity and liberty of all the men who surround me." We cannot be free until we have discharged our responsibilities to do what we can to make our fellow men free also. It has been said that we cannot be happy about anything until we are happy about everything. In other words, happiness requires some central core of security and joy. In the same way, true freedom must be held by everyone, or each person's freedom is reduced in measure. It follows that we cannot obtain our own freedom at the expense of anyone else's. We have as much stake in our brother's freedom as in our own. The free man cannot contract out of the human community.

Experiments with the so-called "consciousness-changing" drugs, like mescaline, psilocybin, and LSD, have led the experimenters to a realization that man's connection with his fellows is profound and inseparable. Under the influence of these drugs, the whole world seems to the participant to fuse into one, including himself. Ego-isolation is replaced by an experience of unity.[40] Alan Watts, who has had such experiences, has argued that the scientific-medical way of looking at an individual as what is contained within a given envelope of skin is inadequate. The individual is rather a reciprocal interaction between everything inside the skin and everything outside it. He is the particular and unique focal point of a network of relations that is ultimately the "whole series," that is, the whole cosmos.[41] Whatever the scientific validity of these drug experiments, the experimenters seem to be rediscovering what has long been postulated by most mystics and many religious leaders: we are all ultimately part of one another; whatever we do affects all; what we do to another we do to ourselves.

Consensus and Leadership in the Democratic Community

There is still no unanimous agreement on how a person should behave in the democratic community. What should be his attitude toward majority decisions, toward his democratically elected leaders, toward heretics and minority groups who wish to speak their minds or organize into parties? It is not uncommon to hear even university professors in democratic countries maintain that, once a government has been democratically elected, it should be left to rule the country, unhampered and unembarrassed by adverse criticism. This is the view of leadership out of which dictatorship is made. It is essential, in a democracy, that the leaders be kept as fully aware as possible of the views of those they lead. In some mountainous districts where sheep are pastured, ranchers put a few goats among them to act as leaders. Usually all goes well, but occasionally the goats lead the sheep into dangerous country where the sheep injure themselves, or are killed, while the goats are safe because of their agility. It reminds one forcibly of the agility of some Latin American dictators in making off safely with their fortunes when the country they have ruined explodes in bloody revolution. This type of leadership— marked by a great gap between leader and follower and a lack of appreciation on the part of the leader of the condition, needs, and views of the followers—is one that always holds potential disaster for the people. But it is one that a democracy *can* avoid—if the people are prepared to exercise their duty of informed and critical watchfulness over the government.

Healthy leadership of a democratic group must represent an accurate expression of the will of the group rather than a domination of it. It is much easier to dominate autocratically—or to abdicate leadership altogether—than to try to understand the group consensus and lead in a way that implements it. Such a concept means that the nature of the leadership given, and perhaps that of the leader himself, must change as the consensus or the function of the group changes. A certain person may appropriately follow on most occasions, but he can be the rightful leader when the group function needs his special talents. The healthy group is one in which such leadership changes can occur easily without destroying or disrupting the group.

Perhaps the most important lesson in democracy to be learned by children in a free society is the best way to reach group agreement, with its implications for the appropriate treatment of minority viewpoints. We need to eradicate the notions that democracy is the same as taking votes, that a majority has the right to implement its program without considering the minority, and that a minority has no responsibilities for constructive discussion and co-operative implementation of majority programs. If we seek a desirable model of the duties of the individual and the group in a democratic framework we should look not at the clever tricks, sly maneuvering, and ruthless debating of modern parliaments, or even the United Nations, but rather at the way in which, at its best, a Quaker meeting reaches the "sense of the meeting." [42] In coming to a corporate decision, the group attempts to find out the will of God in the matter. All members have a part to play. There is no voting, no chairman with powers of discipline. Everyone may speak his mind and the Clerk is responsible for gathering the sense of the meeting. Everyone has a measure of responsibility for the meeting and for the achievement of unity. There is often controversy, but there is no belief that a large majority on one side has learned the will of God in the situation. If one member is convinced the action is wrong, the meeting will wait for his agreement. A minority will often express its opposition, then withdraw from dispute, leaving the way clear for action. But on important matters the minority can delay action until it or the majority is convinced, or (more likely, and usually more creative) until a new solution is found preserving the convictions of all members. The process is often slow. But this is the fault not of the method but of man. "If men are slow to apprehend the will of God, they must be slow to act, for it is their business to act only in obedience." [43] Achievement of unanimity is more rapid by this method than by voting. Because there are no party lines, the aim of each side is to understand the other and to be understood. When a decision has been reached, there is no aftermath of bitterness as with a disgruntled minority. Waiting for unity brings a line of action that calls forth the complete dedication of all members to the implementation of the decision.

Finding Oneself in the Community

Helping young people to find themselves and to become what they are uniquely capable of becoming is a profitless enterprise unless they are also impelled to use their talents for the benefit of mankind. A person can realize himself fully only through the community. "His touch of colour contributes, however imperceptibly, to the beauty of the landscape—his note is a necessary, though unnoticed, element in the universal harmony." [44] There is today a widespread realization, on many levels of understanding, of this truth, and it is perilous for educators to underestimate its power. Lack of the experience of genuine community is a dangerous impoverishment for many members of industrialized societies. The desire for it is one of the principal recruiting agents for communism. It is easy to criticize the forceful and violent collectivization characteristic of communist technique, and to see that the collective is in fact the archenemy of the community, but it is more important to appreciate that uneducated or hungry men are always liable to confuse the two, and that the collective is often a sincere, if barren, attempt to satisfy a powerful, basic longing in man. We can be sure that, if we fail to provide for this longing through the creation of genuine communities, the world order will be based on the coerced collectivization of communism.[45]

The process of finding oneself cannot go on in isolation. Once we have come to a degree of knowledge of *ourselves*, the next step should be to let *others* know who we are. Mowrer has shown the connection between mental sickness and secrecy.[46] Sin and mental sickness are both enemies of community: they isolate the individual, withdraw him from the group. And in both cases cure lies in a return to the community—through confession of sin and its expiation, or through discussing one's anxieties with another. We need to open ourselves—including our sins—to our relatives, friends, colleagues, neighbors. This genuine communication is the prerequisite of authentic community. Sin demands to have a man alone. As long as a man is in touch with his fellows he draws strength that helps him to resist the temptation to sin. But if he lapses into the isolation of hypocrisy—that is, he pretends to others to be what in his heart he knows he is not, thus cutting himself off from genuine community—he sacrifices one of his greatest sources of support.

A growth in freedom necessitates a growth through social action and social responsibility. A man cannot operate in freedom when he acts merely for himself: the selfish man's freedom is undeveloped. The less free we are the more we tend to see ourselves in opposition to the world, set apart from it, trying to control it. The freer we become the more we are able to see ourselves in *relation* to the world, to realize that our freedom exists only through our *interaction* with the world. As persons, we find our highest possibilities of freedom through responsible participation in community.

V   EDUCATION FOR AUTONOMY WITHIN COMMUNITY

Education for Citizenship

Just as education must produce at the same time both man and worker, so it must produce both man and citizen. The young child's eagerness to understand his social group and to conform to its demands is an early indication of man's drive to establish bonds of commonality with the rest of his society. As a reaction to the undue emphasis of nineteenth-century education on making children conform to type, there has sometimes been in the twentieth century an equally one-sided emphasis on individualism to an extent that has neglected the need for a minimum of conformity. The young child needs to be inducted into his culture or he will be left without the basis of common experience and knowledge that is essential for civilized living. This will inevitably involve a certain amount of what is often condemned as indoctrination: even learning to read involves indoctrination, and we cannot—and should not—avoid it. Inevitable indoctrination is, of course, different from propaganda: the former is carried out in order, eventually, to expand the area of the child's freedom, while the latter is aimed to reduce it. Conformity through acculturation is necessary to give form and power of expression to the child and to enable him to carry on a genuine dialogue with those who share his culture.

At a later stage, this pervasive and often casual process of acculturation becomes a more conscious education for responsible citizenship. If education fails to foster feelings of social cohesiveness and mutual loyalty there will always lie the threat of social disintegration. And if society does not find a common ground by voluntary means, the State will step in and enforce the necessary unity by forceful means. When that happens, the cost of avoiding conformity has been too great, for individual freedom is largely lost under authoritarian control.

However, the *way* in which local and national loyalties are developed is vitally important. They should be developed not in an exclusive or fanatical way, but with a realization that out of them should grow a steadily expanding and maturing concern for all mankind. Military technology has made more poignant the essential interdependence of all nations today. Nuclear warfare is ironically symbolic in that the attempt to destroy an enemy would result also in self-destruction. We must choose between living together and dying together. Hence, an education for citizenship must today be an education for *world* citizenship. "Now it can never be well with any nation unless it is well with the world," Harry Fosdick has said. "Today being an internationalist is an essential part of being a patriot." [47]

Science as a Paradigm of Individual Submission

The scientific method might be cited as a paradigmatic example of the justifiable submission of the individual to the group. The essence of the scientific method is the idea of public verifiability—that all conclusions arrived at by the individual scientist are held tentatively by him, that his findings and methods are made public, and that the conclusions will be modified in accordance with the results of future relevant research. Anyone with the necessary curiosity, training, and apparatus can repeat the original experiment and, if identical conditions prevail, identical results should follow. This is the essential commonality of the scientific community. Whitehead has shown how Christian discipline and asceticism carried over into the field of science. The scholastic view of a rational order of nature contributed to a common use of the experimental method, based on the faith that the separate findings of scientists would eventually fit together and make sense.

John Dewey, who was opposed both to external authority exercised as dictatorship and to an individualism that denied the need for any authority, saw the need for a complementary relationship of authority and freedom best satisfied through the scientific method. He saw the collective authority, the co-operative use of organized intelligence, and the scope for individual initiative and enterprise that characterize science as providing the greatest hope for achieving a synthesis of individual freedom and group authority.[48]

The objectivity of the scientist demands that, as far as possible, he exclude himself, his personal hopes, passions, prejudices, and assumptions from the laboratory. He must follow the inexorable route of the experiment wherever it leads, however undesirable and inconvenient the direction may be. In science, personal submission is the only path to truth.

Education for Individual Autonomy

Education is all too liable to be an instrument of excessive conformity. When children must be handled in groups there is a constant temptation for the teacher to encourage the development of the conformity that produces docile, obedient, similar pupils. Unthinking conformity to society's traditions is also a common product of defective education. In preliterate societies, this conformity is virtually total, and individual nonconformity is either unknown or severely punished. But even more advanced societies are liable to use education for the reactionary purpose of ensuring strict acceptance of their own traditions or, what is worse, an alien tradition. Victor Murray has recounted that on a visit to an African school in Nigeria he asked the African headmaster what was the most popular subject in the school. Without hesitation, the headmaster replied, "Latin." When asked why, he said, "Latin is what you have in your English schools: therefore, we want it here also." [49] This sort of conformity to tradition, without consideration of its relevance or value, can do nothing to make education an agent of individual freedom.

Education has the responsibility to free the individual from the tyranny of a narrow provincialism through the sympathetic study and appreciation of the ideas of other groups, systems, nations, and epochs. The alternative has been poignantly and repeatedly brought home to us in the forms of Nazi crematoriums, *apartheid*, Hiroshima, and the Ku Klux Klan. The people of a free society must be educated to an awareness of the limits and perils of in-group fanaticism. Groups and sects provide a certain security for the individual growing up, but his maturity will be severely limited if he stays within the group that gave him initial security. For these groups enable him to measure himself by more favorable standards than would be available to him in the outside world. That is, they enable him to avoid the rigors of self-knowledge. One of the key tasks of education is to help the individual to gain the strength to step outside these protecting but limiting circles and take stock of himself in the widest possible context.

This will mean that we must be ready for young people to cast an increasingly critical eye on the groups they transcend, including perhaps their own society. James Baldwin has said,

The paradox of education is precisely this—that as one begins to become conscious one begins to examine the society in which he is being educated. The purpose of education, finally, is to create in a person the ability to look at the world for himself, to make his own decisions. . . . The obligation of anyone who thinks of himself as responsible is to examine society and try to change it and to fight it—at no matter what risk. This is the only hope society has. This is the only way societies change.[50]

The school as an institution is too closely integrated with society to be expected to controvert society. But the individual teacher has an unlimited responsibility to try to produce morally autonomous individuals. One of education's most valuable functions is to enable us to put some evaluative distance between us and our immediate world. There is a sense, as John Wild has pointed out, in which the individual is *bigger* than the group, and education can give him this realization of transcendence. "Humanistic disciplines, and especially philosophy, may give him a sense of the radically different alternatives that are open to him, and may stimulate him to work out global meanings of his own." [51]

Education for Diversity

The idea of freedom is essentially linked with individual uniqueness. If human beings were all alike the aim of being free to find oneself, to live one's own life, would be meaningless. Freedom would lose its value. How can education be improved to encourage this type of freedom? Roger Williams has suggested that children, as early as their preschool years, should be made aware of their own individuality. Even at an early age, their senses of taste and smell, their reactions to colors and textures, their ways of doing things, their likes and dislikes in stories, will be sufficiently diverse as to be striking and revealing.[52] We should encourage students to examine themselves, to see that they are unusual, and to accept their unusualness without psychological disturbance. By this means they are more likely to accept other people's unusual features.

In studying human beings, we need to examine not only the averages, types, statistical means, and generalizations that constitute so much of psychological enquiry but also the particular qualities of a unique person—what Allport has called "the Johnian quality of John." [53] Specific knowledge of individual students is essential for the teacher who would apply rules wisely. Children should have freedom to the extent that they are able to use it well. But while rules are uniform, individuals vary infinitely. Therefore, it is common to find a pedagogical situation where some of the children have too little freedom, and others too much. The best hope of successfully handling this dilemma is through the teacher's knowledge of and appreciation for each unique person.

This regard for individual differences was an original impetus behind the progressive education movement, and still forms the basis of some of its best manifestations. The better progressive educators believe it is important to try to understand each student, to deal with him at his particular stage of development, and to build individual programs suited as nearly as possible to his unique requirements. Along with this, there is the belief that the school's respect for personal differences will encourage the students to respect others who differ from them. The house of truth has many entrances, so that people can enter from any point of the compass. It is necessary to foster the attitude that prompts the individual to ask, concerning a problem, "How does it look from *your* position?"

The school can also help by showing the child the importance of solitude and how he can obtain it in the midst of a gregarious society. It should convince him that, in the last analysis, he alone is the agent of his own education and must bear a lonely responsibility for it; that the book that puts him into a condition of silence and solitude may be a better aid to self-understanding than the radio or television that fills his life with noise and gregariousness; that he must learn to live well with himself before he can live well with others. The school can make provision in the timetable for silent and solitary activities, as well as social, co-operative ones. Children do not know without guidance how to use silence properly and need help in learning this vital lesson.

An education for diversity among human beings would probably be enhanced by diversity among educational institutions. One way to encourage this, admittedly a very "un-American" way, would be through a system of government subsidies for people who want to set up small, private, experimental schools. Anyone with an educational idea he wants to try out, and who can find staff, building, and pupils, would be given financial backing by the government, with no questions asked. Later, government inspectors might come to see if it is justifiable to continue the grant or end it. The history of religious freedom in America shows clearly the connection between diversity and freedom. We are less likely to enhance freedom by ordering it by legislative decree or by putting "freedom" on the curriculum of all public schools than by "letting a thousand flowers bloom."

Education for Personal Excellence

The task of education is even more complex and difficult than that of helping the child to find himself, for he has several "selves," not all of which are worthy of being fostered or expressed. This is why self-expression is in itself an inadequate aim. The duty of the adult is to help the child come into his deep self, his *best* self. We are helped in this task by a natural striving in healthy young people to achieve personal excellence. We are hindered by the lack of excellent models to which they can look. The authority of good models is crucial in the process of maturing. Much of the current rebellion of young people can be ascribed to their own search for integrity, and their despairing rejection of the models they see manifested in a hypocritical adult society. Irving Levin, the principal of a New York City school, has said of contemporary youth:

> We try to make them act the way we don't. . . . We try to teach them to be polite, to be generous, to believe in the sacredness of human life, to respect the rights of others. But the kids have eyes. They look around. They see that ultimately individuals and nations use force to solve their problems. . . . We do not practice the virtues which we preach in private life, community life or in foreign relations.[54]

The free man is one who, through study, comes to know his best self and then *acts* in accordance with its demands. In preliterate societies man largely lacks individual freedom because responsibility and guilt are collective and heriditary. Responsibility for sin is passed on to subsequent generations. The free man must take full individual responsibility for all his acts: he cannot slough it off onto his ancestors, contemporaries, or descendants. An education for freedom is one that encourages the individual to act in accordance with the inner law of his own being when he is at his best. It helps him to gain the strength to live from his center out, following the lead of conscience, rather than from the environment in, following the lead of group opinion. To avoid dissolving in the faceless crowd we need to develop the kind of personal certainty that comes only through direct experience of the dimension that both transcends us and is part of us. Some call this God, some cosmic law, some the inward light, some the unconscious.

By whatever name it is known it will involve the steady pursuit of a goal of personal excellence. This means a constant striving for the highest standards we can reach. The best that we can envisage will always be above our present level of performance, and so there must always be an attempt to transcend the present self. In terms of knowledge, this reaching out to something greater involves necessarily a loss of innocence. As did Adam and Eve, we imagine that knowledge brings greater freedom, but, as they did, we find that it both brings freedom and takes it away. It brings freedom by increasing our range of potential action. It takes away freedom because gaining knowledge is an experience, and once we have undergone an experience we can never return to our previous condition. The freedom of innocence that we previously enjoyed has now gone forever. In a sense we both possess our new knowledge and are possessed by it. But the freedom of innocence is not the only, or the greatest, type of freedom open to man. He can also achieve the type of freedom that flows from what he strives for. Education brings with it the duty of trying to be intelligent and responsible in our conduct. There is perhaps some defense to be made for the ignorant person who acts in conformity with mass standards, but there can be none for the man of education who does so. Because of his knowledge, which has forcefully ejected him from the state of primitive freedom, he must strive to attain the highest standards of personal excellence that he can envision. In this vision and this striving lies the possibility of a higher freedom. The person who aspires to this level of freedom can never rest content with his present knowledge, insights, and beliefs. The man who loses the spirit of curiosity, quest, and criticism soon loses his freedom; he becomes the prisoner of his present beliefs. The educated man must constantly reappraise himself and the most cherished items of his intellectual and moral furniture. Only in this way can he achieve the freedom of personal excellence.

Education for Community

All of the efforts toward achieving individual autonomy and excellence will be stunted and without their crown if the educational task is not seen as focusing ultimately on preparing the individual for responsible participation in a community of free persons. Much of the recent concern with community, with communication and interaction, with relationships, seen in the work of men like Heidegger, Jaspers, Buber, and Marcel, constitutes in part a response to the challenge of collectivism contained in communism and fascism.[55] We must study the form and spirit of collective education, for we have much to learn in order to reduce our individualistic complacency. But collective education is inadequate, for it fails when it is needed most. Helmut Gollwitzer has written of the breakdown of community spirit among German soldiers in Russian prison camps after the Second World War. "If our own moral powers, our own sense of community and of belonging together had been stronger we could have stood this test. Why was it that the years of collective education under the Hitler regime resulted only in the fact that, at the first test, any sense of community gave way at once and turned into cynical egoism?" [56] One might answer that it is because collectivism and egoism are not far removed from each other. A collective is a coerced and premature grouping of unfree individuals: the authority is arbitrary and imposed, and it comes from without. A community is an uncoerced grouping of autonomous persons who come together only when they are ripe for the experience: the authority is still there, but it is relevant and self-assumed, and it comes from within.

An education that fits people to live in such a community will not stop at the level of individual autonomy. It will be concerned to bring to the person a realization of his connections with others. It will show him, as Marcel has pointed out, that even knowledge of oneself cannot be self-centered. "We can understand ourselves by starting from the other, or from others, and only by starting from them. . . . Fundamentally, I have no reason to set any particular store by myself, except in so far as I know that I am loved by other beings who are loved by me." [57] A person who has been educated for living freely in community will be self-directed without being self-centered. He will be other-centered without being other-directed. He will be free from the domination of others' wills but able to give himself fully in terms of insight, sympathy, and talents to fulfill others' needs.

The education of such a person must sail between the twin dangers of Puritanism and hedonism. The Puritan would have us suppress our passions, our awkward energies and socially embarrassing drives. He would save us from egocentricity by sacrificing our creativity. The hedonist would have us express ourselves freely, without regard to consequences or social implications. He would save us from frustration by sacrificing community. An education for freedom in community must avoid these destructive formulas by the *transformation* of passion, energy, and drives into creative and productive concern and compassion for others. In the last analysis, the problem of the individual and the group must be resolved in terms of paradox. We lose our lives by trying to save them: we find ourselves, we save our lives, only by losing them for the sake of our group, our community, our neighbor.

NOTES

1 See Daniel Bell, *Work and Its Discontents* (Boston: Beacon Press, 1956), 7. The same is true in countries like Japan where the group orientation is dominant: see Yoshiharu S. Matsumoto, "Contemporary Japan: The Individual and the Group," *Transactions of the American Philosophical Society*, New Series, vol. 50, Part 1 (Philadelphia: The American Philosophical Society, 1960), 59–66.

2 David Riesman, et al., *The Lonely Crowd: A Study of the Changing American Character* (New York: Doubleday, 1955), 60.

3 For illustrations of the difficulties of maintaining this stance, see John R. Seeley, et al., *Crestwood Heights* (Toronto: University of Toronto Press, 1956), 229.

4 Karl Stern, *Through Dooms of Love* (New York: Farrar, Straus & Cudahy, 1960), 138.

5 H. Richard Niebuhr, *The Responsible Self: An Essay in Christian Moral Philosophy* (New York: Harper & Row, 1963), 71. For a popular treatment of this subject, see John W. Gardner, *Self-Renewal: The Individual and the Innovative Society* (New York: Harper & Row, 1965), ch. 9, "Individuality and Its Limits."

6 Robert H. Carr, "Those Wise Restraints Which Make Men Free," *Oberlin Alumni Magazine*, vol. 58, no. 7 (November, 1962), 4–9.

7 Henry David Thoreau, *Walden, or, Life in the Woods* (New York: Mentor, 1957), 22.

8 Charles E. Bish, "The Academically Talented," *N.E.A. Journal*, (February, 1961), 33–37.

9 See Bernard Bergonzi, "Strictly for the Beat," *Manchester Guardian Weekly*, September 22, 1960, 11.

10 The *Observer* (London), March 12, 1961, 13.

11 From the Zoroastrian *Gathas*, in *World Bible*, Robert O. Ballou, ed. (New York: Viking Press, 1950), 213.

12 From the *Koran*, *Ibid.*, 468.

13 Douglas V. Steere, "On the Power of Sustained Attention," *Then and Now: Quaker Essays, Historical and Contemporary*, Anna Brinton, ed. (Philadelphia: University of Pennsylvania Press, 1960), 295.

14 André Schwarz-Bart, *The Last of the Just*, Stephen Becker, trans. (New York: Atheneum, 1960). See, particularly, ch. 5, "Herr Kremer and Fräulein Ilse."

15 *Eighth All-China Congress of Trade Unions* (Peking: Foreign Languages Press, 1958), 106–25. Quoted by Theodore Hsi-en Chen, *Teacher Training in Communist China* (Washington, D.C.: U.S. Department of Health, Education, and Welfare, 1960), 40.

16 See Hannah Arendt, "A Reporter at Large: Eichmann in Jerusalem-I," *The New Yorker*, vol. XXXVIII, no. 52 (February 16, 1963), 40–113.

17 See Aldous Huxley, *Brave New World Revisited* (New York: Harper, 1958), 127.

18 See Charles Morgan, *Liberties of the Mind* (London: Macmillan, 1951), 34.

19 See, for example, Charles Morgan, *op. cit.*, ch. 1; Aldous Huxley, *op. cit.*, ch.7, 11; Arthur Koestler, *The Yogi and the Commissar* (New York: Macmillan, 1945), 3–14, 218–47; *Darkness at Noon*, Daphne Hardy, trans. (New York: Modern Library, 1941); George Orwell, *Nineteen Eighty-Four* (New York: Harcourt Brace, 1949).

20 E.M. Forster, "What I Believe," *Two Cheers for Democracy* (London: Arnold, 1951), 79.

21 John Stuart Mill, *On Liberty* (Chicago: Regnery, 1955), 18.

22 Perry Miller, "The Location of American Religious Freedom," *Religion and Freedom of Thought* (New York: Doubleday, 1954), 15–16.

23 Quoted by Dan Wilson, *Promise of Deliverance* (Wallingford, Pa.: Pendle Hill, 1951), 20.

24 Martin Buber, *Good and Evil: Two Interpretations*, Ronald Gregor Smith, trans. (New York: Scribner, 1953), 142.

25 Martin Buber, *The Legend of the Baal-Shem*, Maurice S. Friedman, trans. (New York: Harper, 1955), 41.

26 See David Riesman, *op. cit.*, 278–97.

27 Sylvia Ashton-Warner, *Teacher* (New York: Simon and Schuster, 1963), 96.

28 Quoted by Victor Gollancz, *Man and God* (Boston: Houghton Mifflin, 1951), 395.

29 Quoted by G. H. Bantock, *Freedom and Authority in Education: A Criticism of Modern Cultural and Educational Assumptions* (London: Faber & Faber, 1953), 164.

30 Arthur Miller has cited some poignant examples to show that the juvenile delinquent is not a rebel, but rather a strict conformist who runs in packs and is afraid of solitude. "The Bored and the Violent," *Harper's*, vol. 225, no. 1350 (November, 1962), 50–56. For a vivid account of the dependence of the young gang member on the gang, see Warren Miller, *The Cool World* (Boston: Little, Brown, 1959), 9, 224.

31 Thoreau, *op. cit.*, 216.

32 Quoted by Herbert Schneider in *Dialogue on John Dewey*, Corliss Lamont, ed. (New York: Horizon Press, 1959), 75.

33 Thoreau, *op. cit.*, 95.

34 Christopher Burney, *Solitary Confinement* (London: Macmillan, 1961), 170.

35 Howard Thurman, *Mysticism and the Experience of Love* (Wallingford, Pa.: Pendle Hill, 1961), 7–8.

36 Philip Rieff, "The American Transference: From Calvin to Freud," *Atlantic* (July, 1961), 105–107.

37 Douglas V. Steere, "The Christian Approach to World Religions," *Friends Journal*, (August 4, 1956), 6.

38 James Baldwin, "The Black Boy Looks at the White Boy," *Nobody Knows My Name: More Notes of a Native Son* (New York: Dell, 1962), 218–19.

39 See John Macmurray, "Freedom in the Personal Nexus," *Freedom: Its Meaning*, Ruth N. Anshen, ed. (New York: Harcourt Brace, 1940), 517–23, for a stimulating discussion of this distinction. The present argument is based partly on Macmurray's ideas.

40 See Gerald Heard, "Can This Drug Enlarge Man's Mind?" *Psychedelic Review*, vol. I, no. 1 (June, 1963), 7–17.

41 Alan W. Watts, "The Individual as Man/World," *Psychedelic Review*, vol. I, no. 1 (June, 1963), 55–65.

[42] The following description draws largely on Harold Loukes, *Friends Face Reality* (London: Bannisdale Press, 1954), 109–10.

[43] *Ibid.*

[44] Herbert Read, *Education Through Art* (London: Faber & Faber, 1943), 5.

[45] The experiment of the Israeli kibbutz is a challenging direction that deserves careful examination. Bettelheim claims that the products of its communal education are in important ways superior to the products of American upbringing and education. Bruno Bettelheim, "Does Communal Education Work? The Case of the Kibbutz," *Commentary* (February, 1962), 117–25. See also Melford E. Spiro, *Children of the Kibbutz* (Cambridge, Mass.: Harvard University Press, 1958).

[46] O. Hobart Mowrer, *The Crisis in Psychiatry and Religion* (Princeton, N.J.: Van Nostrand, 1961), 180.

[47] Harry Emerson Fosdick, *The Living of These Days: An Autobiography* (New York: Harper, 1956), 306.

[48] See John Dewey, "Authority and Social Change," reprinted as "Science and the Future of Society," in *Intelligence in the Modern World*, Joseph Ratner, ed. (New York: Random House, 1939), 343–63.

[49] A. Victor Murray, *The State and the Church in a Free Society* (Cambridge University Press, 1958), 138.

[50] James Baldwin, "A Talk to Teachers," *Saturday Review*, December 21, 1963, 42.

[51] John Wild, *Existence and the World of Freedom* (Englewood Cliffs, N. J.: Prentice-Hall, 1963), 189.

[52] Roger J. Williams, *Free and Unequal: The Biological Basis of Individual Liberty* (Austin: University of Texas Press, 1953), 73.

[53] Gordon W. Allport, *Becoming: Basic Considerations for a Psychology of Personality* (New Haven: Yale University Press, 1955), 23.

[54] Harrison E. Salisbury, *The Shook-up Generation* (New York: Harper, 1958), 138–39.

[55] See F.H. Heinemann, *Existentialism and the Modern Predicament* (London: Black, 1953), 147.

[56] Helmut Gollwitzer, *Unwilling Journey: A Diary from Russia* (London: S.C.M. Press, 1953), 96.

[57] Gabriel Marcel, *The Mystery of Being* (London: Harvill Press, 1950–51), 2 vols., II, 8.

V

THE AUTHORITY OF EXCELLENCE
The Freedom to Enjoy Equal Opportunities

I EXCELLENCE

Excellence and Democracy

Democracy introduces more possibilities than does a totalitarian system. On the one hand, it makes possible the release of greater and purer forces of energy and creativity. On the other hand, however, it also makes possible the release and spread of the forces of baseness, vulgarity, triviality, and shoddiness. It offers greater freedom to rise but greater freedom to fall. The relative absence of external authority means greater opportunity to be self-ruled and greater opportunity to be self-indulgent. It is for this reason that democracy is constantly faced with the threats of vulgarization, loss of quality, and leveling down to a low common standard. Precisely these threats have impelled some critics to demand a continuous emphasis on excellence as an essential feature of a healthy democracy.

One of the most eloquent of these critics is Sir Richard Livingstone, who has warned:

The spread of democracy will not help us; indeed it makes our task more difficult. To call the masses into power is to dilute existing culture. They must be humoured and satisfied; attention must be paid to their interests and tastes, and if these are trifling, ignoble and base, the level of civilization will fall. . . . We have called a new class on to the stage, but done little to prepare it for its role.[1]

He has called our era the "Age without Standards," and said:

The life without standards exists in all epochs, but it is the peculiar danger of a rich society at whose feet every kind of facility, distraction and

167

pleasure are poured in indiscriminate profusion. . . . Of all lives the life without standards is the most ignoble and barren, sweet in the mouth but bitter in the belly.[2]

G. K. Chesterton once described the British working man as profoundly uninterested in the equality of man but deeply interested in the inequality of racehorses. Livingstone would no doubt attribute such a state of affairs to the trivializing and vulgarizing of proletarian life, the result of the failure of the educated to provide adequate cultural leadership. It is not necessary to accept or reject Livingstone's concepts of *noblesse oblige* and the "dilution" of culture (the concept of cultural leadership will be dealt with, more relevantly, later) to recognize the validity in his warning that unless the process of democratization is accompanied by a constant regard for standards of excellence the gravest cultural, educational, and social dangers impend.

Discrimination and the Vision of Excellence

If it is precisely in a democracy that we need to maintain the vision of excellence, it is precisely in a democracy—apparently paradoxically—that we need to encourage the practice of *discrimination*. The kind of discrimination that people in a democracy need to develop is that which enables one to distinguish the excellent from the second-rate, the lasting from the transient, the authentic from the phony. It is another part of the apparent paradox that one must become more aware of *inequalities* —but this is a feature of the development of a critical sense. It is necessary to be prepared to pass *judgment*, that is, not to accept all things as equally good. But this judgment should not be capricious or casual: rather, it should be based on study and knowledge, it should be relevant, and it should be combined with an openness to new or unusual forms of excellence—those that depart from traditional standards of worth.

The pursuit of excellence can be carried on only at a cost. The cost is not, as is often supposed, the sacrifice of the ideal of equality (the relationship between these two goals will be discussed later) but the sacrifice of a degree of ease and comfort. If we seek to encourage excellence in our children it will involve introducing them to challenge and difficulty, even seeing them experience failure if they are not giving enough of themselves to the task. It will involve also the nurture of a measure of discontent: if people are satisfied with themselves as they are they will not fully discover the talents and potentialities that lie dormant with them. For us to understand ourselves and achieve whatever brand and level of excellence is possible for us we must be *stretched*: excellence is not reached by staying within the cocoon of present performance.

The vision of excellence is a double vision. It must be conceived in terms of the closeness to perfection with which the task itself is carried out and in terms of the measure of one's relevant talent and energy that is given to the task. The excellent worker gives of his best to the material, or person, or situation. For the teacher, for example, this means trying consistently to achieve excellence in teaching—with all kinds of students and in all sorts of circumstances. It is inconsistent with this attitude, therefore, to classify a student as "hopeless," or to give up trying with a certain group, or to give one's second-best because one judges the students to be second-best.

Restraints on Excellence

Societies are apt to pay lip service to the goal of excellence while they organize themselves in ways that hinder its development. Some restraints on excellence are inevitable, but many are deliberate, and we should be aware of their cost.

The principle of hereditary privilege is such a restraint. In a society where hereditary privilege is the rule, one's status, power, and chances of achieving desires are largely determined by one's position in a particular family, class, or caste. Natural ability is important only within strict limits. Men of talent may be kept in subordinate positions because they are born into an unprivileged group. Such unrewarded individuals often contribute to the accretion of a mass of frustration, which provides material easily ignited by the spark of violent revolution. Prerevolutionary France failed to see the need for due outlet and reward for all talents and paid a heavy price. Plato, in the *Republic*, showed greater wisdom in that, while leadership was to be based mainly on heredity, room was to be found at the top for the unusually able child of lowly birth. The English aristocracy have similarly recharged themselves from the lower classes for centuries, and as a result have retained an unrivaled hold on political power.

In "democratic" America, apart from the hereditary privilege inherent in the racial caste system, a ubiquitous restraint has been the prevailing attitude of conformity. "The idea that men are created free and equal," wrote Riesman, "is both true and misleading: men are created different; they lose their social freedom and their individual autonomy in seeking to become like each other." [3] It has been widely observed that there is in contemporary America an often forceful pressure to hide or depreciate one's talents. One must avoid arousing envy or resentment by an obvious display of intelligence or ability. One must not threaten another's self-esteem. In this atmosphere, said Gardner, "deliberately slovenly speech, the studied fumble and the calculated inelegance have achieved the status of minor art forms." [4]

Affluence, despite its benefits, represents another possible hindrance to the nurture of excellence. The affluent society easily and dangerously develops attitudes of comfort and ease that prompt a complacent satisfaction with the *status quo* and an unimaginative inability to envision anything better than material affluence. Such affluent insulation, moreover, discourages the development of the sensitivity to perceive that many people all over the world are not affluent, and that unprecedented heights of achievement and sharing will be necessary before they can reach a decent level of material well-being.

In America, one of the most serious restraints on excellence has been the fact that private affluence has been combined with public stinginess. Americans have never been prepared to curtail private consumption for the sake of adequate public investment in education. The picture of an unnecessarily large, vulgarly opulent, uselessly high-powered automobile driving past a dilapidated, overcrowded, understaffed, slum school is a sad commentary on a major American problem. Frederick Rudolph, in his inquiry into who financed the nineteenth-century American college and supported it through its days of infancy and immaturity, has concluded that it was the professors, and that it was done at a tremendous cost to the intellectual quality of American life. The American nineteenth-century college, Rudolph has shown, developed through systematic faculty exploitation, which enabled it to keep down both faculty salaries and student fees. In the process, it robbed a profession of dignity and alienated a large body of American intellectuals from the mainstream of American life, to their mutual impoverishment.[5] More recently, we might cite the attitude of many toward the Higher Horizons Program in New York City, which has achieved dramatic results with culturally deprived children by providing a high proportion of staff to pupils, more guidance staff, many field trips and visits, and other services. Detroit, a city with one of the worst Negro slum-school problems in the country, sent observers. When they discovered that the program cost an extra $50 per annum per pupil (about a third of what many people spend on tobacco) they decided against it as being too expensive.

If we are to break through this barrier to individual excellence, there must be federal educational intervention, planning, and aid on a scale never attempted in America. We are still suffering from the hangover of an anachronistic *laissez-faire* attitude, which permits us to exploit the young through educational deprivation today, just as it permitted the nineteenth-century employer to exploit his workers. Galbraith [6] and others have shown the necessity in modern society of regarding education as an investment—indeed, the most important investment; perhaps it could be more important in establishing an effective national position than many military expenditures. Educated people should be regarded as a country's capital, not its expenses.

There is in America an unreasoning fear of federal control that draws carefully selective and misleading analogies from countries that are in crucial ways different from America and, at the same time, ignores the evidence of this country's own history. The Federal Government has already intervened heavily in education—through land-grant contributions, the G.I. Bill of Rights, the National Defense Education Act—without showing the least inclination to control. National concern and support for education on a large scale are now the only means of effectively reducing valueless inequalities of material circumstance. Suffering, hardship, and deprivation *can* be stimulants to growth and creativity, but more often they are depressants. The cost, in terms of unused, unexplored talents, of permitting avoidable deprivation to continue is out of proportion to the possible learning that men might gain from such misfortunes.

The purpose of such national concern should, of course, be to protect and support the weak and nurture the able, not to crush all into the same Procrustean mold. We have the warning example of some trade-union practices, which themselves constitute restraints on individual excellence by putting limits on what a man may produce and by demanding equal treatment for all irrespective of ability. But there is no ineluctable reason why greater federal intervention should lead to greater uniformity. One can plan for diversity as well as for uniformity. Indeed, there are good reasons why a national department of education would be willing to leave more decisions to teachers and schools than would a local school committee.

In this endeavor to support and nurture all the human talent we have, one note of warning must be interposed. The emergence of a society into a state of great technological complexity means that it needs ever greater supplies of trained manpower. But there is a danger of a debasement of man in thinking of him in terms of manpower. He becomes conceived of as a resource or commodity useful for raising national production, winning hot or cold wars, or achieving other national goals. One of the most eloquent fictional accounts of this threat is John Hersey's *The Child Buyer*,[7] which constitutes a formidable attack on the attempt to use children as weapons, to process and store human talent for profit and defense. If a free society ceases to regard each individual as an end in himself, then it has lost its chief claim to distinction and virtue.

Excellence and the Mass Media

Every society must be constantly examining the kinds of excellence it is honoring. It may be honoring types of talent that do not serve it well and neglecting some whose loss would be grievous. No country is so rich that it can afford to squander its resources by encouraging trivial or pernicious talents (such as are often seen on television or in football stadiums) at the expense of creative talents that could nourish the whole of society (such as those of artists, musicians, and writers).

The problem is greatly aggravated in a society where commercialism, advertising, and the mass media of communication are influential or dominating features. In such societies there is a persistent intensification of the threats of vulgarity, triviality, a low level of conformity, and other symptoms of the debasement of standards. "Where commercialism is given its head in an inappropriate setting," wrote Jenkins, "as in its television services and its burial arrangements, it achieves a fatuous vulgarity without parallel in all the world." [8] Advertising is usually a trivializing influence because it appeals to the superficial elements of human attention in its attempts to stimulate quick response. The aim of commerce and advertising is not to sell what the consumer needs or what would be best for him but merely to sell: the standard by which they abide is that of the successful sale.

In an era of mass production—of goods and messages—it is in the narrrowly conceived interest of the advertiser that people should become more alike. Eccentricity and nonconformity are harmful to him because he depends on reaching, quickly and easily, the largest possible number of people and persuading them to like his message and buy his product. He must, therefore, emphasize those things that are common to large numbers of people, and the more he can make people alike the larger will be his potential market.

What are the responsibilities for the fostering of excellence of those who control the mass media of communication in such a setting? Should the press, radio, television, and other media lead or follow the public? Should they form cultural standards or reflect them? In America, it is often claimed that the task of these media is to give the public what it *wants*, and that it would be undemocratic and authoritarian for them to give the public what they think is *good* for it. This argument represents a dangerous irresponsibility: it holds a grain of truth, which it uses misleadingly to disguise a narrow self-interest. It is an approach that gains more readers, listeners, and viewers, that sells more newspapers, magazines, and products; but it does so by abandoning the responsibility of leadership that their undeniable power thrusts on the mass media.

Responsible leadership does not mean patronizing the public, talking down to it, or exploiting it; nor does it mean trying to impose one's own ideas, beliefs, and attitudes. It means adhering faithfully to one's own professional standards of excellence, to standards of truth and impartiality. It means respecting the tastes and attitudes of the public, but bringing new ideas to widen its horizons; presenting a wide variety of viewpoints, but encouraging the public to judge them itself.

II EQUALITY AND DISCRIMINATION

The Meaning of Equality

The concept of equality is an important but often underexamined factor in many of the principal controversies of contemporary education. Slums and suburbs, social-class influences on learning, the neighborhood school, the integrated classroom, excellence, growing up female or absurd—the list of topics that embrace the concept of equality as a vital component is virtually endless.

What might it mean to say that all men are created equal? Clearly, it is easier to answer this question negatively than positively. It is not difficult to adumbrate what it does *not* mean. Little investigation is needed to establish that we are not created equal in certain attributes: physique, appearance, color, race, sex. And there are strong indications that we should add other attributes: temperament, energy, sensitivity, and certain kinds of aptitude and ability. Most people outside of communist countries (and many inside) would agree that, however much or little heredity governs our potentialities, it is sufficient to make us all different.[9] It is arguable that the most important human datum is that all men are created unequal.

However, it might be that to say that all men are created equal is to make not a descriptive statement but a prescriptive statement. That is, although men are not *created* equal in all respects, nevertheless they should be *treated* equally in all respects.[10] But a moment's reflection will convince us that we do not really want this. We do not, for example, consider all men and women deserving of equal freedom to teach. We try to reserve this freedom for those who have shown they possess certain abilities and have undergone certain training. Furthermore, once the teacher is qualified, we do not want him to treat all his students equally in the sense of providing the same educational experiences for children of all ages, any more than we want doctors to prescribe the same medicine for all illnesses, or governments to impose the same taxes on all incomes. As Aristotle pointed out, it is no more just to treat unequals equally than to treat equals unequally.

The equality that men claim for themselves and others is not, then, an equality of talent or merit, or a uniformity of treatment under all circumstances; it is an equality of political and legal *rights*. It was equality in the sense of political rights that was proclaimed by the liberals and radicals of the late eighteenth and early nineteenth centuries, by the American and French revolutionaries, and by the English reformers. Political rights are often held to be due to all equally, although many countries (such as Switzerland, South Africa, and Rhodesia) have not yet reached this position, and all countries impose some qualifications, such as age, nationality, citizenship, and legal freedom.

Moreover, the provision of formal *rights* is different from providing a genuine *opportunity*. This difference was underlined by Anatole France when he suggested that equality before the law meant that the rich as well as the poor were forbidden to steal bread or sleep under bridges. It is possible for me to possess a legal right that I cannot in fact exercise because of attendant social or economic circumstances. And drastic social reforms may be necessary before this right can be made effective.[11]

When we advocate equality of rights or opportunities we advocate nothing until we make clear what right or opportunity we think should be exercised. Equality is an empty concept until invested with some substantive content. This is a function of its comparative nature. Equality implies comparison, and two things can be compared only if they possess a common quality. We cannot compare an orange and a lemon: we can compare only one or more of their qualities, such as size, shape, weight, color, or taste. To compare two men we must select a quality that they both possess, such as height, intelligence, running speed, and so on. Only thus can we talk of superiority, inferiority, and equality. Comparison requires analysis and abstraction.

Dorothy Lee has pointed out that this approach to the concept of equality is cultural: not all people compare in this way. In some societies it is not true that some are superior to others, because both the notion of comparison and the practice of choosing a quality out of the totality of the individual are notably absent. She mentioned the Trobrianders of the South Pacific, the Wintu Indians of California, and the Lovedu of South Africa as cultures that have this view of "natural equality;" the uniqueness of each man is recognized, and an absolute respect for all replaces comparison, competition, and achievement assessment.[12]

Accepting our cultural limitations for the moment, it must further be recognized that, just as equality itself is an empty concept, equality of opportunity means nothing until we know what it is that we seek the opportunity to do. Nor should we expect equality of opportunity to lead to equality. Greater equality of educational opportunity at the beginning of the formal educational process, for example, may lead to greater inequalities of performance at the end. Unless we attach some substantive content to the concept of equality of opportunity, it is quite possible to both attack and defend a particular program in the name of this cause. The English tripartite system of secondary education, for example, can be defended on the grounds that it provides different programs relevant to genuine differences in children, thus providing equal opportunity for all, rather than forcing everyone into the rigidity of a common program. Equally, it can be *attacked* on the grounds that it perpetuates class differences, discriminates unfairly in favor of the child with academic leanings, and discriminates unfairly against the child from a poor or unintellectual home background. Clearly, neither equality nor equality of opportunity is a self-justifying term. If we wish to think clearly about these concepts, we must invest them with substantive content and then be prepared to examine each case carefully.

Fundamental Equality

(Equitable – better term

Belief in equality has been assimilated by many systems, including utilitarianism, theories of natural rights, and various religious doctrines. But, as Isaiah Berlin has pointed out,[13] it has entered them less by way of logical connection than by psychological affinity or because supporters of these doctrines believed in equality for its own sake. When we demand equality for all (in the absence of good reason for discrimination), we imply that there is something in human nature that supports this. This widespread assumption of a kind of "fundamental equality" among men is sufficiently important and consequential to warrant some examination.

Since this idea is often thought to be embedded in the Western tradition, it is important to note that the Greeks and Romans did not hold it. The Greek citizen viewed as most precious his freedom, which for him meant to be in a class superior to a slave. The Greeks, it is true, emphasized intellect and reason and regarded all men as having the potentiality for engaging in rational activity; but the quality of individual intellects varies enormously, and reason is at least as much a divisive and differentiating factor in human life as it is a uniting and equalizing one.

The major component of the Western tradition that gives support to the idea of fundamental equality has been Christianity. Christians believe that the doctrine of the Fatherhood of God implies a brotherhood of man. That is, all children of God are of equal concern to him, despite their differences, just as in a good family the parent loves his children equally yet uniquely. The intelligent child is valued for his intelligence but the dull child matters just as much. This Christian position must be accepted on faith, if at all. We cannot *prove* that the Fatherhood of God means that all his children should be regarded equally. God may intend us all to be valued differently.

This religious belief has received some support from psychiatric studies. The work of C.G. Jung, in particular, points to certain common features of all men, revealed in explorations below the conscious level. His discovery of recurring archetypal images in his patients and his hypothesis of the "collective unconscious" lend weight to the assumption that fundamental equalizing links exist among mankind.

There is a link between the concept of fundamental equality and the concept of human uniqueness. In their totalities, men cannot be considered superior or inferior because their uniqueness makes them immeasurable and, hence, incomparable. How does one compare, for example, an inefficient clerk who is a thoughtful husband and kind father with a brilliant physicist who is selfish and greedy? Lee has suggested that democracy derives from the postulate of the intrinsic dignity, infinite worth, and incomparable and ultimate nature of man. When we measure man and try to evaluate him on the basis of comparison with others, we do not regard him as infinite and do not value him as of ultimate worth.[14] Comparison begins not with the individual but with an external principle or standard. This, she has suggested, is at variance with the idea of democracy, which can be realized "only when human dignity is valued without measure, and when the rights of others are respected in their integrity, without comparison or utilitarian calculus." [15]

Fundamental equality is manifested most clearly in human relationships at their best. It is the immeasurable reciprocation of a good friendship or marriage. Such a relationship recognizes the equality inherent in our mutual dependence on one another. It recognizes, in Karl Mannheim's words, that "all embody the *same ontological principle of human-ness*." [16] All other members of the human race share with me a fundamental kinship, the nature of which cannot be fully explained or measured in quantitative terms. "The equality in nature among men," said Jacques Maritain, "consists in their concrete communion in the mystery of the human species." [17] At best, this type of equality is expressed in the love of one person for another. "Equality," said Reinhold Niebuhr, "is love in terms of logic." [18]

Inequalities and Discrimination

Even those who believe in this fundamental equality among men, however, do not want to treat all men alike in all respects. The most extreme egalitarians recognize, if only tacitly, that some differences among human qualities justify treating their possessors differently. It is revealing in this connection to examine the distinction between the words "difference" and "inequality." When we are speaking of the treatment accorded to people, the word "inequality" has usually a pejorative sound about it. "Difference" is at least neutral in connotation. But the two words can refer to the same thing. We may want to defend an inequality in treatment, but if we do we usually call it a difference. The words will be used here as synonyms, although it is recognized that they have different emotional content.

Most people favor the extension of inequalities of treatment to whole groups of people under certain circumstances. For example, few people would want to see all forms of discrimination between men and women removed. We willingly tolerate the exclusion of women from certain occupations, such as coal mining, heavy construction work, professional football, and so on, presumably on the grounds of relevant physical differences between the sexes, although some would add social and cultural grounds.

We must also expect to suffer certain inequalities of treatment or opportunity because of the age and the society in which we happen to live. To a degree, we must accept the contemporary preferences of our society, and it may be that we are out of luck—born too early or too late. If my talents are for head-shrinking or bullfighting or lyre playing, it is unlikely that they will be granted wide opportunity for development in twentieth-century America. Nor can the young man or woman with academic talent and professional aspirations who lives in a technologically undeveloped country expect the same opportunity to attain his vocational aspirations as his counterpart in a technologically advanced country. Failure to appreciate this fundamental inequality leads to much frustration among Asian and African university graduates.

In education, we often deliberately discriminate in favor of certain groups and defend this as a justifiable inequality. For example, we are prepared to discriminate in favor of blind, deaf, crippled, and mentally defective children, in terms of the amount of money spent per child, teacher-pupil ratios, the building of special schools, and so on. How far is it justifiable to go in this sort of discriminatory treatment? What sort of minority groups can claim specially favorable educational treatment? Gifted children? Left-handed children? Jews? Lower-class children? Blue-eyed children? Slow learners? And what about remedial discrimination in favor of groups previously discriminated against? Is it justifiable, for example, to provide Negroes with unequally favorable educational opportunities, on the grounds of past disadvantages? Galbraith has suggested [19] that it is the responsibility of the affluent society to see that the misfortunes of parents (deserved or undeserved) are perpetuated as little as possible in their children. This may involve a compensating treatment, which would invest heavily in the children of disadvantaged groups to give them a good chance of reaching maturity without marked handicap.

Most difficulties in the realm of equality of opportunity arise when we try to decide *how far* we should go in compensating for inequalities or in equalizing opportunities. There are wide differences of opinion concerning the factors we should try to equalize. Most advanced countries (the United States being a remarkable exception) try to reduce avoidable health inequalities through state health services. Some schools insist on a school uniform to remove inequalities in dress.[20] If the value of equalization is high enough in our system of priorities, there is almost no end to the measures we can take to further this end. We could, for example, increase equality of opportunity by removing all children from their parents at birth and raising them in state nurseries, so that differences in home background would be eliminated; by abolishing all fees for education at all levels, from kindergarten through graduate school; by removing all hidden costs of education by providing all books and equipment and paying parents who keep their children in school beyond the statutory leaving age an amount equivalent to what the children might earn if working; and by paying college students a stipend of at least as much as they could learn elsewhere.[21] Needless to say, some of these steps might conflict with other values we hold. How to decide among these competing claims is a problem to be discussed in the next section.

Analysis of equality of educational opportunity often concerns the treatment of children of different intellectual aptitudes. The whole structure of curriculum planning, testing, grouping, and the application of standards is fraught with complexities for the concept of equality. It is clear to most people by now that equality of opportunity does not mean identity of treatment for all. If a slow child is given a program that fully stretches and challenges him intellectually, and a bright child is given the same program, which bores and stupefies him, they do not enjoy equal opportunities. Even when we put children of different abilities into different groups we do not remove inequalities, for there is a tendency to treat all members of any one group alike, whereas in fact they are all different.

We may deliberately insist on inequality of treatment of different students to increase equality of opportunity. For example, we may demand that an able student achieve a higher level of work to pass than a less able student. The passing grade really signifies "performance in relation to ability," and the pass of the able student represents a higher measure of achievement than the pass of the less able student. We might defend this by arguing that the same absolute standard for all would mean that the weak students would not enjoy equal opportunities because they would be constantly penalized by failure.

The provision of special courses for students with special talents or interests can be viewed as another way of increasing equality of educational opportunity. Business, secretarial, and auto-mechanics courses are often provided in high school, for example. But how far should we go in providing such courses? What about the student who wants to be trained as a beautician or mortician or jockey? Is he being unfairly discriminated against if we fail to provide special training for him? In a country like America, where local control of education prevails, opportunities of this kind are usually determined by what the local majority judges to be appropriate. There is no uniformity in this matter: opportunities are predominantly affected by local employment possibilities. But it should be noted that the proliferation of special courses in schools makes it ever more difficult to justify ceasing to provide new courses at any particular point.

Some institutions frankly follow discriminatory admission policies and defend their practices as justified. Many schools openly declare that they give special consideration to applications from children of alumni. That is, they are encouraging a hereditary system. This is certainly not furthering equality of opportunity among all potential applicants, but it can be defended on a number of grounds. For example, it might foster elements of continuity in the school, encourage support from parents, develop school spirit and tone, and so on. These consequences have to be weighed against the opposing consideration of equality of opportunity.

In other words, equality is not an absolute value; it must take its chance among other competing values. If we want to weigh these various considerations, one of the central tasks is to establish some working criteria by which we can justify the practice of specific discrimination in favor of or against certain individuals and groups.

Criteria for Warrantable Discrimination

We must take care to distinguish between an equal right to education and a right to equal education. Richard Wollheim has suggested that it is the principle from which the former is derived—that is, what he has called the principle of Proportional as opposed to Quantitative Equality—that belongs integrally to the liberal tradition.[22]

Clearly, we do not want identical educational experiences for all. More-over, we must distinguish between equality of *outcome* and equality of *procedure*. Whatever educational policy we advocate, it would be foolish to demand that all children come out of the educational process equal. Rather, we are concerned that equal procedures should be fol-lowed during the educational process, unless good reason can be given for departing from this general principle. We are concerned that pro-cedures are, and appear to be, just and fair. But how can we judge whether they are just and fair? The purpose of this section is to explore this question.

As we have already suggested, we do not want to promote equality of opportunity at all costs. We do not want to arrange our procedures so that all inequalities will be removed. Some educationally significant inequalities, such as sex and race, cannot be removed by educational means. We are stuck with the inexorable fact of diversity. Furthermore, some inequalities, such as color of eyes, are trivial and can be ignored for educational purposes. Again, some inequalities are important, but the cost of removing them would be too high in terms of other values.

However, we meet some inequalities on the borderline, where it is very difficult to decide what, if anything, should be done about them. We might consider the distance from school as such a borderline area. If one child lives one mile from school and another child lives two miles from the school, the first is at something of an advantage, but normally we do not think of compensating for this inequality. However, if a white child may go to school a mile away and a Negro child in the same area must travel 15 miles to a Negro school, we might well con-sider that the matter has crossed the borderline and warrants some change or compensation.

We must recognize that neither complete equality nor complete equality of opportunity can be attained in education. A reasonable as-piration would be to attempt to compensate for natural disadvantages and to remove differential disabilities in pursuing educational aims up to the point where the process becomes too costly in terms of the sacrifice of other values.

If we accept the notion of fundamental equality we are impelled toward a position maintaining that members of the class of human be-ings should be treated alike unless there is a sufficient reason for treat-ing them differently. Equality seems to need no explanation: inequal-ity usually does. If we propose to treat men alike, there is a sense in which this is regarded as self-justifying and natural. If we propose to treat men differently, we need to explain our actions, to account for them by some special justification.[23] In other words, the burden of proof lies on the one who would discriminate. If no grounds are produced, the assumption is that there will be equal treatment.

What sort of grounds would be considered adequate? [24] A prime criterion would be that the proposed difference in treatment should be *relevant* to genuine differences in the person who is to experience the discrimination. The reasons we adduce must be relevant to the differences accorded: they must not be based on whim, desire, greed, or prejudice. If we treat people differently it should be because they differ in an important way that is relevant to the difference we make. The administration of a professional school, for example, might warrantably discriminate against those who fail an entrance examination (that is, by refusing to admit them) in the interest of maintaining high standards in the school. This can be defended on the grounds that the refusal to admit a student is relevant to his demonstrated failure to show promise that he would achieve the required standards if admitted. Hence, it can be demanded that examinations for admission should test for qualities that are relevant to the studies to be pursued.[25]

Another criterion would be that the degree of discrimination should be *proportionate*, as far as we can judge it, to the degree of difference in the relevant respect. This cannot be quantitatively measured, but this fact does not permit us to make it purely arbitrary. Reasons should be given for the degree of difference and these can then be assessed and criticized.

This brings us to a third criterion: the difference in treatment should be *public*. The relevant criteria for discrimination should be publicly spelled out. Unless the procedures of discrimination are known by all we cannot plan or predict. Nor should they be vaguely stated, for then they are open to all sorts of interpretations. Educational institutions that exclude certain applicants should give clear and precise reasons for their exclusions, so that the public can criticize the criteria used. Discrimination that is not explained leaves the door open to prejudice and favoritism. Our judgment of a quota system, for example, will be much affected by whether it is public or secret.

Finally, the discriminatory treatment should be *consistent*. If we discriminate against or in favor of a person because he fits certain criteria, we should discriminate similarly against or in favor of all others who fit the same criteria. All cases should conform to the criteria enunciated and there should not be particular exceptions. If a particular case seems unfair, the general criteria should be examined and, if necessary, changed, so that the particular case can be justly treated in the framework of a general rule of discrimination.

In all of this, we are not advocating greater equality of treatment in any absolute sense. We are advocating that we maintain inequalities but change the type of discrimination. We suggest that some inequalities are unjust or unreasonable or inappropriate because their application is irrelevant or disproportionate or secret or inconsistent, and we suggest new inequalities based on relevant, proportionate, public, consistent usage. We are trying, in sum, to make discriminations more reasonable.

III THREE DIFFERENTIATING FACTORS

Race

Racial discrimination in education is a fact. The question to be explored here is whether it is justified. In America this problem is epitomized by the fact that there are usually educational penalties attached to being a Negro. We shall not attempt to grapple with the problem of what might be meant by the concept of "race." This is much too complex a matter to be dealt with in this space.[26] If we were all thoroughly informed with the knowledge that is available about the concept of race, the so-called "racial" problem would without doubt disappear. But since this happy state does not yet exist, we shall speak as if it were possible to say exactly what a race is, and as if Negroes and whites were scientifically distinguishable.

It is clear that the educational discrimination against the American Negro is closely tied to the fact of segregation. The United States Supreme Court has decided (Brown v. Board of Education, 1954) that "in the field of public education the doctrine of 'separate but equal' has no place. Separate educational facilities are inherently unequal." [27] In its judgment, the Court cited the authority of psychological and sociological research to show that separating the races is interpreted as denoting the inferiority of the Negro group. A sense of inferiority affects the motivation of a child to learn. Segregation therefore, tends to retard the educational and mental development of Negro children and to deprive them of some of the benefits they would receive in an integrated school system.

The Supreme Court, of course, was trying to judge not whether whites and Negroes should go to school together, but whether they should go to school together *according to the Constitution*. The task of the Court was to interpret the Fourteenth Amendment, which conferred citizenship on all people born or naturalized in the United States and prohibited the states from abridging the privileges and immunities of citizens or from denying equal protection of the laws. The interpretation of the law does not, in itself, tell us what is or is not morally justifiable. For this we have to determine whether race is an *educationally relevant factor* as a basis for discrimination and segregation.

There has been an interesting reversal in the liberal position on this in recent years, corresponding somewhat to the process of legal desegregation. Until recently, and still today in segregated areas in the South, there has been a tendency for the liberal to say that race should not be regarded as educationally relevant, that children should go to their neighborhood school without consideration of race. Now, however, especially in Northern cities, there are many who would use race as an educationally relevant factor and move children out of their neighborhoods to attend racially mixed schools. We must examine both the short-term and long-term implications of these and other recommendations.

Let us examine first the claim that race is an educationally relevant factor because of the Negroes' innate inferiority in intelligence, which makes it inappropriate for them to go to school with the superior whites. This field of inquiry has attracted much research, but most of it has been inconclusive. Many studies have claimed to prove that Negroes *are* innately inferior in intelligence to whites, but the studies have many defects. Some failed to control socio-economic influences, some did not eliminate the influence of the Southern milieu and education, few considered the students' cultural background, some used tests that had not been sufficiently validated, and most failed to consider the motivational and cognitive structure of the students and their environment.[28] On the other hand, it is virtually impossible to prove positively that Negroes are *not* innately inferior in intelligence to whites. Too many variables—such as the effects of upbringing, social class, schooling, cultural and motivational differences, imperfect tests and test administration, lack of agreement on the meaning of "intelligence," and so on—make the task insuperably formidable.

Moreover, even if we could prove it, we would have proved very little in the context of the present problem, for the claims for separation are made on grounds of intelligence rather than race. It would be a simple matter to test all children and assign them to schools in such a way as to make the schools intellectually as homogeneous as possible, if that is really what we want to do. However, the segregation would then be made by a criterion other than race, whatever the subsequent correlation between race and test performance turned out to be.

It is sometimes argued that race is an educationally relevant criterion because Negroes are *morally* inferior and will adversely affect whites if brought together with them in school. It is true that Negroes show up badly on various rough moral criteria like the incidence of crime, delinquency, drug-addiction, vagrancy, and so on. But it is impossible to say with our present knowledge whether this is a product of race or of poverty, living conditions, education, parental circumstances, and other nonracial factors. Moreover, it is by no means certain that we want moral homogeneity in schools, even if that were possible. It might well be, if there are children of different moral standards, that we would want deliberately to bring them together in a controlled situation like that of a school.

The United States as a nation (in contrast to remnants of reaction in the South) has turned its official face consciously against the use of the criterion of race to keep Negro and white children *apart*. What about the use of this criterion, however, to bring them together? This matter is more complex and takes us into the shadowy obscurities of *de facto* segregation. The problem is especially acute in the large Northern cities, where legal integration does not mean *de facto* integration, because school district lines follow residence lines, which follow color lines. Should we accept the degree of educational segregation that is determined by housing segregation or should we transport Negro and white pupils out of their own districts to force racial integration in schools?

Some of the arguments against enforced integration are: much time is wasted in traveling; bringing whites and Negroes together may increase mutual contempt rather than mutual respect; it may result in having all whites in college-preparatory classes and all Negroes in vocational classes; it is associated with the traditional and mistaken American faith in the power of education to achieve social reforms that are beyond its competence; it is difficult to make a fair selection of the students who are to be transported and impossible to persuade the selected white parents to accept the decision. Some of the counter arguments are: enforced integration *has* changed people's attitudes (for example, in the United States Army); America is a multiracial society, and the school may be the only place to bring the full implications of this fact to millions of children; the best way to raise the standards of education in Negro areas may be to involve the concern of white parents through their own children.

The cruel truth is that it is impossible to be both color-blind and color-conscious at the same time. That is to say, if we discriminate in favor of the Negro to ameliorate the short-term problem of his previous and present disadvantages in American society, then we are making race an educationally relevant criterion and being color-conscious. While there may be good reasons for doing this, we should recognize that we may not be thus serving our long-term aim, which should be to be color-blind in the sense of cherishing, evaluating, and educating each individual as a unique person, whatever his race.

However, many Negro leaders claim that most American whites are at present "color-blind" not because they are able to value each man for qualities more fundamental than color, but because they hide their heads from awareness of the Negroes' problems and disabilities by living in segregated, suburban, white ghettos where they and their children can grow up, go to school, live, and die without ever coming into personal contact with a Negro. To the extent that this is true, it constitutes an argument in favor of short-term, compulsory, racial integration in schools, for we may have to go through the stage of color-consciousness (in the sense of *seeing* the Negro and his problems more clearly and deeply than we do now) to make it possible for us some day to reach the stage of genuine color-blindness.

Social class

The close connection between housing segregation and educational segregation demonstrates the degree to which opportunities in school are linked with those that exist in society. Further evidence comes from an examination of the social-class influences on equality of opportunity. Social justice does not demand that all men have the same; it requires that men's inequalities stem from their individual qualities of mind, character, physique, and so on, and not from their accidental membership in a social class. Moreover, there are good reasons for attempting to organize society so that even genuine individual differences do not lead to exaggerated inequalities of privilege and opportunity. Marked class differences exert a poisonous influence in society because they foster feelings of superiority, arrogance, snobbishness, envy, and resentment; they hinder the development of wide human sympathy, common concerns and interests, and a sense of unity. In his classic plea for the reduction of marked inequalities, R.H. Tawney placed great emphasis on human relations, "of a kind that violent disparities of income and opportunity are apt to impair." [29]

In relatively open societies, the school represents a means for the able and ambitious to achieve upward social mobility. But we are just beginning to collect evidence of some of the costs of such mobility. In England, a country with an amazing capacity to withstand drastic threats to the sanctity of its class structure, a thorough recent study by Jackson and Marsden [30] has illuminated some aspects of that cost. They made an intensive study of 88 "successful" working-class children, that is, children who had passed the infamous "11+" examination, gone into a secondary grammar (college preparatory) school, and thence into some form of higher education and professional career. Many of these young men and women had developed into snobs, sometimes taking pride in retrospect in the fact that one or two boys used to come to their grammar school in cars and that fees had been charged before 1944. The majority of them were hostile to working-class movements and the trade unions. Their education typically had broken them away from their neighborhood and from their parents. Many became rigidly orthodox, ready to accommodate, tactful, suspicious of nonconformity of any kind, eager to engrain themselves in "established" society, and overly concerned with the *status quo*. Their main concern was often to forget their working-class background.[31] Sadly, even the intellectual gains that are often held up as the principal fruits of such selective and segregated schooling were often conspicuously absent. There was little intellectual development among these young people after formal schooling was finished. The investigators found a wide gap between the claims made for these pupils ("Those who can learn from books") and the extremely light recreational uses to which literacy was actually put. There had been a failure of their grammar school education to "address the whole being, not merely the apt and cognitive self; and a failure to accept that self without divesting it of the most enriching parts of family and social life." [32]

The relatively greater social mobility in American society does not always mitigate these problems—in fact, sometimes it exacerbates them. Although there are probably greater opportunities (at least for whites) to rise in American society than in European societies, the real opportunities are fewer than supposed. Since expectations are created by belief rather than reality, American life is marked by considerable disappointment and frustration. Moreover, when it is widely believed that success or failure is the result of individual talent and virtue rather than hereditary privilege or injustice, it is harder for the unsuccessful to live with the fact of their own failure.

Some of the disillusioning effects of the Higher Horizons Program illustrate some aspects of this American problem. Often the result of the program is to tear children away from family and cultural roots without providing an adequate substitute. The customary substitute is some congeries of middle-class values, but many slum children, especially Negroes, find the reality of middle-class life frustrating and disillusioning. They may want it, but they quickly find that they are not allowed fully to enjoy it. Furthermore, the guidance program focuses largely on the lure of social and financial advancement through education. This may be the only effective contemporary motivation, but, as Martin Mayer has suggested, "there is something sickening about the spectacle of a society which can reach its children's minds only through their stomachs or their vanities." [33]

Advocates of equality of educational opportunity must grasp the painful nettle represented by the fact that social class and academic success are universally linked. An important English study examined this phenomenon in a thorough analysis of the children who succeed and fail in the secondary grammar schools.[34] The study found that there is a highly positive correlation not only between social class and chances of admission of grammar school but also between social class and chances of success in the sixth form (the highest grade). That is, not only is the child of a professional man more likely to be admitted to grammar school at eleven than the child of an unskilled laborer, but the least promising children of professional men are likely to overtake the most promising children of unskilled laborers by the time they leave at eighteen.[35]

It is perhaps unpalatable but nevertheless undeniable that, if the English want their schools to operate most efficiently (in the sense of giving most return for money invested, fewest drop-outs, and so on), it would pay them to discriminate *against* bright children from poor homes and in *favor* of less bright children from wealthier and professional homes, since the latter stay in school longer and succeed better in the kind of curriculum at present offered. Needless to say, this type of efficiency is not the only criterion in determining educational policy. Nevertheless, such studies demonstrate clearly that schools, as organized at present, are predominantly middle-class institutions, and unless we are prepared to intervene on a massive scale to reduce the social and economic handicaps that penalize the lower-class child as he progresses through the school, he is going to continue to do badly academically and, often, to leave school rather than experience continual defeat.

An important part of the reason for this correlation between social class and educational success lies in the nature of the tests and examinations used to discriminate among students. The testing movement can be considered a factor encouraging the perpetuation of inequalities when it serves to classify and segregate children according to traditional academic criteria. Many studies have shown the high correlation between social class and performance on academic and intelligence tests.[36] When children are segregated according to the results of these tests, with curricula of different difficulty and type for the different groups, we find the groups tending toward social and economic homogeneity. This means that, even if curricular changes keep lower-class children in school longer, quantitative inequalities between social classes may be reduced, but qualitative inequalities are often increased. That is, a slum child does poorly on a test because he is, as a slum child, culturally deprived, and most tests—including intelligence tests—have a high cultural content. The test results are then used to put him into a curriculum or school whose program will go far toward ensuring that he will be denied entry to the occupational level that could raise him and his children from slum status.

The American public school is intended to be an instrument for compensating for certain natural disadvantages, such as cultural deprivation, ignorant and unsupporting parents, lack of medical and optical aids to learning, and so on. But the school is less effective in this compensating role than it might be, because it usually reflects the deprivations of the community in which it is placed. That is, slum schools tend to be understaffed, they have relatively poorly paid and poorly trained teachers, and they have lower per capita financial support. Social segregation means that educational inequalities compound social inequalities, because local control and financing ensure that wealthy suburbs will have schools that are better in virtually all respects than urban slum schools.[37] The public school often compares badly as a "crucible of democracy" with the private school that has a deliberate policy of selective recruitment and scholarships for students from underprivileged groups.

It would seem that little can be done about the educational inequalities that stem from social class differences until America is willing to attempt two measures that so far it has been reluctant to adopt. In the first place, there is a need for what Gunnar Myrdal has called a a new Marshall Plan for the bottom stratum of American society.[38] It is important to recognize that the "affluent society" is a term that applies only to the majority of American people. Large and important minorities are left out of this prosperity. Michael Harrington has estimated that the poor in America constitute about 25 percent of the total population: they number somewhere between 40,000,000 and 50,000,000, depending on the criterion adopted.[39] These people are liable to *continue* to be left out, because of changes in the economy. Just as there is a tendency for rich countries to get richer and poor countries to get poorer, so there is a tendency for the affluent and the poor in America to grow farther apart. This is because technological changes like automation are leading to a demand for more and more highly skilled labor and less and less unskilled and semiskilled labor. Unemployment in America is no longer cyclical but structural. There is a danger that a deep and permanent class schism will develop, with an affluent class that is concerned only with its own affluence on one side and a poor class that can do nothing for itself on the other. The needs of these poor must be clothed with effective demand by national planning and intervention in a most "un-American" manner. Otherwise they will continue to lack the power to bring their schools up to adequate standards.

Secondly, and related to the first measure, there is a need for a drastic revision of values and practices in the public school. We need, in particular, to prick the bubble of complacency that middle-class values are sacrosanct and superior: they should be examined critically and fearlessly. Students should be introduced to the facts of class differences in American life through study and field trips. Opportunities should be made for students from different class backgrounds to spend time studying in each other's schools and living in each other's homes.

Sex

When we come to discuss the problems of equality between male and female, we enter a perilous area. It is impossible to find anyone who can discuss this matter entirely objectively and dispassionately, since everyone is a member of one of the two groups involved.

The basic factor in the situation is that, so far, no mechanism has been invented that would enable men to bear children. Pregnancy, parturition, suckling, and nurturing all take time and energy. Meanwhile, men are talking politics, making laws, setting up governments, writing books, creating styles and fashions in ideas. It is in this sense that this is a "man's world:" it is on the whole the male of the species who has decided what ideas will be believed and what notions and rules will be followed. One of the most important ideas he has propagated in almost all societies and eras is that women are inferior to men and, hence, not worthy of equal opportunities.

This belief in the natural inferiority of women has taken a wide diversity of forms. In educational terms, it has usually meant either that girls should be wholly excluded from formal schooling or that their schooling should be inferior in quality and quantity to that of boys. Even Plato, who was prepared to admit girls to the education suitable for Guardians on an equal basis with boys, "because the nature to be taken in hand is the same," [40] did not expect that many girls endowed with the requisite qualities would arise, since the male sex is superior to the female in virtually all respects: "in almost everything one sex [female] is easily beaten by the other." [41] Usually, schools have not gone even as far as Plato in admitting and treating qualified female students equally with males. It is almost universal, for example, for schools and colleges to have different social rules for men and women. Until recently, girls at Oxford University who invited men to tea in their rooms were made, first, to push their beds into the corridor.

In America, for reasons that have been exhaustively explored elsewhere, women have come unusually close to equality of treatment. In the elementary and secondary stages of education girls have reached a state of quantitative parity with boys. In 1962, the high school graduating class included 872,000 boys and 966,000 girls. The median number of years of schooling completed was 12 for women and 11.6 for men.[42] Women have entered almost all fields of activity, many of which were previously sacrosanct to men and have proved that their admission was justified. Almost the only activity, indeed, in which women have failed to equal male performance is cooking. All the world's great chefs are still men.

At the level of higher education this near-parity falls away. Of the students entering American colleges in 1962, only 42 percent were women. Women earn one out of every three bachelor's and master's degrees and only one out of every ten doctorates. The major dilemma facing female education in America today is the fact that, before genuine *equality* has been achieved, the problem of *differentiation* must be faced. Since sex is a differentiating factor that will affect virtually every aspect of the person's life, it is at least probable that it is a factor that should influence the formulation of a suitable educational program for that person. The mental abilities of men and women may be equal in power and yet different in quality. It is noteworthy that, especially in the Eastern states, women's colleges often arose out of embittered feminism. Hence, there was an understandable desire to prove women's minds the equal of men's. It was not surprising, therefore, that these colleges tended to emulate the men's colleges, following their curriculum and trying to become identical in all academic respects. Now, however, we recognize that identical education does not necessarily provide different people with equal opportunities, and the task is to determine what differentiations are appropriate between male and female education to come closer to equality of opportunity.

It is important in this connection to observe the pattern of female employment in American society. One out of every three workers is a woman. Three out of every five women workers are married. One out of every three married women is working outside the home.[43] With an increasing affluence and household technology it becomes ever more possible for married women to carry the double career of home and profession. Some of the opportunities and dangers of this situation might well be explored in female education, to avoid pitfalls like competitive aggressiveness, domestic frustration, neglected children, envious husbands, and other unfortunate dividends of an unsuccessful compromise. Female education must fulfill a multiple function in preparing women for their multiple roles. The working life of a typical woman follows a much more broken and complicated pattern than that of a typical man, whose working life is relatively less affected by such milestones as marriage, birth of the first child, enrollment of the youngest child in school, departure of the youngest child from the home, and so on. Women differ from men not only in that they bear children, but also in that they are, in most cultures, expected to run the home, they live longer, and they often have more leisure in middle age.

Despite the opportunities for employment outside of the home, it would be unfortunate if all married women were frightened by the strictures of Betty Friedan,[44] Bruno Bettelheim,[45] and others into feeling guilty for not following a career. The boredom of a mother at home with young children is often a testimony not to her vital intellectual energies but to her lack of creative insight into the possibilities of her home situation. Many challenging opportunities are lost by women at home whose education has not helped them to visualize how they can make their homes into creative centers for their husbands, children, and communities.

Without doubt the most difficult part of a woman's education is the task of preparing her for just the right blend of firmness and flexibility. It is clear that the demand for human flexibility made by rapid technological change is increased in the case of women, who in many cases will interrupt and later resume a field of study or career. Both educational and employment opportunities for women need to be made more flexible in response to this demand for individual flexibility. Female education should be marked by a wide diversity of approach, much experimentation, many part-time opportunities, second chances, refresher courses, irregular programs, and flexible admission procedures. The field of teacher-preparation offers a specially suitable area for such modifications.

But there is also a danger that a woman's education will help her to become an adaptable creature at the cost of a desirable firmness of character and purpose. If a woman is merely an auxiliary to a man it is unlikely that she will develop her unique, autonomous talents. Marion Hilliard has suggested that women are often trapped by their own adaptability into trying to be all things to everyone—responding quickly and automatically to all the disparate demands of their environment.[46] A woman is primarily a person and cannot find herself or fulfill herself by reflecting other people any more than a man can. Women run the risk of losing some of their intellectual creativity through dissipating their energies in the vitally important task of being the reconcilers and harmonizers of their environment, instead of exercising, disciplining, and believing in their own insights, which might be more costly emotionally to themselves and their men. They also run the danger of losing intellectual power through suppressing their intellects on the assumption that men dislike women who may threaten them intellectually. Hence, a woman's educational opportunities cannot be maximized unless her education is so arranged (and some may argue that this means sexual segregation at some points) as to help her discover and develop her own talents independently and confidently.

The educational opportunities offered to a female as a *person* may be quite different from what would be offered to her as a *woman*. For example, in the matter of admission to professional school, a woman stands the chance of obtaining roughly the same treatment as a man, if she is regarded as a person for whom such training might constitute a form of self-realization and self-improvement. Regarded solely as a woman, she might suffer a worse fate. For example, since professional men have a longer professional life than professional women, a state or an institution might argue that, provided enough qualified men applicants can be found, it would benefit society in the long run to admit only men to professional training.

In this, as in other differentiating factors, equality of opportunity is not an absolute value: its worth and priority can be gauged only when set into a matrix governed by the purposes of the educational enterprise.

IV   ARISTOCRACY AND DEMOCRACY

Functional Élites

If a democracy is to attain a creative growth alongside a measure of social justice, it must be prepared to live with a tension between the demands for justifiable equalization adumbrated here and the demands for hierarchy inherent in progress toward excellence. This is an enormously difficult tension to maintain, and it is a constant temptation to escape from it into the apparent simplicities of a traditionally aristocratic or dogmatically egalitarian position.[47] A democracy must attempt both to enhance the freedom to enjoy warrantable equality and to nurture the authority of excellence in leadership.

We must recognize that cultural attainments in the past have been largely the product of the leisure and commitment of *élites* in society. It would be foolish to believe that the democratic ethos of equality forbids, or the power released by democracy makes unnecessary, the existence of *élites* in the future: such a belief will lead to cultural stagnation. Rather, our efforts should be directed toward establishing and applying democratic criteria for the selection and training of such *élites*. In particular, democratic *élites* cannot be permitted to flourish at the traditional cost—the cultural isolation and impoverishment of the majority.

We are no longer willing to abide by Plato's injunctions about the importance of hereditary factors in leadership, and we are impatient with his compulsive desire for stability.[48] But we should beware lest this impatience prompt us to neglect the value of excellence in our concern to avoid certain types of inequality. Thomas Jefferson was one who had read his Plato, and this fact was reflected in his constant concern for both democracy and aristocracy, equality and quality, the public and its leaders.[49] Jefferson's specific educational recommendations may be largely anachronistic today, but his voice is still needed as a reminder that an aristocracy can be a functional aristocracy of virtue and talent rather than an aristocracy of birth and wealth.

A society that chooses social justice over hereditary privilege is to be commended. But it is also to be warned that an age of rapid change and social revolution demands leaders who have submitted to the sternest demands of educational excellence. It would be an unnecessary tragedy if we were to rid ourselves of the social waste and injustice of old aristocracies at their worst only to fall into the trap of assuming that democratic leadership can be developed without the submission to discipline and the recognition of responsibility that characterized aristocracy at its best.

One of the great defects of the neo-Jeffersonian view, however, is that of seeing the functional aristocracy as a single, unitary, or at least interlocking, body that gives leadership to the "masses." Such a view perpetuates the pernicious dichotomies that have marred societies in the past and is anachronistic in the light of the growing demands that the expansion of knowledge has placed on expert leadership in many fields. What is needed today is a multiplicity of *élites*, operating in various spheres, selected by different criteria, making use of diverse talents, and emphasizing many values. Suzanne Keller has examined the growth of what she has called "strategic elites" and viewed their proliferation and diversification as a protection against exploitation and despotism.[50] Diversity is in this sense the best route to freedom.

Leadership, Intelligence, and Human Classification

One who defends the idea of functional *élites* has to be prepared to outline how such *élites* should be selected and educated. Who shall lead? For a multiplicity of reasons, the criterion that would be most accepted for selecting leaders today is intelligence.[51] Leaders, whatever else is demanded of them, must be able to get things done—by themselves or by others. There is, in other words, a strong efficiency or effectiveness component in good leadership, which therefore correlates positively with intelligence, whose most general definition might be the power to cope successfully with whatever problems life presents. Intelligence has some rather obvious advantages as a criterion: intelligent leadership is under most conditions preferable to stupid leadership. But it also has some pitfalls, which deserve special consideration.

The use of intelligence as a criterion in education usually involves having students compete with each other and ranking or classifying them according to the outcomes of their competition. James Conant has argued that the events of the past two decades have made necessary the development of Jefferson's natural aristocracy. He has suggested that the revolutionary course of world history has forced Americans to accept the principle of academic competition as a basis for the selection of leaders.[52] However, wherever people are classified there is a danger that justifiable claims to equality of opportunity will be ignored or contemned. In order to avoid this, some of the pitfalls of classification need to be held in mind.

It was argued earlier that all men are basically equal in the sense that each one is an irreducible self. At this level, clearly, all ranks, labels, and classifications are irrelevant. Nevertheless, it is possible to think of men, under certain circumstances, in other terms and at levels other than this basic one. In such cases, classification may be added over and above this basic equality for purposes of temporary efficiency and convenience. Classification is not in itself unjust. Injustice is involved only when we classify people wrongly, according to irrelevant or otherwise invalid criteria.

What, then, constitute defensible criteria of classification? In the first place, the classification should be made according to function rather than heredity. Status should be associated with the way a person performs in a given situation or system rather than with a label that supposedly denotes some innate quality. Hence, so-called "intelligence tests" are safer and less pernicious when thought of as tests of performance than when regarded as revealing inborn, immutable qualities.

Secondly, classification should be made *a posteriori* rather than *a priori*. That is, we should classify only in the light of the contribution a person makes to a specific task, not according to previous doctrine. John Dewey has suggested this approach as characteristic of democracy.[53] In Dewey's view, authoritarian regimes assume that intelligence is confined to a superior few who, because of inherent natural gifts, are endowed with the ability and right to control others. In a democracy, on the other hand, there is the assumption that, although intelligence is distributed in unequal amounts, it is sufficiently general so that everyone has something to contribute, and the value of each contribution can be assessed only as it enters into the final pooled intelligence constituted by the contributions of all. Authoritarian schemes assume that its value can be assessed by some *prior* principle, if not of family and birth, or race and color, or material wealth, then by the position and rank a person occupies in the existing social scheme.

Thirdly, classification should be temporary rather than final. It may be a useful device for a specific purpose or period of time, but it becomes increasingly dangerous the longer it lasts. This is one reason why it is easier to defend grouping children according to their performance in an academic subject than by curriculum or "stream" or school. It is easier to move into another classification for another subject than it is to move into another curriculum or school. The latter type of classification has a way of becoming a self-fulfilling prophecy.

Lastly, classification should be considered partial and not total. It should be looked on as denoting something about one aspect of a person rather than a label that completely summarizes and exhausts him. This is why classification according to intelligence, while the most widely acceptable, is also the most perilous of criteria. John Gardner has suggested that Americans see appraisals of intelligence as total judgments on the individual and as central to his self-esteem. We discriminate nicely between excellence and mediocrity in athletics, he has suggested, but are reluctant to be equally precise about intelligence. Gardner maintained that this is because we do not take judgments on athletic ability as total judgments on the person and so can be more coldly objective about them.[54]

In a society where the success ethos prevails, we are liable to deify intelligence because of its power of effectiveness. We are also liable to attribute an individual's intelligence to him personally rather than remember that high intelligence is—at least initially—an unmerited gift, to be revered as such, but not automatically conferring on the recipient any special virtuousness. Clever men, Tawney pointed out, are impressed with their differences from their fellows; wise men are conscious of their resemblance to them. Superior intelligence does not give us any *a priori* claim to superior privilege.

We should, then, approach the problem of classification and the criterion of intelligence with caution and skepticism. It is a good rule of thumb *never* to classify unless we are quite convinced of a clear purpose for doing so. If we use the common criterion of intelligence as a prime factor in the selection and education of *élites*, we should bear in mind the dangers associated with its use. If we regard it as functional, partial, and subject to change, if we value it in terms of its contributory effectiveness, and if we do not associate it *eo nomine* with virtue or privilege, we can use it with a minimum of danger. But, above all, we should resist any kind of straitjacket of classification and should be constantly open to a diversity of criteria of human worth and leadership.

Meritocracies and Social Mobility

In addition to the general dangers mentioned in the use of intelligence as a prime criterion in the selection and education of leaders, there are also some particular dangers that attend its use in a highly educated, affluent, socially mobile, war-minded society. The most brilliant analysis of these dangers is that of Michael Young, in his biting satire, *The Rise of the Meritocracy*.[55] Young showed clearly how rule by a meritocracy, where merit equals I.Q. plus effort, can be both a logical development of the democratic value of equality of opportunity and a destruction of the most precious of democratic ideals. It achieves this by holding too narrow a view of the criteria by which a man's worth is judged and repudiating the democratic ideal of respecting every man for the unique good that is in him.

It may well be that some of Young's strictures hold more relevance for English conditions than for American.[56] An important difference between England and America is that English leadership is more homogeneous and interlocking than American. Through such institutions as the English Public School and the London club, English gentlemanly leaders in many fields know each other and manage to keep power and influence in amazingly few hands.[57] In America, even the *Power Elite* described by C. Wright Mills is neither as homogeneous nor as centralized. There is greater geographical decentralization and diversity in America. The relationship of London to England is vastly different from the relationship of Washington, D.C. to the United States. America not only has a larger population, but a larger proportion of that population is college educated. The leadership in one field is often totally out of touch with leadership in other fields. This may mean that cocktail party conversation in America tends to be more stilted, more professional, and less sparkling than in England, but it also means that there are more possibilities in America for wide diffusion of leadership and responsibility among all talented people.

A more exigent and critical problem in America arises from the fact of, or rather the belief in, social mobility. Socially stable societies tend to hold down both ambition and anxiety. Socially mobile societies, in which many people believe they have the opportunity to rise (whatever may be the truth about their actual possibilities to do so), tend to release energy, stimulate aspiration, and increase expectation. At the same time, however, they tend to increase anxiety, through the fear of either downward mobility or the failure to rise. Moreover, if expectations are aroused far above the realistic possibilities of fulfillment, large-scale frustration and social discontent may ensue. One estimate has indicated that four-fifths of young Americans aspire to high-level jobs of which there are enough to occupy only one-fifth of the labor force.[58]

The Soviet Union faces a similar problem: the principal bottleneck in Soviet education occurs between the end of secondary and the beginning of higher education. Only a fraction of qualified applicants are admitted to university. The official Soviet explanation for this is that the country lacks the economic resources to expand higher education to meet the demand. But this argument is dubious because of the degree of control the government has over the economy. It could divert economic resources in this direction if it chose to. A more likely explanation is that the Soviet government is reluctant to produce more intellectuals than the society can absorb, because underemployed and disgruntled intellectuals are a notorious cause of trouble.

Stable societies and societies characterized by hereditary privilege protect their members from the astringent privileges of self-knowledge. The able may never discover their talents: the stupid may never be forced to admit their limitations. In mobile societies with wide opportunities these protections are removed or lessened. The individual who fails in such a society cannot claim—as he can in a stable, privileged society—that he would have risen to the top if opportunity had been granted. He is faced with the painful fact that in open contest he tried and lost. He is at the bottom of the heap not because of unfair discrimination but because that is where he rightly belongs. An important prop for his self-esteem has been removed.

How can a free society maintain a high level of energy, aspiration, and creativity among its members and yet avoid these perils? The most important route to be explored is the increasing diversification of goals and values. Many of these dangers stem from excessive stereotyping of individual aims. Intelligence can be used in a much greater variety of ways. Many kinds of excellence should be fostered.[59] In America, for example, we unduly limit ourselves by our foolishly exclusive focus on the liberal arts college as the monopolistic source of educational excellence. We also limit ourselves by our anachronistic allegiance to the demands of an economy of scarcity and war-preparedness. Material affluence means that producing more is no longer the virtue it used to be. And military technology has rendered preparation for a Third World War a suicidal waste of resources. Under these circumstances, we ought to be moving away from the single criterion of judging a man by the amount by which he increases material production. In the second half of the twentieth century a society like America should be strong and confident and far-sighted enough to be able to encourage many criteria, diverse values, and a multiplicity of aims.

Cultural Leadership and Minority Values

A democracy that is concerned to attain a high level of culture must be aware of the danger that the pursuit of equality can lead to a mediocre uniformity. Some critics of democracy are prepared to sacrifice equality for what to them is the greater value of differentiation. T.S. Eliot, for example, opposed equality of opportunity on the grounds that it leads to excessive social fluidity. The *élites* thus chosen, he warned, "consist solely of individuals whose only common bond will be their professional interest: with no social cohesion, with no social continuity. They will be united only by a part, and that the most conscious part, of their personalities; they will meet like committees." [60]

Moreover, the standards of taste, sensitivity, and appreciation that we associate with the minority values of cultural *élites* are riches that we would be foolish to jettison in the name of an ill-defined term like "democracy." "There is . . . no escape," G.H. Bantock has suggested, "from the problem of 'minority' values and the needful acceptance, by the common man, of the authority inherent in them. All men necessarily rest in incompleteness; it is in the nature of life that some must be more incomplete than others." [61]

However, although the arguments of men like Eliot and Bantock contain some valuable truth, they also slide dangerously over some vital flaws. The fact is that the "common man" does *not* accept the "authority" of these minority values. Shut out from the benefits of *élite* culture by a variety of economic, social, and psychological barriers, he has formed his own culture, which at best has produced some of the delightful authenticity and spontaneity of folk music and folk tales, but at worst has descended into the depths of insipid banality and superficial sentimentality. The aristocratic form of cultural leadership has resulted in a serious schism that impoverishes both the *élite* (who become more snobbish, fastidious, and effete) and the masses (who become more vulgar, unrefined, and insensitive). We make a mistake when we identify mass culture with popular culture. Mass culture is the vulgarized consequence of denying the masses the benefit of the refining influence the *élite* could bring. A genuinely popular culture would not be that which appeals only to the "common man" but that which is capable of enriching and uniting *all* people. This concept of popular culture is similar to what Richard Hoggart has called a "common culture." By a common culture, he has written,

. . . we mean a culture not irrelevantly divided either by old social distinctions or by new status distinctions. We mean also a culture which, though it is varied, flexible, and allows a free movement of interacting minorities, has this common ground: that in all its aspects it gives room for individuality, idiosyncrasy, the play of mind and heart true to their own observation and to the substance of the things observed.[62]

Raymond Williams, in the course of an excellent discussion of mass culture and popular (or common) culture, has said,

The inequalities of many kinds which still divide our community make effective communication difficult or impossible. We lack a genuinely common experience, save in certain rare and dangerous moments of crisis. What we are paying for this lack, in every kind of currency, is now sufficiently evident. We need a common culture, not for the sake of an abstraction, but because we shall not survive without it.[63]

The development of such a popular or common culture is the prime cultural need of most industrialized nations today.

Formal education in the past has done little to help to bring about such a development. Sometimes the consequential lack of social unity has had tragic effects. Herman Eschenbacher has indicted the American college in the pre-Civil War period for failing to serve as a source of social unity at a critical time. Higher education in the first half of the nineteenth century, he has suggested, was unable to help solve the social conflicts that divided the nation because it had lost contact with the aspirations of the masses.[64]

Perhaps we need the aristocrats to remind us of the degree to which we can enrich our lives by recognizing the authority inherent in the best of our cultural traditions. But we also need the democrats to remind us of the importance of providing equal access to those traditions for all who wish to enrich themselves. The development of cultural insight, sensitivity, and knowledge must ultimately be carried out *by* oneself, but it need not be done *for* oneself. The school can help by rigorously upholding cultural standards while making clear that a rich culture is not an esoteric concern of a peculiar view. It can help by showing gifted children how they can assist less-gifted children to enjoy, appreciate, and contribute to the cultural treasures of their own society. It can help by creating an atmosphere in which young people are encouraged to go beyond existing cultural standards, to establish new cultural values, to create a culture that is both popular and growing.

V EDUCATION, EXCELLENCE, AND EQUALITY

Opportunity and the Nurture of Excellence

In education, we must somehow find a way to live with the continuing tension between the emphases of the Classical tradition and those of the Romantic tradition. If we insist, as many do, on breaking the tension and elect one or the other alternative, we must settle for less than the best. We need both the Classical vision of standards of excellence and the Romantic reverence for the unique and incommensurable individual. How we achieve this synthesis in any particular situation depends largely on the purpose of our educational endeavors. To take two widely separated examples, the standards of excellence that people must meet before entering a profession should be strictly demanded, for their own sakes and for that of society, while the elementary school teacher should hold in the center of her concern the unique possibilities for growth and progress that lie within each child.

Isaiah Berlin's view that the Romantic philosophers favored inequality, while the Classical philosophers favored a Procrustean equality,[65] is a specious oversimplification. The Romantic influence—especially as manifested in progressive education—has favored equality of *opportunity* (with a wide base of recruitment and a minimum of segregation) but inequality of *treatment* for each individual (with an emphasis on individual differences). The Classical influence has favored inequality of *opportunity* (not all should be admitted to higher or even to secondary education) but equality of *treatment* (all should follow the same academic curriculum). The Classical focus is on the school and the curriculum: those who cannot meet the established standards show that they are unable to profit from the program offered and, hence, do not deserve educational opportunity. The Romantic–progressive focus is on the child: all should have the opportunity to gain something from schooling, and it is the school's responsibility to adjust accordingly.

In the past, the common fault has been to impose the Classical rigor too soon. We know now that, if we are to foster individual excellence, the Romantic emphasis must prevail in the early stages of schooling. Every individual should be regarded as potentially capable of achieving the highest understanding and use of himself. Educators should strive for the maximum liberation of capacity in each of their students. Rather than concentrate on precise *equality* of opportunity for all—which drains our energies away into the tasks of measurement and comparison—we should seek *maximum* opportunity for each, with the social, economic, and cultural conditions that permit each person to grasp his opportunities.

This means rigorously eschewing the temptation, to set *prior* limits to any child's achievements. "Within the range of what we loosely call normality," said Ernest Johnson, "no known facts about the equipment and limitations of any given child will warrant a prediction that sets boundaries to his achievement in a favorable cultural environment." [66] Jackson and Marsden, in their important study of education and class in England, have revealingly documented Johnson's claim. Although their main study was of working-class children, they also followed up a number of middle-class children in secondary grammar (that is, selective, academic) schools. Sometimes teachers advised middle-class parents that their child was not capable of doing certain kinds of academic work. But the parents interfered and insisted that the child take the full course, and usually, at the "best" level. In the event, the parents were right: the children's abilities flourished and multiplied when favorable conditions were secured.[67] This throws light on the problem of "innate" ability and working-class children's difficulties. Teachers tend to make quick and immutable judgments on a child's potentiality: but support and opportunity can make nonsense of their prognostications. Education for excellence is distinctly different from the education of the most easily educable.

Education for excellence means that all children, not only the gifted, should be stretched to their utmost. They should be taught to be constantly discriminating but not necessarily condemning. They should be encouraged to respect excellence wherever it may be found. They should be helped to gain that generosity of spirit that enables one to recognize excellence in others and to enjoy it without envy.

Excellence and Diversity

It has already been implied that there is an essential relationship between equality and diversity. The kind of equality to be encouraged in human relations is not that of identical cogs in a machine but that of diverse members of a family bound together by love, respect, and equality of concern.[68] We need this respect for diversity urgently on the international level. Ernest Hocking has suggested that the individual quality of different countries remains one of the great values of travel. "While this variety constitutes one of the chief obstacles to the successful codification of international law, a developed appreciation of difference promises to be a major help in bringing about a warless world." [69] It is doubtful that humanity can survive unless a larger proportion of us learns to regard differences among men as potentially creative rather than potentially threatening. One is warranted in striving for one's own values, as long as he recognizes the richness provided by other views and does not try to snuff out all opposition to produce uniformity.

There is also an essential relationship between excellence and diversity. Healthy societies (and this includes both nations and schools) will not only tolerate but positively encourage diversity among their members. If they do not, they can have little hope of growth and progress. A confident, creative society will cherish many different kinds of excellence. John Gardner has put it this way:

> An excellent plumber is infinitely more admirable than an incompetent philosopher. The society which scorns excellence in plumbing because plumbing is a humble activity and tolerates shoddiness in philosophy because it is an exalted activity will have neither good plumbing nor good philosophy. Neither its pipes nor its theories will hold water.[70]

The sort of school that will best serve such a creative society is one in which a student is accorded the right to be different and is valued for precisely that difference. This means that every child must be recognized by the school as precious and his talents thought worthy of development, even if they do not fit well into the academic or occupational structure of this society. The only alternative to this admittedly stringent demand is for the school to rob millions of boys and girls of their dignity and self-esteem.[71]

Some of the most sophisticated investigators in the field of mental health (for example, Marie Jahoda, M.B. Smith) are positing that rather than a single entity called "positive mental health" there are *several* types of health: the price paid for one of them (for example, self-actualization) may be a lower level in another (for example, accurate perception of reality).[72] If this is so, it should make us more accepting of ourselves and give us more respect for differences in others' personalities. If a person's "defects" may be the price of his "virtues," of his being uniquely himself, then instead of picking out and emphasizing his defects we should look at him as a whole person and enjoy his uniqueness.

Seen in this light, the task of the school is to help the student to find his own brand of excellence. This has obvious implications for the problem of general versus specialized education. Finding one's own bent, discovering one's talents, requires an early and sustained exposure to a wide variety of experiences and subjects. At the same time, however, it requires an early opportunity to specialize in depth at whatever one is good at. Communication necessitates common experiences; opportunity necessitates wide exploration; excellence necessitates specialization. The challenge for the school is to nurture the differences among students in such a way that, instead of justifying exclusiveness, the differences serve to enhance unity, just as the differences in a good orchestra enhance the unity of music.

Excellence in diversity is threatened by the monopolistic prestige of certain curricula and certain educational institutions. Maximum opportunity in education for all does not mean that all children, or even all intelligent, middle-class children, should go to college. On the contrary, it means opening up a great range of routes to excellence. It means recognizing that one can become liberally educated without going to a liberal arts college, that some people can be prevented from or hindered in gaining a liberal education by going to a liberal arts college. Life-long opportunities for growth and education should be provided for all who want to take advantage of them: through industrial apprentice and training programs; through trade-unions and government-sponsored educational programs; through evening courses and extension courses; through art, music, and craft schools; through correspondence study; through radio and television; through creative work experiences; through work camps in conservation and urban renewal; through Peace Corps and Poor Corps; through work in repertory theaters, local newspapers, local radio and television stations; and so on. The list is almost endless, and it is all in addition to the opportunities offered to those who choose the liberal arts college.

The problem of finding the best route for each individual is complicated in America by the habits of identifying the good life with the successful life, of defining success in material terms, and of urging a college education as a formula for material success. The prediction that a college education is necessary to become a respected and successful person becomes, if shared by enough people, a self-fulfilling prophecy. Unless we can break this circle with some nonmodish diversification of educational values, we shall needlessly impoverish ourselves as individuals and as a society.

The task is not made any easier by the restricting values of the cold war and the narrowly intellectual pressures that accompany military preparations. We should be instructed in this respect by the similarity between Athens and Sparta in the seventh and eighth centuries B.C. and the contrast between them in the fourth century B.C. The cultural decline of Sparta can be seen clearly from 550 B.C., when power came strictly into military hands. The educational curriculum was "tightened up" as a reflection of a cold-war mentality: "frills" like art, music, poetry, and dancing were removed. Discipline, obedience, military preparation, and uniformity were stressed. The results were disastrous. Our advantage over the Spartans is that we have their example to profit from—if we choose.

Teacher-Student Equality

The learning process and the achievement of excellence are crucially affected by the relationship between teacher and pupil. What should this be, at its best? A.S. Neill has insisted that the good school, like the good home, is one in which children and adults act and relate on a basis of *equality*. He has castigated both the situation in which children have *no* rights and that in which children have *all* the rights. The "proper" situation is one in which neither adults nor children have any special rights or disabilities by virtue of their age or position.[73]

Like many of Neill's ideas, this theory of teacher-pupil relations serves to stimulate thinking in fruitful directions and, yet, suffers from an undue simplicity that hides some important complexities. It is doubtful that Neill would object to the superior authority wielded by the conductor of an orchestra and his position of inequality *vis-à-vis* the other musicians. This is because the purpose of the orchestra demands a certain distribution of authority. Similarly, if we want to know what is the proper relationship between teacher and pupil we should look not to the past (as Neill would agree) or to a simple egalitarian formula but to what we conceive the purpose of the teaching-learning situation to be.

When we look at the teaching-learning situation in this way we notice immediately that its purposes are manifold and complex. It is necessary to break down the situation into a number of functions: some functions will suggest a relationship of equality, others a relationship of inequality. For example, the functions of teacher and pupil as contributors to the achievement of the purpose of establishing a human relationship at its best will often demand equality. For this they must treat each other with courtesy, respect, and honesty; must treat each other as ends rather than as means; must not seek to achieve power over each other; and must regard each other as of ultimate, immeasurable value. Similarly, when they are discussing, arguing, seeking the truth, they should be equal partners in the dialogue.

But there are other purposes in the situation where we are seeking the attainment of certain standards of excellence, where evaluation of performance is involved. Here the functions of teacher and pupil are unequal. Indeed, the teacher is employed precisely because he *is* unequal—in wisdom, knowledge, skill, experience, or maturity. His task is to guide and judge, sometimes to direct and order. In this role equality means irresponsibility.

The Comprehensive Principle

The discussion of specific educational provisions that might foster students' ability to submit to the authority of excellence and simultaneously foster the maximization of opportunity could be virtually endless. Instead of attempting to cover all or a large number of such provisions, we shall conclude by examining a single educational recommendation— the principle of comprehensiveness. The defense of this focus is that this principle offers the single most important means for closely approximating to these twin goals.

If we follow the comprehensive principle, we should attempt to bring together in one school as great a diversity of children—judged by economic, social, racial, religious, vocational, and intellectual criteria— as circumstances permit. The restraining circumstances would include, notably, geographical factors. As suggested above, there are formidable arguments against the large-scale transportation of children to increase the range of, say, racial comprehensiveness, although these arguments should not deter us from reforming zoning arrangements, selecting school sites, and permitting individual transfers, to follow this principle. Another restraining circumstance includes parental freedom of choice. The loss of freedom involved in preventing parents from patronizing private schools would not be sufficiently compensated for by the increased comprehensiveness gained by compelling all parents to send their children to the same public school.

One of the great defects of noncomprehensive education is that it is enormously difficult to bring the ablest children, who will often become leaders in their society, to a realization of their fundamental (as opposed to specific) equality with their fellows. Segregated schooling makes it less likely that they will enrich all, rather than only themselves, through their talents. This is the great weakness of the English Public School: although it represents important values of excellence, its separateness and aloofness from the mainstream of English life have prevented its products from acting as a leaven through the whole of English society. They have served rather to deepen the schism between Disraeli's "Two Nations." [74] Similarly, the English segregation of the academically able into the secondary grammar schools and the average and below average into the secondary modern schools has resulted in socially debilitating feelings of superiority and inferiority. Too many students in secondary grammar schools have developed into social snobs without adequate compensation in terms of intellectual excellence. [75]

As a product of such a school, I can remember clearly the complacent superiority with which I and my fellows looked down on the unwashed masses who had not been selected for our school. I have also taught in secondary modern schools and can attest to the lack of student leadership and the consequent deterioration in moral and intellectual standards resulting from the congregation under one roof of children who are united only by having been rejected as too unintelligent for higher education.[76]

The comprehensive principle implies that classifying, testing, labeling, segregating, and selecting should be avoided wherever possible, carried out only where clear gain to all will ensue, and regarded always as provisional. The comprehensive school scores over the special or selective school in that, in the former, necessary classification can be postponed longer; groupings tend to be tentative; individuals can transfer easily from one category to another; rigid, determining labeling can be avoided; the principle of multiple chances prevails; groupings can be more easily made by educationally relevant criteria, such as motivation and talent in a specific field of study; and it is easier to create a large number of patterns of excellence.

Comprehensive education gives the best chance of coming effectively to grips with the tension exerted by the contending demands of specialized and general education. Talented people tend to be talented in many areas, not all of which can be fully explored in a lifetime. The exploration of one means the neglect of others. Morever, the successful development of one talent tends to lead to reward and reinforcement for this talent, leading to further neglect of other talents. Comprehensive education avoids rigid, premature specialization, thus enabling gifted students to explore a wide range of talents before inevitable specialization leads them to concentrate and narrow their concerns.

At the same time, the flexibility of this type of schooling makes it possible for all students to follow and develop in depth a specific bent or interest within a broad framework of common culture. This makes it more likely that genuine talents of all kinds will be discovered and nurtured and less likely that all students will be either crowned or broken by a single criterion of excellence. Finally, the comprehensive principle is our best hope for evading as long as possible the educational classification of students according to the powerful and often vicious social-economic-racial pressures of society. These will operate to a large extent in any case, but the comprehensive school will give the student a chance of finding out who he really is and what he is really good for, instead of fitting him into an educational and, hence, vocational category according to his origins.

NOTES

[1] Sir Richard Livingstone, *Education for a World Adrift* (Cambridge University Press, 1944), 7-8.

[2] *Ibid.*, 10-13.

[3] David Riesman, *et al.*, *The Lonely Crowd: A Study of the Changing American Character* (New York: Doubleday, 1955), 349.

[4] John W. Gardner, *Excellence: Can We Be Equal and Excellent Too?* (New York: Harper, 1961), 14.

[5] Frederick Rudolph, "Who Paid the Bills? An Inquiry into the Nature of Nineteenth-Century College Finance," *Harvard Educational Review*, vol. 31, no. 2 (Spring, 1961), 144-57.

[6] John K. Galbraith, *The Affluent Society* (Boston: Houghton Mifflin, 1958).

[7] John Hersey, *The Child Buyer* (New York: Knopf, 1960).

[8] Daniel Jenkins, *Equality and Excellence: A Christian Commentary on Britain's Life* (London: S.C.M. Press, 1961), 46.

[9] Roger J. Williams, *Free and Unequal: The Biological Basis of Individual Liberty* (Austin: University of Texas Press, 1952). See especially ch. 7.

[10] In an ingenious paper, Jerrold R. Coombs and B. Paul Komisar have argued in favor of equality of treatment by the simple device of defining equality as "fittingness." "The Equality Principle in Education," *Proceedings of the Nineteenth Annual Meeting of the Philosophy of Education Society* (Lawrence, Kan.: Philosophy of Education Society, 1963), 112-20. However, equal treatment is not the same as "fitting" or "appropriate" or "proper" treatment. To say that A and B deserve *fitting* treatment is one thing: but, since this may mean *different* (that is, *unequal*) treatment for each, it is difficult to justify calling this *equal* treatment. See also B. Paul Komisar and Jerrold R. Coombs, "The Concept of "Equality in Education," *Studies in Philosophy and Education*, vol. III, no. 3, (Fall, 1964), 223-44, for a restatement of their view. C.J.B. Macmillan, "Equality and Sameness," *Studies in Philosophy and Education*, vol. III, no. 4 (Winter, 1964-65), 320-32, has adequately refuted some of Komisar and Coombs' basic points, although he seems strangely reluctant to draw the full implications from his own argument.

[11] For an interesting discussion of equality of rights and opportunities, see John P. Plamenatz, "Equality of Opportunity," *Aspects of Human Equality*, Lyman Bryson, *et. al.*, eds. (New York: Harper, 1956), 79-94.

[12] Dorothy Lee, "Equality of Opportunity as a Cultural Value," in *Aspects of Human Equality*, Bryson, ed., 255-69; "Comment," *Ibid.*, 386-88; see also Dorothy Lee, *Freedom and Culture* (Englewood Cliffs, N.J.: Prentice-Hall, 1959), 39-52.

[13] Isaiah Berlin, "Equality," *Proceedings of the Aristotelian Society*, 1955-56 (London: Harrison, 1956), 325-26.

[14] Lee, *Aspects of Human Equality*, 386-88.

[15] Lee, *Freedom and Culture*, 41.

[16] Karl Mannheim, *Essays on the Sociology of Culture* (London: Routledge & Kegan Paul, 1956), 176. Italics in original. See also his section on "The Principle of the Ontological Equality of All Men," 180-88.

[17] Jacques Maritain, *Redeeming the Time*, Harry Lorin Binsse, trans. (London: Geoffrey Bles, 1943), 15. Chapter I, "Human Equality," is an eloquent if one-sided critique of the "empiricist, anti-Christian philosophy of enslavement" and

the "idealist, pseudo-Christian philosophy of egalitarianism" and a defense of the "realist, Christian, true philosophy of equality."

18 Reinhold Niebuhr, *Faith and History* (New York: Scribner's, 1949), 189.

19 Galbraith, *op. cit.*, 330.

20 It is interesting in this respect, however, to notice that in the English Public School, where uniform is mandatory, social distinctions are maintained through fine differences in the quality of cloth and tailoring. See Paul Nash, *The English Public-School Gentleman* (Harvard University: unpublished doctoral dissertation, 1959).

21 Myron Lieberman, in an excellent analysis of "Equality of Educational Opportunity," has listed many other means of increasing equality of opportunity: *Language and Concepts in Education*, B. Othanel Smith and Robert H. Ennis, eds. (Chicago: Rand McNally, 1961), ch. 9.

22 Richard Wollheim, "Equality," *Proceedings of the Aristotelian Society, 1955–56* (London: Harrison, 1956), 284. Jacques Maritain has written: "such notions as that of equality of opportunity or equality of conditions, which egalitarianism would make chimerical, become true and proper if they are understood in the sense not of an equality pure and simple, but of a *proportional* equality." *Op. cit.*, 24.

23 On this point, see Isaiah Berlin's enlightening treatment, *op. cit.*, 302–305.

24 For a cogent discussion of the importance of choice of criteria, see S.I. Benn and R.S. Peters, *Social Principles and the Democratic State* (London: Allen & Unwin, 1959), ch. 5.

25 One of the best treatments of the importance of the criterion of relevance can be found in R.M. Hare, *Freedom and Reason* (Oxford: Clarendon Press, 1963), ch. 11.

26 For an introductory treatment of this vast subject, see Clyde Kluckhohn, *Mirror for Man* (New York: McGraw-Hill, 1944), ch. 5, "Race: A Modern Myth."

27 David Fellman, ed., *The Supreme Court and Education* (New York: Teachers College, Columbia University, 1960), 80.

28 See William M. McCord and Nicholas J. Demerath III, "Negro Versus White Intelligence: A Continuing Controversy," *Harvard Educational Review*, vol. 28, no. 2 (Spring, 1958), 120–35.

29 R.H. Tawney, *Equality* (London: Allen & Unwin, 1931), 239.

30 Brian Jackson and Dennis Marsden, *Education and the Working Class* (New York: Monthly Review Press, 1962).

31 *Ibid.*, ch. 5.

32 *Ibid.*, 220–21. For a fictional account of the cost of rising in English society, see George Hitchin, *Pit-Yacker* (London: Cape, 1962); and for a fictional portrayal of one who refuses to pay this high price and prefers to remain outside the "system," see Alan Sillitoe, *The Loneliness of the Long-Distance Runner* (New York: New American Library, 1961).

33 Martin Mayer, "The Good Slum Schools," *Harper's* (April, 1961), 51.

34 Ministry of Education (England), *Early Leaving: A Report of the Central Advisory Council for Education* (London: Her Majesty's Stationery Office, 1954).

35 *Ibid.* See especially pp. 17–19 (Tables K and L), 34, 56.

36 See, for example, Allison Davis, *Social-Class Influences upon Learning* (Cambridge, Mass.: Harvard University Press, 1962).

37 See James B. Conant, *Slums and Suburbs* (New York: McGraw-Hill, 1961), especially ch. 1, 4.

38 Gunnar Myrdal, "The War on Poverty," *New Republic* (February 8, 1964), 14–

16. This was written before President Johnson's "War on Poverty."

39 Michael Harrington, *The Other America: Poverty in the United States* (Baltimore, Md.: Penguin, 1963), 185.

40 Plato, *Republic*, Francis M. Cornford, trans. (New York: Oxford University Press, 1945), 154.

41 *Ibid.*, 153.

42 *American Women: Report of the President's Commission on the Status of Women* (Washington, D.C.: U.S. Government Printing Office, 1963), 11. Indeed, it is sometimes suggested that, in the primary grades, it is the boys who are discriminated against. Some observers have pointed out that, when boys enter public school in America, they leave a female-dominated home for a female-dominated classroom. Their "male" characteristics of physical aggressiveness, adventurousness, restlessness, and noisiness are not appreciated in either place. They react to this unrewarding situation, it has been suggested, by becoming poor students. It is perhaps not coincidental that most teachers in the early grades are women and most backward students in those grades are boys.

43 *Ibid.*, 27.

44 Betty Friedan, *The Feminine Mystique* (New York: Norton, 1963).

45 Bruno Bettelheim, "Growing up Female," *Harper's* (October, 1962), 120–28.

46 Marion Hilliard, *Women and Fatigue* (New York: Doubleday, 1960), ch. 12.

47 For an indication that this is a widespread problem, see Paul Nash, "Quality and Equality in Canadian Education," *Comparative Education Review*, vol. 5, no. 2 (October, 1961), 118–29.

48 The most mordant critique of Plato's principles of leadership is Karl R. Popper, *The Open Society and Its Enemies* (Princeton, N.J.: Princeton University Press, 1950), ch. 7.

49 A useful statement and critique of Jefferson's educational views are contained in Gordon C. Lee, ed., *Crusade Against Ignorance: Thomas Jefferson on Education* (New York: Teachers College, Columbia University, 1961). See also Robert D. Heslep, "Thomas Jefferson's View of Equal Social Opportunity," *Educational Theory*, vol. XIII, no. 2 (April, 1963), 142–48.

50 Suzanne Keller, *Beyond the Ruling Class: Strategic Elites in Modern Society* (New York: Random House, 1963), ch. 11. She described strategic élites as follows: "Only certain leadership groups have a general and sustained social impact. . . —those whose judgments, decisions, and actions have importance and determinable consequences for many members of society. We refer to these groups as *strategic elites.*" *Ibid.*, 20.

51 For a classic statement on the importance of trained intelligence in leadership, see Eric James, *Education and Leadership* (London: Harrap, 1951).

52 James B. Conant, *Thomas Jefferson and the Development of American Public Education* (Berkeley: University of California Press, 1962).

53 John Dewey, "Democracy and Educational Administration," *School and Society* (April 3, 1937); reprinted in Joseph Ratner, ed., *Intelligence in the Modern World: John Dewey's Philosophy* (New York: Modern Library, 1939), 402–404.

54 Gardner, *op. cit.*, 68–69.

55 Michael Young, *The Rise of the Meritocracy, 1870–2033* (London: Thames & Hudson, 1958).

56 For a comparison of the nature of élites in the United States and other countries, see Suzanne Keller, *op. cit.*, ch. 5. For an acute analysis of the Canadian situation, see John A. Porter, *The Vertical Mosaic* (Toronto: University of Toronto Press, 1965).

57 Paul Nash, *The English Public-School Gentleman*, ch. 6, 7.

58 Donald Paterson, "The Conservation of Human Talent," (Walter Van Dyke Bingham Lecture, Ohio State University, April 17, 1956), quoted by Gardner, *op. cit.*, 20.

59 "Why should no marks be given for saintliness, generosity, compassion, humour, beauty, assiduity, continence, or artistic ability? . . . It is the injustice of isolating, as a basis for extreme inequality, certain selected ones out of the multiple strands that go to make up the human personality, which constitutes the fundamental ethical case against any élite or aristocracy." C.A.R. Crosland, *The Future of Socialism* (New York: Schocken, 1963), 168.

60 T.S. Eliot, *Notes Towards the Definition of Culture* (New York: Harcourt, Brace, 1949), 46.

61 G.H. Bantock, *Freedom and Authority in Education* (London: Faber & Faber, 1953), 53.

62 Richard Hoggart, "Culture—Dead and Alive," *Observer* (London), May 14, 1961. For his critique of mass culture in working-class England, see Richard Hoggart, *The Uses of Literacy* (London: Chatto and Windus, 1957).

63 Raymond Williams, *Culture and Society, 1780–1950* London: Chatto & Windus, 1958), 317. See also 295–338, for his analysis of culture and equality.

64 Herman Eschenbacher, "Education and Social Unity in the Ante-Bellum Period," *Harvard Educational Review*, vol. 30, no. 2 (Spring, 1960), 154–63.

65 Berlin, *op. cit.*, 310–11.

66 F. Ernest Johnson, "The Concept of Human Equality," *Aspects of Human Equality*, Bryson *et al.*, eds., 31.

67 Jackson and Marsden, *op. cit.*, ch. 2.

68 A generation ago, R.H. Tawney wrote: "What a wise and good parent would desire for his own children, that a nation, in so far as it is wise and good, must desire for all children. Educational equality consists in securing it for them. It is to be achieved in school, as it is achieved in the home, by recognizing that there are diversities of gifts, which require for their development diversities of treatment. Its aim will be to do justice to all, by providing facilities which are at once various in type and equal in quality." *Op. cit.*, 206.

69 William Ernest Hocking, "The Freedom to Hope," *Saturday Review*, vol. XLVI, no. 25 (June 22, 1963), 13.

70 Gardner, *op. cit.*, 86. See also Rockefeller Report, *The Pursuit of Excellence* (Garden City, N.Y.: Doubleday, 1958), 16–17, for a discussion of diversity and excellence.

71 For evidence that this, unfortunately, is exactly what the American public school is doing, see Edgar Z. Friedenberg, *The Vanishing Adolescent* (New York: Dell, 1959), especially ch. 5, "Five Exemplary Boys."

72 See Joseph D. Havens, "Psychology," no. III of *Faith Learning Studies* (New York: Faculty Christian Fellowship, 1964), 8–9.

73 A.S. Neill, *Summerhill* (New York: Hart, 1960), 107.

74 See Paul Nash, "Training an Elite: the prefect-fagging system in the English Public School," *History of Education Quarterly*, vol. I, no. 1 (March, 1961), 14–21.

75 See Jackson and Marsden, *op. cit.*, ch. 5.

76 Richard Farley, a teacher in a secondary modern school, has suggested that "Ninety per cent of the work in a Secondary Modern School is control and discipline." *Secondary Modern Discipline* (London: Black, 1960), 59.

VI

THE AUTHORITY OF DETERMINISM
The Freedom to Choose

I DETERMINISM AND FREEDOM

Fate

To what extent is man able to choose and act freely? To what extent
are his choices and actions predetermined by causes outside him? Is man
an autonomous creature, making decisions of his own free will, or is he
a puppet, acting out a part that has already been foreordained for him,
reading lines that have been meticulously written by someone or something else? These questions have been exercising the world's best minds
for centuries, without our having arrived at a consensus or a solution.
Thus, the problem of human freedom is reopened here only with much
hesitation, and because its examination is essential for the purpose of
clarifying our beliefs concerning the extent and limitations of man's
responsibility.

At one end of the spectrum of opinion in this matter we have the
doctrine of fatalism: the belief that all events in the universe are in-
eluctably predetermined, that nothing man can do can affect their
course in any way, and that a submissive acceptance of all that happens
is man's appropriate role. Fatalism is more common in periods and
areas in which man is relatively powerless to tame or control the threatening forces of nature that bring disease, suffering, or death. It usually
declines when he begins to control and modify his environment and, consequently, to feel his power to affect his own fate. In modern industrialized societies it is usually confined either to the ignorant, who keep
astrologers and horoscope makers in business, or to the emotionally
stunted, who cannot bear to carry responsibility and so cast it off by
postulating their inability to affect events in any way.

The idea of fate has recurred throughout history in the beliefs of men. Greek tragedy was characterized by the dominance of Fate. The Romans referred to the ruling will of Fortune. The Islamic concept of Kismet or Destiny is similar. The ruling law in Hinduism and Buddhism is Karma, that is, the sum of a person's actions in one state of existence, carrying over and inexorably deciding his fate in the next. Every man reaps in his lifetime what he sowed in his previous existence. He receives what he is fated to receive, and even a god cannot make it otherwise.

Christianity

The controversy over determinism and freedom has been waged continuously within Christendom and continues today. The doctrine of predestination, for example, has long been associated with Christianity, although it also appears in Hebrew and Islamic thought (orthodox Islamic theology teaches absolute predestination). In Christianity, the idea of predestination appeared to a degree in the writings of St. Paul, prominently in those of Augustine, and most completely in those of Calvin. According to the doctrine of divine predestination, God imposes on all creation a rigid conformance to his will. Everything is decided for the future. Men are divided into two predetermined classes: those destined for salvation and those destined for damnation. This decision is taken by God before the birth of the individual and nothing that man can do can in any way alter the decision. The Protestantism of Luther, and more especially of Calvin, taught that man is incapable of saving himself by his own efforts and is dependent for redemption on the unpredictable grace of God. This doctrine effectively undermined the foundations of the Church's faith in, and profit from, good works like penances and indulgences, but it also made more complicated the problem of man's attitude toward his personal freedom and his responsibility for his own fate. Writers like Fromm and Mowrer have suggested that this theology encouraged the feeling of personal helplessness that is modern man's most serious moral defect.[1] This is a somewhat oversimplified interpretation that contains an important aspect of the truth. In fact, early Protestantism encouraged a logically difficult mixture of personal freedom (the true Christian, according to Luther, was free to defend his religious conscience against false ecclesiastical interference) and utter metaphysical dependence (the true Christian always lived in the consciousness of his complete dependence on God).[2]

In contemporary Christianity, the doctrine of predestination has largely disappeared in its strictest, Calvinist form, although the consequences of the latter are still with us, especially in North America. However, Christianity still has not resolved the problem of freedom.

One of the thorniest aspects of the dilemma concerns the possibility of man's freedom in the face of God's omnipotence and omniscience. If God is all-powerful, does it make sense to say that man is free to act as he wishes? If God can at any time divert or nullify man's little plans, where is man's autonomy? Moreover, if God is all-knowing, He must have complete foreknowledge of all events: does it make sense to say that man is free if everything he decides and does has been already foreseen by God?

Finally, what validity can there be in claiming man's freedom if we admit the reality of God's grace and providence? According to the doctrine of grace, God is not a passive spectator of the human scene but actively intervenes in the universe to achieve his will. It has been suggested [3] that chance and accident are in reality examples of God's grace and providence at work in the world.

. . . what is it other than the chance happening and the accidental development which foils the plans which men in their pride make for themselves? What else prevents man from making himself the captain of his soul and the master of his fate? So the Christian does not resent or rebel against the barrier of chance or accident, but welcomes it gladly for what it is, humbling himself before it instead of vainly combatting it, because he knows that through it the lovely mystery of grace comes to him in his own life.[4]

However, persuasive as this argument is, it can be reconciled with the idea of man's freedom, as we shall see later, only at the level of paradox.

Science

The belief that man is able to make free choices and decisions, which cannot be determined in advance, is challenged also by scientific or mechanistic determinism. The scientific determinist regards the whole of nature—including man—as a harmonious system governed by uniform, regular, and unchanging laws. These laws are conceived in terms of rational connection and causal determination. All events, including human acts, are rigorously conditioned by a continuously linked chain of cause and effect. The future is completely determined by a closed system of natural law, in accordance with which every element of nature must necessarily behave. No alternative modes of behavior are possible.

The great French mathematician and astronomer, Laplace, expressed the strict determinism of classical mechanics with his "mathematical demon." Laplace envisaged the invention of an infinitely intelligent computing machine, of which he would demand to know the precise position and velocity of every particle in the universe at a certain moment. With this data he would be able, he claimed, through the laws of classical mechanics, to predict the future with absolute certainty. This dream was abruptly shattered by the German physicist, Werner Heisenberg who, in 1927, formulated the Uncertainty Principle, which states that it is impossible to determine both the position and velocity of a particle simultaneously. The degree of indeterminism is very small and consequently of no importance in most fields, as for example in ballistics. But it becomes crucial in the field of atomic physics. Heisenberg's principle prevents the determination of the initial conditions necessary for Laplace's demon and cuts the ground from under classical mechanics, replacing it with quantum mechanics. According to quantum mechanics, an electron can move in any one of a number of possible ways. The future can be predicted only statistically. That is, with large numbers of electrons it can be predicted what proportion will move in a particular way, but we cannot predict the path for any particular electron. It is similar to the lack of power of life-expectancy tables to predict the death of any individual, although they may be statistically valid for a large group. The twentieth-century scientist, consequently, is much less sanguine about the possibilities of predicting the future than were some of his nineteenth-century predecessors.

Psychology and Psychiatry

Much of the eighteenth- and nineteenth-century enthusiasm for democracy stemmed from the Enlightenment view of man as a rational creature, capable of solving his personal and social problems through the process of reason. This one-sided and optimistic picture of man has been shaken in this century by World Wars, concentration camps, racial discrimination, and the threat of the total destruction of civilization. It is not surprising that a similarly one-sided—but pessimistic—view of man has crept in to occupy the vacuum caused by disillusionment. This second picture has received strong reinforcement from those theories of psychology and psychiatry that emphasize man's irrational side and show the power of the unconscious to affect his decisions, beliefs, prejudices, and choices. The discovery of the unconscious cast further doubt on the idea of man's freedom: psychiatry has shown us that often, although we believe we are the rational, conscious determiners of our behavior, in fact we are virtual slaves of unrecognized unconscious forces.

Moreover, Freudian psychology and the kindred science of sociology have contributed to the feeling of helplessness in man by demonstrating that he is often the victim of circumstance rather than the master of his destiny. In this century, more and more people who previously were regarded as evil, but free, have been looked on as unfortunate sufferers from unkind fate. Studies showing the positive correlation between juvenile delinquency and poor home conditions, for example, engender an attitude that hesitates to condemn the young wrongdoer, on the grounds that he is not a free agent but an inevitable product of his experiences. The idea that the individual's personality is largely formed in the first few years of life leads to a tendency to regard with skepticism his freedom to develop or change in any fundamental way later.

Strengthening these determinist forces was the development in the first two of three decades of this century of the theory of behaviorism. This theory cast doubt on the idea of an autonomous, self-determining human being and emphasized the importance of antecedent stimulus conditions in determining the responses of the individual. The work of Pavlov and J.B. Watson on conditioning and of Thorndike on S-R connections and habit have contributed to an attitude that is prepared to see all behavior as the inevitable product of external stimuli.[5] Accordingly, man has been progressively relieved of moral responsibility for his acts. Since everything we do is ultimately caused by outside forces, we cannot be held personally accountable for our behavior and should not feel guilty for our misdemeanors.

Determinism and Causation

There can be no doubt that these determinist claims contain a great deal of truth and that they have done a useful service inasmuch as they have helped to bring about a more balanced view of man's power to act and decide with complete freedom. We have gained immeasurably from the realization that there is traced around every man what de Tocqueville called a "fatal circle" beyond which one cannot pass. Our freedom is strictly circumscribed, and those who are not aware of this are dangerously lacking in maturity and humility. "We are adaptable creatures," wrote Christopher Burney, "and flatter ourselves with the conceit that by adapting ourselves to events we master them; therefore it is the irrevocable which causes our greatest humiliation." [6]

What marks out the fatal circle for each one of us? In the first place there is the authority of the laws of the physical universe. All men are subject to the law of gravity, and whoever ignores or fails to make allowance for it must pay the harsh penalty. In Whitehead's view, the main limitations to freedom arise not through our fellow men but through "the massive habits of physical nature, its iron laws. . . . Birth and death, heat, cold, hunger, separation, disease, the general impracticability of purpose, all bring their quota to imprison the souls of women and of men. Our experiences do not keep step with our hopes." [7] Jean

Piaget has shown [8] that the primitive mind of the child is dominated by the feeling that he is omnipotent and can command the universe at will. He makes no clear distinction between the self and the external world. Progress toward maturity is marked by a realization that there is a difference between the self and reality, that the external world is governed by physical laws, that one cannot command the universe in accordance with desire, that there are limits to one's powers over the world, and that the external world represents an authority over the self. This realization is the beginning of freedom, because one is freed from illusion and closer to an aspect of the truth.

In the second place, our freedom is conditioned because of the authority of heredity. To some extent, our behavior is caused by the unique combination of genes that we have inherited. Exactly what part is played by heredity in determining our future cannot be ascertained, but it is fairly certain that heredity places a ceiling on our physical and mental growth, as well as affecting the development of our personality. Genetic and endocrinological studies have suggested that certain behavior probably stems in part from differences in glandular secretion, and that one inherits tendencies for under- or over-secretion of certain glands.[9] Heredity may be partly responsible for emotional and social behavior.

A third force exerting influence on our freedom is our social heritage and environment. Benjamin Bloom, in summarizing a great deal of relevant research, has pointed out that certain human characteristics can be drastically affected by the environment, especially during their most rapid period of growth. He also showed that for these selected characteristics (height, general intelligence, aggressiveness in males, dependence in females, intellectuality in males and females) there is a negatively accelerated curve of development that reaches its midpoint before five years of age. Thus, especially in these crucial early years of rapid growth, the power of environmental influences is great. Bloom's findings confirmed "the tremendous power of early learning and its resistance to later alteration or extinction." [10] We admit the power of the environment to influence choice and decision when we give careful attention to a child's early upbringing, or spend large sums on advertising, or undertake the task of universal education, or set up institutions for the reformation of criminals. Alan Paton has told a poignant story [11] about Jacky, a Negro who came to Paton's South African Reformatory. He was torn between his desire to be a priest—which made him ready to study long hours, pray, work hard—and his desire to smoke *dagga*—which made him steal to buy it. Paton showed that the struggle was destined to be won by the forces of evil, because in contemporary South Africa the environment is unhelpful to the African who tries to work out a decent life for himself. Most of us become more humble when we pause to reflect on the degree to which a favorable environment has helped us to come as close as we do to the level of conduct that we hold up as our ideal.

Our actions are determined also by our habits and passions. It is widely recognized that a man has lost some of his freedom when he is governed by passion or obsession. Similarly, unthinking obedience to habit implies lack of free, conscious control over actions. Bergson has pointed out the connection between habit and necessity in social life.[12] He likened society to a system of more or less deeply rooted habits, corresponding to the needs of the community. These habits exert a pressure on our will. We may evade the pressure, but we are drawn back, like a pendulum that has swung away from the vertical. A certain order of things has been upset; it must be restored. We feel, through these habits, a sense of obligation, which is always exerting a determining influence on our behavior.

Finally, it is necessary to recognize that the Uncertainty Principle does not demonstrate the existence of human freedom. It is true that, having shown that there is, in the last resort, an unpredictability in nature, the Uncertainty Principle destroyed the old classical determinism that rested on the assumption that it is theoretically possible to forecast the future from a complete knowledge of the present. But modern determinism is more modest and tends to confine itself to the assumption that there is an operative power in the universe giving rise to regularity in nature and that, in accordance with this regularity, all events are determined by antecedent causes. In human terms, this means that all behavior is *caused*. My decisions are determined by the strength of various motives, even though these motives may not be fully explicable or discernible.

This type of determinism is not incompatible with the existence of accident in human affairs, although some writers seem to entertain this delusion. The historian, E.H. Carr, has criticized the point of view that confuses accident in history with a lack of causal determination. He suggested that the "Cleopatra's Nose" theory of history—the theory that history is a succession of accidents (typified by ascribing the result of the battle of Actium to Anthony's infatuation with Cleopatra)—in no way refutes determinism. Anthony's infatuation with Cleopatra was just as much causally determined as every other event: "the relation between female beauty and male infatuation," Carr pointed out, "is one of the most regular observable sequences of cause and effect in everyday life." [13]

II FREEDOM TO CHOOSE AND ACT

Causation and Freedom

There seems little to commend in the attempt of the orthodox indeterminist to defend man's freedom. He maintains that it is, and will always be, impossible to predict the behavior of an individual, because there is in human affairs a perennial unknown—the factor of free will. This free will the indeterminist envisages as the ability of the individual to act with complete unpredictability, in a manner that may flatly contradict the ruling traits of his character and bear no relation to the surrounding and conditioning circumstances. The motives behind this attempt to defend free will may be laudable, but the method of proof must be condemned. Such a contention strikes at the laws of regular causation in the universe, by which, it has already been suggested, man is consistently governed. It substitutes for this regularity only the operation of chance and repudiates the universality of rational connection. Moreover, it cuts away the ground of individual moral responsibility. I cannot be held responsible for acts that are the result of chance. Only as acts issue from my character and are expressions of my purposes can they be ascribed to me as "mine" and made the basis of moral judgment on me.[14]

However, the main point to be emphasized here is that there is no need, in fact, to disguise or deny causation in man's life, for causation is in no way incompatible with the existence of individual freedom. The misapprehension that it *is* incompatible has led men into ridiculous paths in an attempt to demonstrate the reality of freedom at any cost. In attempting to clarify the relationship between causation and human freedom we must distinguish between actions whose causes can be discovered and actions that could not have been avoided. We have been misled in this matter by false analogies with science, mechanistic interpretations, and misinterpretations of the writings of Marx and Freud.[15] It has been argued that all human behavior is caused or compelled by certain forces (the laws of history, one's personal past, the laws of a mechanical universe, and so on), and hence it could not have been otherwise.

But not all causes compel us to act in a certain way: they may be *necessary* but not *sufficient* causes. Only a sufficient cause compels an effect. Causal explanations of human behavior may be sufficient explanations when we are talking about things that *happen* to an individual, but they are only necessary (and insufficient) explanations when we are talking of deliberate choices and actions—where responsibility, blame, praise, reward, and punishment are considered appropriate. In other words, we have not discovered any *sufficient* causes of actions that can be called *free*, that is, actions for which the individual can be held accountable. When a man acts deliberately, trying to achieve certain ends or purposes, we judge his behavior according to moral criteria. We cannot completely explain the causes of his behavior in naturalistic terms because moral acts are normative and, hence, cannot be wholly accounted for in terms of factors (such as brain changes, body chemistry, and so on) that are naturalistic. Natural explanations can give an account of necessary conditions (such as the existence of a brain) for free actions but not of sufficient conditions.

There is an essential residual ignorance in connection with our attempts to explain causation in human conduct. There are two types of ignorance: predictive ignorance and posterior ignorance. We have no psychological, sociological, historical, or anthropological laws that would enable us to predict human behavior with absolute certainty. If I am faced with two choices, no one can predict unerringly which of the two I will choose. The situation is complicated by the fact that, once a prediction is made public, I am able to learn it and take it into consideration before I act. The prediction itself becomes part of the causal picture. This makes prediction uncertain, because once I know it may deliberately act contrarily. A statistician might be able to predict correctly the proportion of a large number of people who would choose each alternative, but he would be unable to determine unerringly into which group I would fall. Each man is unique. This uniqueness implies the impossibility of describing him fully in his present state. Laplace maintained that if we knew the present precisely we could forecast the future. But we cannot know the present condition of a man precisely. Therefore, infallible, particular prediction is impossible.

This predictive ignorance is well-known, of course, but even *after* the event there remains a posterior ignorance. After my choice has been made, psychiatrists and others could study me in depth, and by lengthy analysis of my nature and motives could reconstruct a substantial plan of the causes of my choice. But there will remain a partial mystery: the complete story of human action and its causes cannot be told with our present knowledge and techniques. What the future holds with regard to possible advancements in ways of analyzing human behavior is irrelevant. Future developments will demand the modification of future opinions. Present opinions must be formed on the basis of present knowledge. The incompleteness of the explanation of causation does not, of course, demonstrate human freedom, but it means that the ideas of causation and freedom can coexist, and it makes it illogical to hold any theory of determinism that depends on the sure prediction or total posterior analysis of human choice.

God and Man

The relationship between God and man complicates the problem of freedom, it has already been suggested, in two principal ways: through God's omniscience and foreknowledge of all of man's actions, and through God's active intervention in the world through grace and providence. The apparent contradiction between God's foreknowledge and man's freedom arises only because we mistakenly think of God in temporal terms. To talk of God's foreknowledge means to put God on man's timescale and, hence, make Him finite and subject to the same limitations as man. But this is clearly incompatible with the concept of an omnipotent and omniscient God who is infinite and, therefore, beyond time. In terms of an eternal and infinite God, concepts like *post* and *ante* have no meaning.

The problem of grace and providence is more complex, and perhaps no intellectual solution will suffice. However, there would seem to be room in the world for *both* free men and an active God. We feel that we can do much to control and determine our own destiny. And yet we cannot effect our desires infallibly, or predict or explain everything about the human condition. This can be regarded as unfortunate and temporary, or it can be seen as affording some elbowroom in which grace can appear. Accidents can be regarded as unnecessary failures of our predictive techniques or as tokens of God's purpose working in the universe. The first interpretation denotes pride: the second, humility. The paucity of our present exact knowledge of human behavior would seem to indicate that a degree of humility is an appropriate posture. Abraham Heschel asked,

Considering the itinerary of one's life who could comprehend where the goals lie? One might go on a journey for the purpose of transacting business, while the true end was to worship in an inn, where the thought of God had never pierced the air, or to render help to a weary man encountered on the road. One might fulfill his destiny by the way.[16]

Animal Compulsion and Human Choice

Man shares part of his nature with the lower animals and this animality usually constitutes an impediment to his freedom. Animals are not free to deny their destiny. The salmon *must* go up the river to lay eggs and die; the swallows *must* build the mud nests typical of their species; the migrating bird *must* respond to the call to fly south for the winter. It is not within their power to disobey such summonses. Observation of human infants leads to the impression that they, too, are often inexorably ruled and determined by the demands of their nature.

It must be admitted, further, that the human adults are often unfree. What we choose is a function of what we are; and what we are is largely a result of what has happened to us. The very fact that we must make an effort before we can overcome the effects of heredity, environment, and our own animal impulses, shows that we are not free from their influence. We are, moreover, often unfree even when we believe we are free. For instance, we often believe we are free simply because we do not want to do something that, in the event, we would be unable to do.[17] Or we feel free because we have a false belief in our power to achieve our desire, either through an overestimation of our capacities or means, or through ignorance of obstacles to the achievement of our intentions.[18]

When all this has been said, however, the most important fact about man remains to be mentioned. That is, that although real limitations on man's freedom undeniably exist, he retains at the heart of things an all-important area of freedom. "It is true, that around every man a fatal circle is traced, beyond which he cannot pass," said de Tocqueville; "but within the wide verge of that circle he is powerful and free." [19] Human life takes its significance not from the outer limitations but from the inner element of freedom. Like the migrating birds, many of us hear a call to fly south for the winter—to Florida or the Côte d'Azur. But we can obey or disobey. We can even, if we choose, fly *north* for the winter. To be called, and to be able to disregard that call: herein lies man's freedom. Such freedom is, of course, widely assumed in common experience. Even the most rigorous determinist will strenuously defend his own ideas and try to persuade others of their validity, presumably on the assumption that individuals are able to choose and that their choices and beliefs will affect the future. Predestinarian preachers do not hesitate to exhort the individual to mend his ways and conform to God's will, as if man had the freedom to respond to or disregard divine grace.

The human situation is marked by both ineluctable authority and genuine freedom, and the wise man will not ignore either. James Baldwin has suggested: "Europe has what we [Americans] do not have yet, a sense of the mysterious and inexorable limits of life, a sense, in a word, of tragedy. And we have what they sorely need: a new sense of life's possibilities." [20] The existence of alcoholism is strong evidence of the existence of authority: the alcoholic is enslaved by the authority of his compulsion. But the existence of Alcoholics Anonymous is equally strong evidence of the existence of freedom: here are men and women who were unfree but who, through personal efforts and the help of others, have regained their freedom—albeit a knife-edge freedom maintained tenuously above the abyss of a reversion to the authority of their former compulsion.

There could hardly be a more testing situation for the existence of human freedom than the deadening and conditioning circumstances of life in a concentration camp. Yet Viktor Frankl has concluded as a result of his concentration camp experiences that freedom was clearly demonstrated.

There were enough examples, often of a heroic nature, which proved that apathy could be overcome, irritability suppressed. Man *can* preserve a vestige of spiritual freedom, of independence of mind, even in such terrible conditions of psychic and physical stress. We who lived in concentration camps can remember the men who walked through the huts comforting others, giving away their last piece of bread. They may have been few in number, but they offer sufficient proof that everything can be taken from a man but one thing: the last of the human freedoms—to choose one's attitude in any given set of circumstances, to choose one's own way. . . . In the final analysis it becomes clear that the sort of person the prisoner became was the result of an inner decision, and not the result of camp influences alone.[21]

The essential element of freedom, which distinguishes man from the animals, can perhaps be best seen in man's ability to frame and pursue distant goals. Maslow has distinguished two types of motives: deficit motives and growth motives. Deficit motives, which are common to animals, infants, and adults, call for the reduction of tension and the restoration of equilibrium. Growth motives maintain tension in the interest of long-range purposes and distinguish human from animal development and adult from infant development. Growth motives are allied to what Adler called the "life-style" of the individual and what Allport has called the "proprium." Allport's concept of the proprium includes all those aspects of the personality that make for inward unity—the "central interlocking operations of personality." [22] Propriate striving confers unity on the personality, but not the unity of fulfillment, repose, or reduced tension. It concerns our insatiable interests and purposes, which last throughout life. These propriate aspirations are the mark of the free man.

"To be freed from belief that there is no freedom," wrote Buber, "is indeed to be free." [23] In other words, man is not free to do anything until he believes he *can* do it. For otherwise his execution of the task can be only accidental and not intentional. It is in the identity of the intention and the execution that lies freedom. We are least free when we are purposeless, or when our actions do not reflect our purposes, or when we fail to execute our purpose through inattention, ignorance, or the pursuit of incompatible goals. We are most free when the ends we pursue have our wholehearted support, and when these ends represent long-term goals, the products of mature reflection.

Responsibility and the Existential Predicament

One of the greatest contributions of the existentialist philosophers has been to show that man is free to choose and that he *must* choose. The existential predicament is simply this: man is condemned to choose and to bear responsibility for his choices. He cannot escape this situation by passivity, for to fail to make a decision still involves choice and responsibility. The world can be just as affected by man's refraining from decision and action as by his active choice. If he fails to decide he has in effect chosen in favor of the *status quo*. Like it or not, it is our nature to be free and, under the sting of suffering, to choose between good and evil. According to Kierkegaard, it is the fact of freedom that produces "angst"(anxiety)—the fear that we may abuse our freedom. In Sartre's view, man has no essential nature apart from his existence—that is, apart from the existential choices and decisions he makes from day to day. Man makes himself through his free choices: he becomes what he wills. Moreover, his choices affect others, and for this, too, he must carry responsibility.[24]

The concept of responsibility is the crucial aspect of the idea of human freedom.[25] That we ascribe moral responsibility to ourselves and others for our acts assumes freedom; ethical judgments depend on the existence of freedom. We may curse or kick a stool when we trip over it, but when our passion subsides we do not impute to it any moral blame for our painful shin. Nor would we blame or praise men for their decisions if they were but the pawns of external forces and not free. There is no virtue in behaving well if we cannot do otherwise. Thus, it is freedom that lends dignity and stature to human existence.

Freedom in responsibility is a strenuous affair. To exercise it means that one must be constantly girded for decision. There are no periods of rest or relaxation: one must always be ready to take part in the struggle against anonymity and anarchy. Because this struggle is so demanding, many have tried to avoid their human sentence by surrendering their freedom to some form of authoritarianism. Such men seek an authority that will make pronouncements that will stand for all time: the awful responsibility of repeated free decisions is thereby removed from the individual. His responsibility is thenceforth only a matter of learning and applying the dogma. Of this development, Buber has said:

Our age is intent on escaping from the demanding "ever-anew" of such an obligation of responsibility by a flight into a protective "once-for all."

The last generation's intoxication with freedom has been followed by the present generation's craze for bondage; . . . . He alone is true to the one Present Being who knows he is bound to his place—and just there free for his proper responsibility.[26]

Mowrer has claimed that Luther, Calvin, and Freud are largely to blame for engendering an attitude of irresponsibility in modern man.[27] Luther's Protestantism, especially as interpreted by Calvin and his followers, taught that man has freedom and responsibility in only one direction: he can choose the wrong and must bear the full consequences of doing so, but he is wholly dependent on God's grace for choosing the right. In Mowrer's view, Freud tacitly agreed with Luther and Calvin that man cannot save himself, but went further by holding no one accountable for falling into sin (neurosis) in the first place. By emphasizing that man is a product of his past, Freud relieved him of all responsibility for good or evil. Mowrer agreed with Richard LaPiere [28] that we are a sick generation and that it is our sickness to resort to the Freudian ethic of moral irresponsibility rather than to hold ourselves and others accountable.

It is doubtful whether the truth is as simple as Mowrer maintained, and his interpretation of the views of these three men, especially Freud, tends to be one-sided. Nevertheless, there is no doubt that the teachings of Calvin and Freud, whatever their intentions, have sometimes borne fruit in the way that Mowrer condemned. And we need to recognize that taking the responsibility of human freedom means assuming the burdens of anxiety and guilt. The free person is not free from anxiety and guilt but is able to live with them without being destroyed by them. Anxiety is the vertigo of freedom—an inevitable consequence of gaining height. It can be productive if it is a manifestation of thought about an unresolved conflict: it may be resolved by bringing the person to a higher and more creative level of operation. Guilt is a concomitant of freedom because the free person is responsible and because no one ever completely lives up to his responsibilities. The responsible person sees a gap between what he judges to be his responsibilities and his performance. Guilt, which is formed by this gap, can be a healthy force if it is accepted as an inducement to personal excellence. It is precisely when guilt is *not* accepted, *not* faced, that it becomes neurotic and, hence, destructive of freedom.

Freedom and Excellence

A danger in the existentialist emphasis on man's responsibility to choose is that a concentration on the act of choosing can divert attention from the nature of the choice. Man has the freedom to choose, but the choice he makes in turn affects his degree of freedom. When a man is faced with a choice between good and evil (or, as is more common, between a greater and a lesser good, or a greater and a lesser evil), if he chooses the evil he is subsequently less free, for he has become more enslaved to his lower nature. If he chooses the good, it might be said that he is enslaved by his higher nature, but this is exactly the kind of bondage that paradoxically liberates us. Paul, the bondslave of Christ, rejoiced in the bondage with which Christ had made him free.

The free man is he who chooses the good, or in religious terms, who chooses God. The freest man is he who chooses the best. "The most freedom we can have," said Austin Farrer in his 1957 Gifford Lectures, "is to make the best of ourselves." [29] If we aspire to be free we must work to determine ourselves by the highest possible standards. In the words of Dean Inge, we need "the resolution to stand by the noblest hypothesis." We need, that is, the vision to see what is the highest choice we can make and the courage to follow that choice. Man grows in freedom by deliberately making brave choices and glorying in them.

The task of achieving freedom thus consists largely in unburdening ourselves of those complications and distractions that prevent us from pursuing this highest aspiration. Victor Murray has called freedom "a release from all hindrances to excellence." [30] Choosing implies both a liberation and a limitation: a liberation because the decision opens new possibilities; a limitation because every road chosen means other roads unexplored. A choice cuts us off forever from numberless other choices. This is why we must put our freedoms into a hierarchy. It is by the hierarchy of freedoms we construct that we can be estimated. We are all bound—sinner and puritan, ignoramus and pedant, hypochondriac and muscle-bound athlete. The differences among us are determined by what we choose to allow to bind us. The parish priest who works ceaselessly in the slum and the profligate who indulges himself in riotous living may both ruin their bodies and lose the freedom of good health. But we do not estimate both men equally, because they have sacrificed this freedom to demands of different value. The freest man has himself bound by the highest demands of excellence.

III FREEDOM AND THE SELF

The Nature of the Self

The free man, it was suggested above, is he who acts wholeheartedly to achieve long-term purposes. In our personal experience, we know, according to this criterion, that we *are* free to a degree, because we *do* frame and pursue such purposes. These purposes are expressions of our character, of our selves. But who are these selves who choose, decide, and pursue goals? An examination of the nature of the self is crucial to an understanding of freedom.

If an alcoholic gets drunk and beats his wife, is he sick or wicked? The common supposition is that, if he is sick, he is under the pressure of an undeniable compulsion and is not free to act in any other way. We judge him wicked, on the other hand, if he is free to get drunk or to remain sober and, hence, to beat his wife or to treat her decently. Aristotle would have said that the man is acting freely when the cause of his action comes from within himself; he is acting under compulsion, and hence not freely, when the cause of his action lies outside himself.[31] Up to this century, drunken wife-beaters, youthful criminals, and misbehaving schoolboys, were widely assumed to be freely and culpably wicked. Recent developments in psychology and psychiatry have made us less certain.

The alcoholic, many would say, is acting under a compulsion, as the delinquent who is unloved and unrecognized is compelled to seek recognition in socially forbidden ways, as the bored and unstimulated schoolboy is compelled to try to compensate for his boredom through adventurous misbehavior. In other words, if the motives for this behavior lie outside the agent, then he is held to be not free and, hence, not responsible. Psychopathology has shown us that some people are not free to choose whether to steal or not steal: they *must* steal. The alcoholic, we know, is physiologically different from the nonalcoholic. How do we know that the delinquent, the naughty child, and the criminal are not similarly left without real alternatives to their behavior? Our inability to explain human motives completely makes us hesitate to dogmatize.

But we must beware that we are not unthinkingly led into the assumptions and methods of the psychologist when they are inappropriate to our task. The psychologist wishes to explain behavior, and to do this he tries to isolate and analyze individual motives. This is a useful exercise, but if we are concerned with the freedom of man we must not forget to synthesize afterward, for only thus will we be able to see man whole—and it is the whole man who exercises freedom. Paul Tillich has said that freedom comes from what he has called the "centered self," that is, the self acting as a whole. He has disagreed with the idea of part of the mind controlling the rest, or the will being separate or controlling, or the ego or the unconscious being the sole source of freedom. The more we separate man from his motives, the more we reduce the area of the free self, and the more we enlarge the area of determining causes. But we do not need to submit to this reduction of the area of the self. We can—are surely justified in so doing—include a man's motives as *part* of his self, and so render him responsible for them. Far from having to envisage a tiny core of self acted on and controlled by numerous causes and motives, we are entitled to see a man's motives as expressions of his total personality. This seems a more fruitful and realistic concept of the self.

This may sound like a harsh doctrine, for it can involve saying that the young delinquent who has had all the hereditary and environmental cards stacked against him from the beginning is free to act lawfully and, hence, when he does not, is guilty. But holding the individual responsible does not prevent us from showing him sympathy and affording him treatment. And the alternative of personal irresponsibility is more dangerous. We must bear a degree of responsibility, in other words, not only for our decisions but for who we are. Carl Rogers has suggested that freedom is "the quality of courage which enables a person to step into the uncertainty of the unknown as he chooses himself. It is the burden of being responsible for the self one chooses to be. It is the recognition by the person that he is an emerging process, not a static end product. . . . Freedom, rightly understood, is a fulfillment, by the person, of the ordered sequence of his life." [32]

Self-knowledge

The individual, then, is responsible for what he makes of himself. Moreover, the degree of freedom he achieves will be determined largely by his degree of self-knowledge. If he is largely ignorant of his own nature, he is likely to be driven and compelled by forces within himself, ignorance of which prevents him from controlling and modifying them. "Freedom from the constraints that emanate from the non-rational parts of our own natures," Maurice Cranston has said, "is indeed the most important freedom we can have or strive for." [33] Self-knowledge also enhances our freedom by bringing the realization that our drives, impulses, and desires are not unitary but ambivalent and often conflicting. In life, we must constantly decide. The man with self-knowledge is able to face up to the fact that his decision will involve giving up other desirable alternatives. The man ignorant of his own nature is incapable of this degree of insight and will not resolve the underlying conflict that decision-making involves. Often he will avoid deciding at all, without knowing why he cannot decide. If this indecision continues, without a resolution of the conflict, a neurosis develops. The neurotic lacks freedom because his self-ignorance separates him from firm decision and committed action.

Donald Soper tells a story of the Cockney evangelist who recounted to his audience his own version of the parable of the prodigal son. He went into a far country, said the evangelist, and there he had a hard time.

First he was forced to pawn his overcoat. Then he had to pawn his jacket, then his shirt, then his undershirt. And when he came to himself he had to go home. This is what we, too, must do in effect. We must strip away the outer coverings of self-deception until we come to ourselves. We must get down to what T.E. Hulme called the vital axioms deep within us, which may not correspond to the ideals to which we pay lip service but are the real sources of our choices and decisions. The free man is ruthlessly honest with himself. And since our capacity for self-deception is almost limitless, the task of winning freedom through knowing and facing ourselves is not an easy one.

It is interesting to note in this connection that even deterministic psychiatrists tacitly assume the possibility of human freedom. Otherwise, it is difficult to see what purpose there could be in their treatment. They seem to assume that the patient who gains a measure of self-knowledge will be better able to cut away those factors that hinder him from making a decision and carrying it out. "Psychotherapy," wrote Allport, "gives hope that a corrected self-image, a more rational assessment of one's behavior, will reduce compulsions, induce order, and free channels of development to accord with chosen aims." [34] In other words, its operational assumption is that self-knowledge can enhance man's power to choose and act freely.

Self-consciousness and Self-transcendence

Psychology and psychiatry have brought us the realization that we act freely less often than we had supposed. Lawrence Kubie has suggested that the deepest form of enslavement is to unconscious forces that govern our behavior despite our conscious efforts. Our thoughts, feelings, and acts may become enslaved to an internal tyranny.

To the psycho-analyst, the ultimate freedom is the fifth freedom: the freedom to know what goes on inside us. Until we solve this most basic problem of education, of morals, and of spiritual development, all other efforts to seek human freedom are relatively superficial makeshifts.[35]

But the realization of the danger of this enslavement does not need to dishearten us if we perceive that there is also opportunity here. The opportunity comes because freedom is the complement of self-consciousness. Our greater knowledge of the human psyche makes it more possible for us to open a channel between the conscious and the unconscious realms and to become more aware of the whole working of our personality. There is an objective aspect to history: necessity does exist. But this is not all: there is a subjective aspect too, a place where man's freedom can exert an effect. In the same way, the unconscious is important in influencing man's choices. It would be foolish to ignore or under-rate it, for we know it can be decisive. Nevertheless, its operations can be resisted and overcome or combined harmoniously with the intentions of the conscious mind.

We are coming to realize that part of being free means being one-self in the deepest sense. This implies the achievement of a degree of integration of personality wherein the conscious and unconscious are, at best, working in harmony or, at least, not operating in mutually nulli-fying conflict. Self-consciousness extends the potential range of my free-dom by enlarging my control over, or at least my understanding of, all the forces—conscious and unconscious—that impel me.

The peculiarly human quality of being able to stand back from oneself and examine oneself, to be both object and subject at the same time, is essential to the exercise of freedom. It can be termed self-tran-scendence.[36] Freedom requires both self-transcendence and existential choice. Unless we transcend ourselves through reflection on our total nature and the meaning and direction of our lives, we act as unthinking automata and not as free men. But if we *merely* reflect and contemplate, operating always at the meta-level and never at the level of choice, de-cision, and action, we forfeit our freedom through passivity.

Guilt, Conscience, and Self-respect

Self-knowledge is important to enable us to deal with the problem of personal guilt. We recognize the deficiency of the individual who feels no guilt or remorse and, hence, has no impulsion to improve his level of behavior. On the other hand, we do not wish to encourage the devel-opment of the kind of guilt feelings that can immobilize or destroy a person. The only way to sail between this particular Scylla and Charyb-dis is to be fortified with a calm knowledge of our own abilities, limita-tions, noble motivations, and base drives. Only with such a level of ma-turity can a person hope to handle his guilt productively.

Crucial to the development of this degree of maturity is the growth of conscience. It was suggested earlier that man is most free when he chooses the good. When he chooses evil, or behaves in a way that does not conform to his ideal image of himself, it is conscience that reduces his freedom. What the theologian calls sin produces, if there is no ac-knowledgment or attempted expiation of it on the part of the sinner, what the psychiatrist calls neurosis or psychosis. The neurotic or psy-chotic has forfeited his freedom, or a part of it. He can regain his free-dom only through becoming whole again—that is, by bringing his be-havior in line with the demands of his conscience.

It is also possible, of course, to narrow this gap by reducing the demands of conscience down to the level of present behavior. And there are some who criticize psychiatry on the grounds that it results in just such a lowering of moral aspiration. But such a "solution" is effective only at the cost of bringing the individual down to a diminished level of freedom. We cannot help a sinner or a neurotic back to a life of freedom unless we help him to regain his self-respect. And he will recover self-respect not by tranquilizing his conscience, but by acknowledging his shortcomings and engaging in an active program to atone for them.

IV EDUCATION FOR CHOICE AND ACTION

Education for Better Choice

Education serves to increase our personal freedom by increasing the number of choices open to us. If, when faced with a problem, we can envisage only one possible course to take, we possess relatively little freedom. If, however, through greater knowledge, awareness of consequences, reflective power, or other products of an effective education, we become able to envisage several possible courses, our personal freedom is enlarged accordingly. The effective educator then, is one who makes his pupils' choices less predictable by opening possibilities that were hitherto closed.

The educator, however, must be concerned not only with increasing the *number* of choices open to the student but also with improving the *quality* of those choices. It is in this sense that the whole process of education rests on the assumption of human freedom. If man's choices were wholly determined by forces outside his own mind and character it would be useless to try, as teachers try, to change the quality of mind and character. It is because man's choices and decisions *are* determined in part by himself, by his own mind, that the massive institution of education is worth supporting. Education at its best is an attempt to develop the mind and character in such a way that the best possible choices and decisions are made.

An education for freedom, therefore, must include opportunities for gaining knowledge of the physical, social, economic, and other forces that exercise authority over us. Men who have knowledge of the laws of nature can anticipate the consequences of acting in various ways and can thus guide events, to some extent, to desired outcomes.[37] It was pointed out earlier, for example, that all men are subject to the authority of the law of gravity. But knowledge of its workings can alter its effect on us. Both primitive man and modern man are subject to its authority. But by studying its operation, modern man has learned to live with it differently from the way primitive man lives with it. He has invented the airplane, for example, which does not ignore the law of gravity but operates within it and under its authority. Knowledge of the authority of nature has opened up new areas of freedom.[38]

It can be objected that by introducing a student to this knowledge the teacher is changing him, influencing him, molding him, *determining* him. That is, the student becomes less free because his decisions are partly determined by the teacher's influence. Such an objection makes the error referred to earlier of confusing determination with causation. It is true that antecedent influences contribute to the causal pattern behind the student's decisions. But it does not follow that his freedom is thereby reduced. All behavior is caused, it has been agreed, but one is most free, it has been argued, when he is purposefully and consciously making the *best* decisions. If, therefore, through teaching, I help a child to gain knowledge and understanding, help him to see more clearly, help to emancipate him from paralyzing inhibitions, from unnecessary fears and superstition, I am not determining him in the sense of making his choices for him. Rather, I am enlarging his freedom by bringing the possibility (but not the certainty) that he can make better, more enlightened, more insightful choices.

If the school would educate people to live in a free society, then, it must assume squarely the responsibility to educate for discrimination in the widest and deepest senses. Training in language and literature is crucial here. There must be systematic and rigorous analysis of all those influences, especially commercial advertising and political propaganda, that hinder the development of discrimination and taste and that flourish only by encouraging inferior or unthinking choices. Furthermore, students must be shown that the educated person knows not only *how* to read but also *what* to read, and that this implies knowing what *not* to read. The educated person does not subject himself undiscriminatingly to all sorts of influences, through books, magazines, newspapers, radio, television, movies, and other people, but chooses carefully (inasmuch as his knowledge permits him to forecast) those experiences that he feels will best nurture his development. This does not, of course, mean cutting oneself off from all ideas contrary to one's own. Often it will mean just the opposite: a deliberate confrontation and fair examination of the unfamiliar, the unorthodox, the unpopular. But it also means becoming acquainted with the best that has been written and said in the world. The training in discrimination that is made possible through being introduced to the greatest classics of the world's literature should be a prime criterion in framing a literature program in school or university.

Just as one cannot learn to swim well except by practice in swimming, so one cannot learn to choose well except by practice in choosing. It is foolish to expect a young person to make wise decisions immediately after graduating from school if his school experiences have not given him the opportunity to make all sorts of decisions in an atmosphere where unwise or immature decisions do not carry disastrous consequences. And yet, many of our schools constantly appear to hold such expectations, if we judge by the state of juvenile dependence in which they keep their pupils. In the high school, the student must be given a growing responsibility for framing his own program of study, even though this includes the right to make wrong choices. Hence, the importance of guidance facilities that give genuine help in the making of good decisions rather than merely furnish information. Hence, also, the necessity for opportunities to specialize in school. "Ignorance of most of the universe is an inescapable aspect of the human condition," wrote Martin Mayer, "most gracefully borne by those who are not equally ignorant in all directions." [39] By being permitted a degree of specialization, the student is likely to be more interested in and committed to his studies, for his is not then constantly diverted from the pursuit of the field of his own choice.

We can help children to learn to choose well by knowing when as adults we should intervene in their lives and when we should stand back. It may be necessary for us deliberately to refrain from intervention even when we know we could make a better decision for them. We can also help them by ensuring that they become faced by real problems that have relevance and significance for their lives, whatever their ages. Otherwise, their "choices" are phoney and have no educative value. We can help them by distinguishing clearly between decisions that the adult should (and ultimately does) make and those that the children can genuinely make for themselves. Nancy Gayer has criticized those teachers who pretend to be more democratic and permissive than they really are. They confuse and manipulate the children, she maintained, by using "may" when they mean (and the children are aware that they mean) "must," as in, "You may take out your arithmetic books now," and by asking children to make up their own rules of behavior when there are some suggestions that the teachers would not accept (that is, the teachers really make the rules but get the children to suggest them). [40] If we are honest enough to distinguish between those issues that *we* will decide and those that the children can genuinely decide for *themselves*, the children will be less confused and will learn to take the responsibility for choosing, knowing that their choices are real.

In the last analysis, it is the *ultimate* choices of the young person that will decide the quality of his life. These ultimate choices are made in terms of his basic values, the things he finds most worth living and striving for.[41] If the school is to have any influence on the quality of these basic choices it will have to provide experiences in school wherein the student is forced back onto the bedrock of his values. This cannot be done through a continued emphasis on catechistical teaching and the repetition of verbalisms. It can be done only if the student is encouraged to gather the information necessary for making a choice; to make the choice himself; and to bear responsibility for the consequences of his choice. Only in this way are mature people made.

Education for Living with the Unpredictable

It is a truism that the rate of change in our world is increasing. What implications does this bear for those who wish to frame an education for children who will be able to make good choices and decisions? R.M. Hare has pointed out that, if we are teaching someone, it is foolish to teach him such a fixed and strict set of principles that he will never have to make an independent decision. It is equally foolish to leave him to find his own way of acting, unaided by the accumulated wisdom of previous generations.

What we do, if we are sensible, is to give him a solid basis of principles, but at the same time ample opportunity of making the decisions upon which those principles are based, and by which they are modified, improved, adapted to changed circumstances, or even abandoned if they become entirely unsuited to a new environment.[42]

However, the balance we strike between the teaching of principles and the encouragement of decision-making depends on the nature of our society and especially on the rate of social change. In a virtually static society it may be acceptable to inculcate certain principles by which young people should govern their conduct. If they always act automatically according to the principle they will be all right because the world in which they are acting is essentially the same as the world for which the principles were originally designed. But in a rapidly changing world, children brought up in this way will not have had enough practice in making decisions that they have had to think out for themselves, while the changed conditions are apt to have rendered the principles by which they have been educated no longer valid. At this point individual breakdown occurs. Hence, in a time of rapid social change, it is essential that children have every opportunity to test, modify, and live with the principles we ask them to adopt.

Of course, we must beware of insisting on too much decision-making too soon. If we force the child to choose before he is ready there is a danger that he will reject the whole idea of autonomy and responsibility. G.H. Bantock has said,

> To face young children with the continual necessity to choose, which is what in effect progressive theorists do, is to remove from children the sense of security which an imposed ritual can often afford immature minds. To have to perform set tasks at a set time creates with young children a background of security that is vital for their development . . . some of the difficulties inherent in our culture arise . . . from the disintegrative aspects of too great a freedom of choice.[43]

There is just enough truth in this to make it dangerously misleading. It is true that the young child needs security, for without it he will lack the confidence to stretch out into new ventures. It is also true that he can often gain this security through teacher-imposed tasks, routine, and repetition. But Bantock seems to be avoiding two important facts: the young child *can* choose without suffering disintegration if the choices with which he is being faced are within his power of understanding and execution; and it is only through the experience of such appropriate freedom of choice that these "immature minds" can be changed into mature ones. Unless the child is encouraged to choose as much and as soon as he is able, his security will enable him only to be a comfortable vegetable.

In order to bring up a child to live with the unpredictabilities of a changing society, the school needs to train him to reason deductively, inductively, and what C.S. Peirce called abductively. In authoritarian societies the emphasis is placed on deductive thinking. The premises are laws set out by the authorities. The conclusions follow inexorably. In a predominantly pragmatic society, inductive thinking is favored. Evidence is patiently gathered and principles and laws cautiously framed. Abductive thinking means thinking in terms of possibilities. It is particularly important in a dynamic society for the school to train children in abductive reasoning. Once the child is made aware of the possible solutions to a problem, he chooses the one that *appears* to be true. The accuracy of his guess is then tested by inductive inference. The test need not be made in the external world: he can conduct mental experiments to determine the conceivable consequences of the choice.[44] Through training in deductive, inductive, and abductive reasoning, the child learns what it means to choose wisely in a world where events can not be fully predicted.

Perhaps the most we can do to help children to live confidently and productively in an unpredictable world is to emancipate them from fear—in particular, fear of spontaneous impulses in themselves and others. In John Wain's novel, *The Contenders,* the rivalry implied in the title is between Ned, the hard, driving, meticulous business man and Robert, the wild, unpredictable painter. At one point, Ned shows his friend, Joe, a secret that he has had since boyhood: a room in his house where he has laid out a tremendous, elaborate, model railway. He plays with it to show Joe how it works. Joe is not impressed: "My facetious private guesses about that room had been inaccurate, but hardly more horrifying than the truth. There it had been all along, his private fantasy-world; the world where *everything* arranged itself along foreseeable lines, and acted predictably according to the amount of power you played through it." [45] In Ned's case, this desire for predictability stemmed from his fear: fear in particular that Robert, his rival, would surpass him, and fear in general of the unpredictable nature of life, with its spontaneity, its vital force, its mystery, which Robert with his wild painter's genius epitomized. A liberalizing education will help children to enjoy confidently their own spontaneity, to meet life without a desire for complete foresight and prediction, to face whatever the future brings them, to accept eagerly the fact of life's mystery and freedom.

Education for Purposeful Action

The education of a free man must be an education for action. It is in action that the fruits of freedom are manifested, and an education cannot be considered adequate unless it encourages the translation of purposes into active form. Such an education must, therefore, constantly guard against giving aid to the many forces in society that engender in young people a passive, accepting attitude toward life. We are concerned here with curriculum but even more with methodology. The nature of the subject does make a difference. For instance, if we want to teach children to write well, it is more effective to have them write than to have them read, although one would not guess this from the number and length of written assignments given in many North American high schools.

But *how* we encourage our students to learn is even more important in this respect than *what* they learn. Any subject can be studied creatively or destructively. Reading, for example, which occupies a large part of the student's time, can be a helpful or a harmful experience, an active or a passive process. Passive reading, it should be stressed, is not a neutral but a directly harmful practice. I have written elsewhere:

If we are not absorbed in what we are reading we are not only wasting time but building up dangerous habits of intellectual torpidity. . . . In order to learn from and be stimulated by what we read we must *act upon* the book in a precise and aggressive fashion, taking from it only that which we need to enrich ourselves. This involves exchanging our habits of *passive* for those of *active* reading. A much smaller part of our total "reading" time should be spent in passing our eyes obediently over tyrannous lines of print, and a much larger part spent in meditation upon and utilization of what we have read. Not only will we thus *understand* more of what we read, and make more of it our own, but we will avoid the boredom, restlessness and semi-attention which are the products of passive reading and the causes of one of the most common and virulent diseases of our age: lack of concentration.[46]

A similarly critical attitude should be taken toward the field of educational technology. One of the criteria that should be used in judging the extent to which techniques like radio, television, films, and teaching machines should be introduced into the schools is the degree to which they will encourage activity or passivity on the part of the learner. Charles Morgan has issued an important warning in connection with the use of films. Subjection to films, he wrote, "is habitual acceptance of ready-made imagining, designed to require a minimum effort of the receiver. . . . The evil of its regular use is . . . in the film's collective, habit-making power to satisfy imaginative hunger 'out of a can' and so to discourage the secret, individual imagination from following its own quarry." [47]

The same applies with even greater force to television. The great danger in the use of this teaching tool is that even more will be given to, and less asked of, the student than is customary even in the active-teacher, passive-pupil classrooms of today. It is extremely difficult to devise television programs that demand an active role from the student: the medium lends itself best to the dissemination of information. The imaginative powers of the student are not *stimulated*, as they might be by reading, but *satisfied* by the full provision of visual and aural images.

Needless to say, it is not activity for its own sake that is advocated here. Generations of inferior teachers have discovered the trick of keeping children busy to keep them quiet. There is nothing to recommend in this busy-work. At best it is an unproductive force in the children's lives. At worst it misleads teachers into thinking that the children are usefully occupied and, hence, no further pedagogical effort is needed. We are all prone to be misled by our own activity into thinking that we are virtuous and productive: busyness is a great solace to the conscience. J.K. Galbraith has said: "One of the best ways of avoiding necessary and even urgent tasks is to seem to be busily employed on things that are already done." [48]

How can we avoid both passivity and busyness in the school? There is no simple answer. On the negative side, we should avoid as far as possible all trivial activities—even when the children seem happy to engage in them. We should avoid subjecting children to constant distraction and changes of focus of concentration; we should allow them to develop as deep a concentration on a subject as they can attain. We should encourage them to be increasingly dissatisfied with conventional answers and to engage actively in a search for their own answers, and even better, their own questions. We should devote thought and care to making the activities they pursue meaningful to them on their own terms. And finally, we should help them to develop those long-term interests and commitments that provide the focus for purposeful action.

Education for Responsibility

One of the greatest hindrances in modern society to the kind of education advocated here is the steadily increasing size of institutions and the corresponding complexity of decision-making. When events are decided on such a large scale the individual is assailed by a feeling of personal helplessness. Even when they recognize a social evil, young people are liable to say, "There's nothing *I* can do about it." Much more dangerous than the actual powerlessness of the individual in modern society is the paralysis that results because he *believes* he is powerless.

The school must show the young person that individual freedom is won by constantly taking on greater responsibility as judgment and wisdom mature. But it cannot succeed in this attempt if the individual is convinced that his actions and decisions are impotent. Young people will respond eagerly when they scent that things are being changed, but they are quick to reject what is dead and incapable of producing fruit. If the education we offer them is to provoke a response from them, therefore, it must, while aiming at serious and worthwhile ends, be capable of ready application with a good chance of effective results.

It is up to the school to apprise students of their personal responsibilities for the reform of their society. This does not include laying down the *direction* of that reform, but it does include helping each individual to comprehend the effective range of his freedom and to understand the ways in which he can exercise it. Norman Cousins has said,

An individual needs instruction in the techniques of action and decision. He needs to be convinced that individuals and groups changed history in the past—and to learn how they did it. He needs an awareness of the fact that vital fractions have moved whole societies—and that the essential ingredient had something to do with the inspiration by which a man comes to recognize his own possibilities for effective action. Surely in the lives of men who have been able to harness this power there may be essential nourishment for people who are starved for purpose.[49]

When people try to rationalize their failure to assume responsibility for action by asking, "What can I do?" they need to be shown that there is a great deal they can do if they trace out the periphery of their potential circle of action, study the nature of change, ally themselves with like-minded fellows, and have the courage of their convictions.

Education for responsibility involves us as teachers in combating, wherever we find it, the attitude that considers people to be victims of circumstance and upbringing and, hence, not responsible for what they make of themselves or for the choices made by those selves. While affording sympathy and understanding to those who have suffered from unfortunate environments, we should nevertheless make it clear that we expect them to try to rise above their difficulties, and that we have faith in their ability to do so.

At the same time, however, we can help students toward responsibility and freedom by urging them to make their demands and aspirations personally relevant. We can encourage the dreams and ambitions of our students and yet still encourage them to study themselves and the relationship between their talents and their dreams. Where this relationship is realistic, the student is more likely to be successful in effecting change, in exerting leverage. This success can then encourage him to further aspiration and effort. But where the relationship is drastically unrealistic, it is hard for him to escape the disillusionment that follows failure to carry out grandiose schemes, or the resentment that ensues when one refuses to accept any limits on his freedom and has them forced on him unwillingly and uncomprehendingly. He who insists that "where there's a will there's a way," who believes that will power is the only prerequisite for successful action, who refuses to accept the intractability of nature, will be broken by nature—perhaps broken into neurosis or psychosis.

Children who are to feel at home in a free society must be helped to grow in self-knowledge. They need to become aware of the factors in their personal history that have affected their development, of the urges within them and the restrictions society places on those urges, of the limitations placed on them by their membership of various groups—social, religious, racial, national, and cultural—and of the authority inherent in their various deficiencies and talents.[50] As they advance in this sort of self-knowledge they will be able to perceive more exactly what they can and cannot do. Illusions of power lead to disillusionment and subsequent passivity. Illusions of impotence lead to an underassumption of responsibility. Self-knowledge also saves us from the rationalizations that permit us to slough off our appropriate and even urgent responsibilities. It is tempting to focus our attention on abstract or ultimate problems or distant causes, on which it is impossible for us to take action, as a substitute for immediate action on problems that are near us. These latter often lack the glamour and fascination of the distant: we tend to find them mundane and dull. This temptation must be fought against, for it leads to complacency and inertia.

Finally, it is necessary to show that there is a connection between choice and responsibility. It is not enough to allow and encourage an individual to follow his own strong interests. He must also be shown that this sort of freedom involves responsibility; that is, he must be held *accountable* for his choice. This means that he should be responsible, according to his age, for a certain degree of autonomy, thoroughness, perseverance, and integrity in working through the implications of his choice. Moreover, this freedom also carries a *social* responsibility, in that he should bring back the fruits of his line of interest and inquiry to his fellows.

Responsibility and Punishment

What are the implications of these views on freedom and responsibility for the question of punishment? Punishment of the individual wrongdoer has been defended by those who see man as wholly determined and by those who believe in his freedom. The determinist may advocate punishment on the grounds of deterrence or restraint. According to the deterrence theory, the wrongdoer, although not personally responsible for his actions, is used as an example to deter others who might be tempted to repeat the crime. According to the restraint theory, the individual is forcibly restrained, by isolation or imprisonment, to protect society from him. In both cases, the individual, though not culpable, is sacrificed for the good of society.

The determinist must adopt a legal or sociological argument for applying punishment. It is not *just* (as opposed to lawful) to punish the individual unless he has freely done wrong and could have acted otherwise. Hence, only the believer in human freedom can punish with justice. The view supported here is that, in the last analysis, man is free, must bear responsibility for his acts, and, therefore, can be justly punished. When we claim to punish an individual justly we assume that he is a free agent—that is, he can reason and understand consequences, and he had the possibility of having acted otherwise. If these conditions are absent, the individual cannot be considered free. We can consider him, for example, as a mental patient. He is then not blamed or punished but treated. Hegel and some of his followers regarded punishment as an indication of the wrongdoer's moral freedom, as his right and privilege. Hegel wrote,

> Punishment is regarded as containing the criminal's right and hence by being punished he is honoured as a rational being. He does not receive this due honour unless the concept and measure of his punishment are derived from his own act. Still less does he receive it if he is treated either as a harmful animal who has to be made harmless, or with a view to deterring and reforming him.[51]

We do not punish justifiably unless the individual did the act deliberately, he was old enough and sane enough to know what he was doing, he knew it to be wrong (or at least had the opportunity to find out that it was wrong), and he was not forced to do it. Exceptional temptation or provocation may persuade us to temper the punishment if it does not seem that this would encourage a general rash of offenses. For example, if a child lies to protect a friend, and is detected, we may decide that this is a special case deserving unusual consideration; whereas, if a child lies casually and for personal gain we may judge that if allowed to go unpunished the offense would become habitual.

It is one thing to examine the conditions under which punishment is *just*: it is another to consider when it is *wise*. The wisdom of including punishment in an education for responsible choice and action must therefore be examined. In the first place, if it becomes a choice between using punishment and encouraging an atmosphere of determinism, fatalism, or personal unaccountability, it is preferable to choose the lesser evil of punishment. The long-term consequences of promoting in the young person an attitude that refuses to admit personal responsibility and pushes responsibility onto extrapersonal factors (such as parents, upbringing, luck, fate, schooling, and so on) are almost certain to be more dangerous than the consequences of punishment. In an important study of juvenile delinquency, William Kvaraceus has pointed out that children who are liable to become delinquents frequently have a prevailing philosophy reflecting a reliance on fate or luck.[52] Fatalism is common among delinquents. Their attitude is reflected by statements such as: "I was unlucky, I was caught," or "He's lucky, the police didn't catch up with him." This philosophy inhibits a purposeful seeking for long-term goals and provides a handy excuse for any misadventure. Any evil that befalls the delinquent is explained away by him not in terms of personal responsibility but by invoking an ill-fated destiny.[53]

Secondly, there is some evidence to suggest that mental illness may be associated with unexpiated guilt. Mowrer has suggested that, because they lack the formal means to confess and atone, modern men and women make use, unconsciously, of the stigma, disgrace, and suffering connected with being "crazy" and hospitalized. The insane, he has said, are the self-condemned and self-punished.[54] External punishment can be a way of helping the individual feel he has atoned for his misdeed and, hence, enable him to live in peace with himself and society. We know that people who commit deeds that depart from their own moral code and who are not found out and punished often punish themselves in roundabout and sometimes excessively severe ways, such as accidents, physical or mental illness, or even suicide.[55] Equally, of course, external punishment may be too *easy* a way of ridding oneself of guilt. Most teachers are familiar with the discouraging impotence of punishment to effect moral reform. This is often because, especially in healthy young people, external punishment leads them to believe they have "paid for" their crime and can now go ahead with a clear conscience and do the same again (perhaps taking greater care this time not to be caught).

Is there any way out of this dilemma? We need to recognize that, when the free, responsible individual does wrong, he is genuinely guilty and that, even if we do not recognize his guilt, or even know about his crime, he will recognize it, at some level, if his conscience is normally active. We should show compassion and concern for the wrongdoer, without suggesting that his guilt feelings are groundless. We should show him that we expect him to atone for his misdeeds, but we should realize that our punishment of him is an unproductive technique and may make it easy for him to avoid genuine change. The individual must come to grips with his own guilt or offense. We can help him to do this in a creative, productive way by showing him a way of *action* through which he can atone and, hence, actually *become* less guilty, rather than wallow passively in his own guilt feelings or neurotically punish himself to excess.

The school should set up opportunities for service and even sacrifice on the part of its students. One great advantage of this generalized opportunity is that the school can never know all the secret crimes and misdemeanors of which its students are guilty. By showing the young person that there is limitless need for service to others in the world, and that service and sacrifice are legitimate ways to expiate our sins, the school provides a process through which the individual can constructively and harmoniously deal with his private and public crimes and deficiencies.

Finally, this whole problem of responsibility and punishment is one in which, pre-eminently, a sense of proportion is needed. Children must be held responsible, and punishable, only in proportion to their age, experience, and maturity. This is a case where ignorance *is* an excuse, although this does not permit us to refuse to accept an opportunity to relieve our ignorance. Moreover, our fallibility of judgment should make us patient of our own lapses and those of others. In the last resort, we should not take ourselves or other people too seriously and should live a life of sufficient flexibility so that a sense of humor can exert its salubrious influence.

NOTES

[1] Erich Fromm, *Escape from Freedom* (New York: Rinehart, 1941), ch. 3; O. Hobart Mowrer, *The Crisis in Psychiatry and Religion* (Princeton, N.J.: Van Nostrand, 1961), ch. 11.

[2] See Robert Ulich, "Freedom and Authority in Education," *Freedom and Authority in our Time*, Lyman Bryson, *et al.*, eds. (New York: Harper, 1953), 674.

[3] For example, by William G. Pollard, *Chance and Providence: God's Action in a World Governed by Scientific Law* (New York: Scribner's, 1958).

[4] *Ibid.*, 87.

[5] For a radical extension of the view that control over human behavior is possible, see B.F. Skinner, *Walden Two* (New York: Macmillan, 1948).

[6] Christopher Burney, *Solitary Confinement* (London: Macmillan, 1961), 11.

[7] Alfred N. Whitehead, *Adventures of Ideas* (Cambridge University Press, 1933), 84.

[8] Jean Piaget, *The Child's Conception of the World*, Joan and Andrew Tomlinson, trans. (Paterson, N.J.: Littlefield, Adams, 1960), ch. 4, "Realism and the Origin of the Idea of Participation," especially 162–68.

[9] C.R. Stockard, *et al.*, *Genetic and Endocrine Basis for Differences in Form and Behavior* (Philadelphia: Wistar Institute of Anatomy and Biology, 1941).

[10] Benjamin S. Bloom, *Stability and Change in Human Characteristics* (New York: Wiley, 1964), 210–16.

[11] Alan Paton, "The Divided House," *Tales from a Troubled Land* (New York: Scribner's, 1961), 107–116.

[12] Henri Bergson, "Freedom and Obligation," *Freedom: Its Meaning*, Ruth N. Anshen, ed. (New York: Harcourt, Brace, 1940), 613.

[13] E.H. Carr, "Causation in History," *Listener* (May 11, 1961), 816.

[14] See A.E. Taylor, *Elements of Metaphysics* (London: Methuen, 1961), 369–79.

[15] For an excellent discussion of the latter, see Richard Peters, *Authority, Responsibility and Education* (London: Allen & Unwin, 1959), part II, "Freud, Marx, and Responsibility."

[16] Abraham J. Heschel, *The Earth is the Lord's: The Inner World of the Jews in East Europe* (New York: Schuman, 1950), 58–59. H. Richard Niebuhr has suggested that the interactive relationship between man and God can be exemplified by the Joseph story, summarized in Joseph's statement to his brothers: "You thought to do evil but God thought to do good, to bring it about that many people should be kept alive." Niebuhr commented: "Here the clear distinction is made between the particular intentions that guide a finite action and the divine intention that uses or lies behind such actions. So Joseph can and does forgive, responding to the infinite in his reaction to the finite. . . . To discern the ways of God not in supernatural but in all natural and historic

events, to respond to his intention present in and beyond and through all finite intentions, that is the way of responsibility to God." *The Responsible Self: An Essay in Christian Moral Philosophy* (New York: Harper and Row, 1963), 169–70.

17 "If we had no desire to do things, we should hardly know the meaning of constraint." Maurice Cranston, *Freedom: A New Analysis* (London: Longmans, Green, 1953), 5.

18 For a discussion of these types of illusory freedom, see John Macmurray, "Freedom in the Personal Nexus," *Freedom: Its Meaning,* Anshen, ed., 511–12.

19 Alexis de Tocqueville, *Democracy in America* (New York: New American Library, 1956), 317.

20 James Baldwin, "The Discovery of What It Means to Be an American," *Nobody Knows My Name: More Notes of a Native Son* (New York: Dell, 1962), 11–12.

21 Viktor E. Frankl, *From Death Camp to Existentialism: A Psychiatrist's Path to a New Therapy,* Ilse Lasch, trans. (Boston: Beacon Press, 1959), 65–66.

22 Gordon W. Allport, *Becoming: Basic Considerations for a Psychology of Personality* (New Haven: Yale University Press, 1955), 54.

23 Martin Buber, *I and Thou,* Ronald G. Smith, trans. (New York: Scribner's 1958), 58.

24 "What happens to me happens through me, and I can neither affect myself with it nor revolt against it nor resign myself to it. . . . There are no *accidents* in life." Jean-Paul Sartre, *Being and Nothingness: An Essay on Phenomenological Ontology,* Hazel E. Barnes, trans. (New York: Philosophical Library, 1956), 554.

25 For a radical empiricist's statement of the view that the free man is the responsible man, see John Wild, *Existence and the World of Freedom* (Englewood Cliffs, N.J.: Prentice-Hall, 1963), ch. 6–8.

26 Martin Buber, *Between Man and Man,* Ronald G. Smith, trans. (Boston: Beacon Press, 1955), 70.

27 O. Hobart Mowrer, "Psychiatry and Religion," *Atlantic* (July, 1961), 88–91.

28 Richard LaPiere, *The Freudian Ethic: An Analysis of the Subversion of the American Character* (New York: Duell, Sloan & Pearce, 1959). See especially ch. 2–6.

29 Austin Farrer, *The Freedom of the Will* (London: Black, 1958), 96.

30 A. Victor Murray, *The State and the Church in a Free Society* (Cambridge University Press, 1958), 74.

31 Aristotle, *Nicomachean Ethics,* J.A.K. Thomson, trans. (Harmondsworth, Middlesex: Penguin, 1955) Book III, ch. 1.

32 Carl R. Rogers, "Learning to be Free," *N.E.A. Journal,* vol. 52, no. 3 (March, 1963), 28. But for an eloquent critique of Rogers' view of the self and freedom, see George Kateb, *Utopia and Its Enemies* (New York: Free Press of Glencoe, 1963), 154–55.

33 Cranston, *op. cit.,* 52.

34 Allport, *op. cit.,* 84.

35 Lawrence S. Kubie, "Psychiatry in Relation to Authority and Freedom," *Freedom and Authority in Our Time,* Bryson *et al.,* eds., 390–91.

36 See Robert Ulich, *The Human Career: A Philosophy of Self-Transcendence* (New York: Harper, 1955), especially ch. 10, for an excellent discussion of this concept. See also Wild, *op. cit.,* ch. 11, "An Existential Argument for Transcendence."

[37] Sterling P. Lamprecht, "Metaphysical Background of the Problem of Freedom," *Freedom and Authority in Our Time*, Bryson et al., eds., 603, makes this point clearly.

[38] This point is well discussed by Simon Greenberg, "An Outline for a Comprehensive Inquiry into the Problem of Authority and Freedom," *Ibid.*, 582.

[39] Martin Mayer, *The Schools* (New York: Harper, 1961), 329.

[40] Nancy Gayer, "On Making Morality Operational," *Phi Delta Kappan*, vol. XLVI, no. 2 (October, 1964), 42–47.

[41] "The problem of the academic world is that although it judges everything—politics, religion, art, science—and judges brilliantly, our judgment leads away from decision rather than toward it. . . . While universities and churches are concerned with how people spend their money, they aren't concerned with how they make it in the first place. Universities know that the acquisiton of knowledge is second to its use, yet still allow public relations aspects to dictate which moral concerns they will make their own. Every responsible university should see and present forcefully to its students the moral dimensions of job choosing." William Sloan Coffin Jr., "Moral Values and Our Universities," *Prospector*, vol. V, no. 3 (March, 1965), 2–3.

[42] R.M. Hare, *The Language of Morals* (Oxford: Clarendon Press, 1952), 76.

[43] G.H. Bantock, *Freedom and Authority in Education* (London: Faber & Faber, 1953), 67.

[44] See C.S. Peirce, *Values in a Universe of Chance*, Philip P. Wiener, ed. (Garden City, N.Y.: Doubleday, 1958), 230, 368–71; George W. Smith, "Peirce's Philosophy: Some Educational Implications with Particular Reference to the Teaching of Science" (unpublished dissertation, McGill University, 1961), ch. 2, 3.

[45] John Wain, *The Contenders* (New York: St. Martin's Press, 1958), 231.

[46] Paul Nash, "Reading and the Professional Conscience," *American Association of University Professors Bulletin*, vol. 46, no. 4 (Winter, 1960), 366–68. Valéry, as a general principle, condemned all reading as a passive and stultifying habit. A constant diet of printed matter, he thought, produces only a gray, pulp-like deposit in the brain. He was fond of saying, "Nos cerveaux sont faits d'une pâte grise de livres." See Laszlo Borbas, "Valéry and the Education of Youth," *French Review*, vol. XXXIV, no. 4 (February, 1961), 369.

[47] Charles Morgan, *Liberties of the Mind* (London: Macmillan, 1951), 50.

[48] John K. Galbraith, *The Affluent Society* (Boston: Houghton Mifflin, 1958), 3.

[49] Norman Cousins, "Education Against Helplessness," *Saturday Review*, vol. XLIII, no. 2 (March 19, 1960), 22.

[50] For a discussion of some of the implications of this for school counseling, see Paul Nash, "Some Notes Toward a Philosophy of School Counseling," *Personnel and Guidance Journal*, vol. XLIII, no. 3 (November, 1964), 243–48.

[51] Georg Hegel, *Philosophy of Right*, T.M. Knox, trans. (Oxford: Clarendon Press, 1942), sec. 100, 70–71; see also sec. 220, 141.

[52] William C. Kvaraceus, Walter B. Miller, et al., *Delinquent Behavior: Culture and the Individual* (Washington, D.C.: National Education Association, 1959), 134.

[53] *Ibid.*, 67.

[54] Mowrer, *op. cit.*, 100.

[55] See Karl Menninger, *Man Against Himself* (New York: Harcourt, Brace, 1938), parts III, IV.

VII

THE AUTHORITY OF TRADITION
The Freedom to Create

I THE NATURE AND SIGNIFICANCE OF CREATIVITY

Nature of Creativity

Creativity thus derives from available exuberance; it is an ebullience of personal energy and power focused in what for the individual is a significant direction. It is an outgiving of insight and awareness which is productive and fertilizing, releasing and free-flowing. It is a condition of controlled euphoria in which fulfillment is experienced, novelty becomes a reality and a noble tension is released. It is best accomplished with humor and with love. It has its moments of self-transcendence in which the little self is lost in a selfless absorption in a sublime creation; at this stage it seems timeless and noble.[1] Thus Ordway Tead described creativity.

The freedom to create has been frequently and eruditely analyzed and discussed, and yet we are still not sure what it is or in whom it exists. Creation is described in the Bible in the myth of the Creation and in the parable of the talents. But mystery obscures our clear vision of its true operation. "The mystery of creativeness," said Berdyaev, "is the mystery of freedom." [2]

There is no universal agreement concerning this mystery. Some men claim that creation is something of which only God is capable. "Man, the creature," said Buber, "who forms and transforms the creation, cannot create." [3] Others suggest that, while man is potentially capable of creativeness, few men attain it, and that the term "creative" should not be used loosely but reserved for human activity at the highest level. "Of all the numerous activities of an individual or a group," said Sorokin, "only the activities which add something new and constructive to the highest values of Truth, Goodness, Beauty, and to other positive values can be called creative." [4] Jacques Barzun has added his voice to many others in deploring the undiscriminating use in North America of the term "creativity" for a wide range of commonplace activities.[5] Finally, there are those who insist that *all* men and women are not only capable of creativity but constantly being creative in even the most prosaic aspects of their lives. Viktor Lowenfeld has suggested that an outstanding difference between man and the animals is precisely this—that man intentionally creates and the animal does not.[6] It is, thus, a specifically human characteristic to be creative.

To some extent, these apparent differences can be dissolved away by semantic analysis. Clearly, if we use the word "create" to mean to make something that has never existed before and to make it out of nothing, then we must acknowledge God as the sole owner of such talent. If the only creative ideas are those that have never before been conceived by anyone else, we must admit that the creators of such ideas compromise a tiny *élite* group.

The view taken in these pages, however, is somewhat different. While admitting the danger of using the term "creativity" loosely to describe all sorts of self-important childishness, it is nevertheless suggested that all men and women are *potentially* creative. We are all capable of creating and almost all of us do so at some times in our lives. For example, solving a difficult personal problem, adapting a piece of equipment to an unfamiliar use, creating a friendship or marriage, being original in conversation, planning an aspect of our life in an ingenious way, or intervening to bring harmony to a bitter human situation, are all examples of human creativity at work.

Certain fields are commonly thought of as providing special opportunities for creativity: art, music, crafts, drama, dancing, and language.[7] Almost all young children show the bases of potential creativity in these fields: they paint, draw, make up songs, build things, play-act, try new physical movements, make rhymes, experiment with words, and tell stories, with singular freedom and lack of self-conscious inhibition. Usually, however, these creative stirrings are killed or maimed, during the years of growing into adulthood, through indifference, ridicule, stereotyped teaching, inappropriate criticism, or lack of suitable training.

The poet, the artist, the original thinker [8] and the visionary keep all their lives something childlike about their natures. We all shared, as small children, their spontaneity and power to some degree. We all had a skin that was growing. The artist goes on growing after childhood, but most of us concentrate on the task of making ourselves relatively invulnerable by building a shell of protection around our personalities. Too late we discover that the shell that keeps out hurtful experiences also keeps in our creative powers. These powers, if long unused, atrophy.

There is a shrinkage within the shell. The shrunken kernel may, however, remain unperceived from the outside because of our skilfully built exterior. But our creative life has, in effect, died when we cease to grow in this way.

It is a mistake to think of creativity only in terms of the production of tangible objects. To be sure, a great painting, a piece of sculpture or architecture, a poem or novel are manifestations of individual creativity. But man can also create experiences—joy, happiness, intensity of emotion. He can create love and friendship. A mother can be creative through bringing up a healthy child capable of joy and through building a home whose atmosphere encourages peace, harmony, delight, and the other intangible qualities of a good life. Some men create through stimulating other men's minds with their spoken words, or through supporting the despairing, encouraging the weary. One can be perhaps most creative of all in the creation of his own personality. Man can take a hand in the process of shaping himself.

It is important to differentiate creativity, discovery, and appreciation. There is a danger in North America, under the influence of pragmatism, of using the term "creativity" when we would do better to say "discovery." The principal example is that we discover truth, rather than create it. But we can create without making something out of nothing: it is creative to put existing things into fresh combinations and arrangements to throw a fresh light on them. Although the term "creative appreciation" is an unfortunate one, and one can understand the non-pragmatist squirming under it, nevertheless genuine appreciation can be a creative act. Certainly, much that goes under the name of appreciation is uncreative passivity. But if it involves the re-creation of the imaginative insight of the original artist or composer or writer, then it can be on another level a creative experience for the appreciator. It is in this sense that imaginative looking, singing, music-making, and reading can be creative.

Creativity and the Divine

Man is free to create and yet, paradoxically, he is not autonomous in his creativity. Despite the popular image of the artist as an egocentric person, there is a great deal of evidence to suggest that creativity stems not from egocentricity but from the opposite—from the individual's connection with and sensitivity to forces outside of the ego. The creative person is impelled by a power that is not his own. It comes to him from elsewhere: he is only the carrier of it, the instrument through which it passes. What is the source of this power? The point of view put forward here is that creativity is both human and divine. It is within man and yet has a divine origin: it is the most vital expression of the divine spark that is in all men.

Beethoven, Schelling, W.H. Auden, Berdyaev, and many other creative spirits have attested that in their moments of creative inspiration a cosmic or divine influence seemed to be operating within them, lifting them up to a level that they could not themselves attain. "What we conquer for ourselves through art," wrote Beethoven, "is from God, divine inspiration. . . . Every genuine creation of art is independent, mightier than the artist himself . . . it bears testimony to the mediation of the Divine in him." [9] In the words of Schelling, "The artist . . . seems to stand under the influence of a power which . . . compels him to declare or represent things which he himself does not completely see through, and whose import is infinite." [10] In his *New Year Letter*, Auden wrote:

> We can love each because we know
> All, all of us, that this is so:
> Can live because we're loved: the powers
> That we create with are not ours.[11]

And Berdyaev has affirmed that, "True creativeness is always in the Holy Spirit, for only in the Spirit can there be that union of grace and freedom which we find in creativeness." [12] One of the most vivid accounts of the experiencing of this divine power has come from Thomas Kelly, in his description of a flash of creative insight:

> It is as if a fountain of creative Mind were welling up, bubbling to expression within prepared spirits. There is an infinite fountain of lifting power, pressing within us, luring us by dazzling visions, and we can only say, The creative God comes into our souls. An increment of infinity is about us. Holy is imagination, the gateway of Reality into our hearts.[13]

There are, of course, certain philosophical and theological difficulties about this position. Is it man who creates, or God? If God is the source of creative power, has man any genuine freedom? But these and some related problems are the consequences of an unnecessary exclusiveness of approach. The atheistic existentialist, for example, would say that there are no essences, no universal "oughts," no transcendental values. Therefore, man is free to create his own standards and values. He is a free, autonomous, potentially creative individual. Man can make himself. The Thomist neo-scholastic on the other hand, would say that values are universal and established. Man's nature is fixed: he is made by God. All creation comes from God: man only discovers and interprets. The truth is that both are right in their main emphasis, but both are wrong in their exclusiveness. Man and God are *both* freely and creatively at work in the universe. Man is made by God but is able to modify himself and his environment by his own creative efforts. As men like Berdyaev and Froebel have pointed out, God made man in his own image and likeness, and man is therefore called in his turn to creative work. Creativity is the God-like part of man.

This view, then, questions the assumption of a static, unchanging, self-sufficient God and posits instead an active, creative God constantly at work among men, whose co-operation he needs as much as they need his. Creativity is conceived as an interdependent partnership. If the question is pressed whether God's will or man's will prevails, it must be answered that, although man must seek to know and execute God's will, this will is not preordained but capable of change according to man's creative response and initiative. The will of God is perceived by man in the creative opportunity of the moment.

The Creative Process

What is the evidence of this creativeness operating in the universe? How does the creative process work? Two aspects of creativeness are often suggested: what Berdyaev called *inner* and *outer* creativeness, or what Lowenfeld called *potential* and *functional* creativeness. Inner creativeness is the primary creative act in which man, facing inward, hears a symphony, conceives an idea or poem or picture, becomes aware of invention, feels love for a person. This is an inner knowledge not known to the world: the individual is not concerned with realization. Potential creativeness is the creativeness a man has within him but does not necessarily use. Often, upbringing and education have neglected, inhibited, or buried it. Outer creativeness is the secondary creative act in which man faces outward—faces the world and other men. Now comes the realization through action of the creative intuition. Functional creativeness is that part of a man's creativeness that he uses, that expresses itself through his work and effort.[14]

The creative process is usually thought of as having a number of observable phases. In the views of various writers, these vary in number and nomenclature. However, they are usually reducible to the following four, and if the names differ from these they are usually close synonyms: *preparation, incubation, inspiration, revision.*

The phase of *preparation* involves the often long and laborious process of gaining experience by steeping oneself in the field. The emphasis often placed on the moment of inspiration can divert attention from the necessity for hard preparatory work. Inspiration comes only within the strict bounds of the discipline in which the individual is working.

Painters do not obtain inspirations about new mathematical theories; physicists are not inspired with great symphonies.

There usually seems to be a need for a period of *incubation* to bring the creative act to fruition. This is helped by a clear sense of direction, by steady effort, deep concentration, and fairly lengthy periods of work, interspersed with periods of rest and relaxation. Although external interruptions are harmful to the creative process, periods of deliberate inactivity are not only helpful but essential during this incubation phase.

The stage of *inspiration* or illumination is difficult to write about, since it is hard to predict. It may be a moment of sudden insight or it may be a more gradual process. It cannot be forced or demanded, but, as pointed out, it will not come without preparation. Moreover, its nature depends fundamentally on the culture in which the creator has grown up. For example, no Beethoven could arise among the Australian aborigines, no Shakespeare among the Eskimos, no Einstein in New Guinea.

The form of the fourth stage of *revision* is affected by the nature of the creative work. In the arts, it may consist of reworking, polishing, rebuilding. In other fields, it may amount to verification, testing the original hypothesis or insight. The best creative work is almost always the result of much revision—a fact that is unpopular with the undisciplined performer.

Needless to say, these phases are neither chronological nor necessarily distinct. There is often merging and overlapping. To an outside observer, their sequence and even their appearance may be undetectable. But usually, in some form or other, they will together represent the development of the creative process.

This is an appropriate place to raise the question of the extent to which the creative process is a *conscious* process, and to what extent *unconscious*. Ghiselin has suggested [15] that the unconscious part of man's mind is the greatest asset to creativity. In a way, he maintained, the conscious and the unconscious act in opposition to each other. The conscious is a conservative tendency, hindering the introduction of anything new. The old order is associated with that which is readily realizable in the focus of the conscious attention. The unconscious is the realm of obscurity, of a potential new order, which threatens the conserving and persisting tendencies of consciousness. If we want to open ourselves to creative innovation, therefore, we must beware of that which easily imprints itself on our conscious attention and give an opportunity for unconscious influences to operate.

The theory that the unconscious is an important element in the creative process has been energetically opposed by Sorokin.[16] He maintained that, contrary to the claims of Freud, Jung, von Hartmann, Janet, and others, the unconscious does not create anything. Such beliefs are the result, he thought, of a mistaken identification of the *superconscious* (which is above the conscious level) with the *unconscious* (which is below the conscious state of mind). It is this superconscious which is the "starter and supreme guide in making all notable discoveries, inventions, and masterpieces of man." [17] However, since this is a realm about which very little is known with certainty, Sorokin's dogmatic refutations and claims seem ill-judged. Perhaps he has been influenced by the fact that psychiatrists have concentrated on the destructive, rather than the creative, power of the unconscious, thereby rendering it something to be feared instead of nurtured.[18] All that it seems wise to say at this point is that there appears to be a source of creative activity that is different from the sensory and rational modes of cognition and that operates on an intuitive level, free from the limitations of the conscious. This source has been frequently identified with the unconscious, and I shall adhere to the use of this term.

When these unconscious forces are permitted to operate, the creative worker seems to catch hold of a power greater than his own. The work of creation develops its own momentum and the worker is in a sense transformed and created anew by the work. Jung has written of poetry that the poet's work

outgrows him as a child its mother. The creative process has feminine quality, and the creative work arises from unconscious depths—we might say, from the realm of mothers. Whenever the creative force predominates, human life is ruled and moulded by the unconscious as against the active will, and the conscious ego is swept along on a subterranean current, being nothing more than a helpless observer of events. The work in process becomes the poet's fate and determines his psychic development. It is not Goethe who creates *Faust*, but *Faust* which creates Goethe.[19]

It must be remembered that Jung was a practicing psychiatrist and, therefore, apt to overemphasize the importance of the unconscious, the evidence of whose power he was constantly facing. The conscious mind, too, has a part in the creative process. It is most important in the stages of preparation—storing the mind, cultivating the ground—and revision—verifying and correcting one's intuitions and inventions. Nevertheless, Jung's dramatic description is a salutary reminder that in a technological and would-be rational society it is perilous to ignore the unconscious. If we would create anything new we must learn to sit loosely to life. To grit the teeth and set the will merely reinforces the hold of the conscious mind on the problem in view. Conscious willing helps to solve problems that are already formulated, but it is less useful in reaching out to the undiscovered, where the unconscious mind sets its own unpredictable pace.

Qualities of the Creative Person

Potential creativity is universal in man. But we know that, functionally, not all men live creative lives. What is the difference between the more, and the less, creative personality? What are the distinguishing characteristics of the person who is markedly creative? A number of investigators have tried to answer these questions, and there is a remarkable degree of agreement among them. Harold Anderson, in summarizing a number of studies on the subject, wrote,

The consensus of these authors is that creativity is an expression of a mentally or psychologically healthy person, that creativity is associated with wholeness, unity, honesty, integrity, personal involvement, enthusiasm, high motivation, and action.[20]

Theresa Haney, as a result of her experiences at the Akron Creative Arts Center, has summed up her findings about the creative person.[21] The creative child, she found, is the unpredictable child, the one with the gift for seeing and saying the different, the unconventional, the surprising. He has a sense of humor. He has an appreciation for the life about him and reacts to it with energy. His personality is never flat; he is never indifferent. His curiosity impels him to an awareness of the details of the world. He observes them and is sensitive to the experience they provide.

One of the most careful studies is that made by Frank Barron of the originality displayed by 100 United States Air Force captains. He found significant relationships between originality and the following six qualities: "disposition towards integration of diverse stimuli . . . energy, fluent output, involvement . . . personal dominance and self-assertion . . . responsiveness to impulse and emotion . . . expressed femininity of interests . . . general effectiveness of performance." [22]

Let us examine one or two of the more important qualities in greater detail. There is good reason for listing first among the qualities of the creative person that of openness or flexibility. The creative person is ready to see new possibilities in old situations, has the flexibility to take advantage of the unexpected, is able to profit from mistakes, is excited and challenged rather than disturbed by sudden changes in conditions. Arthur Koestler has noted these qualities in most of the geniuses responsible for the major mutations in the history of thought. They combine a marked skepticism toward traditional ideas, dogmas, and assumptions with a remarkable openmindedness toward promising new concepts. Out of this combination results the crucial capacity for perceiving a familiar object, situation, or problem in a new light or new context.

This act of wrenching away an object or concept from its habitual associative context is . . . an essential part of the creative process. . . . Every creative act—in science, art or religion—involves a regression to a more primitive level, a new innocence of perception liberated from the cataract of accepted beliefs.[23]

Closely related to this quality of openness is the tendency toward unity and integration. The creative person combines his openness to a wide range of phenomena and experiences with a strong desire to arrange these experiences into some sort of coherent and meaningful pattern. Followers of the holistic theory of J.C. Smuts would say there is throughout the universe a tendency toward the creation of wholes—from the atom nucleus to the integrated personality of man, the creation of friendships and communities, scientific principles, laws, paintings, sonatas, poems, and so on.[24] What are disconnected fragments to the unimaginative person can be organized by the creative person into a uniting configuration, bearing a significance previously undetected. This ability to integrate our experiences is associated with the degree of integration of our own personality. Speaking of the relationship between self-knowledge and creative activity, which he called "spontaneous" activity, Fromm wrote, "Only if man does not repress essential parts of himself, only if he has become transparent to himself, and only if the different spheres of life have reached a fundamental integration, is spontaneous activity possible." [25]

The greater degree of self-knowledge of the creative person permits him to realize his own inconsistencies and ambiguities and, hence, makes him more tolerant of complexity and ambiguity in the outside world. This is demonstrated in Barron's finding expressed femininity of interest among creative men. They were able to recognize in themselves impulses or interests considered more appropriate to women. This is an aspect of the disposition to allow more complexity and contradiction into one's consciousness. The more original men allowed themselves to be aware of tabooed interests and sought to integrate them into a more complex whole.

Clearly, then, such a personality is characterized by a relative lack of fear, which, in turn, is associated with the confidence and energy of the creative person. The fears that impede creativity are fear of the unknown, fear of others, and fear of oneself. We are all to some extent afraid of the unknown: we feel safe with the familiar and cling to it.

The creative mind, however, tolerates and welcomes the unknown as a source of opportunity and inspiration, is unafraid of the unstructured and the unfamiliar, is unthreatened by the new and the changing. Fear of others is also destructive of the creative impulse. The creative person is relatively unafraid of the weight of society's opinion, he can operate with a degree of autonomy, he finds competition, opposition, and criticism stimulants rather than disasters. He has also overcome to a degree fear of himself, can trust his own judgments, has faith in the validity of his own unique experiences, and can change his mind and admit his errors because he is unafraid of his own inconsistencies and deficiencies.

There remains to be discussed the elusive quality called "general effectiveness of performance." Despite the possession of many of the qualities of the creative person, some people still fail to be notably creative. What is the missing ingredient? It is suggested that the clue to the creative personality is a factor of *balance:* the outstandingly creative person has achieved a harmonious balance in his personality, between freedom and control, between imagination and discipline, between primitivism and rationality.[26] The second part of each of these polarities is less frequently mentioned in analyses of creativity than the first part, which has more fashionable appeal. But it is unwise to ignore either part. Without imagination there can be no creativity, but without the use of reason to discipline the imagination, potential creativity too often dribbles away like water through the fingers. The creative person, moreover, must discipline and control himself to be creatively productive: he must apply to himself the same sense of form and order that is the essence of a work of art.

It is this balance, above all, that distinguishes the unusually creative person from the mentally ill person. Clemens Benda has examined carefully the connection between mental illness and artistic creativity. He studied the lives of Van Gogh, Friedrich Nietzsche, Edvard Munch, and Strindberg, and he concluded that these cases prove that mental illness is not necessarily a productive factor in the creative process; it is often a destructive one.[27] He admitted that creative artists share with neurotics and schizophrenics a tendency toward "primitivism"—that is, the ability to identify with objects on a primitive level. But artists differ from mentally ill people in their ability to control and integrate their experiences. Both can descend to the primitive level, the source of much imagery and symbol, but the artist can return to the level of rationality and creative performance. Studies of the unconscious alone put the creative artist close to the neurotic or even the schizophrenic, in their imagery formation, but the neurotic is an ineffective person, while the artist has strong powers of control and discipline. It is the ability to transform the imagery into symbolic forms that distinguishes the artist. Thus, the creative person, Barron suggested, may be "at once naïve and knowledgeable, being at home equally to primitive symbolism and to rigorous logic. He is both more primitive and more cultured, more destructive and more constructive, occasionally crazier and yet adamantly saner, than the average person." [28]

Significance of Creativity

The primary significance of man's creativity is that it represents for him the core of genuine freedom. Only a free man can create, and to be creative is to show irrefutable evidence of personal freedom. Henri Bergson argued, in *Time and Free Will*, that the most free act of which man is capable is the creative act.[29] The outstandingly creative person is the highest type of human being, one who is marked by what Riesman has called "autonomy," [30] what Fromm has called "spontaneity" [31] (which he later expanded into the concept of the "productive orientation" [32]), and what I would call freedom. This is the type of person who can relate to other people through love and to the world in general through creative work. It is centrally important that through love and creative work one becomes forgetful of the self: herein lies an important source of freedom. And this is why the artist has greater hope of becoming free than the ascetic. The ascetic life tends to make the individual concentrate on himself, on his own moral progress and chances of salvation. The artist who loses himself in creative work, on the other hand, is able to transcend his own petty level and become absorbed in a timeless, sublime dimension.

Furthermore, to develop a point raised earlier, it seems that there is a significant relationship between creativity and mental health. It is true, of course, that creativity has sometimes been associated with the compensatory efforts of a mentally sick person to create under the compulsion of a deficiency or frustration. But consider how much finer and more productive these lives are than those of the mentally sick who are hopelessly without any creative outlet.[33] We can guess what a difference creativity might make to such lives from our knowledge of the contribution of creative work to the harmony and fulfillment of the lives of healthy people. Ordway Tead said,

> Creativity properly conceived is perhaps the most important of the several outlets of personal expression which is self-fulfilling and intrinsically rewarding. It is an indispensable quality of a full and rich personality. . . . It almost seems true that we *are* as we are creative.[34]

Michael Andrews has suggested that creativity and mental health are related because creativity is a self-integrating force, because it stems from well-being, because its source is man's tendency to actualize himself, to become his own potentialities—all of which are the marks of the mentally healthy person.[35]

We must be aware that in an industrial society and in a heavily armed world the alternatives to creativity are costly and dangerous. When our creative impulses are penned within us, as they often are by the conditions of factory work or of mass education, they apparently die away. In fact, these repressed urges can serve to poison our unconscious lives. This "unlived life" can be the cause of our embitterment and, ultimately, our destruction. Douglas Steere has warned that

> It is still to be ascertained how much of the bitterness, the projection of blame upon an enemy country or group of countries that characterizes modern wars (whether they be hot or cold wars) or that marks class conflict is really a blind, frustrated, free-hanging hate that comes from this unused creativity in the worker. Thus this reservoir of mass hatred is available for demagogues to draw up and to direct now to this enemy and now to that, and when these whipping boys fail, much of it may come back upon the wife or husband and the family.[36]

Similarly Sir Herbert Read has suggested that "Destructiveness and creativity are opposed forces in the life of the mind. To create is to construct, and to construct co-operatively is to lay the foundations of a peaceful community." [37] Sylvia Ashton-Warner saw the mind of the young child as "a volcano with two vents; destructiveness and creativeness. And . . . to the extent that we widen the creative channel, we atrophy the destructive one." [38] Erich Fromm maintained that it is when man senses his failure to transcend his situation by creating that he tries instead to transcend it by destroying: in the act of destruction he proves himself superior to that which he could not create—life.[39]

There is one immediate reason why an emphasis on the creative process is so important in contemporary North American society: it is that this society is predominantly product-centered rather than process-centered and would benefit by having the balance altered somewhat. Such a society needs to be brought to the knowledge that possession as such provides neither power nor security. The race to possess material goods or destructive weapons or academic qualifications is doomed to fail to provide the strength that is hoped for. It is often not until the end of one's life that one looks back and realizes, too late, that the benefit, the joy, and the fulfillment lay in the process of work or study, not in their material rewards. The experience of creative activity is the best means to bring to men a realization that it is through *doing* and *being*, rather than through *having*, that life is to be created, lived, and enjoyed.

There is also a danger in a society that is satiated with material goods that its members will come to take their material environment for granted, ceasing to appreciate or even see it. The experience of creative activity can do more than anything else to arouse these dormant senses and increase sensitivity to the world's beauty. One cannot become more creative in art, music, literature, religion, or human relationships without becoming more sensitive. The artist might be thought of as one who sees further and more clearly. His sensitivity, attuned through his creative activity, enables him to see beauty and color where the ordinary man sees only familiar drabness. It has been said that "Nature copies art." What does this mean? Perhaps that artistic creativity opens our eyes, shows us how to look, affects the way in which we see and understand nature, and hence virtually determines what our conception of nature will be. In a country where almost all are half-blind, the sensitive vision of the creative artist is something to be treasured and nurtured.

One of the by-products of creativity that we might reasonably hope for in our industrialized society is that it will make the worker who enjoys it more demanding of the aesthetic quality of his conditions of work, as well as more aesthetically sensitive to the quality of his own work. This may be temporarily embarrassing for many managements, but its long-term effects should be to raise the whole aesthetic tone of our lives. And there is no need to emphasize the factor of the increasing leisure time made available in industrialized societies. With the postponement of the beginning of the working life, shorter working hours, and longer years of retirement, the place of creative activity becomes crucial. We must note in this connection the difference between creative activities and recreational activities. There is a great danger today of organizing the recreation of young people and adults to the degree that their leisure time becomes as routine and uncreative as their work time. Much better than this formal organization is to help children find joy in an appreciation of the creative process, so that they will constantly seek creative opportunities in work and leisure.

Lastly, creativity bears significance not only through its successes but also through its failures. This is especially true in the field of artistic creation. No one can be considered liberally educated who has not attempted to be creative in some field of art. This is not because the educated man must be an artist, but because only through experiencing the joy and pain of artistic creation can he understand the nature of art. And it is also only through art that he can come close to the knowledge of perfection, for although man cannot achieve perfection in this world, artistic creation is the field in which he comes closest to breaking the bonds that keep him from it.

II EDUCATION FOR CREATIVITY

Creative and Aesthetic Education

An education that is designed to produce sound, mature people cannot fail to include an aesthetic component. Today in the West we are generally aware of the need to nurture in young people an appreciation of the *true* and the *good* but are more likely to forget the importance of the *beautiful*. Not only are all three vital, but they need to be related to each other through the educational process so that the individual can integrate the rational, the ethical, and the aesthetic within himself. Without this integration we are in danger of producing the narrow intellectual snob, the preaching moralist, or the affected aesthete, none of whom can be considered mature or soundly educated people, because they lack perspective and breadth of vision.

One of the greatest fruits of an aesthetic education is that it gives the individual an opportunity to find within himself the hidden sources of his creative energies. This means finding an activity that helps him meet and come to an understanding of that most difficult of all entities —himself. In an eloquent statement on the significance of art education, Archibald MacLeish has said,

> It is only by establishing the relationship between the poem, the picture, and the experience of life *as he knows the experience of life*, that any human being reaches an understanding of what is happening before his eyes: happening to *him* now and here, no matter when or where the work was done. Unless, as reader of this poem, he is able to make *his* way back through this movement of images upon a pattern of music, into a context of meaning which is real for him, which is alive for him, which is human for him, he will not have shared in the creative act. . . . it is by sharing in the creative act that education in humanity advances.[40]

It is a mistake to think that certain activities—such as poetry, literature, art, music—touch the aesthetic and creative part of man, while others—such as science, mathematics—do not. Creative imagination is important in all fields, although not equally so at all levels. In recent years its importance in science has been increasingly recognized, and certainly one of the earliest lessons in aesthetic education can be taught by insisting on clean arithmetic papers.

Nevertheless, all fields are not equally valuable in nurturing creativity and aesthetic sensitivity. The great enemies of creativity are fear and passivity, and these reactions are often engendered in children as a result of their growing realization of the vastness of the universe and its limitless power. The consequent feeling of personal powerlessness carries the danger of the dissipation of energy. One way of combating this danger is to give children the opportunity to deal with material that is tractable and malleable, on a scale that is comprehensible to them, so that, at one level, they can experience the feeling of mastery and control. Hence, of outstanding value in this educational process are painting, pottery, woodwork, metalwork, sculpture, and all work that gives the child the chance to alter the material form of the world. Lowenfeld has suggested that creative aesthetic experiences stimulate general creativity.[41]

Creative and aesthetic education need special attention in America, where we still suffer from the vestiges of a Puritan tradition that combines a philistinic contempt for many art forms with a moral distrust of the artist himself. In Nazi Germany many artistic forms (expressionism and surrealism, for example) and creative expressions were rejected and proscribed. If such forms and expressions are rejected in America, it will not be because of Nazi passions but because of philistinic indifference. And indifference is much more dangerous than suppression, because its effects are more permanent. If we are indifferent to art and creativity and their place in the education of men, we shall, in effect, have achieved the same as the Nazis.

The Nurture of Creativity

Creativity cannot be taught. Nevertheless, the environment can be arranged so that enabling rather than disabling conditions operate on the creative potential of the individual.[42] What guidelines can be laid down that will make the educational process one that nourishes rather than destroys the potential creativity of all men and women? The basic challenge that presents itself to parents and educators arises from the phenomenon that almost all children are promising, from a creative point of view, but very few adults are functionally creative. Between the promise and the performance is a gap that can be reduced by the skilful parent or teacher. Instead of hastening the apparently inexorable process by which the potentially creative child grows into the dull, uncreative adult, the wise and ingenious teacher can help the child to release the creative forces within him and to mold them into effective performance.

The surest way of nurturing this creativity lies in leading the child through an experience of harmonious balance between the qualities of *discipline* and *freedom*. Creative activity is the product of an appropriate blend of restraint and flexibility, conservatism and progressivism, control and experiment. Creative ideas are essential but insufficient: there must also be discipline and skill to translate the idea into reality. In the rest of this section we shall explore some of the aspects and implications of this necessary blend.

How much control and pressure is suitable to evoke the creative response of which a child is capable? The fault of most traditional education has been to apply too much control and pressure, on the assumption of the wickedness and laziness of children, thus effectively discouraging the potential creativity of slow or unconfident children and producing mental breakdown in sensitive ones. The fault of some types of progressive education has been to apply insufficient control and pressure, on the assumption of the goodness and self-direction of children, thus producing a large number of complacent, self-satisfied, uncreative nonentities. The solution to this dilemma lies in distinguishing between two types of pressure. The first type presents a problem or challenge that the individual can solve—or try to solve with a good chance of success—with the ideas, skills, background, and knowledge that he possesses or can foreseeably gain. The second type presents a problem or challenge that the individual cannot, or feels he cannot, possibly solve or overcome with his own resources. The first type is often the stimulus to creativity: the second is often the cause of passivity and despair.

Once we have presented a challenge that is appropriate for this child, we must show him that there can be no creativity without submission to the discipline of work. The creative worker ultimately achieves a complete identification with his work. It is the responsibility of the teacher to arrange the classroom situation so that the child can involve himself deeply with the material studied and with the learning process. This involves a ruthless pruning of the curriculum to exclude all meaningless, irrelevant material. Arbitrary, imposed tasks, whose function and relevance to his own sense of purpose the child cannot grasp, are destructive of creativity for they accustom the child to working without involvement. For example, the study of grammar should evolve only as a natural outgrowth of the desire for accurate and elegant expression and should be toppled from its place as a separate, functionless, and unfruitful activity. Opportunities for the child to participate actively in the planning and execution of his school program will further serve to involve and, hence, discipline him.

The skilful teacher will realize that the kind of discipline that nurtures creativity has little connection with mere external control. This kind of control has served in the past largely as a means of stamping out creativeness; discipline should be used as a means of controlling those forces that impede creativeness, thus making possible a release of creative energy. Fundamentally, the discipline required involves a mastery of the *self* in relation to the *material* or to other *people*. Gradually the child should become aware that the discipline necessary for the productive expression of creativity takes the form of self-control, unabating effort, deep concentration, renunciation of transient but interfering pleasures, sacrifice of time, leisure, and material goods, vigorous and honest self-examination, and self-criticism.

Discipline is related to order in the life of the creative person. It is easy to underestimate the importance of material and mechanical factors in the nurture of creativity. The painter needs physical space, the writer a clean desk, the child space and time, uncluttered with trivia, if they are to perform as they might. A regular place and time of work and a tidy arrangement of workthings are often aids to creativity. It is a fallacy to think that the creative worker needs to be untidy, disorganized, chaotic, and temperamental. This is a popular stereotype that has done much harm.

Not only in his working habits, but also in the work itself, should the quality of order manifest itself. All creativity involves a putting together, a putting into an ordered whole what was previously a disparate chaos. It is, therefore, important in a creative education to give the child manifold opportunities to see relationships between different parts of his experience, to put together his experiences into various combinations, and to understand wholes rather than fragments. Much contemporary education is an anticreative force precisely because of this tendency toward the fragmentation of knowledge into meaningless portions.

The child, moreover, should be brought to realize that in a creative work there is order in the form of a high degree of *economy*: nothing should be wasted, nothing superfluous. In a great work of art, for example, it would be almost impossible to add anything or take anything away without impairing it. The teacher must encourage the child to strive for the kind of order that is reflected in the utmost economy of expression—the idea he conceives must be expressed with the minimum of material.

Interwoven with these manifestations of discipline in the creative process there must be at the same time manifestations of freedom. There must be freedom for the child to penetrate deeply into his experiences and to absorb them. This means above all that the teacher must give the child *time*—time to sit quietly and reflectingly before knowledge and events to gain real insight into them, instead of memorizing facts, quickly using them, returning them to the examiner, and forgetting them. There is a crucial need for more reflection and contemplation in school. Instead of always insisting on quick answers, the teacher should sometimes ask the children to sit in quiet contemplation of a question before attempting to answer. Freedom for the child to become deeply involved in his studies means also that the teacher must not teach too much, not cover too much ground, not teach too many subjects, not be afraid of leaving gaps. Only by concentrating on depth in whatever is studied can the teacher give the child time to penetrate below the superficial level.

John Richardson, who lived for several months with Pablo Picasso in an attempt to discover the roots of Picasso's creative genius, has given us a vivid insight into the artist's powers of concentration:

What struck me about Picasso was his total absorption in the task of the moment. The huge, owl-like eyes would get an intent, rapacious look, and appear to devour whatever was in front of them. . . . I realized that part of Picasso's genius lies in his ability to concentrate all his faculties on whatever he is seeing, doing or saying. If he looks at a book he looks at it as if he had never looked at one before; even signing his name is never an automatic gesture. Nothing is done unthinkingly or absent-mindedly. Picasso pays attention to everything and everybody. When he drinks a glass of water he *thinks*, deliberates even. One feels this throughout his work; this concentration is also the driving force of his life: the reason why he is capable of such intense warmth and friendship. . . . And yet there is seldom any feeling of strain or nervousness on his side or, for that matter, on anybody else's. When you know him well, you can relax, even if it is like going to sleep with the light on.[43]

Another important freedom that creativity demands is the freedom to *feel*. If children are to be creative they must be enabled to experience their *own* genuine emotions and to be unafraid of them. Only through recovering our deep emotional life can we escape the stifling influence of the artificial sentimentality that pervades our society. Fromm has expressed the danger well:

While there is no doubt that any creative thinking—as well as any other creativity—is inseparably linked with emotion, it has become an ideal to think and to live without emotions. To be "emotional" has become synonymous with being unsound or unbalanced. By the acceptance of this stand the individual has become greatly weakened; his thinking is impoverished and flattened. On the other hand, since emotions cannot be completely killed, they must have their existence totally apart from the intellectual side of the personality; the result is the cheap and insincere sentimentality with which movies and popular songs feed millions of emotion-starved customers.[44]

Too often our education teaches us *what* to feel, what is respectable or fashionable to feel, thus hindering the process by which the person frees himself from conventional sentiment and gains the courage of his own spontaneous, creative feelings.

Freedom from inflexibility is yet another aspect of creative freedom. Its nurture is always difficult and is probably impossible with inflexible teachers. To help the individual's creativeness we must teach him how to be *ready*—ready to take advantage of the unexpected, the unforeseen, the unusual. This means encouraging a certain skepticism toward things as they are, an eager readiness to entertain new ideas, to see familiar things in unusual ways, to be on the lookout for unusual analogies and patterns of relationships. Needless to say, only the secure teacher can afford to maintain a classroom atmosphere in which such flexibility can flourish. It is helpful to point out to children that, although familiar external conditions and working materials may be aids to creativity, a slavish dependence on them reduces our flexibility and, hence, narrows our freedom. It is better if possible to be independent of idiosyncratic devices.

In order to be creative it is necessary to be sensitive, to refine the senses so that one becomes acutely aware of one's surroundings. The skilful teacher can help the child toward freedom from the purblind condition in which most people face the world. The creative teacher can teach the child to *see*, to use his eyes for observing and comparing as well as recognizing. What to the untrained eye may be only the numerous branches of the trees in winter can become to the creative observer a wonder and delight of changing shapes, patterns, colors, and relationships—an effect of dynamic beauty that can stimulate and renew his own creative efforts.

Obstacles to Creativity

On the other side of the coin of the nurture of creativity can be seen the obstacles to its development. These can largely be inferred from the preceding discussion, but something can be gained by outlining more concretely one or two of the major obstacles, so that we have them clearly before our eyes.

Education for creativity is especially important in a technological age: the machine affords us more leisure in which creativity can blossom; but it also destroys creativity by increasing the use of repetitive, simple, fractured operations, often devoid of meaning and context. Meaninglessness, atomization, interruptions, noise—these are all prime threats to creativity that are aggravated by the machine. "We arrest our inner creativity," wrote Lewis Mumford, "with external compulsions and irrelevant anxieties, at the mercy of constant interruptions by telephone and radio and insistent print, timing our lives to the movement of a production belt we do not control." [45] Unfortunately, many of the destructive features of industrial life have been carried into the home and school. In the home, creativity is impeded by the constant noise and kaleidoscope of confusing experiences presented by the ubiquitous television and radio. In the school it is impeded by short periods of work, frequent bells, rigid timetables, and enforced gregariousness, all of which militate against the deep and sustained concentration and periods of reflective solitude that are necessary to bring the creative spirit to the surface.

Another threat to creativity stemming from the assumptions of an acquisitive, technological society is the predominant emphasis on material productivity. The values in such a society are concerned with the efficient exploitation of natural resources and human beings for maximum productiveness and acquisition. This operates against the creation of an atmosphere in which can be encouraged the unpredictable, spontaneous, apparently "unproductive" impulses of man. A society that stresses the producing, gaining, and hoarding of material objects will discourage the careless generosity of spirit needed for creativity. In North American education, the influence of pragmatism and instrumentalism has been to emphasize the type of creativity that produces tangible objects with practical utility. This is valid but narrow. If adhered to exclusively it cuts us off from some of the most vital creative experiences, such as the pursuit of truth and understanding, the achievement of virtue and harmony, and the creation and enjoyment of beauty.

In the schools and universities, this dominance of productivity takes the form of a concentration on examinations and marks, the outward signs in the academic world of successful production. Oscar Handlin, among many others, has deplored this development in American colleges, whose students, he has claimed, are so grade-hungry that they have no time for genuine education. The ablest, potentially creative, young people secure an admirable training in what he called "the techniques of the right answer. They learn to remember; to be accurate, neat, and cautious. But they are rarely called on to use their ability autonomously or speculatively, to deal with situations in which the answers are not known but must be discovered. . . . With what pain, if ever at all, will they learn how to know what they do not know, how to probe alone beyond the limits of what is handed to them, how to be creative original thinkers." [46] The schools, too, emphasize the production of results to the detriment of creativity. Holland and his research associates at the National Merit Scholarship Corporation found consistent, though small, *negative* relationships between school grades and measures of originality, independence of judgment, and complexity of outlook among their scholarship candidates.[47] In other words, at the upper end of the ability scale at least, school grades may reflect only the ability to follow direction, obey the teacher, be docile, and memorize. If this is so, it is a severe indictment of the school system as a creative influence.

Teachers who are concerned to encourage creativity among their pupils must resolutely oppose the concept of education as information-feeding. It is, of course, wasteful for children to have to rediscover for themselves everything that has already been discovered. And it is necessary to gain some basic knowledge to use it as a springboard for creative work. The problem is how to help children to gain this knowledge without, in the process, killing their creative drive because of the *way* in which the knowledge is assimilated. We know that spoon-feeding and mechanical, ground-covering [48] methods are most likely to kill creativity. Teaching children thoughts rather than how to think is one example of this approach. Readymade thoughts that have to be absorbed into the memory work against the encouragement of originality. If we insist that children memorize hundreds of isolated scraps of information, we must be prepared for the fact that, with their time totally taken up with absorbing mountains of data, there will be no time or energy left for thinking. If we insist on continually hurrying to cover the curriculum, to complete the book or assignment, we must be prepared to sacrifice those vital moments of insight that are so rare that everything needs to be stopped to assimilate and cultivate them.

We must view with caution and use with care the range of audiovisual techniques that technology is making available to us. While these have many valuable uses, they often tend to nurture a passivity in the student that is a severe threat to creativity. A prime example is the use of television, which tends to capture and satisfy the imagination rather than stimulate and liberate it. A good teacher, like Socrates, should make us feel a little uncomfortable, should prod us into creative activity. Television, with its rich supply of visual images, tends by contrast to saturate us, to fill in all the gaps, to provide the missing pieces, so that there is little or nothing left for us to do.

Closed-ended pedagogical techniques of all kinds are impediments to creativity. This includes objective examinations,[49] true-false tests, and a host of minor techniques, most of which have the "virtue" of keeping energetic children busy. Busyness is itself not only a misleading sign of the degree of genuine activity going on in the classroom, but a major obstacle to creativeness. In his autobiography, Richard Church wrote, "I became conscious that to be 'busy', to be up and doing some immediate job, was always a good excuse for putting off the *real* exercise of the mind, that agonising, racking athleticism of creative thought, which exhausts us body and soul, and usually gives such intangible results." [50]

One of the commonest ways in which we, as adults, suppress the creative freedom of children is through what I would call the *authority of expectations*. We limit the creativity of many children by holding unduly low expectations of what they can become. Children arrive at their own evaluation of themselves partly through their perception of what we expect of them. In large measure they docilely become what we appear to expect them to become. We can help children by showing that we have faith and confidence in them, without making our expectations so specific in terms of role or performance that we in effect mold them according to our preconceived notions. And there is a mutuality between this concern for the creativity of children and our own creativity: parents who help children to solve their problems creatively are themselves strengthened. Just as teachers who suppress children's creative endeavors must pay the cost of this suppression in terms of their own personal development, so teachers who help children to become more creative will themselves benefit in terms of the growth of their own creative powers.

Finally, we must not ignore one of the commonest and most serious obstacles to creativity—fear. In the family, the primary enabling conditions of creativity are parental love and loving family relationships. The primary disabling conditions are parental and family relationships that breed fear and insecurity. In the school, it is necessary to arrange the environment with extreme delicacy, if we want the emotional and unconscious life of the child to feed the springs of creativity. It is unlikely that high-quality creative work can be nourished from these sources if there is a harsh, unsympathetic, authoritarian teacher who motivates by fear. Creative work should be expected only in a warm, supporting, secure atmosphere. We shall never get children to frame important questions for themselves, to wonder deeply, or to play with ideas—all ways of releasing creative energies—unless we can reduce their fears. There is a case to be made for removing much of the personal risk from education, for encouraging children to play with ideas in a largely risk-free situation. But we have a long way to go in this respect. John Holt, who has vividly documented the failure of schools to nurture creativity in children, has maintained that our substitution of fear for creativity is deliberate. It is no accident that the child in school is afraid, he has charged. "We have made him afraid, consciously, deliberately, so that we might more easily control his behavior and get him to do whatever we wanted him to do." [51]

Despite their drawbacks in some fields, progressive schools, on the whole, produce richer creative work than do traditional schools. In the same way, despite their greater sloppiness and wastefulness, politically liberal regimes engender greater creativeness than do totalitarian regimes. The fear of censorship or punishment in modern totalitarian regimes has rendered largely nugatory their creative achievements in the fields of art, literature (especially poetry), philosophical speculation, and pure science. Even in more liberal countries, the massive size of the problems of industrial societies leads to a fear and distrust of one's own powers and creative capacities. The belief that social, political, economic, and religious problems are too complex for children to study in school is a reflection of the belief that, in a complex civilization, people should not try to think out their problems creatively but should wait for experts and specialists to pronounce authoritatively on them.

Creativity and Values

Is it enough to educate for creativity and leave it at that? Certainly, the parent or teacher who succeeds in freeing the latent creative urges of the child, and in disciplining them into functional creative power, might justifiably feel that he had done more than most adults do for the children in their care. But even this is insufficient. Just as we need to examine more carefully the link between the aesthetic and the ethical, so we need to study the link between creativity and values.

On the practical level, we need to show children that their creative gifts should be used not for selfish or destructive ends but for the service of their fellow men. We have already seen examples of the ghastly possibilities for the abuse of creative power in the fiendish ingenuity used to destroy, torture, and experiment on the inmates of Nazi concentration camps. Closer to home, we must be prepared to raise and examine the case of the creative research scientist who puts his talent at the disposal of his government to create more efficient ways of destroying his fellow human beings through atomic, bacteriological, and chemical weapons. It is clear that we cannot afford to raise and educate creative but conscienceless men and women.

How, then, are we to help people to distinguish between productive and destructive creativity, between positive and negative creativity? As an initial guide, we might suggest that the kind of creativeness we want to encourage will be characterized by the two criteria of *love* and *joy*. If the creative worker works in a spirit of love—love for life, love and respect for himself, his work, and his fellow men—we can be happy if we have helped to nurture this creativity. If, on the other hand, a research scientist says, "If you're doing the kind of creative work you want to do, you can't afford to enquire too closely into where the money comes from or how your work will ultimately be used," then we are justified in doubting whether this is the kind of creative worker we should like to have produced. For these are the men who create cancers in the body of the world. "Cancer," wrote Karl Stern, "is life created by parthenogenesis, new life created without love . . . cancer is a case of loveless creation, a paradox. A paradox right out of hell." [52] In the end, there is no positive, productive creativity except in a spirit of love.

Furthermore, while shamefaced, apologetic, joyless creative work must be viewed with some suspicion, we can rejoice in the kind of Creativity that is marked by an open, expansive joy. Bergson wrote,

> Philosophers who have speculated on the significance of life and the destiny of man have not sufficiently remarked that Nature has taken pains to give us notice every time this destiny is accomplished; she has set up a sign which apprises us every time our activity is in full expansion; this sign is joy. I say joy; I do not say pleasure. . . . True joy . . . is always an emphatic signal of the *triumph* of life. . . . We find that wherever joy is, creation has been, and that the richer the creation the deeper the joy.[53]

III UNIQUENESS, CONFORMITY, AND CREATIVITY

The Particularity of Man

In planning an educational program that will help to foster the creative powers of the child, we must be aware of the special opportunities and special difficulties presented by the fact of the uniqueness of each individual. Every new human being who arrives in the world represents a completely new set of creative possibilities. There has never been anyone quite like this before. No theory or prediction can wholly explain him or exhaust his potentialities. Indeed, his humanity lies precisely in this unique potentiality for unpredictable creativeness.

It is the responsibility of the adult to show the young person that he has a duty to develop his own uniqueness and to have faith in the value of his own unique experiences, to show him that if he were not unique in the world, his presence would be superfluous, for another could discharge his special responsibilities. "Every single man," Buber has written, "is a new thing in the world and is called upon to fulfill his particularity in this world." [54] Buber has described better than anyone the lonely responsibility of each person to nurture and exercise his special powers. Elsewhere, he has written: "You must hear the claim, however unharmoniously it strikes your ear—and let no-one interfere; give the answer from the depths, where a breath of what has been breathed in still hovers—and let no-one prompt you." [55]

Respecting and Enjoying Uniqueness

Distrust of one's own powers and drives, it was suggested above, is a prime factor in killing creativity. This distrust is largely engendered in our society by the contempt and suspicion and scorn with which the insecure treat the obviously "different." A major task in the preservation of creativity is, therefore, the development of respect for and enjoyment of the differences of others. Maurice Friedman wrote,

An animal does not need confirmation because it is unquestionably what it is. A man needs confirmation because he exists as a self, at once separate and in relation, with unique potentialities that can only be realized when he is confirmed in his uniqueness.[56]

Cantor has pointed out that we tend to be afraid of the genuine creative forces in people that demonstrate their *differences* from us. We use praise or blame concerning them but rarely completely *accept* them. We want to control and be loved, rather than to love and help unreservedly: rarely do we permit a child or an adult an effective margin of self-determination, he maintained. "It is difficult, wholeheartedly and unaffectedly, to accept those who differ from us." [57] Ralph Ojemann has suggested that, while creativity and mental illness are not positively correlated, nevertheless the *different* nature of the markedly creative person raises special problems in terms of his acceptance and adjustment.[58]

In order to permit and encourage the unusually creative child to flourish (which means, among other things, safeguarding his mental health), we must help *all* children to develop their own security and sense of adequacy. Otherwise they will, in their insecurity, attack or ridicule those who are different and creative. We must engender an atmosphere that tolerates—induced encourages and enjoys—nonconformity, uniqueness, difference, for the creative person does not conform. To bring out this security it is necessary to teach children how social forces operate (as we teach them how physical forces operate), to teach them about the ways in which a person grows and becomes different from his fellows, about the value of those differences, about the consequences of suppressing them, about the consequences of frustrating creative impulses through ridicule or persecution. Moreover, each individual must be helped to gain his own sense of satisfaction through achievement, so that he does not need to oppose or belittle others' achievements. Those who find fulfillment in their own efforts are more likely to be able to share and rejoice in the fulfillment that comes through the creative accomplishments of *others*.

The appearance of genius raises a special problem. While creativity is universal in man, genius is rare. The conscious nurturing of creativity in school will certainly help the majority: it is doubtful whether it will do much to affect the development of the potential genius, who will set his own laws. But it will serve to create a climate in which genius can be *appreciated* by the majority, as a result of their own creative experiences. Many of us have experienced that refinement of critical appreciation for an artist of genius that follows our own painful attempts to create beauty in his particular field. Thus, indirectly, we can assist the creative productivity of the genius by helping to build an environment in which his work is better evaluated and enjoyed.

Conformity and Creativity

A corollary to the importance of preserving and fostering the unique qualities of each individual in the nurture of creativity is an awareness of *conformity* as a danger to the creative process. One can be creative only to the degree that he is *himself*. Conformity to patterns set by others is, therefore, an enemy of creativity. When we act in accordance with others' expectations or unexamined convention; when we strive for safety, status, and respectability; when we seek to avoid controversy, differences, and clashes; when we pursue predictability, control, and a cautious neatness in our lives; and when we proceed only on the basis of well-established rules and habits, we fail to grow and our creative powers are impaired. In the depths of conformity life loses much of its meaning: we gradually lose the capacity to feel genuinely our own emotions (as opposed to making conventional responses); we come to doubt our own capacities, especially in untried fields; instead of developing the ability to create new things, ideas, and relationships, we become satisfied with what is; we look to authority figures for leadership rather than try to use our own resources and experiences as guides to conduct; and although we appear to bear a reassuring similarity to other people, in fact, we are separated from them, because we can relate to others only if we have a real self with which to relate.

Insecure or unhappy parents, incompetent teachers, dictatorial governments, all try to ensure safe conformity and, hence, destroy unpredictable creativity. The unique vision of the creative person is not welcomed: instead, conventional reactions that can more easily be understood and handled are encouraged. In a typical speech in Munich, Hitler stormed,

As for degenerate artists, I forbid them to force their so-called experiences upon the public. If they do see fields blue, they are deranged, and should go to an asylum. If they only pretend to see them blue they are criminals, and should go to prison. I will purge the nation of them, and let no one take part in their corruption—his day of punishment will come.[59]

One of the most delicate problems raised by the desire to avoid conformity and preserve the uniqueness of the individual concerns the best way to handle the expression of emotion in young children. If we might indulge in a rough generalization, we might say that European schools, especially in the past, have tended to leave the emotional life of the child too much alone, while many American schools, especially in recent times, have tended to interfere with the child's emotional life too aggressively. Both errors have unfortunate consequences for the creative development of the child: the "European" error makes the child un-accustomed to expressing his emotions and afraid that they will be unacceptable; the "American" error makes the child so aware of others' emotions that he comes to accept them in lieu of his own. By constantly digging into his hidden motivations and unearthing his deeper feelings, we can make it more difficult for the child to resist the forces that in-fluence him to feel as others feel. This, in turn, makes it harder for him to feel as only *he* can feel. And life is duller when we all feel alike. On the other hand, by allowing the child to express his feelings openly and showing him that such expressions do not bring fatal consequences, we make it possible for the child to have more confidence in his own emotional life. Perhaps the answer is to encourage children to bring their feelings to the surface but then to emphasize that we are *not* looking for agreement; that what we seek is peaceful coexistence with differences; that we should tolerate, respect, and enjoy people who are different from us; that this brings more interest, zest, and excitement to life.

Somehow or other, the creative person has to find his own unique way. This is not easy, for going one's own way in our society tends to produce guilt feelings in the individual. How this guilt is handled becomes crucial: the contrast between the creative artist, who resolves the problem constructively, and the neurotic, whose attempted resolu-tion is destructive and repressive, represents one of the basic polarities in our civilization. The experience of formal education can also render it difficult to become oneself. Henry Miller has described the difficulties he met in learning to write: "The facility of speech which I possessed was a handicap; I had all the vices of the educated man. I had to learn to think, feel and see in a totally new fashion, in an uneducated way, *in my own way*, which is the hardest thing on earth." [60] Ben Shahn, in *The Biography of a Painting*, has described vividly his growing realization that his art, however professional and original it might have been, was somehow foreign to him, was not really deeply his own, did not contain the central person which, for good or ill, was himself.[61]

An education that helps the individual to resist the tendencies toward conformity and come to a knowledge of and confidence in himself will give him the experience of solitary activities and the guidance that will enable him to stand alone. "As an originator," [62] wrote Buber, "man is solitary. He stands wholly without bonds in the echoing hall of his deeds." [63] It will also avoid the kind of imitative and stereotyping teaching procedures that are as popular with poor teachers as they are devastating to potentially creative children. Lowenfeld has exploded over these techniques: *"Never prefer one child's creative work over that of another! Never give the work of one child as an example to another! Never let a child copy anything!"* [64] He has heartily and unreservedly condemned coloring books and workbooks, which require the child to fill in or copy stereotyped animals and objects. Such techniques, he insisted, make the child dependent in his thinking (he is not given the freedom to create what he wants); render him inflexible (he has to follow what he has been given); do not provide emotional relief (he is denied the opportunity to release his emotions through expressing his own experience); and condition him to adult concepts, thus frustrating his own creative ambitions.[65]

IV   SELF-EXPRESSION AND STANDARDS

Self-expression

A central aspect of the task of sustaining and developing individual uniqueness lies in the encouragement of self-expression and a subjective approach to problems. Self-expression is inadequate as an *end* of education, but it is a valuable *means* toward the achievement of creative individualism. Subjectivism can be dangerous in isolation, and a subjective interpretation will need to be checked by other means at some stage. But the neglect of the subjective in education has been one of the factors mainly responsible for the loss or failure of creative power.

One of the great educational contributions of experimentalism and progressivism has been the emphasis they have placed on aesthetic subjectivism, self-expression, the release of emotion, and creative activity. Some progressive schools, of which Summerhill is a prime example, have put self-expression, through such means as spontaneous acting,[66] craft work, and art, at the center of their educational philosophy and program. Such ideas stem in part from the influence of the Romantic Movement, which demanded that the artist be free in all aspects of his work and conceived art primarily as a mode of self-expression.

Those who are concerned mainly with self-expression are interested in the effect of the creative process on the person, rather than in the tangible product of that process; in the refined sensitivity that flows from aesthetic experience, rather than in the quality of the aesthetic creation. They can find support, among other sources, in Bergson's philosophy of creative evolution and Whitehead's philosophy of organism. Both of these are philosophies of process rather than of substance; both accept the nonrational as ultimate but not dominant; both look on the connectedness of the passing stream of becoming as essentially aesthetic, in the Platonic sense of "harmonious wholeness." [67]

In the field of art, no one has given clearer and more insistent expression to this point of view than Lowenfeld, who adamantly maintained that, for the child, art is purely a means of expression. Any correction by an adult that refers to reality rather than to the child's own experience interferes drastically with the child's *own* expression and, hence, inhibits creativity.[68] Tremendous harm has been and is being done to children's creative powers through the imposition on them of adult standards of evaluation. The meaningfulness of creative work to its creator, Lowenfeld demanded, must never be disturbed by "objective evaluations." Evaluation of children's creative works must differ from individual to individual and from one stage of development to another. It should be made only to gain insight into the child's growth and not to confront him with his own weaknesses or strengths. By discriminating "good" from "bad" without regard for the child's own desires we set rigid standards. These standards encourage the child who lacks confidence in his own work to copy the preferred one. Unable to compete with it, he gives up his own work. The result is discouragement, lack of confidence, inhibition in the majority, and a go-ahead signal for a selected few.[69]

In the field of art, there is no doubt that Lowenfeld's views, based on many years of careful observation, teaching, and study, must be treated with respect. No one who has watched the joyous freedom of the young child, the painful self-consciousness of the adolescent, and the miserable stiffness of the adult, as they try to express themselves artistically, can fail to realize that some disastrous process of gradual hardening of the emotions is at work in most people. Anything that can postpone or mitigate this process will provide a positive support to the creative forces of the world. The child's artistic vision is different from the adult's and should be respected. Nothing is to be gained by imposing adult standards on the creative work of a young child. A severe threat to the development of personal creative power in the child is represented by the reiteration of adult demands for correspondence to reality. The typical adult question, "What is it?" may be the beginning of the end of individual expression for the child. If such treatment is continued, the child's efforts become stereotyped in an attempt to fit in with existing and approved forms. He sees that adults are satisfied when he conforms, when he is not individualistic or original, when "he draws a tree that *looks* like a tree." He, therefore, ceases to grow in his ability to express his feelings uniquely and personally. We do need to encourage self-expression in children's art, not because it is an end in itself but because it is the only means to high-quality creative work, which is the product of a free and expressive personality.

Similarly, in language and literature, we should concentrate with young children on encouraging them to express themselves freely. The stress should be on quantity rather than on quality. In poetry, the emphasis should be on enjoyment and on free composition, unencumbered by considerations of analysis, form, or technique. This, of course, is why we need good teachers at this primary level: because it is much easier to teach formal features like grammar, spelling, and technical terms than to try to unlock the child's creative powers, easier to impose uniform standards and demands than to seek the unique expression of which each self alone is capable.

Standards

Difficult as it might be to foster, self-expression alone does not constitute or ensure creativity. The subjective element is vital but insufficient: an objective element is also required. This is where some progressive education has been justifiably criticized—in its abandonment of educational objectivity in an excessive swing away from the dry, repressive objectivity of traditional education. When self-expression and creativity are identified, we find ourselves in danger of the arrogance and complacency that regards any childish doodle as sacred and all the achievements of the past as unworthy of study. "The most foolish of all errors for foolish young men to believe," said Goethe, "is that they forfeit their originality in recognizing a truth which has already been recognized by others."

The recognition of and growth toward objective standards are, like self-expression, essential features of creativity. Standards *can* be harmful to the creative process, but only when they mean slavish imitation, meaningless copying, thoughtless conformity. They are helpful to the creative process when they are used to show us something that has been done superlatively well, bringing a realization of our own inadequacies. When many different examples of others' work are studied, compared, and analyzed, we gradually attain that knowledge of superior creative achievement that is necessary to develop taste and humility, to avoid the repetition of what has already been achieved, and to stimulate us to creative excellence. Creativity is not just a throwing over of accepted standards in art, literature, music, and so on. This sort of destructive iconoclasm is usually the refuge of the incompetent. Creativity is essentially constructive and reconstructive and takes place within the canons and standards of one's own cultural tradition.

One of the great and continuing contributions of aesthetic objectivism, idealism, scholasticism, and much traditional education has been to hold before us these objective standards. Classical rather than romantic in emphasis, such an education tries to show that beauty is an intrinsic quality, independent of man's feelings, that there is a rational element in art and creativity, and that the function of aesthetic education is to introduce the individual to the objectively beautiful, to help him to know and appreciate it, and to civilize him by raising his standards of taste. Naturally, in such an education, the stress will not be so much on self-expression as on *communication*. There is less interest in art education, with its concern for the process and the person, and more interest in fine arts, with a concern for the aesthetic product and its effect on others.

Besides attaining to a release of the subjective and emotional forces within him, the creative individual must submit himself to the relevant demands of objective standards, discipline, form, and order. "Human activity must impose limits upon itself," Igor Stravinsky has written. "The more art is controlled, limited, worked over, the more it is free." [70] There is a danger that in seeking to foster creativity through tapping the emotions and the unconscious, we will neglect the intellectual, rational, conscious components of the creative process. Both are essential. Conscious control, it was suggested above, is the significant characteristic that distinguishes the productive creative worker from the unbalanced neurotic. Most creative artists—even the most anarchistic and recusant—have recognized the need for this balance between freedom and order. "The task which the artist implicitly sets himself," wrote Henry Miller in *Tropic of Cancer*, "is to overthrow existing values, to make of the chaos about him an order which is his own, to sow strife and ferment so that by the emotional release those who are dead may be restored to life." [71] Even the iconoclastic Miller was aware of the necessity for order, albeit one that expressed himself.

Self-expression, which is personal and particular, must eventually be checked and tempered by standards that are ultimately universal if it is to lead to genuine creativity. Although child-art may safely concern itself with self-expression, by the time adolescence is reached an appeal to universal standards becomes increasingly appropriate. This is not to deny that much art and other creative work (folk music, for example) is particular and parochial. But great art has a universal quality, although it does not, of course, appeal to all men at any time.

Genuine creativity, then, requires a balance, a harmony, an integration of free self-expression and disciplining standards. The creative person must be both accepting and critical: he must accept himself but also the unyielding demands of the external world; he must be critical of the world's customs and conventions but also of his own spontaneous efforts. There must be an integration of the subjective and objective, of the emotional and intellectual, of the unconscious and the conscious. If European education has tended to stifle self-expression, in North America there is the danger of finding it sufficient.[72] If North American education has tended to neglect standards, in Europe there is the dangerous habit of applying them mechanically and uniformly. Although there are times when standards must be rigid, this is not true in the nurture of creative work, where above all the standards must be *appropriate*. Dogma and rigidity are the death of creativity, for we are dealing here with the unique experience of the individual and the particular expression that only he can give to that experience. As long as we remember the criterion of appropriateness we will never, for example, judge children's art by adult standards; at the same time, however, we will not forget or belittle those standards.

Imitation and Models

"Down with imagination in school, down with self-expression. Let us have a little severe hard work, good, clean, well-written exercises, well-pronounced words, well-set-down sums: and as far as head-work goes, no more. . . . Let us have a bit of solid, hard, tidy work. And for the rest, *leave the children alone*." [73] The danger that D.H. Lawrence was afraid of is a real one: children are imitative and seek to please. Give them opportunities for self-expression and they will look around for someone to imitate. Hence, we obtain from them only conventional responses. This will not contribute to their unique development but merely make them more alike.

But leaving them alone will not solve anything either. It will lead them to suppose that all that the school ignores—which for Lawrence should include the whole range of the emotional, the unique, the idiosyncratic—is uninteresting and even unacceptable and, hence, make them timid about affirming their own essence. We need self-affirmation with two caveats. First, we need sensitive and skilful teachers: sensitive enough to distinguish between genuine and faked or assumed feelings; skilful enough to evoke the former and discourage the latter. Second, we need to stress the desirability of differences among individual expressions. The child's desire to please us can be used positively if we show him that what pleases us is that he should act differently from others. If a child imitates another, we can say, "Now can you do it *differently* from John?"

However, it is futile and unwise to attempt to prevent *all* imitation among the young. We can easily see what an overpowering force we are faced with when we observe little children who, from infancy on, zealously imitate parents, older brothers and sisters, other children, other adults. We must moderate our fears of this imitativeness as a destroyer of creativity. Certainly, the child who always copies slavishly is lacking in creative power. But the reason for his lack of creativity lies deeper within his personality and personal history: it does not stem from the *fact* of his copying, which is more symptom than cause. Moreover, the art of imitation need not be passive: at best, it involves the assimilation of the original pattern into one's own person, modified in accordance with one's unique purpose and personality.

William James defended imitation as a constructive force in the development of personality. He said,

> Each of us is in fact what he is almost exclusively by virtue of his imitativeness. . . . The entire accumulated wealth of mankind—languages, arts, institutions, and sciences—is passed on from one generation to another by . . . social heredity, each generation simply imitating the last. . . . Invention, using the term most broadly, and imitation, are the two legs, so to call them, on which the human race historically has walked.[74]

We all imitate respected, loved, admired men and women. This is not necessarily unhealthy. It gives a vision of something better that we can use to hoist ourselves up. Especially in the sphere of conduct, the sight of worthiness in a revered person can be one of the most powerful stimuli to creative endeavor in ourselves. More important than the fact of imitation is the quality of the models. While it is unlikely that there has been a net loss through the imitation of Gandhi or Schweitzer, many admired figures today, especially in the fields of sport and entertainment, are not desirable models. The wise teacher, rather than constantly checking imitativeness in children, will accept some imitation as inevitable and, while concentrating on releasing the springs of creative expression, will lead the children to a knowledge of always better models.

Technique

Subjectivity, self-expression, and freedom can never produce creativity, it has been suggested, without discipline, form, submission, and mastery of technique. Although the self-expression of childhood is a necessary precursor of later creativeness, the attainment of technical skill of a certain standard is necessary before the work is worthy of being considered creative in the sense of communicating the intended impression on the objective world. "The desired new order implicit in the stir of indeterminate activity cannot be seized in the abstract," wrote Ghiselin: "it must crystallize in terms of some medium in which the worker is adept. Without craft it will escape." [75]

Technique arises with Berdyaev's *outer* stage of creativity, when the work comes to be formed. The primary creative fire cools down. Man, in realizing his creative intuition, is limited by the world, his material, other people. Every book, picture, statue, good work, and social institution is an instance of the cooling down of the original flame of inspiration. Some creators never find outward expression: they have the inner fire but fail to give it form because of their lack of technical control.[76] Technique, in other words, can be a means of liberation. Moreover, the actual acquisition of technique and skill can alter the way in which one perceives reality: it can aid the vision and stimulate the imagination.

There is no doubt, then, that technique must be learned—and it can be taught. But skill in teaching consists in knowing exactly what degree of technical skill is *appropriate*. The function of the teacher, as Buber has pointed out, is to absorb the constructive forces of the world, deciding, rejecting, accepting those that his pupil needs: the teacher is, thus, both a protective filter and a channel through which appropriate forces and powers are made accessible to the pupil. In little children, creative desire tends to run ahead of skill. With sensitive and judicious help from the teacher they can learn to express themselves more accurately and skilfully. With "overtaught" children, however, the creative impulse tends to dry up. In such cases, teachers have imposed the learning of techniques unrelated to the children's genuine contemporary needs: the desire to express is too weak to support this degree of skill. Then we enter the stage of manipulation.

The key criteria in determining the appropriateness of the technique to be acquired are the maturity of the child and the nature of the material. For instance, if a young child wishes to make a clay animal, he will be best left alone with his vision and his clay, for he has sufficient control of his fingers and hands to bring his vision to some sort of creative fruition. But if the same child wishes to make a stool or a chair, it is not enough to leave him alone with tools and wood. Direct instruction from the teacher is warranted to help the child attain the technical skill necessary for freedom in this medium.

Although both the desire to express oneself and technical skill are necessary to produce creative work, the *order* in which they occur is crucially important. Too much emphasis on technique *first* can kill the desire and power to express. The traditional fault in pedagogy has been to establish firmly at the outset certain standards and then have the child try to gain the technical skill necessary to meet them. This has led to either apathy or rejection. A modern fault—the result of an exaggerated attempt to remedy the old fault—has been to tell the child nothing, in order that he can be completely spontaneous in his expression. This has led to confusion and a miserable level of achievement. The child must *first* be allowed to hazard himself and his ideas: then advice and criticism must *follow*. Not until he has experienced both the urge to express himself and the frustration that technical inadequacy brings will he be ready to assimilate with profit the technical guidance of the teacher.

In the field of writing, for example, the emphasis on quality must *follow* that on quantity. If we want the child to learn to write, he should first be encouraged to write, freely and copiously, on a subject of genuine interest and concern to him, without being made afraid of committing technical errors of grammar, spelling, punctuation, and syntax. The development of such technical skills can be nurtured once the child has felt creative power flowing through him. There is little profit in the study of technique until students are experienced enough to see the necessity of its discipline for more effective creative expression.

Through the skilful and appropriate teaching of technique we can most happily satisfy the complementary demands of self-expression and standards. It will enable us to get away from the harmful assumption that we can foster creativeness through teaching according to dogmatic rule, without considering the specific intentions and desires of the individual. It will enable us to help each child to produce the best of which *he* is capable. If he makes something that is uniquely his, we can encourage his individual expression and yet, at the same time, press him to excel by urging him to look at his work in the light of his own talents. For example, if he is trying to write a story about an event in his life, we can insist that he should try to communicate as clearly and elegantly as possible. There is no attempt to exact a uniformity of thought or even of style, but if his aim is to communicate we can warrantably demand the highest technical standards that his ability makes possible.

V EDUCATION, INNOVATION, AND TRADITION

Change and Innovation

To create means to change. Creativity necessarily involves a change in the objective world, or in ourselves, or in our relationship with others, or in all of these. An education for creativity must, therefore, be in a sense an education for change.

Moreover, as we are frequently reminded, ours is an age of change. Change is as characteristic of our age as relative continuity and apparent permanence were characteristic of the Middle Ages. The evidence of this feature of contemporary life can be drawn from innumerable fields. Our knowledge in science and technology has been estimated to be doubling every decade; it has been calculated that by the year 2000 the population of Asia alone will be almost twice the present population of the world; about 20 percent of the American population move their residence each year, including about seven million school-age children; Margaret Mead has suggested as the most vivid truth of the age the fact that none of us will live all his life in the world in which he was born; Robert Oppenheimer has said (looking no doubt with the single eye of the scientist) that nearly everything now known was not in any book when most of us went to school. There is no doubt that, in the face of such rapid change, we too must change and adapt ourselves to altering circumstances or, like the brontosaurus, we will be pushed aside by evolutionary forces.

This is not to argue for an education for adjustment. The suggestion that man should adjust, chameleon-like, to his surroundings is ill-considered at any time, but especially so when prevailing patterns are dissolving so rapidly that the attempt to be constantly adjusted can result only in frustration and neurosis. But if man cannot—and should not—adjust, he can—and must—grow. Leaving on one side for the moment the important question of the *direction* of his growth,[77] the *capacity* to grow depends on his ability to keep supple in personality, unfinished in form, open to change, sensitive to innovation. Man must grow because his growth is the prism of all creativity in the world. The human being, Gerald Heard has said, "is the growing edge of life." He does not "fulfill himself by precedent but surpasses himself by pre-science."[78] Man remains, as Buber has pointed out, the center of all surprise, unpredictability, and innovation in the world.

Life itself is characterized by change and activity, just as death is characterized by inertness and immobility. It is well-known that constant change within a framework of continuity is a law of life. Like a candle flame, which bears a persistent, recognizable pattern but whose constituents are always being consumed and changed, the human being is a form of continuous activity, always identifiable as the same person and yet always a changing combination of physical components. Loren Eiseley has eloquently described the phenomenon:

I suppose that in the forty-five years of my existence every atom, every molecule that composes me has changed its position or danced away and beyond to become part of other things. New molecules have come from the grass and the bodies of animals to be part of me a little while, yet in this spinning, light and airy as a midge swarm in a shaft of sunlight, my memories hold, and a loved face of twenty years ago is before me still.[79]

Great creative acts of history have been associated with a breaking of the hold of the established pattern—often at painful cost. We cannot create by simply accepting traditional forms as unchangeable. Important changes in science and art have been foreshadowed by a feeling that traditional criteria were becoming meaningless. This is the point, as Koestler has observed, where the specialist's *hubris* yields to philosophical soul-searching, to a painful reappraisal of his basic axioms and of the meaning of the terms that he has taken for granted, to what he calls "the thaw of dogma." This is the situation that "provides genius with the opportunity for his creative plunge under the broken surface." [80]

An excellent example of the pain and difficulty with which human beings accommodate themselves to changing conditions comes from an incident that occurred in England during the early days of the Second World War. Armaments of all kinds were in short supply, and the British made use of a venerable piece of artillery that came down from the Boer War. After the fall of France these guns were hitched to trucks for mobile coast-defense units. But it was felt that rapidity of fire could be increased. A time-motion expert was called in. He watched the gun crews of five men at practice. Puzzled by some aspects of the procedure, he took a slow motion film. From this he noticed that, a moment before the discharge of the gun, two members ceased all activity and stood to attention for a three-second interval, extending throughout the firing of the gun. He summoned an old colonel of artillery and asked him for an explanation. The colonel was puzzled, and asked to see the film again. "Ah," he said finally, "I have it. They are holding the horses." [81]

The contrast between an attitude of creative change and one of sterile inertia may be seen, sadly, in the contrasting attitudes of the scientific and religious communities through most of modern history. A new scientific discovery or theory is welcomed and looked on as a triumphant vindication of the scientific method. The consequent abandonment of disproved views is not regarded as a disaster but as a manifestation of progress. Change and science are essentially linked. One of Dewey's great contributions was to show the value of the method of science in a democracy, where nothing should be exempt from examination and possible reconstruction. Religion, especially as represented by the Church, has tended, by contrast, to regard change with suspicion, to fight desperately and dogmatically to maintain traditional interpretations and attitudes. Although there is something in religion that is timeless and eternal, there is much that is local and temporal, and even eternal verities require changes of interpretation and expression in the light of contemporary circumstances. The rigidity of religion has been its greatest weakness, just as the flexibility of science has been its greatest strength.

There are those who fear that such an emphasis on change will mean that desirable values of the present will not be sufficiently defended. They need not greatly concern themselves. A German apothegm says, "When Pythagoras discovered the theorem of the right-angled triangle, he sacrificed a hundred oxen; since then, whenever a new truth has been unveiled, all oxen have trembled." There are always plenty of human oxen ready to defend the *status quo*. We all have a stake in it, at least in as much as we are lazy and disinclined to make the changes in our beliefs, customs, and personality that the incorporation of new ideas may involve. Every innovation is going to be a threat to someone. We must always be ready, therefore, to give a sensitive audience to each new voice that speaks, within ourselves and in others. We must practice what Ghiselin has called "an imaginative surrender to every novelty that has even the most tenuous credentials." [82]

Progress and the Creative Person

Change is not the same as progress, but there can be no progress without change. An innovation may, of course, be a deterioration, whereas progress implies an advance, an improvement, a movement in the desired direction. All progress involves a move away from the present position, and it is this move that raises difficulties, provokes opposition, invites retaliation from those who think they have something to lose.

The source of this change, and hence the sole agent of all progress, is the creative person. He is the one whose original insights and inventive work provide the variation from the accepted patterns that is the focus of progress. Therefore, the healthy society will look on him as the one on whom the desirable development of society depends. Too often, however, he is looked on as being on the fringe of society, or even as antisocial. This is most likely to happen in societies where the individual is subordinated to the State, where he is taught to conform and obey, and hence does not rise above the level reached by his predecessors. A classical example of such a society was Sparta, which seems to have been incredibly barren in the production of artists, poets, dramatists, philosophers, and creative geniuses of any kind.

This danger besets all totalitarian regimes. It was already becoming apparent in Nazi Germany, which had only 12 years of Nazi rule. In the Soviet Union, the alternations of liberalization and repression in the arts are symptoms of the uncertainties and frustrations experienced by a regime facing this problem. In a revealing interview with *Literatoura y Jijn,* the organ of the Russian section of the Union of Soviet Writers, Ilya Ehrenburg, one of the Soviet Union's best-known writers, made clear his opinion that creativity depends on the writer's freedom to conform not to an accepted ideology or approved creed but to the truth as he sees it.[83]

Since the creative person is both specially vulnerable and specially precious he must be specially protected by the society that understands his value and values his understanding. This is true in all fields, but particularly so in the arts. Progress in science and technology is not so likely to suffer under a repressive or totalitarian regime, for even a dictatorship is impressed by what works. The revolutionary scientific and technological achievements of the Soviet Union are an indication of the wide freedom granted to the creative scientific worker. The contributions of such workers are plain to see and easy to appreciate. Not only are the findings of science cumulative and open to public verification,[84] but they can often be exploited through technology to produce material dividends.

In the arts, the situation is quite different. It can be questioned whether progress is a concept that can be applied to art at all. How do we compare, for example, the Lascaux cave paintings with the work of Cézanne? Or Homer with Shelley? Or Sophocles with Ibsen? Or Vivaldi with Stravinsky? Art, unlike science, is not cumulative: its insights and truths are special, discrete, individual. Although there is undoubtedly progress in artistic *technique,* the creative vision of the artist may break through to a truth that is not attained by any of his successors. Who can ever replace Shakespeare in the way that Einstein has partly replaced Newton? Artistic creativity thrives on deviation, individualism, particularity. Moreover, its truths are not publicly verifiable, useful in the ordinary sense, or normally exploitable for material gain. For all of these reasons, the creative artist is in special danger of neglect or persecution in societies with materialistic or totalitarian tendencies. And which society today is wholly free from these perils?

Continuity and Tradition

In a time of rapid change, it has been suggested, we must avoid adjusting to every little passing wind, but we must continue to grow— which involves change. When this much has been said, much remains unsaid. *How* should we grow? What should be the determinants and ordering criteria of our growth? If our growth is to be organic it must be determined in part by certain significant elements in our past. It is exactly in a time of rapid external change that we need, through the study of our own traditions, to retain a core of continuity out of which can come order and meaning. Otherwise, there is a danger that human personality and group organization will break down into chaos. Within the flux of change, an important part of us must remain linked to its past if we are to retain a secure and stable identity.

We can observe in little children that, alongside their desire for novelty, experiment, and change, there is also a deep-lying need for repetition, familiarity, and routine. In all human beings there is this twin need (not always satisfied or even expressed) for creation and consolidation. If the newness and change outrun the consolidation of past experience, there is uncertainty, insecurity, and perhaps breakdown, at which time creativity ceases until the past "catches up."

Both the intangibility and the importance of tradition in education are well-illustrated by the development of the *tone* of a school. Impossible to analyze, difficult to describe, it is nevertheless something that affects everyone connected with that school. In William James' opinion, tone constitutes "a mere tradition kept up by imitation." [85] It was perhaps most obvious and powerful in the nineteenth-century English Public School, where headmasters like Arnold of Rugby directly influenced their senior pupils, who in turn influenced the younger boys, who in their turn passed on attitudes, beliefs, and assumptions to subsequent pupils. But it exists in every school and is a formative factor of tremendous importance, whether it is ignored or consciously utilized.

If we wish to be genuinely creative, it is suicidal to jettison the traditions that have made us. Traditional forms of conduct and thought often embody a certain organically accumulated wisdom. "It is folly enough to saw through the branch we are sitting on," said Sir Fred Clarke. "It is worse than folly to saw through the trunk itself." [86] A society cut off from its own roots may thrive for a while on its own momentum, but eventually it will wither like cut flowers in a vase. It is a foolish presumption to think that we can ignore the past, to think that the contemporary scene represents all we need. We must not confuse relevance with contemporaneity. G.K. Chesterton wrote, "Tradition is democracy extended through time. Tradition means giving the vote to that most obscure of all classes, our ancestors. Tradition is the democracy of the dead. Tradition refuses to submit to the small and arrogant oligarchy of those who are walking about." [87] Traditional testimonies grow out of date, of course, but they are nevertheless needed as tools of comparison. We cannot, admittedly, go back to the past, but we must *look* back if we are to see what has been gained and what lost.

Mature creativity is essentially embedded in tradition. John Dewey, who was notably aware of the need for change and adaptability, was also aware of the importance of tradition. Dependence on tradition, he suggested, is an essential factor in original vision and creative expression.

> Even the work of an original temperament may be relatively thin, as well as tending to the bizarre, when it is not informed with a wide and varied experience of the traditions of the art in which the artist operates. . . . Each great tradition is itself an organized habit of vision and of methods of ordering and conveying material.[88]

Similarly, the critic, he insisted, must be familiar with the tradition of his particular art before he can take an informed interest or make valid judgments.[89]

We must not allow ourselves to be dominated by tradition, but in freeing ourselves from its dominance we must be careful not to fall into the opposite error and sweep out all traditional vestiges because they are of the past. This attitude, which often purports to be critical or scientific, is not critical or scientific enough. If it were genuinely critical, it would consider carefully *which* aspects of traditional practice have value and relevance and which are anachronistic.

In appealing for the achievement of what they called the "organic community"—which they contrasted with the mechanical community in which the machine is dominant—Leavis and Thompson insisted that the past should not be forgotten: "for the memory of the old order must be the chief incitement towards a new, if ever we are to have one. If we forget the old order we shall not know what kind of thing to strive towards, and in the end there will be no striving, but a surrender to the 'progress' of the machine." [90] If we are to keep man in the center of the picture, we must be able to *evaluate* change, to judge whether it represents an enrichment of man's life in the deepest sense or whether it is only a change necessitated by the mechanical momentum of industrialization. Such judgments demand a knowledge of tradition and a constant choice and selection to maintain continuity with those elements in the tradition that are most valuable, nourishing, and civilizing.

Tradition and Creativity

The greatest danger that attends tradition is that of formalism. Traditional patterns tend to crystallize and set, becoming hard and unyielding on the outside and dead within. Ramsay Muir, in his autobiography, wrote: "The noblest movements are apt to outlive their usefulness when their zeal develops into formalism: an ideal creates an institution and then the institution suffocates the ideal." [91] Laurens van der Post has pointed out that men have a terrible tendency to institutionalize life. Fear of life, born of their own wilful estrangement from it, makes men build fortresses to hold what they have chosen to select from life. "Instead of striving to make permanent the passing forms and shapes of meaning," he wrote, "it would be more creative if they entrusted themselves to the natural processes of change and so refused to become ensnared in surface patterns." [92] Bureaucrats who administer institutions tend to perpetuate existing forms, even when these have lost their original meaning and relevance, if they contribute to the smooth, uneventful running of the administrative machinery.

Traditional forms spawn vested interests, who naturally become opponents of change. E.H. Carr has suggested as a "law of history" that a group that plays a leading role in the advance of civilization in one period is unlikely to play a similar role in the next period "for the good reason that it will be too deeply inbred with the traditions, interests, and ideologies of the earlier period to be able to adapt itself to the demands and conditions of the next period." [93] However, some members of such groups manage to hold on to power for a disastrously long time, increasing the danger of the fossilization of society.

The fossilized society is a barren soil for the growth of creativity. This tender plant grows best within a *living* tradition, not a moribund one. A living tradition cannot be handed on dogmatically and authoritatively by one generation and accepted passively and mechanically by the next. It must be deeply absorbed by each generation, reinterpreted in the light of their own experience, and transformed to serve in the altered circumstances of the day. Unless every generation procreates a rebirth of its civilization there will be no continuing tradition, but only an increasingly spurious façade.

The living tradition must be regenerated by every society and by every creative person. Tradition is necessary, it has been suggested, to provide a balanced, secure basis for creativity. But it will not serve this purpose unless it is studied, understood, and renewed by the individual. Great creative artists have always taken a tradition deeply into themselves in this way. Dewey pointed out that "Shakespeare . . . was such an insatiable devourer of accessible material that he would have been a plagiarist if the material had not at once antagonized and coöperated with his personal vision by means of an equally insatiable curiosity concerning the life surrounding him." [94] In his "non lectures" at Harvard, the late E.E. Cummings said, "So far as I am concerned, poetry and every other art was and is and forever will be strictly a question of individuality." [95] Such a viewpoint is not incompatible with a recognition of the importance of tradition, if we insist that the tradition enter into the thinking and feeling of the individual and become a part of his deepest self.

The maturing process must take place within a tradition: the mature, creative person transcends his tradition. But only he can transcend tradition who has first immersed himself in it. In creating, the individual transcends the temporal and touches fingers with the eternal: this is the ultimate freedom of creativity. But only he can achieve this eternal freedom who has first submitted deeply to the authority of the temporal tradition.

NOTES

1 Ordway Tead, "The Healthy Person's Creative Outlets," in *Creativity and Psychological Health*, Michael F. Andrews, ed. (Syracuse, N.Y.: Syracuse University Press, 1961), 108.

2 Nicolas Berdyaev, *The Destiny of Man* (London: Geoffrey Bles, 1945), 127.

3 Martin Buber, *Between Man and Man*, Ronald Gregor Smith, trans. (Boston: Beacon Press, 1955), 103.

4 Pitirim A. Sorokin, "General Theory of Creativity," in *Creativity and Psychological Health*, Andrews, ed., 1.

5 Jacques Barzun, *The House of Intellect* (New York: Harper, 1959), ch. 4. and 5.

6 Viktor Lowenfeld, "Basic Aspects of Creative Teaching," in *Creativity and Psychological Health*, Andrews, ed., 130.

7 It will be shown later, however, that creativity is not confined to these fields.

8 The view of originality used here is similar to that followed by Fromm: "By original I do not mean . . . that an idea has not been thought before by someone else, but that it originates in the individual, that it is the result of his own activity and in this sense is *his* thought." Erich Fromm, *Escape from Freedom* (New York: Rinehart, 1941), 242.

9 Quoted by Sorokin, *op. cit.*, 10.

10 *Ibid.*, 11.

11 W.H. Auden, *New Year Letter* (London: Faber & Faber, 1941), 73.

12 Berdyaev, *op. cit.*, 131.

13 Thomas R. Kelly, *Holy Obedience* (William Penn Lecture, Philadelphia: Religious Society of Friends, 1939).

14 Berdyaev, *op cit.*, 128–29; Lowenfeld, *loc. cit.*

15 Brewster Ghiselin, Introduction to *The Creative Process*, Brewster Ghiselin, ed. (New York: New American Library, 1958), 17.

16 Sorokin, *op. cit.*, 5.

17 *Ibid.*, 11. Kubie also maintained that the unconscious, far from making us creative, is our straitjacket, rendering us stereotyped and repetitive. Creativity in his view is a product of what he has called *preconscious* activity. Lawrence S. Kubie, *Neurotic Distortion of the Creative Process* (New York: Noonday Press, 1961), 142–43.

18 "If we grant for a moment that a man's subconscious mind contains both sleeping tigers and sleeping princesses, the psychologist is much less aware of beauty than the beast." David Head, *He Sent Leanness* (New York: Macmillan, 1959), 50.

19 C.G. Jung, *Modern Man in Search of a Soul*, W.S. Dell and Cary F. Baynes, trans. (New York: Harcourt, Brace, 1933), 170–71.

20 Harold H. Anderson, *Creativity and Its Cultivation* (New York: Harper, 1959), 248.

[21] Theresa Haney, "Creativity in a Summer Arts Center," *N.E.A. Journal* (March, 1961), 26.

[22] Frank Barron, "Originality in Relation to Personality and Intellect," *Journal of Personality*, vol. XXV, no. 6 (1957), 730–42.

[23] Arthur Koestler, *The Sleepwalkers: A History of Man's Changing View of the Universe* (London: Hutchinson, 1959), 518–19.

[24] See A.G. Hughes, *Education and the Democratic Ideal* (London: Longmans, Green, 1951), 15–16, for the statement of a disciple of Smuts.

[25] Erich Fromm, *Escape from Freedom* (New York: Rinehart, 1941), 259.

[26] For an extended discussion of this point of view, see Paul Nash, "Characteristics of the Creative Scientist," *Journal of Education*, vol. 145, no. 3 (February, 1963), 26–33.

[27] Clemens E. Benda, "Illness and Artistic Creativity," *Atlantic* (July, 1961), 97–101. Kubie's investigations suggest that neurosis "corrupts, mars, distorts, and blocks creativeness in every field. . . . No one need fear that getting well will cause an atrophy of his creative drive." Kubie, *op. cit.*, 142.

[28] Barron, *loc. cit.*, 740.

[29] For a critique of Bergson's views, see Maurice Cranston, *Freedom: A New Analysis* (London: Longmans, Green, 1954), 141–44.

[30] David Riesman, *et al.*, *The Lonely Crowd: A Study of the Changing American Character* (New York: Doubleday, 1955), 301.

[31] Fromm, *op. cit.*, 258.

[32] Erich Fromm, *Man For Himself* (New York: Rinehart, 1947), 82–107.

[33] Sylvia Sprigge has suggested that Strindberg, who was a schizophrenic, would have quite succumbed to his illness had he not bee able to write. His work was his outlet, his therapy. "Mordant Alchemy, " *Manchester Guardian Weekly* (September 13, 1962), 14. On the other hand, Kubie has said, "Merely to be creative is not enough either to protect us from mental illness or to cure us. . . . Of certain modern artists and writers it is sometimes said that they protect themselves from psychoses by their painting or writing. Unfortunately, no critical studies exist which would make of such claims anything more than superficial and somewhat dubious guesses." Lawrence S. Kubie, *op. cit.*, 2–3.

[34] Tead, *loc. cit.*, 107–108.

[35] Michael F. Andrews, *op. cit.*, preface, vi.

[36] Douglas V. Steere, *Work and Contemplation* (New York: Harper, 1957), 80.

[37] Herbert Read, preface to Sylvia Ashton-Warner, *Teacher* (New York: Simon & Schuster, 1963), 11.

[38] Sylvia Ashton-Warner, *Teacher* (New York: Simon & Schuster, 1963), 33.

[39] Erich Fromm, *War Within Man:A Psychological Enquiry into the Roots of Destructiveness* (Philadelphia: American Friends Service Committee, 1963), 21–22.

[40] Archibald MacLeish, *Art Education and the Creative Process* (New York: Museum of Modern Art, 1954), 11.

[41] Viktor Lowenfeld, *Creative and Mental Growth* (New York: Macmillan, 1957), 4.

[42] "We do not need to be taught to *think*: indeed . . . this is something that cannot be taught. Thinking processes actually are automatic, swift, and spontaneous when allowed to proceed undisturbed by other influences. . . . What we need is to be educated in how not to interfere with the inherent capacity of the human mind to think." Kubie, *op. cit.*, 104.

43 John Richardson, "Picasso in Private," *Observer* (London), October 21, 1962, 21.
44 Fromm, *Escape from Freedom*, 244.
45 Lewis Mumford, *The Conduct of Life* (New York: Harcourt, Brace, 1951), 11.
46 Oscar Handlin, "Are the Colleges Killing Education?" *Atlantic* (May, 1962), 43.
47 Frank Barron, "Creativity: What Research Says About It," *N.E.A. Journal* (March, 1961), 19.
48 Riesman has cited the history of the development of psychoanalysis as an example of the fact that the ideas of inclusiveness, of eclecticism, of covering the ground, are hindrances to creativity. David Riesman, *Constraint and Variety in American Education* (New York: Doubleday, 1958), 112–14.
49 For a criticism of objective examinations as enemies of creativity, see Paul Nash, "The Assumptions and Consequences of Objective Examinations," *Canadian Education and Research Digest*, vol. I, no. 1 (March, 1961), 42–50; and "Objective Examinations and the Process of Education," *Canadian Education and Research Digest*, vol. II, no. 2 (June, 1962), 99–103.
50 Richard Church, *The Golden Sovereign* (New York: Dutton, 1957), 33.
51 John Holt, *How Children Fail* (New York: Pitman, 1964), 68. See especially Part II, "Fear and Failure."
52 Karl Stern, *Through Dooms of Love* (New York: Farrar, Straus & Cudahy, 1960), 400.
53 Henri Bergson, "Life and Consciousness," *Hibbert Journal*, vol. X, no. 1 (October, 1911), 41–42. See also Olive A. Wheeler, *Bergson and Education* (Manchester University Press, 1922), ch. 10, "New Methods in Teaching: Creation."
54 Martin Buber, *Hasidism and Modern Man*, Maurice Friedman, trans. (New York: Horizon, 1958), 21–43.
55 Buber, *Between Man and Man*, 66.
56 Maurice Friedman, "The Existential Man: Buber," in Paul Nash, *et al.*, *The Educated Man: Studies in the History of Educational Thought* (New York: Wiley, 1965), 369.
57 Nathaniel Cantor, *Dynamics of Learning* (Buffalo, N.Y.: Foster & Stewart, 1946), 85–86; see also 139–40, where he has made some suggestions for dealing with this problem.
58 Ralph H. Ojemann, "Are Creativity and Mental Health Compatible?" in *Creativity and Psychological Health*, Andrews, ed., 34.
59 Quoted by E.M. Forster, "What has Germany done to the Germans?" *Two Cheers for Democracy* (London: Arnold, 1951), 48.
60 Henry Miller, "The Wisdom of the Heart," in *The Creative Process*, Ghiselin, ed., 185.
61 Ben Shahn, *The Biography of a Painting* (Cambridge, Mass.: Fogg Museum, Harvard University, 1956), 13–14.
62 Although he did not acknowledge man's ability to "create," Buber suggested that man possesses an "originator instinct," which is autonomous.
63 Buber, *Between Man and Man*, 87.
64 Lowenfeld, *Creative and Mental Growth*, 14–15.
65 *Ibid.*, 18.
66 A.S. Neill, *Summerhill: A Radical Approach to Child Rearing* (New York: Hart, 1960), 70.
67 See Charles F. Virtue, "Creativity and Symbolism," in *Creativity and Psychological Health*, Andrews, ed., 56.
68 Lowenfeld, *Creative and Mental Growth*, 12–13.

[69] *Ibid.*, 44.

[70] Igor Stravinsky, *Poetics of Music in the Form of Six Lessons* (New York: Vintage, 1959), 66.

[71] Henry Miller, *Tropic of Cancer* (New York: Grove Press, 1961), 253.

[72] For a "European" criticism of this tendency in American education, see Jacques Barzun, *The House of Intellect* (New York: Harper, 1959), ch. 4, 5.

[73] D.H. Lawrence, quoted by G.H. Bantock, *Freedom and Authority in Education* (London: Faber & Faber, 1953), 175.

[74] William James, *Talks to Teachers* (New York: Norton, 1958), 48. Dewey did not condemn imitation but suggested that its value is not as a model to copy in action but as a guide to clearness and adequacy of conception. "As a general principle, no activity should be *originated* by imitation. The start must come from the child; the model or copy may then be supplied in order to assist the child in imagining more definitely what it is he really wants—in bringing him to consciousness." John Dewey, *School and Society* (Chicago: University of Chicago Press, 1943), 128–29.

[75] Ghiselin, *op. cit.*, 25.

[76] See Berdyaev, *op. cit.*, 129. The whole of ch. 3, "The Ethics of Creativeness," well repays study.

[77] See ch. 8, below, for a fuller discussion of this important point.

[78] Gerald Heard, *Training for a Life of Growth* (Santa Monica, Calif.: Wayfarer Press, 1959), 7.

[79] Loren Eiseley, *The Immense Journey* (New York: Random House, 1957), 207.

[80] Koestler, *op. cit.*, 520.

[81] Elting E. Morison, "A Case Study of Innovation," *Massachusetts Institute of Technology, Department of Economics and Social Science, Publications in Social Science*, series 3, no. 10, 5.

[82] Ghiselin, *op. cit.*, 31.

[83] Reported in *NATO Letter* (December, 1959), 28.

[84] The Lysenko controversy does not disprove this. The fact that there *was* a controversy shows the power of scientific evidence even in a totalitarian country. Moreover, the facts themselves are not clear: some recent findings by Western geneticists suggest that Lysenko might have been partly right after all.

[85] James, *op. cit.*, 49.

[86] Fred Clarke, *Freedom in the Educative Society* (London: University of London Press, 1948), 88.

[87] Quoted by Dorothy Day, *The Long Loneliness* (New York: Doubleday, 1959), 15.

[88] John Dewey, *Art as Experience* (New York: Putnam's, 1958), 265.

[89] *Ibid.*, 310–12.

[90] F.R. Leavis and Denys Thompson, *Culture and Environment: The Teaching of Critical Awareness* (London: Chatto & Windus, 1933), 96–97.

[91] Quoted by Viscount Samuel, *In Search of Reality* (Oxford: Blackwell, 1958), 151.

[92] Laurens van der Post, *The Seed and the Sower* (New York: Morrow, 1963), 255.

[93] E.H. Carr, "History as Progress," *The Listener* (May 18, 1961), 871.

[94] Dewey, *Art as Experience*, 159.

[95] *Manchester Guardian Weekly*, September 6, 1962, 14.

VIII

THE AUTHORITY OF COMMITMENT
The Freedom to Grow

I COMMITMENT AND FREEDOM

The Need for Commitment

One of the saddest diseases of modern man is the growing tendency to withdraw from personal commitment. More and more of us seem to be trying to live on the income of life without touching the capital. But the sterility of such an existence is ultimately brought home to those who adopt it. Even considerations of mental health demand that we occasionally draw on our capital and commit ourselves to a cause or a purpose larger than ourselves. It is illuminating that there are more suicides in peacetime than in wartime. Even such an unfortunate cause as war can apparently lift people above themselves, out of their petty, egocentric concerns, to a level of self-transcending commitment.

Too often, our minds, bodies, and personalities become meticulously prepared for some unknown enterprise that is never undertaken. If we remain like some finely tuned machine that is never put to work, we shall eventually become oppressed by a sense of personal futility. Unemployment is the quickest route to degeneration. At some level we all yearn to be put to use in a significant cause: life has few deeper satisfactions to offer. "Be worn and you will remain new," is the way *Tao-Te King* puts it.[1]

Similarly, experiences in the critical conditions of concentration camps have shown that even physical survival can be determined by the degree to which a man can commit himself to some meaningful goal. Viktor Frankl, who was in a German concentration camp for three years during the Second World War, has reported that the loss of a sense of meaning in life had a deadly effect on a prisoner. Those who survived were often those who saw a meaning and purpose in their suffering. Frankl quoted Nietzsche. "He who has a *why* to live can bear with almost any *how*." On this basis, Frankl developed his form of psychotherapy, called logotherapy; it does not aim directly at self-fulfillment and self-realization, but at helping the individual to find a unique purpose to which he can commit himself, in the belief that fulfilling this commitment will lead, incidentally, to self-fulfillment.[2]

Of course, in the bewilderment of thought there is relief in action, and we must beware of the temptation to commit ourselves to *any* action, as an emotional release from intolerable indecision. Nietzsche also said, "Convictions are prisons." Only convictions have in them the stuff to be the power of new action, but they also contain the possibility of holding us in a vise that prevents growth. The mind must be always open for reflection, so that its convictions are freshened by new experience and contacts but always closed for resolved action, when distraction, hesitation, and half-tones are fatal.

Thomas Carlyle enjoined, "Do the duty that lies nearest thee, the second will become clearer, nobler." An educated mind is one that has reached a certain equilibrium: it is always committed enough to take the next step, to attain the drive of practical action, and is never made up with consummate completeness, impervious to new impressions, unable to take a fresh standpoint.

Lord Acton is a good example of the dangers of too much open-mindedness. He gathered in his lifetime an immense store of historical knowledge—but it died with him. Apart from fragments, the great books that should have preserved his erudition were never written. He was always waiting for a little more, a few more facts, a missing elusive word, to achieve perfection. Through waiting for an impossible measure of completeness before committing himself to paper, he denied us all the concatenations of knowledge which, to be fruitful, must come within a single mind.

We must be constant seekers. But we must also guard against the temptation never to be finders. To seek means to be open, to be aware. To find means to commit ourselves to a position, at this moment, which may involve costly, sacrificial action. W.H. Auden, in his *Litany of S. Matthew's Day*, offered this prayer: "Deliver us, we pray thee . . . from the temptation, stronger perhaps in our age than in earlier times, to pray, if we pray at all: 'I thank thee, O Lord, that I am an interesting sinner and not as this Pharisee.'"

Victor Gollancz tells an old Rabbinical legend that when Moses struck the Red Sea with his wand nothing happened. Only when the first man plunged in did it open. Commitment involves acting in faith, for we can never wholly forecast the outcomes of our actions.

There is a particular temptation for intellectuals to resist the pull of commitment, for they can play around with hypothetical possibilities for an indefinite time. Unamuno admonished intellectuals to stop treating ideas like concubines. They should, he said, have the courage to marry some great idea and have children. John Bright's advice was: "You should link yourself with a great cause: you may never do the cause much good but the cause will do you a great deal of good." In Henry Wieman's view, "Man's greatness is attained not by devoting himself to the exercise of control over what commands his ultimate commitment but to the very opposite. His greatness is attained by giving himself over to be controlled, shaped, and progressively created by it." [3] C. Wright Mills was particularly scornful of the tendency of the intellectual to evade commitment. In what he called the Overdeveloped Society, he criticized the intelligentsia for failing in its duty to confront the great issues of the day. If the intellectuals abdicate this responsibility, he argued, history will be shaped by *élite* groups without responsibility to those who suffer the consequences of their decisions. Intellectuals must face major contemporary problems with moral passion and energetic commitment.[4]

Commitment and Individual Responsibility

To be committed means to be ready to accept our responsibility to act in the life situation in which we find ourselves. We must not use a yearning for another situation or for other talents as a means to free us from this responsibility. The circumstances may not be as we should like them; we may wish we were better equipped to deal with the problems that life presents to us, but none of this absolves us: we must still commit ourselves. It is all too easy to say, "Yes, I believe this should be done, but the time is not ripe." The time *may* not be ripe, but we must be careful to ensure that we are not just finding specious reasons for postponing acting consistently with principle. Equally, we may say, "Yes, this should be done, but there are others more able to do it than I: my talents lie elsewhere." Undoubtedly it is necessary to use our strength wisely, but we cannot always find the ideal object on which to use our talents: we must be prepared to act in imperfect situations. Moreover, the others who we think are better equipped than ourselves may not act either: they, too, may be effective rationalizers. Buber has put it: "Reduction is forbidden; you are not at liberty to select what suits you, the whole cruel hour is at stake." [5]

Commitment involves an inescapable responsibility, but it nevertheless makes possible a higher freedom. This connection can be epitomized by comparing marriage with divorce. There is a common expression that describes the divorced person as having "gained his freedom." But this is only freedom *from*: freedom from certain legal ties and moral responsibilities that have become irksome or unbearable. This is only an *enabling* freedom: it does not in itself carry us into the higher reaches of life. For this we need marriage, which represents freedom *to*: freedom to accept the responsibility for the life of another person as one's own. Marriage makes possible the exemplary bondage of responsibility wherein lies the highest freedom.

To be responsible and free means to be ready to pass judgment on our actions in the light of the values to which we are committed, to condemn those actions as wrong (or sinful) if necessary, and to attempt to atone for our wrongdoing. It is not enough to claim that we are victims of our upbringing or environment, that we act the way those around us act, or that our commitments are arbitrarily determined for us by our society.[6] Ultimately, we are answerable to our conscience.

The prevailing post-Freudian theory of conscience dismisses it as the interiorized voice of parental authority. The young child is punished and admonished for wrongdoing. After sufficient punishments, he comes to hear his parent's voice even when he is tempted to transgress. He restrains himself because he fears the pain that comes from self-accusation. But such a theory fails to distinguish between what Allport has called the *must* of the child's conscience and the *ought* of the adult's conscience.[7] He has suggested that adult conscience is a sense of *positive* obligation and self-consistency rather than a *negative* fear of punishment. While the prevailing theory may account for the early stages of the growth of conscience, it is not a satisfactory explanation of the later stages. Adults have their own private moral codes, often distinct from those inherited from parents and society. Theories based on the fear of punishment do not explain how such changes occur.

The committed person is answerable not only for his own acts, but also for the acts of the groups of which he is a member. In this respect we might contrast Adolf Eichmann with Claude Eatherly, the man who gave the signal for the dropping of the atomic bombs on Hiroshima and Nagasaki, and who has since been tormented with such self-recriminations. Eichmann's view was that "The question of conscience is a matter for the head of the state, the sovereign." [8] Eatherly, on the other hand, wrote some years after the war:

I believe that we are rapidly approaching a situation in which we shall be compelled to re-examine our willingness to surrender responsibility for our thoughts and actions to some social institution as the political party, trade union, church or state.[9]

Eatherly's fate shows that the decision to follow the guidance of one's own conscience can be a costly and painful one. Nevertheless, this is the only path that offers the chance of attaining a genuinely autonomous commitment.

Individual Commitment and "Objective Truth"

Besides the need for personal commitment through the governance of individual conscience, there exists also a complementary need for some sort of public check of the validity of this personal leading. It would be superfluous to document the history of the evil excesses that have been committed in the name of conscience. The problem is complicated by the heterogeneity of the consequences that can flow from a passionate following of conscience.

There is a sense in which passion is the enemy of freedom. This is the sense implied in the story of Mahomet II who, having fallen madly in love, ordered the object of his affections to be murdered, to regain his freedom. Genuine passion is the most intense experience that man can undergo. It consists of a single-minded, intense concentration on a person or cause. It includes a feeling of being driven by forces stronger than oneself (hence, the impression of a loss of freedom) and involves a concentration of all the resources of one's personality on a single focus. It is an inevitable molder of the personality of the one so committed.

And yet, without passion, no great thing can be accomplished. Achievement and passion are essentially linked. The goal should not be to reduce the passion but to channel it in wholesome directions. But how do we determine what is wholesome in this respect? There can be no simple or doctrinaire answer to this question. It is folly to crush every manifestation of dedication to eccentric commitment. This way lie stagnation and the dreary uniformity that has almost always characterized formal education in the past. Nevertheless, we cannot raise the voice of individual conscience to the level of infallible authority. Men are finite and fallible, and hence conscience is the same. Individual vision can become clouded or perverted. The conscience has been likened to a compass—it can be out of true because of steel nearby.[10]

Under such circumstances, it would be rash to ignore the centuries of experience that are represented in the basic ideas (as opposed to the petty denominational *bric-à-brac*) of the major religions, which are remarkably alike in their insights. Knowing the temptations and rationalizations to which man is prone, one would be well-advised to seek wise guidance, to temper his basic longings with the authority of common belief, and to check his ideas against the accumulated wisdom of the past.

Nevertheless, the greater truth in the past has often been held by one who stood against the world, who saw what common opinion was too blind to see. Moreover, there is the danger of assuming that man can grasp the whole of "objective truth" in such a manner that its message can be incumbent on all men. It may be truer to say that the highest possibility that is open to me is to attain a measure of personal truth, something that has validity for my personal life, but which may have to be translated by another before it can have equal validity for his life.

Similarly, in carving out a personal area of lifework, it may be more important to be fully committed to that which is within one's personal grasp than to attempt to cover all the ground, to include all the factors. Riesman has suggested,

The history of science does not support the notion that the way to make progress is to be eclectic and leave nothing out. In my opinion, commitment is more important than inclusiveness both in teaching and research, provided that the commitment is not merely an inherited one.[11]

Freedom through Commitment

By exacting from ourselves a strict account of the nature and purpose of our actions we come to an understanding of what fruit our lives can bear. One of the highest arts consists of learning how to give one's life in such a way that it will not be dissipated in unending trivia. Such fruitful giving demands the focus of a commitment, an organizing principle for life. The life of a man who has such an organizing commitment is marked by simplicity and integrity. The simplicity comes about because his commitment reflects a hierarchy of values and enables him to separate the central from the peripheral, the essential from the secondary.

The integrity is born of a commitment of the whole self—one in which intellectual conviction is associated with emotional involvement and consistent action. Both simplicity and integrity engender one of the most precious freedoms—freedom from fear—for they reduce the number of things we think we cannot get along without, and whose loss we therefore fear.

Freedom from character defects, such as indolence, boredom, moodiness, and self-indulgence, is also engendered by a wholesome commitment, which takes the focus out of the self and places it on something higher. Reinhold Niebuhr put it thus:

Man is the kind of creature who cannot be whole except he be committed, because he cannot find himself without finding a center beyond himself. In short the emancipation of the self requires commitment.[12]

The kind of freedom the mature person strives for is not the freedom to drift, the freedom of separation, for this is the freedom of the wheel that has come away from its axle and starts to run "freely" on its own: it soon exhausts its momentum and runs down toward its fall.[13] Rather he seeks the strengthening and disciplining freedom that is found only within a framework of commitment.

II RELIGIOUS COMMITMENT AND SCIENTIFIC GROWTH

The Perils of Commitment

The act of self-commitment is ultimately an act of faith. In this fact are implied many of its dangers. A commitment that holds the possibility of greater moral freedom may also hold the possibility of less intellectual freedom. The investment of self in a commitment makes the individual less willing to jeopardize his investment by rigorous intellectual inquiry that may bring into question the rightness of his commitment. Hence, dogmatism and obscurantism are constant attendants on this act of faith.

This danger is particularly acute today, when the pace of change and the ease of communication have combined to present man with an unprecedented number of choices. Faced with a bewildering number of alternatives, one is often beset by acute feelings of conflict and anxiety. One yearns for the certainty and security one felt as a child; there is a strong temptation to give up the wearying task of trying to reconcile the conflicting drives within and put one's faith in a strong authority. Once found, this authority—which may be a dogmatic religion or political philosophy—is fastened on to with infantile dependence. Doubts are silenced by intellectual rationalizations, which obviate the need for casting oneself off into the dark uncertainty of the search. Clearly, this sort of commitment for the sake of peace of mind is only providing a shelter wherein the immature can continue to avoid the pain of growing up.

It should be unnecessary by now to underline the fact that a religious commitment can be a source of evil as well as good. Religious authoritarianism has been the greatest enemy of free rational inquiry throughout history. Christians have tortured and killed each other for centuries because of their differing commitments: in Madrid alone, in three centuries, 300,000 were put to death. The "will of God" has been used as a guide to the most frightful crimes and injustices. S.R. Swart, the Minister of Justice in South Africa in 1955, defended South African policies toward Negroes and coloreds with the claim: "We believe that we are sitting here [on the Government bench] at this moment by the will of God." [14] The Mau Mau oaths in Kenya began, "I truly swear by Almighty God . . ." before going on to promise to commit murder, if necessary of their own mothers, fathers, and children.

Carl Jung pointed out that creeds and dogmas may be substitutes for, indeed protection against, immediate experience of God. Commitment to a firm dogma, religious or political, may constitute a screen between the individual and direct experience. This is safer and less demanding, and it does not risk so much. At the same time, it gives an illusion of having "done one's duty," of having performed a worthy act. Hence, it constitutes a reinforcement to complacency and an impediment to personal growth.[15]

There is in almost all of us a tendency to avoid the rational, a fear of the burdens of the intellect, a weakness for what Spengler called, "Confucius on hand-made paper." There are limitations to rational knowledge, but it is important that they be self-realized. There is a great difference between the mind that is prevented from reaching these limits by dogmatism and the mind that autonomously becomes aware of the limits through personal inquiry.

The Safeguard of Science

If our commitment is to be one that permits and encourages personal growth rather than stifles or hinders it, there must be a constant willingness to subject the grounds of our commitment to intellectual examination. The demand for intellectual freedom, said Robert Calhoun, is "fundamentally a demand that artificial restraint of one sort or another shall not be permitted to contradict the primary reality of human existence." [16] Too often, the religiously committed person is afraid to push his inquiry to the farthest point, in fear that the God he will find there will disappoint him. He is afraid to reach out in an attempt to find God at the frontiers of thought and knowledge and prefers the safety of the little deity of his restricted commitment.

The scientific method might be taken as a paradigm of the way in which especially the religiously concerned person should treat his own commitment. The method of science is marked by a restless intellectual questioning, by a reluctance to accept anything on trust, by an active capacity to doubt, by a refusal to admit barriers to free inquiry, and by a welcoming attitude to new evidence. This is one of the scientist's great virtues—his self-discipline, his self-abnegation, as he follows the rule of nature to whatever end it may lead, without regard for his own desires and aspirations. This ascetic objectivity is exactly the kind of cleansing agent that is needed for the purifying of commitment.

It is important to recognize that the intellectual, rational method by which science tries to discover the truth is not the only method. Intuition, imagination, revelation, feeling, are all valid methods of inquiry. But they lack the tentative and self-correcting features of the method of science, which constitute its great safeguard. These other methods often claim a finality for which there is no corrective, while the ordinary processes of science can be expected to correct its errors through the collection of more facts, through more accurate experiments, clearer thinking, and more consistent application of rational argument.[17]

The Power and Limits of Science

Since we are here recommending an infusion of the scientific attitude into the quest for commitment, it is as well to have clearly in mind exactly what science can and cannot do. Unlike many religions, science offers a message that is universal. To the genuine scientist, secrecy and exclusiveness are repugnant: science transcends political, social, and religious barriers and welcomes all seekers who will submit to its discipline. While most religions claim access to infallible truth through the word of God revealed in their scriptures, science claims no infallibility, but only provisional knowledge to be revised as fresh insights are produced. Hence, through science, we have the possibility of a universal commitment capable of growth.

Nevertheless, the application of science to the formulation of higher purposes of human life is beset with severe limitations. Its power to analyze efficient means cannot be equally applied to the formulation of worthy ends; the nature of scientific proof is not of the same order as the probabilities of existential decision-making; the experimental method has doubtful relevance for the problem of determining human goals, since experiments with humans cannot be exactly repeated, and human groups can never be exactly matched or controlled.

It is only the semieducated who are liable to apply science inappropriately to the problem of human commitment, for the trained scientist rarely makes this error himself. He is well-aware, for example, of the important and limiting gap between scientific observations and theories and the real world. Eddington wrote:

In its actual procedures physics studies not those inscrutable qualities [of the material world], but pointer-readings which we can observe. The readings, it is true, reflect the fluctuations of the world-qualities; but our exact knowledge is of the readings, not of the qualities. The former have as much resemblance to the latter as a telephone number has to a subscriber.[18]

And in the words of Bertrand Russell: "Physics is mathematical not because we know so much about the physical world, but because we know so little: it is only its mathematical properties that we can discover." [19]

Moreover, far from being able to remove the uncertainty from commitment, faith, and love, science is itself based on all of these. Logic and reason are insufficient to ensure progress in science. For this the scientist must have a commitment to the truth, a faith in the rationality of the universe and in its comprehensibility by reason, and a passionate love of knowledge.

Awareness of the limits of science will make us more open to the reception of truth from other quarters. It is a peculiarly modern form of pride to believe in the exclusive power of science to enlighten. Arthur Koestler's *The Sleepwalkers* is a cautionary tale against the *hubris* of science, or rather of a philosophical outlook based on it. "The dials on our laboratory panels," he wrote, "are turning into another version of the shadows in the cave. Our hypnotic enslavement to the numerical aspects of reality has dulled our perception of non-quantitative moral values." He went on to condemn "the worshippers of the new Baal, lording it over the moral vacuum with his electronic brain." [20] He who will accept illumination from no source but that of science is not experimental enough. If he were genuinely experimental in his attitude, he would be ready to frame hypotheses and test them in his own experience —not only in the laboratory, but also through works of art, through literature, through music, through personal acts of generosity and compassion.

Scientific knowledge can present us with the evidence for making a commitment, but in itself it can never push us over the edge into ethical judgment and action. Henry Aiken, in his criticism of Sidney Hook's desire to solve all man's problems by the continued and extended use of science in all domains, has asked:

How can the rationale of the scientific method, as such, serve to make men aware of an obligation to reduce the evils which could be dealt with scientifically? It is one thing to know how to provide a more equitable distribution of raw materials; it is another to believe that such a redistribution really ought to exist . . . the problem . . . is not a problem of knowledge, in the scientific sense, but a problem of conscience and conduct. The despair of man in our time . . . is not so much a despair of his ignorance as a despair of his wickedness, his inhumanity, his passion for self-destruction.[21]

Science provides us with limited and uncertain knowledge about particular aspects of our environment. But when all scientific evidence is in, we must still act according to beliefs that are not fully substantiated. And on some of the most important issues in life, science is almost completely silent. It cannot save us from some of our greatest dangers, and some, such as technocracy, it exacerbates. Wittgenstein wrote: "We feel that even when *all possible* scientific questions have been answered, the problems of life remain completely untouched." [22] Moreover, as science proceeds to discover more and more, we begin to realize our immense ignorance and the depth of mystery that lies beyond. For example, in the field of cosmic rays and in the field of genetic inheritance, to mention only two, recent discoveries here served to indicate the unforeseen complexity and subtlety of nature. Far from reducing the mystery of the universe, science serves to increase our points of contact with its immensity. Scientists on this growing edge of knowledge are unlikely to fall into the error of believing that science alone can form the stuff of commitment.

Toward a Scientific-Religious Synthesis

Science without religion is in danger of worshiping a sterile efficiency. Religion without science is in danger of submitting to a dogmatic obscurantism. It should be recognized that there is a distinction to be made between a religious attitude toward life and the things that are often perpetuated by the churches in the name of "religion." Nietzsche, who called the churches the tombs of God, and Kierkegaard, who accused the churches of making a fool of God, would hardly have been reassured by the contemporary scene. The churches too often represent closed frontiers. They hold up accidental and contingent aspects of their faith as central and essential. They fail to protest against social and racial evils and retreat into material prosperity and moral self-righteousness. They are choked with an obsolete mythology that forces honest and intelligent people to reject them totally—and reject all religious openness at the same time.

Major C.L. Anderson, an American army doctor who was captured during the Korean War and served in P.O.W. camps, claimed that many of the 1500 American prisoners who died in the first five months of captivity could have been saved by a feeling for one's fellow men that runs through all major religions. When reminded that an Army study had not found any correlation between religious affiliation, or lack of it, and becoming a "collaborator" or a "reactionary," Anderson pointed out that he was not referring to "announced adherence on a personnel card to some denomination or other" but to "the kind of religion that touches a man inside and causes him to act, however dark the situation, as an ethical, fearless human being." [23]

Allport has stressed the difference between childish religion and mature religion. We still tend to emphasize the childish aspects of religion—familism, dependency, authority, wishful thinking, and magic. But, he has suggested, the religious attitude can be fully developed only in adults. The adult finds that he needs a mature religion (engaging reason, love, and faith) to face the intellect's almost certain failure to surmount unaided the difficulties of life.[24] The churches up till now have concentrated on planting quickly in the young a "belief" in a statement or creed, which is largely meaningless without greater knowledge and experience. What is needed now is the exploration of a mature religious attitude, one compounded of attempts to form a comprehensive viewpoint that will bring a measure of meaning to the individual's life. All mature people need religion, since all mature people must be concerned with certain problems, such as death, responsibility, and freedom, which are ultimately religious. But for a mature person this religion must not cause intellectual reservations or conflict. There may well be absolutes and universals, but they need to be investigated, studied, and tested, rather than accepted from some revelatory book or institution.

Our age requires a religious response that engages the whole personality and that must, therefore, be both imaginative and rational. Science may itself be the best route to such a response. Lawrence Durrell has suggested:

> . . . given time enough, it seems to me clear that science could lead us back to the central cosmological preoccupations of religion, and actually reinvigorate what one might call . . . "a religious view" of things. . . . I believe that science and religion are now within hailing distance, though churches and governments are trying to row in the opposite direction.[25]

Even scientific humanists seem often close to the religious attitude. Julian Huxley has written, for example, that, "The divine is what man finds worthy of adoration, that which compels his awe." [26] Such feelings of awe are at the heart of the genuine religious posture.

The needed synthesis of science and religion is one that enables religion to face changes in the same spirit that science does. The individual must be encouraged to set out to discover the spiritual world for himself, as the scientist sets out to discover the physical world for himself. Religion, like science, must start not from dogma but from a desire for truth and a commitment to seeking it in a disciplined way. We should not expect truth to come through ritual or formalized repetition, but through personal, active, honest seeking. We should beware of the unthinking use of meaningless words and phrases, but should use our own words to express our experiences and seek to interpret them in terms that are meaningful to our contemporaries.

III GROWTH THROUGH COMMITMENT TO UNITY

Religious Commitment as Unity with God

The problem of achieving both growth and commitment can most fruitfully be approached in the light of the concept of *unity*. A commitment that fosters growth toward unity is the most hopeful answer. Unity itself is a term without much meaning until it is analyzed and qualified. Such analysis and qualification are the task of this section.

The sort of religious commitment that was described and advocated above is clearly not essentially connected with any denomination or sect. In this sense, Christianity has no better claim that Judaism, Buddhism than Islam, Hinduism than many forms of humanism. What is important is that the commitment leads toward a growing feeling of unity with some basic element, force, or spirit in the universe. Whether or not this force is thought of as God is at the moment less important than the fact of the direct, personal experience.

Many accounts support the belief that man's highest development occurs in moments of *ekstasis* in which the individual loses separateness and individuation and feels himself in unity with all beings and with the source of Being. Such experiences have been reported for centuries in accounts of mysticism and have been echoed more recently in accounts of the use of psychedelic drugs like LSD, Mescalin, and Psilocybin.

Paul Tillich has talked of the lack or loss of unity as "estrangement." For Tillich, estrangement means separation from God, but also separation from ourselves, for God is the eternal ground of our being; hence, an attitude toward Him is in effect an attitude toward a part—the divine part—of ourselves. We are free to separate ourselves from God, as the prodigal son was free to separate himself from his father. This is our freedom—our glory and our danger. Tillich maintained that the polar demands of individuality and participation find their truth only in the depth where both are united. The danger of freedom is that we shall commit the "original sin" of estrangement. Our task is to find our way back, in freedom, to unity.[27]

An immense range of commitment is able to encompass this, or a closely similar, concept of unity. The Catholic writer, Bede Griffiths wrote:

Beyond all thought and feeling and imagination, there is an inner sanctuary into which we scarcely ever enter. It is the ground or substance of the soul, where all the faculties have their roots, and which is the very centre of our being. It is here that the soul is at all times in direct contact with God.[28]

In Hinduism there is the concept of *Atman*, the universal soul or Self, which is within each of us and which is the source of all life and being. Through recognition of and devotion of this Self, and through following certain ethical rules, one can achieve union with Brahma and, thus, partake of divinity. Of similar nature are the "formless Self" of Zen Buddhism and the Inward Light of Quakerism—that of God in every man.

Man's commitment to move toward this unity is seen essentially as a *response*. "The highest form of liberty," said a Jesuit writer, "is a response to the ultimate love which is the source of the world's being and is the finality of the world's development." [29] Goethe wrote: "If the eye were not sun-like, how could we ever see light? And if God's own power did not dwell within us, how could we delight in things divine?" [30] Aesthetic enjoyment of natural beauty can be seen as one manifestation of this unifying response of man to the divine. Another is the feeling of being loved by the universe, of dwelling in a place where one is essentially at home, where one belongs. Similarly, Buber conceived man as a partner of God, one who is capable of entering into a dialogue with God and achieving through grace a unity with Him.[31] The Latin word for priest, *pontifex*, means literally a builder of bridges, although it is a matter of debate whether he more often acts as a unifier or a separator.

Love as Commitment to Another Person

Unity with another person through love is an aspect of unity that is open potentially to all and, yet, is realized less often than one might wish. Part of the reason for this failure is that the total commitment required by love is one that, at least ostensibly, reduces the freedom of the lover. In William Golding's novel *Free Fall*, he described how Sammy bound Beatrice to him with threads of love: "I did not see that with every additional thread I myself was bound with another cable." [32] Fear of such a loss of freedom is often inhibiting. Promiscuous sexual activity may be a fearful substitute for a commitment to love one person. And yet it is only through such a commitment that the possibility of a higher freedom is reached. Fromm saw the answer to the problem of freedom in what he called spontaneous activity. He wrote,

Love is the foremost component of such spontaneity; love as spontaneous affirmation of others, as the union of the individual with others on the basis of the preservation of the individual self. The dynamic quality of love lies in this very polarity: that it springs from the need of overcoming separateness, that it leads to oneness—and yet that individuality is not eliminated.[33]

Gerald Heard has described three stages in the developing power of love. The first stage he called Eros: the need for love. Everyone begins here, but many grow into the second stage, which is Agape: the capacity to reciprocate love. We can love those who love us. Finally there is the third stage, Charis: the power to give love without requiring reciprocity, the power to be interested and moved by every living thing.[34]

Although few of us reach the saintly stage of Charis, most can hope to reach the stage of Agape, to break through the stifling wall of our own egocentricity and reach into the heart and mind of another. Those who cannot break out of the prison of the self in this way are in terrible danger. Psychiatry has recently rediscovered what the major religions have taught (by precept rather than example) for a long time: "that love, the drive towards reunion of the separated, is the foundation of life and is rooted in the nature of being itself." [35] Infants deprived of love tend to become morally and socially defective. Love is a powerful antidote against criminal, alcoholic, and suicidal tendencies, against hate, fear, and psychoneuroses.[36]

There is an essential connection between love, health, and freedom. Mentally ill patients can often be cured by a healthy environment, that is, not a place where they can *forget* themselves but a place where they can *be* themselves, or in other words a place where they can be most *free*. If we love a person we can allow him to be himself: this is how love frees and brings health.

This increasing realization of the vital need to give and receive love has been accompanied by a rediscovery of the importance of vulnerability. Too many of us spend our lives carefully building defenses against our neighbors, realizing too late that what we thought was a protection is in fact a prison. We need to tear down our human defenses until we can be touched by others and so touch them. Only vulnerable people can love. Love is the unifying answer to the paradox of growth and commitment: only through a commitment to love can we keep ourselves vulnerable and, hence, open to growth.

We cannot leave a discussion of love without mention of the related concept of tolerance. It has been argued that love is not the answer to the world's problems because we can love only what we know personally, and we cannot personally know very much. "In public affairs," said E.M. Forster, "in the rebuilding of civilization, something much less dramatic and emotional [than love] is needed, namely, tolerance." [37] We should encourage the development of a tolerant attitude, but we should also recognize the differences between tolerance and love. We do not tolerate those we love or causes to which we are committed. Toleration means checking the spontaneous impulse to suppress the person or idea we dislike or think is wrong. Strong commitment makes it more difficult (but also more important) to be tolerant. To tolerate the expression of a viewpoint that opposes our own is to imply that we think there may be something of value in the other viewpoint; we admit the possibility that in the last analysis we may be wrong. The scientific attitude demands tolerance. The scientist does not believe he has gained the final truth but, on the contrary, he hopes that future scientists will modify, correct, and improve his findings. Hence, the tolerance and encouragement of other views will nurture the scientific enterprise.

But it seems unwisely timorous to limit our aspirations to the achievement of tolerance alone. It may be true, as Forster claims, that we can love only what we know personally, but do we *need* to love any more? If we can help children to love those they know, we may also be helping them to tolerate those they do not know, for through a loving commitment to one person we can come to appreciate the unique worth of every person.

Community as Commitment to the Group

Tolerance is content with respecting the individual: love is not. Through love we are committed to seek the fullest possible growth of other persons, and this can be done only through the agency of community. Love means assuming an unlimited liability for one's neighbors, and this involves a concern for the relationships that develop both within and without the community. Nels Ferré wrote,

Love wants each one to become genuinely himself but knows that no one can become his fullest and truest self apart from cooperative enterprise. The authority of love is the organic constraint for a cooperative community of free and genuine individuals.[38]

Freedom can be nurtured only if we maintain the primacy of the personal relationships that inhere in genuine community over the functional relationships that characterize society. Macmurray has suggested a "type" instance to describe the difference between these two kinds of relationship. I am with strangers whose good will is important to me and cannot be depended on ("society"). My behavior and conversation with them are not free; they suffer from constraint. I must be careful, cannot be spontaneous, cannot "be myself," must think carefully before speaking to make a good impression. Then I leave this company and join a group of friends I know and trust ("community"). Constraint is replaced by freedom. I now allow my whole self to appear, say what comes to mind, act "naturally;" I need not fear criticism and so can be spontaneous, speaking and acting without an eye to effects.[39]

Education is usually more effective in fostering tolerance than in fostering love and community. Especially inasmuch as it is intellectual, education often acts as a divisive force. We are divided by our intellects, which we use to argue and dispute. But as we dig more deeply into ourselves and come closer to the source of life, we come closer also to our fellow men in understanding and interdependence, as the spokes of a wheel approach each other as they come closer to the center. This sense of community can be fostered through work, through worship, through contemplation, or through explorations of the unconscious (which perhaps explains in part why patients often fall in love with their analysts). It is in this way that we can develop self-knowledge without becoming self-centered, that we can develop the large, emancipating purpose that will absorb the little, enslaving purposes.

One of the great insights of which Buber has reminded us is that we can reach God only by way of man. Buber said,

> The real God lets no shorter line reach him than each man's longest, which is the line embracing the world that is accessible to this man. For he, the real God, is the creator, and all beings stand before him in relation to one another in his creation, becoming useful in living with one another for his creative purpose.[40]

A commitment to God that avoids man is merely an attempt to escape the responsibility that is laid on us to re-enter the cave in order to help those within to grow into community. We love God, it has been said, as much as the one we love least.

Experience in community must be gained on a small scale, but eventually the community to which we must give our commitment is that of mankind. No smaller groups are viable today, if they carry an aspect of exclusiveness. This is a simple dictate of military technology. In the past, it was possible to fight for one's community in order to protect one's children, land, and ideals. Today, fighting a war to protect one's children means to destroy all children. Science has made pacifists of us all. Civilized countries are beginning to realize that the cost of war is out of keeping with the degrees of difference that distinguish them from each other. It has been pointed out, for example, that to engage in uninhibited general war to promote either the communist or the anti-communist cause would be to show "a failure to appreciate the triviality, *sub specie aeternitatis*, of a conflict between two ways of life each of which resembles the other more than it does any other that exists or has ever existed, and both of which are doomed to be superseded." [41]

Even short of the ideal of the community of mankind, it is still possible for a genuine community to flourish, if it obeys the cardinal rule of community: its purpose must be found within itself, in the quality of the relationships to which its members are committed, and not in some external purpose, such as the destruction or subjugation or exploitation of other groups. Archibald MacLeish has castigated America for just such a neglect of its own sense of commitment and an obsession with the purposes and concerns of other nations. The test of loyalty has changed from love for one's own community to hatred for another, usually communist. "A nation which defines itself in terms of what it is *not* inevitably begins to forget what it is. And a nation which forgets what it is is a dying nation." [42]

Service as an Expression of Unity

How is this commitment to the goal of unity to be expressed? The concept of *service* might be considered a paradigm of this expression. It is at the same time a manifestation of the highest type of freedom—that which comes through transcending oneself and imaginatively "entering into" a life other than one's own. Service in this sense means enhancing another's freedom through the sensitivity and creativity one brings to the relationship.

Raymond Williams has made a brilliant critique of the concept of service, which he views as different from, and inferior to, the concept of community, which involves "active mutual responsibility." He attacked the idea of service because it has served, "at every level, to maintain and confirm the *status quo*." This is wrong, in his opinion, because the *status quo* has been "a denial of equity to . . . the lower servants, whose lives were governed by the existing distributions of property, remuneration, education and respect. The real personal unselfishness, which ratified the description as service, seemed to me to exist within a larger selfishness, which was only not seen because it was idealized as the necessary form of a civilization, or rationalized as a natural distribution corresponding to worth, effort and intelligence." [43] The mordant perspicacity of Williams' analysis compels us to treat it with respect. Strict attention to his ideas can save us from falling into the trap of giving an uncritical allegiance to a traditional, hierarchical, class-corrupted notion of service. Nevertheless, Williams is in danger of throwing away too much. His critique should lead us not to abandon the concept of service but to refine and purify it and make it fit for the larger context of community. Such refinement is the purpose of the present analysis.

We can distinguish between two types of service, one to be guarded against as Williams has warned, but the other to be advocated as holding a key to many of the problems here discussed. The first kind derives from a desire for authority over the person "served": the second derives from a desire for the other's freedom. The latter involves *understanding* the other person, entering into a genuine *relationship* with him, engaging in *mutual* action and responsibility, and seeking always to find out how *he* can serve *us*. In a sense it is much easier to give than to receive, especially when the giving is marked by arrogant self-satisfaction and the receiving by an open humility. It is necessary to be aware of the temptations to arrogance, complacency, self-righteousness, and superiority that inhere in the pernicious kind of service, which might be epitomized by the English Public-School gentleman carrying the white man's burden to darkest Africa and Asia; by the Christian missionary who knows exactly what the heathen needs before he has met him and is determined to serve those needs whether the heathen likes it or not; by the Westerner who goes out to serve people in an underdeveloped country without being aware of the possibility that those people might be able to serve and help him; by the middle-class do-gooder who goes into the lower-class slum to serve the slum dwellers patronizingly for a weekend, a month, or even a year, before returning safely and righteously to the sanctuary of his middle-class ghetto; by the teacher who is unable to learn from his students and relatedly unable to help them to grow creatively because he has such a fixed and dogmatic idea of what he wants to teach. The outcome of creative or freeing service cannot be clearly in one's mind from the beginning. It must evolve gradually in the process of responsible interaction with those we would serve.

We are able to help others to grow in freedom only if we submit ourselves to the discipline of serving them selflessly, without seeking personal advantage, without using them as a means for solving our own problems, without trying to mold them to a preconceived pattern. To love a person means to commit myself to his service in such a way that he can grow into that which he is uniquely capable of becoming. I want him to become ever more capable of achieving a loving unity with others, but he must reach this in his *own* way, not in a way that I prescribe for him. My reward for this service lies in the growth that he enjoys, for this growth fosters the greater unity of which I am a part.

Herman Hesse's *Journey to the East* tells the story of a pilgrimage to the East in which the author took part as a member of a rather mysterious League. A key figure in the story was the servant, Leo, who was always ready to serve all and did so with joy and ease. In the end Leo turned out to be also the president of the League. At one point, Leo said, "That is just what life is when it is beautiful and happy—a game! Naturally, one can also do all kinds of other things with it, make a duty of it, or a battleground, or a prison, but that does not make it any prettier." [44] Service to others, he made clear, is not to be done out of duty but out of pleasure: only then is it done in freedom and love.

Gerald Heard has pointed out the importance of honesty in service. Many of us feel we must be liked, and so we do good deeds to assure ourselves that we are really givers of love (at the Agape level), when we are in fact still only needy (at the Eros level). Hence, we are bound to look for gratitude for our service. This seeking for gratitude makes our charity only money with which we seek to buy love. Those who try to behave beyond the power they possess can only be hypocrites.[45] This is doubtless what Thoreau had in mind when he criticized organized philanthropy:

> I want the flower and fruit of a man, that some fragrance be wafted over from him to me, and some ripeness flavor our intercourse. His goodness must not be a partial and transitory act, but a constant superfluity, which costs him nothing and of which he is unconscious.[46]

Commitment to service is undesirable unless we have reached a stage in our own growth where we can serve others without harming them. Howard Brinton has quoted an old Chinese saying: "The right action performed by the wrong man is the wrong action." He went on:

> As long as there is inward chaos, all outward actions will be contaminated by . . . chaos. In such a case all that we do will promote rather than allay confusion. We seek to bring peace in the world when there is no peace in our hearts and as a result we infect the outer world with our inner conflict.[47]

This is the sad story of much missionary service: it was ultimately destructive because those who served were often unready for service. The same danger is present in teaching: some are attracted to the field, consciously or unconsciously, because it offers opportunities for them to solve their own problems through "serving" others. To serve creatively we must first put ourselves in order. We must start with ourselves, with our own problems and needs, so that our service to others can be unsullied by self-deception, hypocrisy, and an unloving artificiality.

Although service must be rendered in a spirit of love, compassion, and sympathy, this alone is insufficient to affect the unity of the human community. Love must be provided with teeth, with tools, with strength. The surgeon's scalpel can be used as an instrument of love, but only when it is used with skill and knowledge. He who wishes to serve must be prepared for the stern disciplining of oneself that alone can make the desire effective. The translation of loving service into practical terms becomes highly complex, and such complexity means that intellectual training is essential for the servants. Hence, the education appropriate for such men and women is both vitally important and difficult to prescribe.

IV EDUCATION FOR COMMITMENT AND GROWTH

Commitment and Objectivity in Education

If we want our children to grow up to be committed men and women, we are faced with two formidable problems: to what should they be committed, and how should we go about helping them to reach commitment? This takes us again into the problem of indoctrination.[48] Aldous Huxley has suggested that an education for freedom must include the "enunciation of a set of generally acceptable values based upon a solid foundation of facts." [49] The values he suggests are individual freedom, based on the facts of human diversity and genetic uniqueness; charity and compassion, based on the psychiatrically ascertained fact that love is as necessary as food for human growth; and intelligence, "without which love is impotent and freedom unattainable." [50] These facts and values are unexceptionable, but unfortunately Huxley does not meet the problem of how this education is to be achieved. These values have already been widely "enunciated," especially from podia and pulpits, but it is difficult to see what effect this has had. Should the values also be *imposed?* If so, how?

There is no doubt that we all indoctrinate to some extent, and that the process goes on continually in society. Sir Richard Livingstone has maintained that

. . . the firmest believer in freedom moulds, or, if we prefer the phrase, tyrannises over, the mind of his child and takes liberty from it in the cradle. It is fortunate that most people do try to implant a view of life in their children, for if they do not teach, the world does.[51]

Certainly, no thoughtful person can be satisfied to leave children to the unopposed ravages of the indoctrinators of Madison Avenue. And when the teacher first receives the child the latter is already stuffed with parental and parochial prejudices. But, when the school uses the same indoctrinating methods it throws away its own chief value and loses its claim to be an institution that provides anything unique, anything that distinguishes it from the home, the church, business, or politics. Livingstone sought to reassure us on this score by saying,

> The danger, such as it is, of dominating a pupil's mind becomes negligible when the teacher is aware of it, believes in truth and has a respect for human personality; as he must if he has any respect either for Hellenism or for Christianity. . . . Our danger is not too few but too many opinions; not to be penned in a single belief but to be puzzled by innumerable alternatives; not a closed mind but an irresolute one. . . . A major task of education is to help to the right choice.[52]

With this last sentence one can agree, although Livingstone's implication that the right choice must be the same for all is unacceptable. Moreover, the history of schools that consider they have a duty to "implant a view of life" in their students, even some that have a respect for Christianity, such as those controlled by the Catholic Church, does not bring us the reassurance that Livingstone sought.

It is foolish to be dogmatic about this matter, for the age, ability, and background of the students are crucial factors. At any level, from kindergarten through university, it can be said that the good teacher himself has convictions. Moreover, he should be prepared to reveal them, especially if asked directly by a student. But part of the art of teaching is to know when and how to reveal one's convictions, so that they will constitute a basis for the student's comparison and criticism and, hence, for the growth of his own commitment, and not a dogma that stultifies the timid and makes unproductive mutineers out of the strong.

Riesman has suggested a useful "counter-cyclical policy" as a guide in this matter. In urban, sophisticated, or *avant-garde* institutions, where teachers are often confronted with uncommitted, city-wise students who "wouldn't dream of fighting city hall," he suggested that the teacher should emphasize the importance of values and commitment, in an attempt to smoke out the evasions and self-deceptions of empiricism. But in many rural, Southern, denominational institutions, the situation is very different: students arrive full of values, parents' and townsfolk's, and very shy on facts. It is a laudable achievement in this case to bring some detachment by introducing a few facts and inculcating respect for them.[53] Education is faced with the difficult task of having to foster both commitment and objectivity: to strike the right balance in any situation is the challenge of teaching.

As an example of the sort of problem that has to be faced, we might take the teaching of science. It is futile for the humanists to deplore science or to try to "balance" its influence by curriculum adjustments, required courses, and other forms of quantitative juggling. We must acknowledge the fact that this is in some senses a scientific age and educate for it by altering our thinking about *all* subjects to encompass the legitimate demands and refinements that science brings. The avid memorizing of meaningless formulas that has characterized much science study in the past must go, and be replaced by a profounder understanding of the history and method of science. To go back and reconstruct the discovery of important theories and laws can not only give a sense of exciting discovery to the students, but also show them that science has to work largely by insights (into new relationships between familiar facts), intuitions (into the making of fruitful hypotheses), guesses (as to profitable lines of advance), assumptions (about previous laws and continuities), and faith (in the value of science itself).

Children must be shown the need both for adopting the disciplined objectivity and sustained inquiry of the scientific method and for going beyond science. In biology, for instance, the students should be given an opportunity to gain the kind of knowledge that comes only from dissecting an animal. But all the facts of biology will not give the kind of understanding that can come through caring for a live animal. This, too, should be part of the educational experience—the opportunity to enter imaginatively into the lives of other living things.

The education needed in a society where science plays the dominating role it does in ours is one that examines and clarifies the connection between scientific knowledge and method on the one hand and the meaning and purpose of life on the other. Failure to do this has been partly responsible for the production of scientists who are ready to spend their lives devising more effective ways of destroying, poisoning, and maiming their brothers. It has permitted the development of the morally defective scientist who feels his whole responsibility is ended with an examination of the *how*, without any need to examine the *why*. Unless education can introduce the student to the great issues and principles of life to which one might commit oneself, it becomes reduced to a mere training for technical competence, and as such it lacks the power engendered by a liberating commitment.

If we bear in mind that any general plan must be interpreted and modified in the light of local and temporal circumstances, we might suggest the following as a paradigmatic approach to the problem of educating for commitment and objectivity. First, we should be concerned to lay bare the present commitments of our students, especially where those commitments are hidden—perhaps hidden from the students themselves. Secondly, we should engender situations in which different commitments can be genuinely confronted and compared, perhaps through precipitating intellectual crises in microcosm, to see how situations of conflicting commitments would be handled. We may at this stage move toward resolution, although we will be more concerned with full exploration and should be wary of the dangers of premature resolution. Next, we should encourage the students to examine and reflect on their own commitments. This stage should emphasize the collection of relevant data, keeping open to new ideas, thinking as clearly and objectively as possible. Fourthly, we should demand that the students assimilate these data and reflections into their commitments. This may or may not involve changes in commitment, but we should insist that commitment cannot be escaped. The students should not remain detached from or external to their studies but should take the meaning of these studies into their own lives. We should institute a concern for the relative costs of different commitments, bringing a realization that a master commitment can involve the sacrifice of lesser values that are also worthwhile. Next, and perhaps most difficult, we should insist that it is necessary to *act* in accordance with commitment whenever appropriate opportunity arises. There is, of course, room for much discussion on what constitutes an appropriate opportunity, but we must not use this difficulty as an excuse for committing the academic sin of holding purely intellectual commitments. Lastly, we should demonstrate that the whole process must be constantly self-renewing.[54] There must be a constant openness to the correction of our commitments, which must be firm enough to engender action, but flexible enough to be capable of correction by communities of criticism.

Love in Education

Love is the integrating element of the commitment-growth polarity because it is man's commitment to love that makes growth possible. Man's superiority over all other species is the result of his capacity for love: first, the mother's love and care for the child; second, the father's sustenance and protection of the family; ultimately the community's support and nurture of all through educational and welfare facilities. Schools at their best are love institutionalized. The human being is able to remain young longer, to learn more, and so become wiser, because the members of his community are able to love and trust each and are willing to sacrifice to provide him with a protected growing period.

If this cycle is to continue, and to be strengthened, the love that sustains education must be constantly renewed through the development in the school of the conditions that help to nourish loving personalities.

We are still vastly ignorant of how to do this. But we have, with the help of medicine, psychiatry, and penology, gradually amassed a little knowledge, and this much we should use, while still searching for more.[55] Already we know that many emphases that dominate the school are in direct contravention of the approach our present knowledge would suggest.

We know, for instance, that to foster a loving personality we must cultivate the child's sensitivity. To grow in love means to become increasingly open to subtle indications and gentle nuances, to remain able to be hurt, to become more aware of the needs and desires of others. The opposite characteristics are to be brittle, hard-boiled, sophisticated, and callous. Seen in these terms, the cost of having football players as school heroes is extremely high—perhaps too high to be borne. And while the school is not, of course, wholly to blame for such noxious influences in our society, it should consider carefully the consequences of giving support to elements in the community that compound these dangers. The very worst offender on this score is the small town high school or college that allows its football team to act as an agent of catharsis for the frustrated violence of the whole community.

We know, furthermore, that, to feel compassion for another person one must be relatively free of fear oneself. The fearful person cannot afford to reach out for another person with openness and concern, for all his psychic energies are occupied in the task of self-protection against the anticipated threat. This means that the school must be a place where the individual can grow in confidence, free from threats and the fear of harsh punishment. It must also be a place with a minimum of externally imposed rules, taboos, and restrictions, because giving our attention to the task of conforming to or getting around a network of regulations means that we cannot also give it to the task of developing imaginative empathy.

A number of investigations into the phenomena of prejudice and intolerance have given us evidence on the characteristics of the intolerant, prejudiced person and on the kind of educational experiences we ought to foster to remedy these defects, which put severe limits on the power of love. We know, for example, that prejudiced, intolerant people most often grew up in an atmosphere of harsh discipline and fear. Less prejudiced and more tolerant people were usually brought up in an atmosphere of security: they felt accepted. If punished, they considered themselves punished for a particular act, rather than being condemned as persons. Tolerant people tend to be more aware of their own shortcomings, which makes them gentle toward others. Intolerant people tend to be unaware of their own faults, which they project onto others

Hence, they are enthusiastic scapegoat hunters. Intolerant people usually rely heavily on authority: they demand strict adherence to law, doctrine, and custom. Tolerant people tend to be more flexible and are ready to make personal and existential judgments. Tolerant people often criticize those with authority over them, including parents and teachers, but do not necessarily lack respect for them. Intolerant people tend to obey unquestioningly but have more suppressed aggression, which finds outlets in hostility toward others and other groups.[56] The appropriate educational treatment to free the individual from these barriers to the growth of his capacity to love can, therefore, be readily inferred.

In particular, education must provide greater opportunity for the study of our own natures. We must not allow the legitimate study of the conditions in which we live to monopolize the educational program so that there is no time to reflect on the significance of our own impulses, sympathies, and reactions. It is only through self-examination and self-criticism that we can avoid projecting onto others the things we do not want to know about ourselves. Self-satisfaction and self-ignorance are divisive and alienating forces in society. A loving unity cannot be achieved until we withdraw our projections and face ourselves, warts and all.

To be capable of love one must be able to transcend oneself. The person who lives only for himself is incapable of love. We do not need to raise here the issue of whether one ever acts completely selflessly or whether every act is motivated by overt or concealed selfishness. However this might be, there are, nevertheless, marked and crucial differences between the person imprisoned in the self and the one who is able to touch and be touched by other people and their concerns. One of the best ways the school can help to develop the second type of personality is by trying to motivate the student by means other than narrow self-interest. The use of grades, ranks, individual prizes, and the like is injurious to this development. It is perhaps futile to hope for the early abandonment of such encouragements of egocentricity, except in a few enlightened institutions, but at least we can all attempt to de-emphasize such techniques and make their effect, when used, as harmless as possible. A preferable approach is to encourage the student to "lose himself" in a piece of work, to become so absorbed in a task that he becomes virtually identified with it.

This brings us to the most important factor in the whole situation —the development by the teacher of an *atmosphere* of calm, quiet deliberation, in which the delicate, subtle relationships and appreciations that love requires may grow. One of the chief obstacles to the development of love today is the unseemly haste with which modern life is conducted. We do not have time for compassion. Suffering must be passed by on the other side for we have an appointment with our stockbroker. Love is time–consuming and the returns are uncertain compared with investment in a secure company. In the school and college the frequent jangling bells remind us that time is passing and that if we are going to make that junior-executive position before the age of thirty we must press on with our studies and with that careful cultivation of people who may be useful in helping us to get ahead. In contemporary West German universities, this human engineering has become formalized with customary German efficiency through the institution of the "corporation," a sort of fraternity where students can meet influential *alumni* and keep alive the contacts that will ensure future business success. William Temple's indictment of callousness was: "There lies the way to spiritual death." We all know dead people walking around today, but the reponsibility of the teacher is to postpone this sort of dying in his students as long as possible.

As a subject in the curriculum, "Love" would be about as efficacious in fostering love as "Social Awareness," "Latin," "Development of Conscience," "Home Economics," or "Teen-age Problems." Love, like happiness, would seem to call for a less frontal approach. Atmosphere is more important than assignment. But an appropriate atmosphere may be difficult to reconcile with the appropriate demands of discipline. Certainly, for an incompetent, insecure, or immature teacher, the demands of discipline will render a loving atmosphere impossible. Hence, the quality of the classroom teacher remains the vital key.

Religion in Education

What are the implications for education of what has been said about the need for a mature religious commitment? The first implication is that all orthodox religious instruction, reading of the Bible as revelation, compulsory praying, and dogmatic indoctrination should be excluded from the school. We need to question the assumption that youth is the time for religious instruction in the customary sense. There is a strange fearfulness underlying the attempt by the Church to catch the young before the Devil gets them and to elicit quickly a verbal allegiance to some creed or belief that is quite beyond the genuine grasp of children in its historical, theological, and semantical complexities.

For a clear example of the inefficacy of formal religious instruction in attaining its avowed aim, we might study the experience of England, where participation in a religious morning assembly and a course of religious instruction is compulsory for all students in state supported schools, except those few brave souls who ask to be excused on grounds of conscience. It is widely acknowledged that religious instruction is the most despised and ridiculed subject in the curriculum. Discussing his pupils in a contemporary secondary modern school, Farley wrote, "Ten years of Religious Instruction has little effect on them; as far as the lads are concerned, one is punished for being caught." [57] One difficult boy said to him, with understandable bitterness: "God never helped my old girl when times were bad, so why do I have to listen in morning assembly?" [58] One might concur with Farley's judgment that religious instruction has little effect, were it not for the suspicion that in fact it has considerable effect—of an unintended and pernicious kind. Religion becomes looked on as something insufferably boring, not worthy of serious interest, since it is so often taught by clearly uninterested teachers; something with a great deal of mumbo jumbo, with no relation to the problems of real life; and above all something riddled with hypocrisy, since the adults who repeat, and demand the repetition of, these phrases clearly do not follow them in their behavior.

The consequences can perhaps best be described in the words of the Archbishop of York:

> In England, there has been a general retreat from Christianity. There has been no open denial on the part of the State. Christianity is still the accepted religion of the nation. The Monarch is anointed and crowned with Christian prayer, exhortation and blessing. Both Houses of Parliament still open with prayer. The judges and the armed forces have their chaplains. On national days of prayer the churches are crowded, and on civil occasions there is usually prayer and dedication. But the great mass of the people are ignorant of the elementary truths of the Christian faith and treat religion as something irrelevant to their lives.[59]

Even when measured by the lowest possible criterion—the number of people prepared to go through the outward ritual—the indications of the effectiveness of conventional religious training are not reassuring. Seebohm Rowntree's well-known census of the percentage of the population of York over 16 years attending places of worship, taken under similar conditions of weather and time of year, in 1899, 1935, and 1947, produced the following results:

    1899: 35.5   1935: 17.7   1947: 10

Protestant Sunday School attendance figures in England and Wales show a similar trend:

    1887: 5,733,000   1920: 5,008,000   1954: 2,800,000 [60]

However, the most important objection to religious instruction in school is that, by setting aside a period for formal religious instruction, we imply that other subjects are not vehicles for the development of religious understanding and insight, whereas all education should open toward the religious. We need a wider concept of religion that potentially embraces the whole curriculum. The Catholics wisely recognize that, if you want a religious education, religion must permeate the whole educational program rather than remain an appendage to it, although one might take issue with the *way* in which they approach the problem. This denial of religious instruction for the sake of wholly religious education is in line with the Quaker denial of the sacraments on the grounds that all things are to be sacramental. For the Quaker, there is no holy meal, because all meals are holy; no moment of baptism because all growth toward God provides forgiveness and renewal; no sacramental marriage ceremony because the shared life is itself an expression of religious love; no oaths because all speech is sacred to honesty; no sacred ministry because all men are ordained to be vessels of truth.[61]

Under this wider concept of religion, religious growth can be measured not in terms of biblical knowledge, or the ability to recite creeds and perform rituals, but in terms of a developing capacity for seeing with clear understanding what are the central commitments on which one would focus one's life, and a growing ability to make one's everyday actions and decisions in accordance with those commitments. Here is the link between the intellectual and the religious of which Robert Hamill wrote:

> God is praised when the scholar puts pen to paper and the teacher sits down with a student to think together. The neighbor is loved when . . . some wise teacher stirs up his mind, trains his talent, and opens to him the wonders of everything true. Thinking is religious work.[62]

It is difficult to see what it could mean to a child to be told that the Bible represents revelation. And it is easy to see what harm can be done to the child by making him memorize such a verbalism. A book like Loren Eiseley's *The Immense Journey* can take him much closer to an understanding of the meaning of revelation. Through this he can gain some idea of what Gerald Heard called the "vast reciprocation" between man and nature. Through the agency of a teacher who has a genuine reverence for and sensitivity to nature, he can come to realize that all existence is a continuing revelation. Apart from such a realization, no real understanding of a particular revelation is possible.

The clearest description I know of the kind of religious growth and commitment here advocated is contained in an account of the psychiatrist Fritz Kunkel, by a woman who was his patient. She described him as a very religious or spiritual man, although she knew of no affiliation he had with any particular church or creed. She wrote,

> His spirituality lay in the vitality and immediacy of his response to all life, his openness to experience, his depth of awareness of the relatedness of all mankind, and in his unshakeable conviction of the ultimate goodness and beauty of creation, no matter how tragic or terrifying its immediate aspect.[63]

It is these qualities of responsiveness, openness, relatedness, commitment, wonder, confidence, and joy that are suggested as the genuine hallmarks of the religious person.

In an excellent discussion of the place of wonder in education, Thomas Green has reminded us of the difference between wondering *why* or *how*—which is the root of curiosity—and wondering *at*—which comes from the realization that the world, though dependable, is contingent. It exists, but it need not exist. Green suggested,

> One way to destroy the motivation to learn is to effectively abort the childlike capacity for awe and wonder. We do this quite efficiently when in teaching we take the description of a phenomenon to be its sufficient explanation; and thus, losing sight of how contingent is our knowledge, we lead students to entertain contingent truths as though they could not be otherwise.[64]

Moreover, in encouraging children to develop the qualities mentioned above, we encounter a grave danger. Religious groups, along with some other forces in society, are guilty of trying to inculcate what they consider appropriate responses and feelings. What they produce all too often is a counterfeit that is harmful to the development of imagination and authentic experience. One reason why we find it difficult to experience deep and genuine emotion today is that the commercial world has ruthlessly exploited us by trying to overlay our spontaneous feelings with a thick layer of conventional responses. If religion presents its values in this way—imposing them and demanding a standardized emotional response—it will merely add to the ruin caused by commercial exploitation. The child will not be helped to deal with the unpredictable emotional experience; he will be pushed farther along the path of hypocrisy and away from the capacity to recognize and experience his own authentic feelings.

Is the situation hopeless, then? Are we doomed to choose between producing hypocrites and producing materialists? Not quite, for there are some largely unexplored resources waiting to be used. In the first place, we need to be much more open to the possibilities of significant growth among *adults*. If we can resist the temptation to make hypocrites out of our children by forcing them to believe and "feel" what they are incapable of understanding or feeling, then we may later find that we have a group of adults who are capable of genuine religious growth and feeling. Secondly, we have our greatest allies in the children themselves. If we can take time to watch and listen to young children, they will guide us to most of what we need to know. They have already done this to a considerable extent in art education. They could do it in other aspects of education, too, if we would let them. Their sense of wonder, delight, and joy in the world as they discover it is the essence of a sense of the infinite that is integral to true religious feeling, and we wean them from it only at enormous cost. By respecting the child and his uniqueness and by providing opportunities for quiet reflection, questioning, and wondering, we do the most to help him to grow into a religiously committed person.

NOTES

[1] From the *Tao-Te King*, in *World Bible*, Robert O. Ballou, ed. (New York: Viking, 1950), 546.

[2] Viktor E. Frankl, *From Death-Camp to Existentialism: A Psychiatrist's Path to a New Therapy*, Ilse Lasch, trans. (Boston: Beacon Press, 1959), especially 69–80.

[3] Henry N. Wieman, *Man's Ultimate Commitment* (Carbondale: Southern Illinois University Press, 1958), 77.

[4] C. Wright Mills, "The Intellectuals' Last Chance," *Esquire* (October, 1959), 101–102. See also Kenneth Winetrout, "Mills and the Intellectual Default," in Robert H. Bohlke and Kenneth Winetrout, *Bureaucrats and Intellectuals: A Critique of C. Wright Mills* (Springfield, Mass.. American International College, 1963), 16–25.

[5] Martin Buber, *Between Man and Man*, Ronald G. Smith, trans. (Boston: Beacon Press, 1955), 66.

[6] For a valuable discussion of the origins of commitment, see Solon T. Kimball and James E. McClellan, Jr., *Education and the New America* (New York: Random House, 1962), ch. 10, "The Nature of Commitment."

[7] Gordon Allport, *Becoming: Basic Considerations for a Psychology of Personality* (New Haven: Yale University, 1955), 72–74.

[8] Martha Gellhorn, "Eichmann and the Private Conscience," *Atlantic* (February, 1962), 52–59.

[9] In a letter to Dr. Günther Anders, June 12, 1959. Quoted in Günther Anders, "Open Letter to President Kennedy," *Exchange: A Canadian Review*, vol. I, no. 2 (December, 1961), 25–31.

[10] George A. Buttrick, *Sermons Preached in a University Church* (New York: Abingdon Press, 1959), 81–82.

[11] David Riesman, *Constraint and Variety in American Education* (New York: Doubleday, 1958), 112–14.

[12] Reinhold Niebuhr, "The Commitment of the Self and the Freedom of the Mind," *Religion and Freedom of Thought* (New York: Doubleday, 1954), 56.

13 See Mildred B. Young, *Another Will Gird You: A Message to the Society of Friends* (Wallingford, Pa.: Pendle Hill, 1960), 5–7, for an extension and discussion of this illustration.

14 *Observer* (London), May 29, 1955.

15 It is difficult to improve on Wieman's statement, which is, therefore, worth quoting at length: "No appeal to divine revelation can save any man from the imperative need to utter continuously the plea to be corrected, because his human mind claiming to be the recipient of divine revelation is always fallible. No appeal to the authority of Church or Bible or religious tradition, no appeal to reason or science or inner conviction, no claim to have undergone the divine encounter nor to be continuously in the I-Thou relationship with God, can deliver one from presumptuous arrogance in making the ultimate commitment of his life if he seek not to have the structure of his life destroyed when it is wrongly constructed and when this destruction will help reveal the way in which man should live." Wieman, *op. cit.*, 167–68.

16 Robert L. Calhoun, "The Historical Relations between Religion and Intellectual Freedom," *Religion and Freedom of Thought* (New York: Doubleday, 1954), 26.

17 Whitehead suggested that it is above all through philosophy that religious commitment is given scientific rigor and rational strength: "Philosophy frees itself from the taint of ineffectiveness by its close relations with religion and with science, natural and sociological. It attains its chief importance by fusing the two, namely, religion and science, into one rational scheme of thought. Philosophy finds religion, and modifies it; and conversely religion is among the data of experience which philosophy must weave into its own scheme." Alfred N. Whitehead, *Process and Reality: An Essay in Cosmology* (New York: Macmillan, 1929), 23.

18 Arthur Eddington, "The Domain of Physical Science," in *Science, Religion and Reality*, quoted by J.W.N. Sullivan, *The Limitations of Science* (New York: Viking, 1934), 224–25.

19 Bertrand Russell, *An Outline of Philosophy* (London: Allen & Unwin, 1956), 163.

20 Arthur Koestler, *The Sleepwalkers: A History of Man's Changing Vision of the Universe* (London: Hutchinson, 1959), 542.

21 Henry D. Aiken, "Sidney Hook as Philosopher," *Commentary* (February, 1962), 150.

22 Ludwig Wittgenstein, *Tractatus Logico-Philosophicus*, D.F. Pears and B.F. McGuinness, trans. (London: Routledge & Kegan Paul, 1961), 6.52.

23 Eugene Kinkead, *In Every War But One* (New York: Norton, 1959), 149–50.

24 Allport, *op. cit.*, 94.

25 Lawrence Durrell, "No Clue to Living," *Times Literary Supplement* (May 27, 1960), 339.

26 Julian Huxley, "Religion without God," *Observer* (London), March 31, 1963, 11.

27 Paul Tillich, *Biblical Religion and the Search for Ultimate Reality* (Chicago: University of Chicago, 1955), ch. VI; see also Carol Murphy, *A Deeper Faith: The Thought of Paul Tillich* (Wallingford, Pa.: Pendle Hill, 1958).

28 Bede Griffiths, *The Golden String* (London: Harvill, 1954), 104.

29 John LaFarge, S.J., "A Case Study in Freedom through Authority," in Lyman Bryson *et al.*, eds., *Freedom and Authority in Our Time* (New York: Harper, 1953), 644.

30 Quoted by Radhakrishnan, *Recovery of Faith* (London: Allen & Unwin, 1956), 150–51.

31 Martin Buber, *Israel and the World: Essays in a Time of Crisis* (New York: Schocken, 1948), 32–33.

32 William Golding, *Free Fall* (London: Faber & Faber, 1959), 85.

33 Erich Fromm, *Escape from Freedom* (New York: Rinehart, 1941), 260–61.

34 Gerald Heard, *Training for a Life of Growth* (Santa Monica, Calif.: Wayfarer, 1959) 7–60.

35 Paul Tillich, "Love, Power, and Justice," *Listener* (October 2, 1952), 544. See also, Aldous Huxley, *Brave New World Revisited* (New York: Harper, 1958), 133.

36 For a documentation of these claims, see Pitirim Sorokin, *The Ways and Power of Love* (Boston: Beacon Press, 1954); *Religious and Moral Polarization of Our Time* (Princeton Theological Seminary: Sesquicentennial History Department Conference, n.d., mimeo.), 18–19.

37 E.M. Forster, "Tolerance," in *Two Cheers for Democracy* (London: Arnold, 1951), 56.

38 Nels F.S. Ferré, "Authority and Freedom," in Bryson, *et al.*, eds., *Freedom and Authority in Our Time*, 491–92.

39 John Macmurray, "Freedom in the Personal Nexus," in Ruth N. Anshen, ed., *Freedom: Its Meaning* (New York: Harcourt, Brace, 1940), 510–12.

40 Buber, *Between Man and Man*, 52.

41 Hedley Bull, *The Control of the Arms Race*. Quoted by John Strachey, "The Forces of Hope," *Observer* (London), January 7, 1962, 8.

42 Archibald MacLeish, "Must We Hate?" *Atlantic*, vol. 211, no. 2 (February, 1963), 79–82.

43 Raymond Williams, *Culture and Society, 1780–1950* (London: Chatto & Windus, 1958), 325–31.

44 Hermann Hesse, *The Journey to the East*, Hilda Rosner, trans. (New York: Noonday Press, 1957), 72.

45 Heard, *op. cit.*, 32–43.

46 Henry D. Thoreau, *Walden: or, Life in the Woods* (New York: Mentor, 1957), 57.

47 Howard Brinton, *The Quaker Doctrine of Inward Peace* (Wallingford, Pa.: Pendle Hill, 1948), 5–6.

48 See ch. 2 of this book for a discussion of totalitarian and democratic indoctrination.

49 Aldous Huxley, *op. cit.*, 133.

50 *Ibid.*

51 Sir Richard Livingstone, *Education for a World Adrift* (Cambridge University Press, 1944), 114.

52 *Ibid.*, 116–18.

53 Riesman, *op. cit.*, 128–30.

54 "Two kinds of authority should be distinguished. One is dogmatic. The other is authority of a reliable method for detecting error and gathering evidence when this method is used with competence acquired by rigorous discipline. Authority of the first kind is the foe of freedom but authority of the second kind is one necessary condition of freedom. . . . The method for detecting error is reason." Wieman, *op. cit.*, 153.

55 For a prescription from a psychiatrist on how to develop what he has called a "biophilous" or life-loving person, see Erich Fromm, *War Within Man: A Psychological Enquiry into the Roots of Destructiveness* (Philadelphia: American Friends Service Committee, 1963), 19.

56 See J.C. Flugel, "The Psychology of Toleration," *Listener* (September 16, 1954), 441.

57 Richard Farley, *Secondary Modern Discipline* (London: Black, 1960), 72.

58 *Ibid.*

59 *Times* (London), October 13, 1955.

60 All figures cited in Viscount Samuel, *In Search of Reality* (Oxford: Blackwell, 1958), 213–14.

61 See Harold Loukes, *Friends Face Reality* (London: Bannisdale Press, 1954), 125. This same writer has conducted the most valuable study to date of Religious Instruction in British schools and has produced some excellent suggestions for reform. Harold Loukes, *New Ground in Christian Education* (London: SCM Press, 1965).

62 Robert H. Hamill, "The Chapel: Servant of Church and University," (Response delivered at Boston University, November 19, 1962). See also W.R. Niblett, *Christian Education in a Secular Society* (London: Oxford University Press, 1960), 123; and Algernon D. Black, *The Religious Education of the Child* (New York: American Ethical Union, 1950), 4–5.

63 Beatrice Burch, "Dr. Kunkel and the Long-Distance Analysis," *Inward Light*, vol. XXV, no. 63 (spring–summer, 1962), 14–15.

64 Thomas F. Green, "The Importance of Fairy Tales," *Educational Forum* (November, 1963), 95–102.

IX

SYNTHESIS

Although the focus in these pages has been on the problem of authority and freedom in education, the approach used might be considered a way of examining other problems in the philosophy of education. To substantiate this suggestion and to summarize the previous discussion, it is appropriate here to adumbrate the principal elements in that approach.

In the first place, it is worth emphasizing that the student examining such an educational problem should not be in a hurry to espouse a firm definition of the concept under investigation. In these pages we have worked with a rough definition of "authority" as that which exercises a force or influence over us, and of "freedom" as the power to achieve, choose, or become. But these definitions have the virtue of sufficient vagueness and lack of specificity to permit further investigation of their content.

A second element is constituted by the realization that definition of such concepts is largely valueless unless carried on in context. Clarification involves a process of qualification according to context and circumstance. In the case of "authority" and "freedom" (and many other words that are centers of educational discussion), it is important to recognize that these words have been too vastly used to permit them to be neatly encapsulated. Moreover, the facts that "freedom" is usually a "hurrah" word and "authority" is usually a "boo" word increase the difficulty of objectivity. A central task, then, is to ensure, when using such words, that we make clear as far as possible the context and sense in which we are using them. Then there is a chance that discussion can proceed fruitfully.

When we examined "authority" and "freedom" in context, we quickly came to realize that we do not want *all* kinds of freedom:

325

nor do we want to avoid all kinds of authority. We want, rather, to examine and evaluate these key terms and their relationships in a variety of situations and under diverse influences. The purpose is to judge what *kind* of authority and what *kind* of freedom we want to foster or to discourage.

Another important element in such an inquiry is the practice of inferring from the material no more than is appropriate. In this particular inquiry, for example, we discovered that some forms of authority lead to a loss of freedom. But it would be inappropriate to infer from this that freedom is enhanced by the absence of authority. For we found that some forms of authority, under certain conditions, lead to some of the highest forms of freedom. So the enterprise becomes one of *distinguishing*—in this case, between stifling and liberating forms and conditions of authority. In general, we found that liberating forms of authority are marked by frequently recurring characteristics: they are often rational, personally relevant, just, and individually appropriate.

Our inquiry suggested that the relationship between authority and freedom is not a simple one of enmity or opposition; it is of a more complex nature. We concluded that redemption comes through achieving creative syntheses of these concepts. Again, not *all* kinds of synthesis are adequate, but only certain syntheses under certain circumstances. A central concern of this volume has been the scrutiny of the educational aspects of such syntheses.

To bring greater specificity to these general remarks, we shall illustrate them by suggesting some of the forms of both stifling and liberating authority that we discovered in each of the polarities studied and some of the forms of synthesis we found we could advocate. This will at the same time constitute a summary of the whole.

We found, for example, that *work* does exercise a form of authority over us. It restrains and influences us. But that authority may be desirable or pernicious. In how many lives, for example, has work provided a liberating and supporting structure, meaning, and purpose? It is often for a man the principal source of dignity and significance: its absence can lead to loss of self-respect or even mental illness. And yet, work can alternatively be a destructive force in human life, as seen for example in physically degrading labor, in its associations with guilt feelings, and in manifestations of a neurotic obsession with work.

Similarly, *play* does occupy an area of freedom—freedom from the demands of work. But this may or may not be a kind of freedom we want. We need a special kind of rhythm in our lives between work and play. We need to laze, to relax, to *be* as well as to *do*. But much leisure may be merely time-filling, a destructive or deadening waiting between intervals of work. There have never before been so many opportunities (from passive television-viewing to vicariously violent spectator sport) for filling such gaps in meaningless or destructive ways.

Moreover, the problem increases in complexity when we recognize that we can look at it from a different standpoint and regard work as the domain of freedom and "play" as the domain of authority. This may be especially applicable, for example, in an automated, "affluent" society; in such a society, work may be the enviable lot of a fortunate few and leisure, with its yawning emptiness, may exercise an authority over us through its effects in terms of boredom, frustration, and consequent social and psychological problems. Hence, instead of taking these words at face value, we should attempt to investigate their operation under different circumstances to judge what kinds of authority and freedom we want to encourage or discourage, and what kind of synthesis of these concepts we should seek to achieve.

In this case, we have suggested that the kind of creative synthesis of work and play that we would advocate can be epitomized as *art*, in the sense of playful work. When activity is infused with purpose, meaning, personal significance, and a serious concern with outcome (as work), but is also marked by reflective interest in the process itself, by deep involvement and present enjoyment (as play), then we have a form of art that represents a synthesis of authority and freedom. In this sense, an education for work and play becomes the education of artists.

In a corresponding manner, *institutions* can constitute either a constraining or a liberating authority in our lives. The Church, for example, can exercise a form of authority that snuffs out individual self-reliance and discourages personal truth-seeking: it can hinder the individual's task of achieving moral autonomy through seeking insights from his personal experience. This has perhaps been its dominant role throughout history. The State can similarly be a destructive, crushing authority when it attempts to control the outcomes of its citizens' inquiries and discussions. Totalitarianism is the clearest example of this misuse of State authority, but all States are liable to this tendency.

On the other hand, the Church can be a liberating authority, when it encourages man to recognize his responsibilities to his fellowmen, his society, and his God (or ultimate commitment), and his responsibility for the personal creation of criteria of judgment by which he can decide among these other responsibilities when their claims conflict. The State liberates when it acts to maintain and support the individual from below, by establishing the social, economic, and cultural conditions that will enable him to develop his full capacities. This may involve using its authority to intervene actively in the social and economic life of society to protect some (potentially vulnerable) groups or individuals from other (potentially exploiting) groups or individuals.

Much will depend on the extent to which institutional authority is employed relevantly, reasonably, and appropriately. Much will depend on the extent to which the individual is brought into the process (in a manner appropriate to his maturity) of determining the rules by which he will live. This is an important means by which he grows in responsibility and freedom.

The synthesis of this particular dialectic, then, can be epitomized as *responsibility*, especially in the sense that stresses the *response*. The type of response to be encouraged is the type manifested in the dialogue, where there is a genuine exchange of ideas with others, a truthful interaction, or what Buber would call an I-Thou relationship. We urge the type of responsibility seen when leaders of opinion (including those who control the mass media of communication) and institutional authorities respond to the demands of truth and resist the temptations of authoritarianism, cheap popularity, deliberate indoctrination, censorship, and thought-control. Through the prism of responsibility one can see that the concept of academic freedom is appropriately related to the professional responsibility and competence of the teacher. An education for living freely within institutional life thus becomes an education of responsible persons.

It has been suggested that authority in the sense of *discipline* is necessary in the teaching situation. But it should be clear by now that when this much has been said almost nothing has been said. All the important and difficult tasks remain: to determine what *kind* of discipline, how *much* discipline, in what manner it should be administered, and so on. It is perhaps unnecessary to point out the pernicious effects on human freedom of authoritarian forms of discipline—the degeneration of personality in both those who receive it and those who apply it. There is always a danger that strong external discipline will kill *interest*, crush all sense of personal purpose, and produce people with no strong desires or well-developed goals.

But these considerations must be set against the fact that discipline in the sense of order is necessary for the exercise of the freest and most fruitful acts. Children and adults without a minimum of order in their lives will reject freedom as an intolerable state of insecurity and unpredictability. Elements of compulsion and external restraint can be justified in education on the grounds that unrestrained choice and action by the immature can cut them off from the possibility of future freedoms.

The sort of educational synthesis we advocate is an education for *self-discipline*. The adult's task is seen as that of bringing the child to a realization that discipline over himself is necessary to release his most important talents. Self-discipline can be seen in the recognition of the authority inherent in the learning situation, the authority of the material in art, the authority of one's own commitments, or the authority inherent in community. An education for self-discipline will permit the child to take, as he matures, a steadily increasing share in formulating and modifying the discipline by which he will live. But this does not justify all of the strict external discipline that is applied to the very young. The order and manner of imposition are crucial: too much external control arbitrarily applied too soon can effectively kill individual interest and the possibility of future growth. (This, indeed, has been a central feature of the history of education.) And strongly developed interest itself constitutes one of the best sources of self-discipline.

The dialectical nature of the relationship between authority and freedom is clearly demonstrated by the relationship between the *group* and the *individual*. There is an important sense in which man becomes himself through his responses to others. From the beginning he is dependent on other people. The individual grows in freedom through the authority of the group: this is shown by the social nature of the growth of human personality. The closeness of the mother-infant relationship is a model of the kind of human interdependence and interaction that enable the development of individual autonomy. Education for cultural participation and intelligent citizenship is a necessary extension of this model.

But the authority of the group can also crush the development of the individual through such agencies as in-group fanaticism, conformity, and provincialism. This use of authority is most fully realized under totalitarian systems, where "brain-washing," enforced collectivism, severe punishment of heresy, and other techniques can appear. The mature society will make room for individual diversity and for the creative rebellion of the individual against group norms. It will treat the heretic differently from the criminal. To become oneself one must, as the prodigal son, leave the primary group, free himself from its authority. He must, in perhaps a literal sense but at least a metaphorical sense, "leave home" and experience periods of solitude—perhaps physical, certainly mental. Such steps are related to the acquisition of the self-knowledge that is an essential attendant of personal autonomy.

The synthesis is not achieved, however, until—like Plato's Guardian returning to the cave, or the prodigal son returning home—there is a return to the group, a recognition of one's responsibility to the group.

The highest freedom for the individual is found not in isolation but in *community*—that is, not an arbitrary or coerced group of individuals but a voluntary and intentional coming together of autonomous persons. Such a synthesis can best be epitomized by the community of a rich, deep friendship, where one acts freely and joyously under the self-imposed authority of caring for another person.

The authority of *excellence* can be destructive or pernicious when standards of excellence are applied inappropriately or irrelevantly or dogmatically; when we suffer from the dominance of a narrow range of types of excellence (such as the ability to perform traditional academic tasks) or of a single institutional model (such as the English Public School or the American liberal arts college); when partial or temporary human qualities are elevated to the status of total or permanent judgments on a person; when the fact of real or supposed excellence is used as a justification for rigid segregation, for the development of self-perpetuating *élites*, or for tolerating the existence of social, economic, or educational conditions that prevent the entry of certain individuals or groups to specific routes toward advancement or achievement.

It is perhaps less necessary to point out that the authority of excellence can be liberating—that it can free us from baseness, vulgarity, triviality, and self-indulgence. We need to foster discrimination when it is the quality of being able to discriminate between the good and the bad, between the good and the better, between the bad and the worse. It is only by learning to make increasingly discriminating judgments, by becoming more aware of certain *inequalities*, that we can raise standards of taste and civilized living. We need also to create a genuinely popular culture—one in which there is wide recognition of the authority inherent in the best of the cultural tradition, yet in which there is free access to that culture for all people, and in which the task of achieving cultural excellence is assumed by each person.

It is suggested that this educational synthesis can be perceived in the fostering of *diversity within unity*. Instead of focusing on equality in the sense of sameness, we should strive to maximize educational opportunity by making individual judgments of what each person needs. Diversity can be fostered through the creation of a wide range of types of excellence without sacrificing the ethos of unity that is served by the concept of fundamental human equality or immeasurability. The comprehensive principle is an educational attempt to facilitate achievement of this double aim by helping the student to find his own unique form of excellence in a common setting.

All of these aspects of the investigation underline the fact that we are not wholly free, that we act constantly within the matrix of many influencing and partly *determining* forces: natural laws, heredity, early upbringing, social and economic environment, unconscious forces that we neither recognize nor control. Many of these forces influence us in early childhood, at a stage when we have no possibility of judging, criticizing, or combatting them. We are not free from the regulatory laws of an orderly universe: our actions and choices are all caused.

However, education can make knowledge of these forms of authority a liberating experience by enabling us to understand them, come to terms with them, and partly control them, instead of being their unwitting pawns. Knowledge of our lack of freedom liberates us to operate within the area of freedom that we do possess. The fact that, as human beings, we can be "called" and choose to respond or not to respond to that call is a clue to our human freedom. Especially when we deliberately, rationally, and reflectively frame and pursue long-term purposes, we are extending the range of our personal freedom. We similarly demonstrate and enlarge our freedom when we assume moral responsibility for our actions and choices.

The educational synthesis of this polarity can, thus, be seen as an education for *self-determination*: encouraging the development of people who shape themselves (within the circle of possibility) according to the authority of the highest possible purposes, people who have the courage to make autonomous choices and who will bear responsibility for the consequences of those choices.

The authority of *tradition* has in the past usually been a stifling and crushing force in education. Children have been compelled to conform to patterns set by others, in such a way as to prevent them from creating patterns that had any significant relation to themselves. This has resulted in a disastrously large-scale atrophy of young children's *creative* powers. The existence of an objective element in education has constituted a weight that has tended to crush individuality, uniqueness, and creativity. The setting of rigid, traditional, external, and often irrelevant, adult standards has produced inhibition, fear, and lack of self-confidence.

But subjective self-expression is also a danger, often fallen into by those who are aware of the preceding perils. The danger in this case is that of complacency—a premature satisfaction with our own performances. The authority of tradition can liberate by showing us the higher possibilities of which we are capable with self-discipline, by bringing a realization that our complacency is unjustified. Our creative achievements are deepened and enriched when we submit ourselves personally and thoroughly to the authority of our own tradition, when we are not drifting but tied fruitfully to the tree of our own personal and cultural past. Attempts to repudiate the past are enemies of creativity. A living tradition can free the individual for greater creativity if that tradition is absorbed, reinterpreted, and transformed by him in the light of his own unique talents and purposes.

The educational synthesis can be seen in the fostering of *order*— again, not *any* order, or order for its own sake, as it often appears in homes and classrooms. It is, rather, epitomized in the greater order imposed by the creative artist on the chaos of nature; in the order that transcends the ambiguity, openness, richness, and apparent disorder of the life and personality of the creative person; in the integrating configuration that the creative person organizes out of previously unrelated fragments of experience; in the balance that the creative person achieves of imagination and discipline, of primitivism and rationality; in the new order that the creative person imposes on the relevant aspects of his own cultural tradition.

Commitments can be cages in which we trap ourselves. A commitment is always in danger of developing into an ideology, where the perils of formalism and rigidity will inhere. Commitments that fossilize into creeds and dogmas often become substitutes for the direct, personal experience that is the stuff of *growth*.

But commitments can also free us. Indeed, the highest freedom comes from submitting to the authority of a commitment that transcends us and our petty concerns. A commitment can infuse our lives with the liberating qualities of purpose, order, shape, simplicity, and integrity: it can free us from fear, egotism, and the fragmentation of life.

The final synthesis is one that in one sense or another repeats and draws together the preceding syntheses: it is focused in the concept of *unity*. It can be exemplified in the common and public nature of *science*, which provides a method of inquiry into the basis of and support for our commitments that will permit and encourage further growth; in *love* as commitment to the growth of another person; and in *community* as a concern for creative relationships that stems from the realization that my freedom is essentially linked with the freedom of others.

INDEX

(Note: footnotes are not indexed unless they refer to material not mentioned in the text.)